AFTER SCHOOL
NIGHTMARE

Story and Art by
SETONA MIZUSHIRO

6

go!comi

Translation – Christine Schilling
Adaptation – Mallory Reaves
Lettering & Retouch – Eva Han
Production Manager – James Dashiell
Editor – Brynne Chandler

A Go! Comi manga

Published by Go! Media Entertainment, LLC

Houkago Hokenshitsu Volume 6
© SETONA MIZUSHIRO 2006
Originally published in Japan in 2006 by Akita Publishing Co., Ltd., Tokyo.
English translation rights arranged with Akita Publishing Co., Ltd.
through TOHAN CORPORATION, Tokyo.

Visit us online at www.gocomi.com
e-mail: info@gocomi.com

ISBN 978-1-933617-48-0

First printed in January 2008

1   2   3   4   5   6   7   8   9

Manufactured in the United States of America.

Koukoku Senior High School

Table of contents

AFTER SCHOOL NIGHTMARE

Our Story So Far

Mashiro Ichijo is a high school student whose body is half female, and half male. One day he's called down to a secret infirmary to participate in a "special class" he needs to graduate. He learns from another student, Kureha, that each person takes on their true form in this class. When each student reaches their personal goal, their most heart-felt dream will come true. Mashiro decides to use this class to become a true male.

But when another dreamer – a merciless knight – exposes his body's secret and Kureha's tragic past, Mashiro vows to protect the weaker dreamers.

Who is the real person behind the knight? While trying to identify the real people behind the facades, Mashiro is accosted by Sou, a male student he doesn't much like. Sou tells him "you're a girl" and then forces a kiss upon him. Wondering whether Sou could be another dreamer, maybe even the knight, Mashiro becomes obsessed with Sou.

When Sou's sister, Ai, reveals that Sou is the knight, Mashiro is stunned. Vowing that he'll never forgive Sou, Mashiro tries to free himself from his confused feelings by spending a tender night with Kureha. The next day, he faces Sou, announcing that he will settle the score once and for all in the next dream class – but does he have the heart for it...?

Sou Mizuhashi

Mashiro Ichijo

Kureha Fujishima

The form she takes in the class.

Participants in the Class

If you get a hold of the key, you can graduate.

Every time your heart takes damage, a bead on the cord breaks. When all three break, you are eliminated from the dream.

Ai Mizuhashi

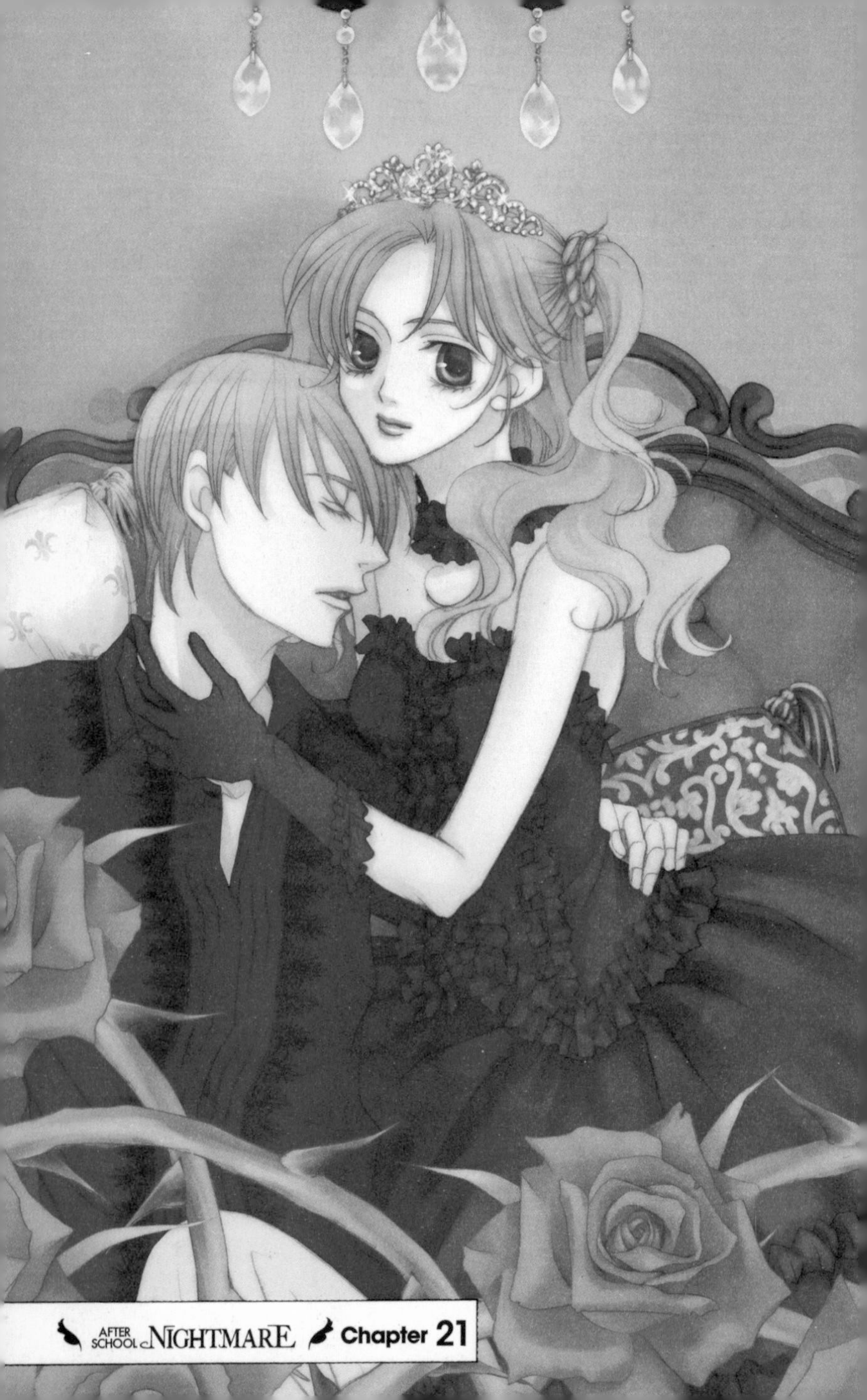
AFTER SCHOOL NIGHTMARE
Chapter 21

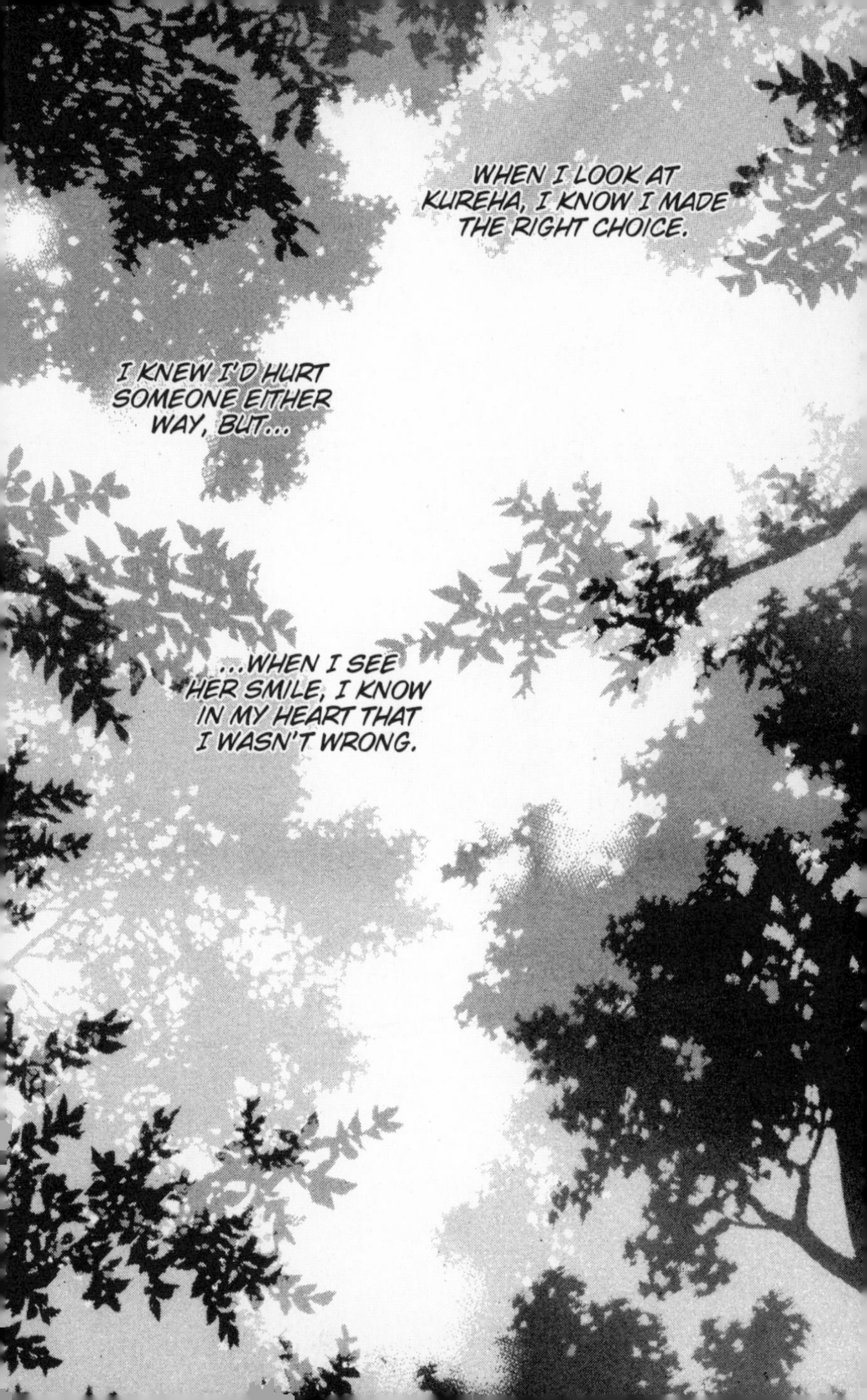
WHEN I LOOK AT KUREHA, I KNOW I MADE THE RIGHT CHOICE.
I KNEW I'D HURT SOMEONE EITHER WAY, BUT...
...WHEN I SEE HER SMILE, I KNOW IN MY HEART THAT I WASN'T WRONG.

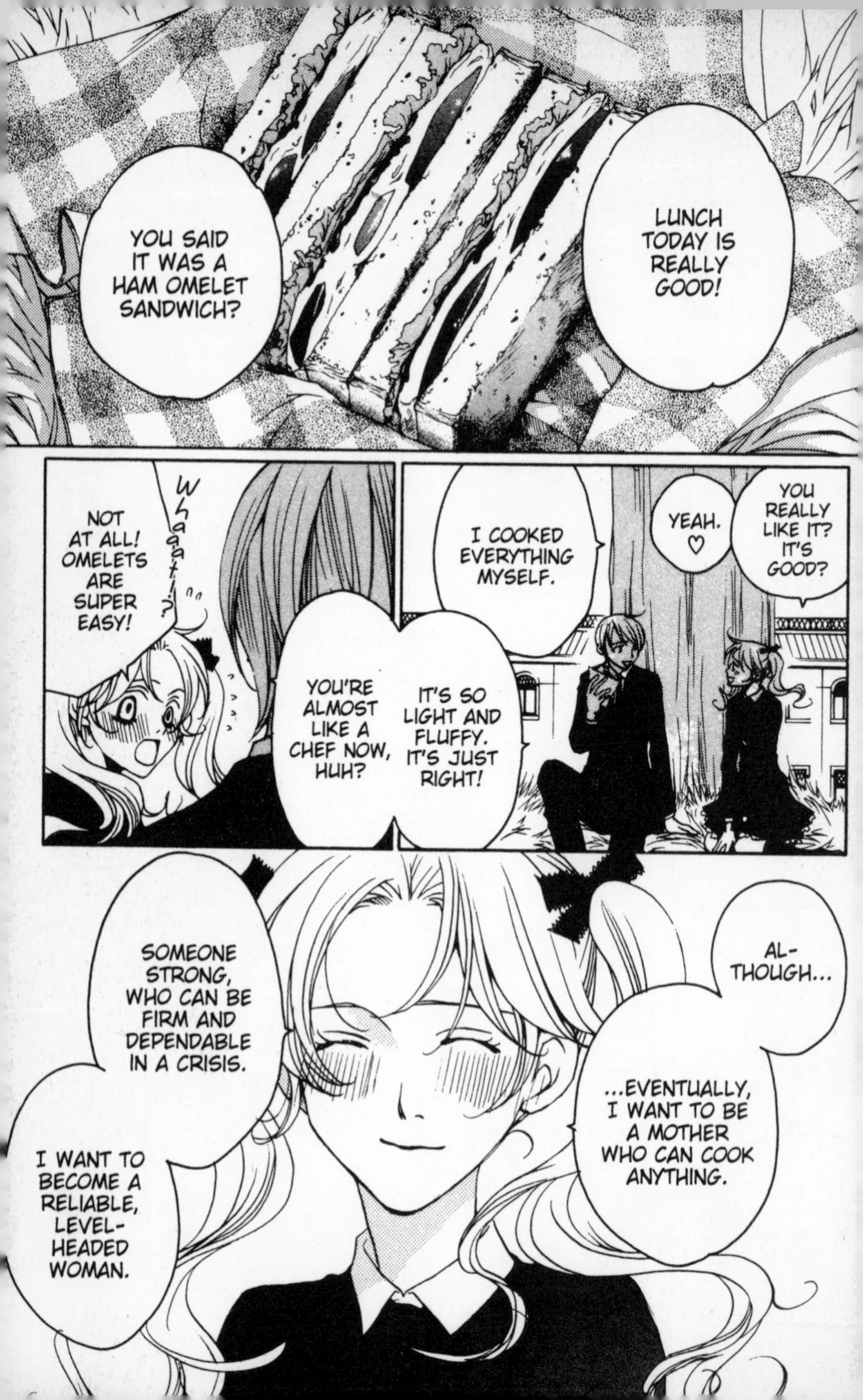
LUNCH TODAY IS REALLY GOOD!
YOU SAID IT WAS A HAM OMELET SANDWICH?
YOU REALLY LIKE IT? IT'S GOOD?
YEAH. ♡
I COOKED EVERYTHING MYSELF.
IT'S SO LIGHT AND FLUFFY. IT'S JUST RIGHT!
YOU'RE ALMOST LIKE A CHEF NOW, HUH?
Whaaat!?
NOT AT ALL! OMELETS ARE SUPER EASY!
AL-THOUGH...
...EVENTUALLY, I WANT TO BE A MOTHER WHO CAN COOK ANYTHING.
SOMEONE STRONG, WHO CAN BE FIRM AND DEPENDABLE IN A CRISIS.
I WANT TO BECOME A RELIABLE, LEVEL-HEADED WOMAN.

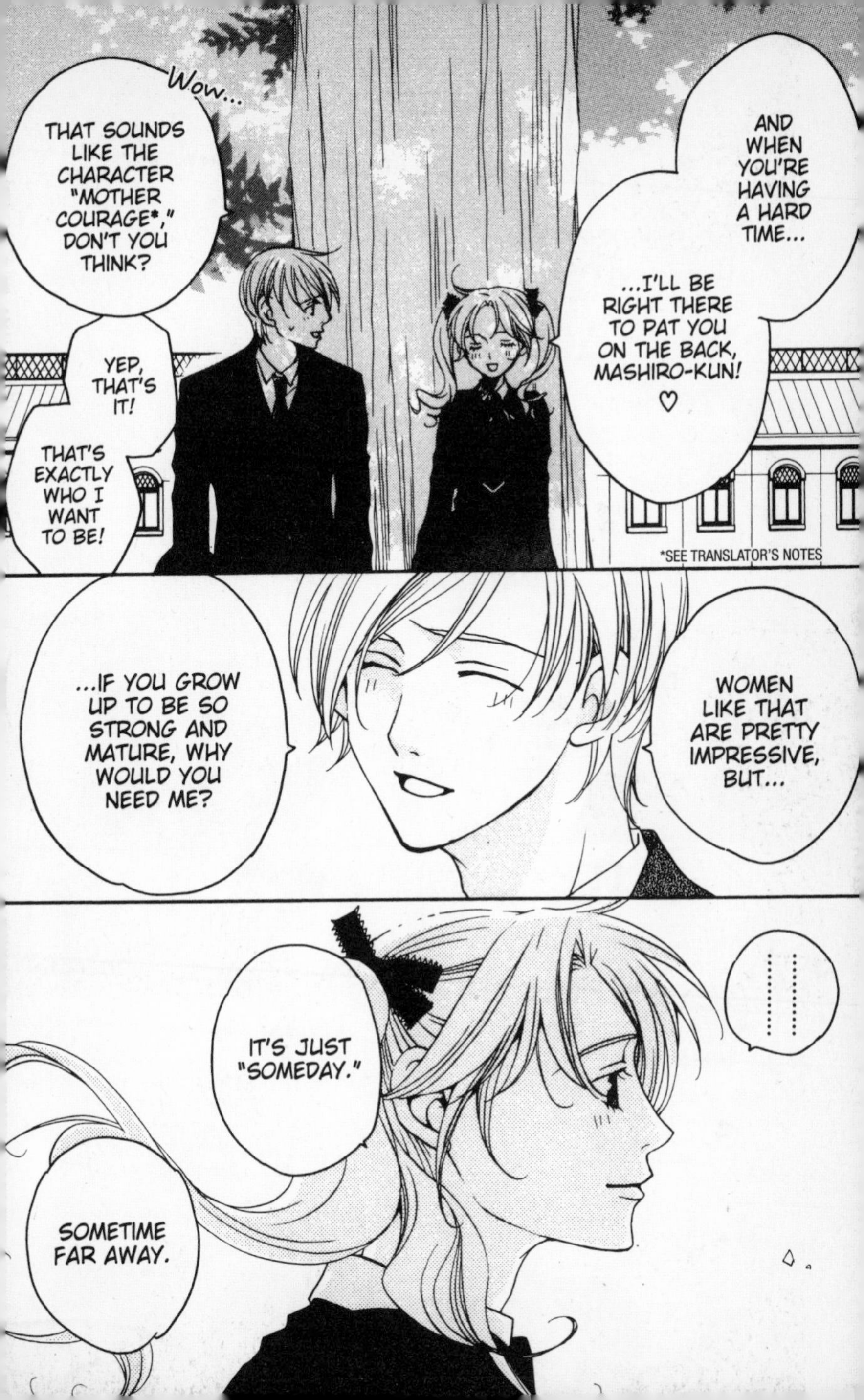
AND WHEN YOU'RE HAVING A HARD TIME...
...I'LL BE RIGHT THERE TO PAT YOU ON THE BACK, MASHIRO-KUN! ♡
Wow...
THAT SOUNDS LIKE THE CHARACTER "MOTHER COURAGE*," DON'T YOU THINK?
YEP, THAT'S IT!
THAT'S EXACTLY WHO I WANT TO BE!
*SEE TRANSLATOR'S NOTES
WOMEN LIKE THAT ARE PRETTY IMPRESSIVE, BUT...
...IF YOU GROW UP TO BE SO STRONG AND MATURE, WHY WOULD YOU NEED ME?
......
IT'S JUST "SOMEDAY."
SOMETIME FAR AWAY.

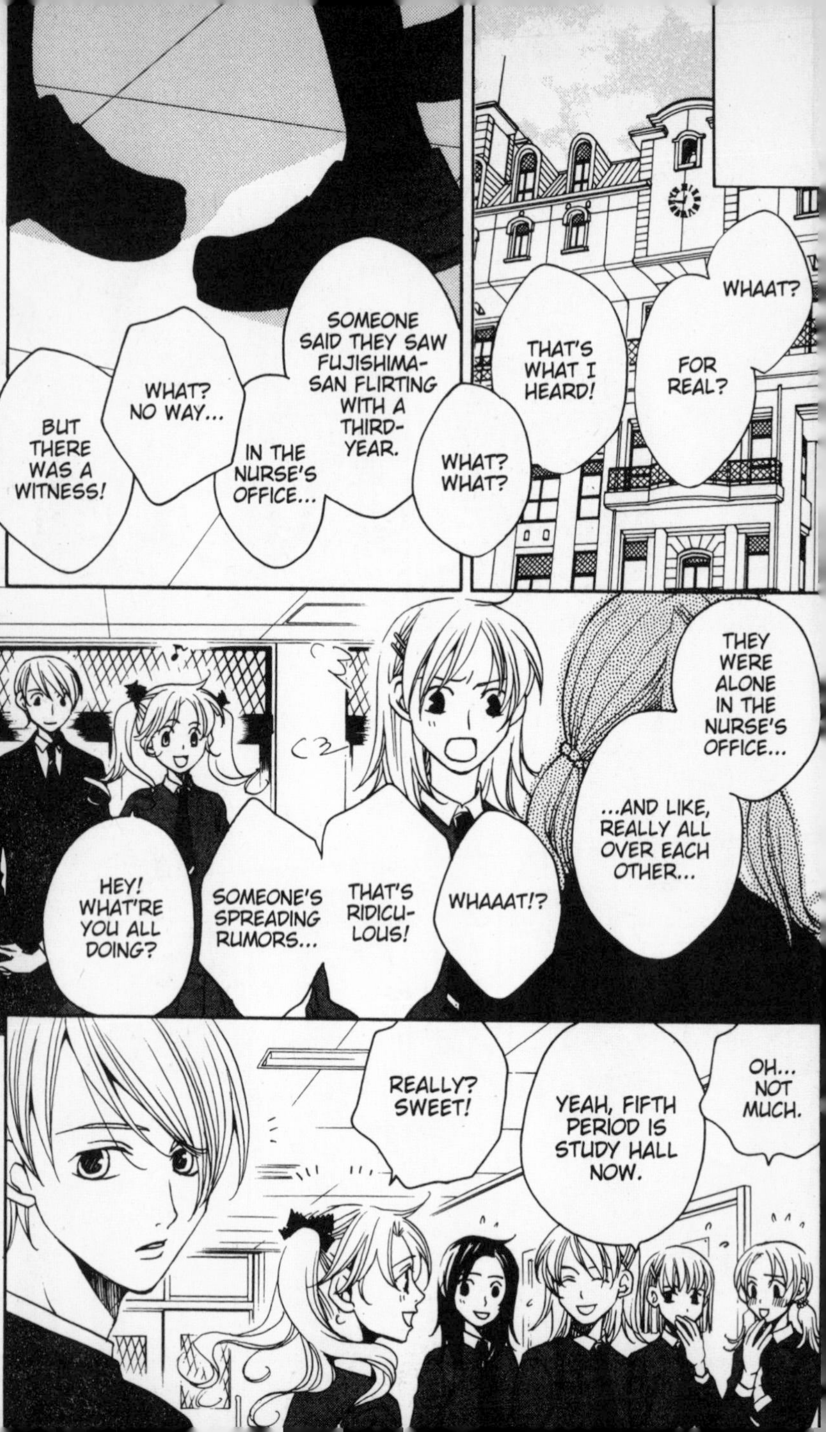
WHAAT?
FOR REAL?
THAT'S WHAT I HEARD!
WHAT? WHAT?
SOMEONE SAID THEY SAW FUJISHIMA-SAN FLIRTING WITH A THIRD-YEAR.
IN THE NURSE'S OFFICE...
WHAT? NO WAY...
BUT THERE WAS A WITNESS!
THEY WERE ALONE IN THE NURSE'S OFFICE...
...AND LIKE, REALLY ALL OVER EACH OTHER...
WHAAAT!?
THAT'S RIDICULOUS!
SOMEONE'S SPREADING RUMORS...
HEY! WHAT'RE YOU ALL DOING?
OH... NOT MUCH.
YEAH, FIFTH PERIOD IS STUDY HALL NOW.
REALLY? SWEET!

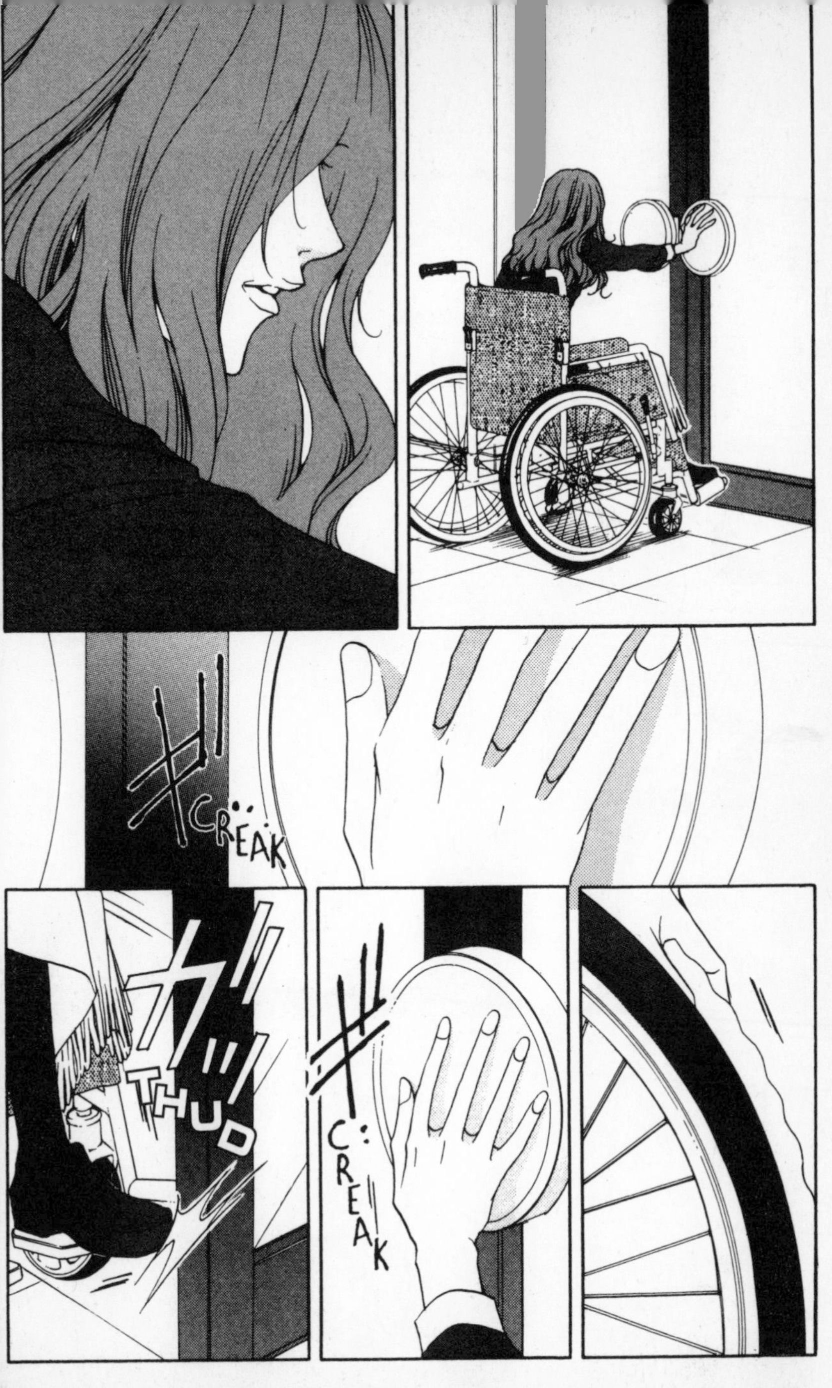
CREAK
CREAK
THUD

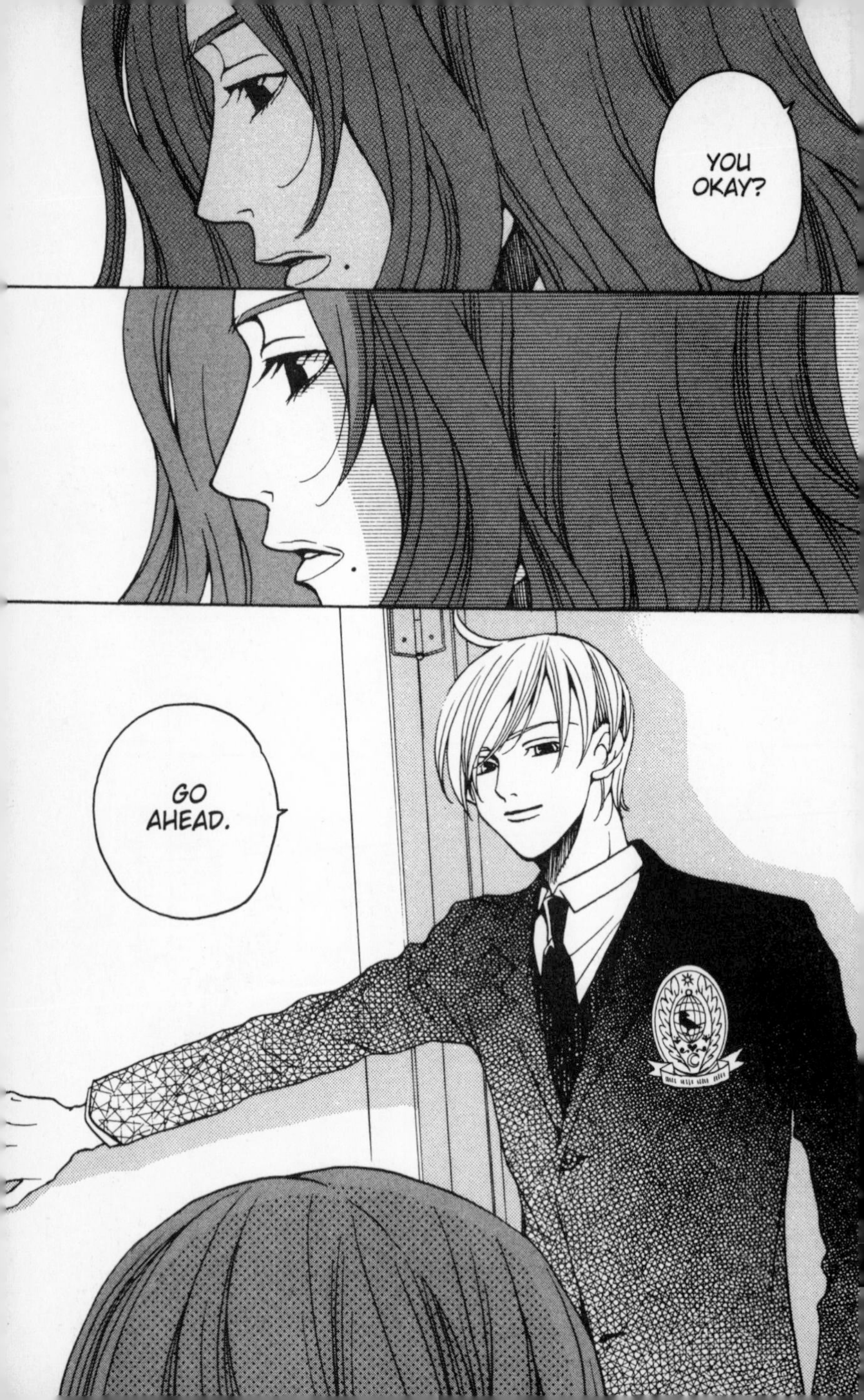
YOU OKAY?
GO AHEAD.

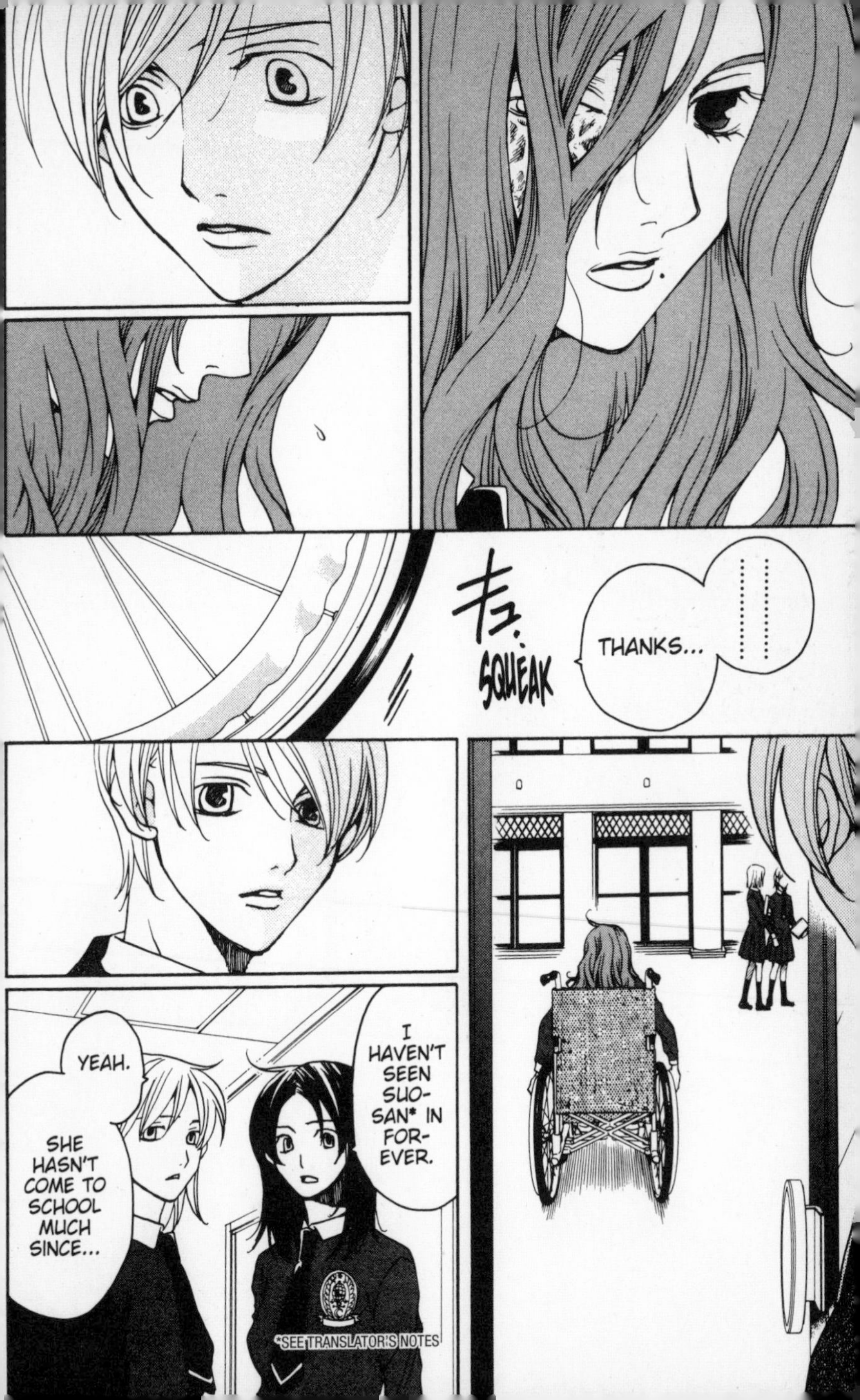
......
SQUEAK
THANKS...
I HAVEN'T SEEN SUO-SAN* IN FOREVER.
YEAH.
SHE HASN'T COME TO SCHOOL MUCH SINCE...
*SEE TRANSLATOR'S NOTES

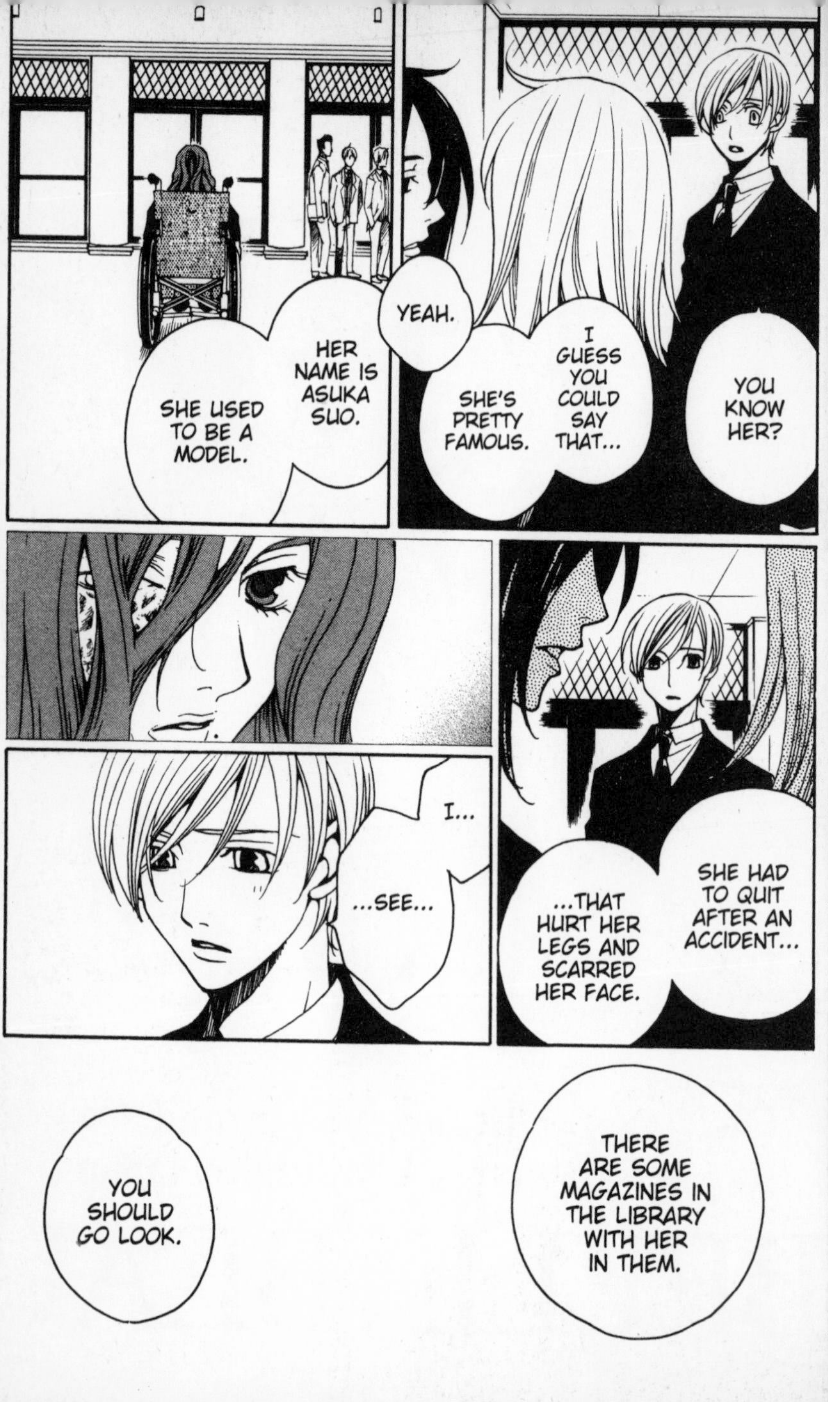
YOU KNOW HER?
YEAH.
I GUESS YOU COULD SAY THAT...
SHE'S PRETTY FAMOUS.
HER NAME IS ASUKA SUO.
SHE USED TO BE A MODEL.
SHE HAD TO QUIT AFTER AN ACCIDENT...
...THAT HURT HER LEGS AND SCARRED HER FACE.
I...
...SEE...
THERE ARE SOME MAGAZINES IN THE LIBRARY WITH HER IN THEM.
YOU SHOULD GO LOOK.

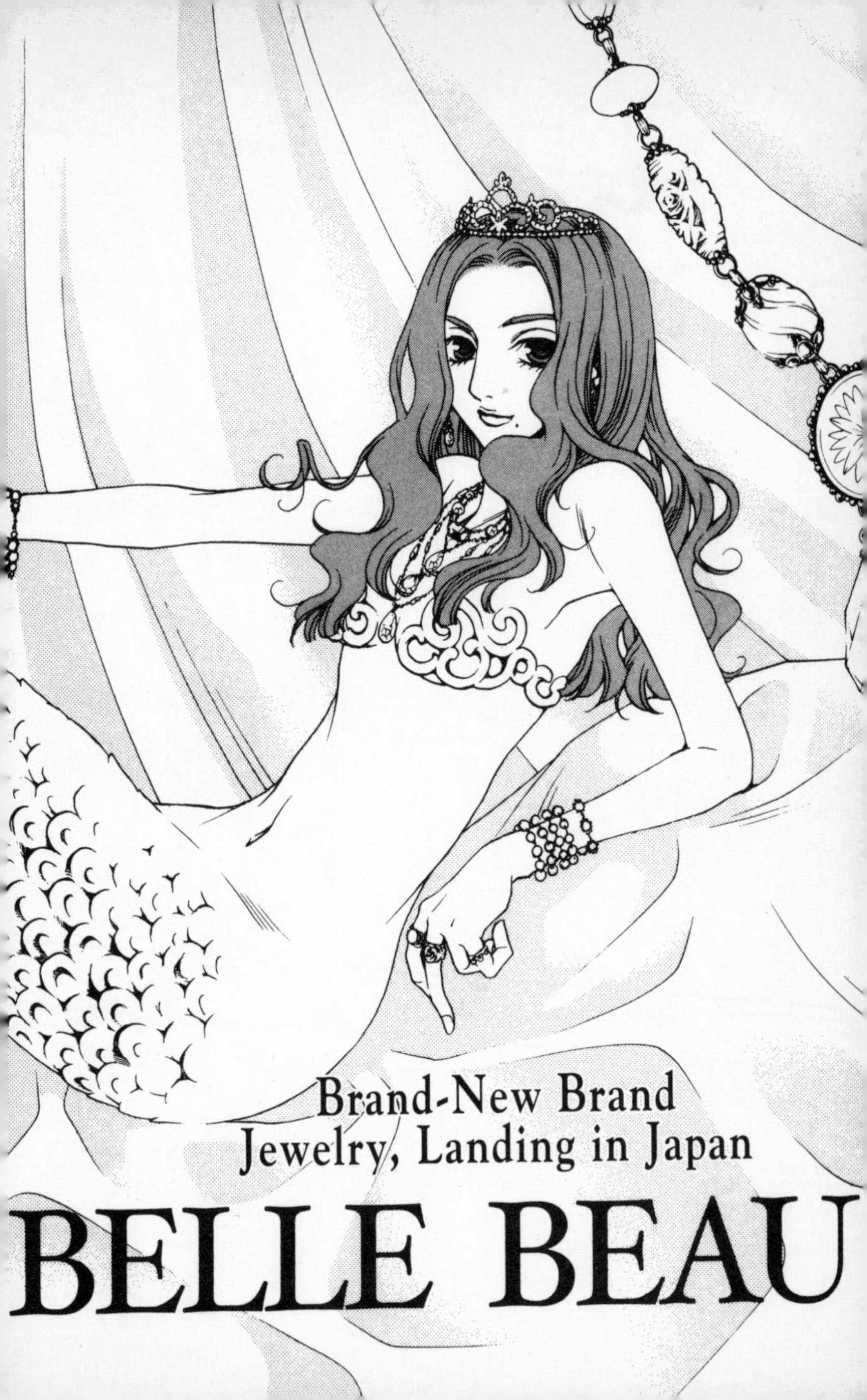
Brand-New Brand
Jewelry, Landing in Japan
BELLE BEAU

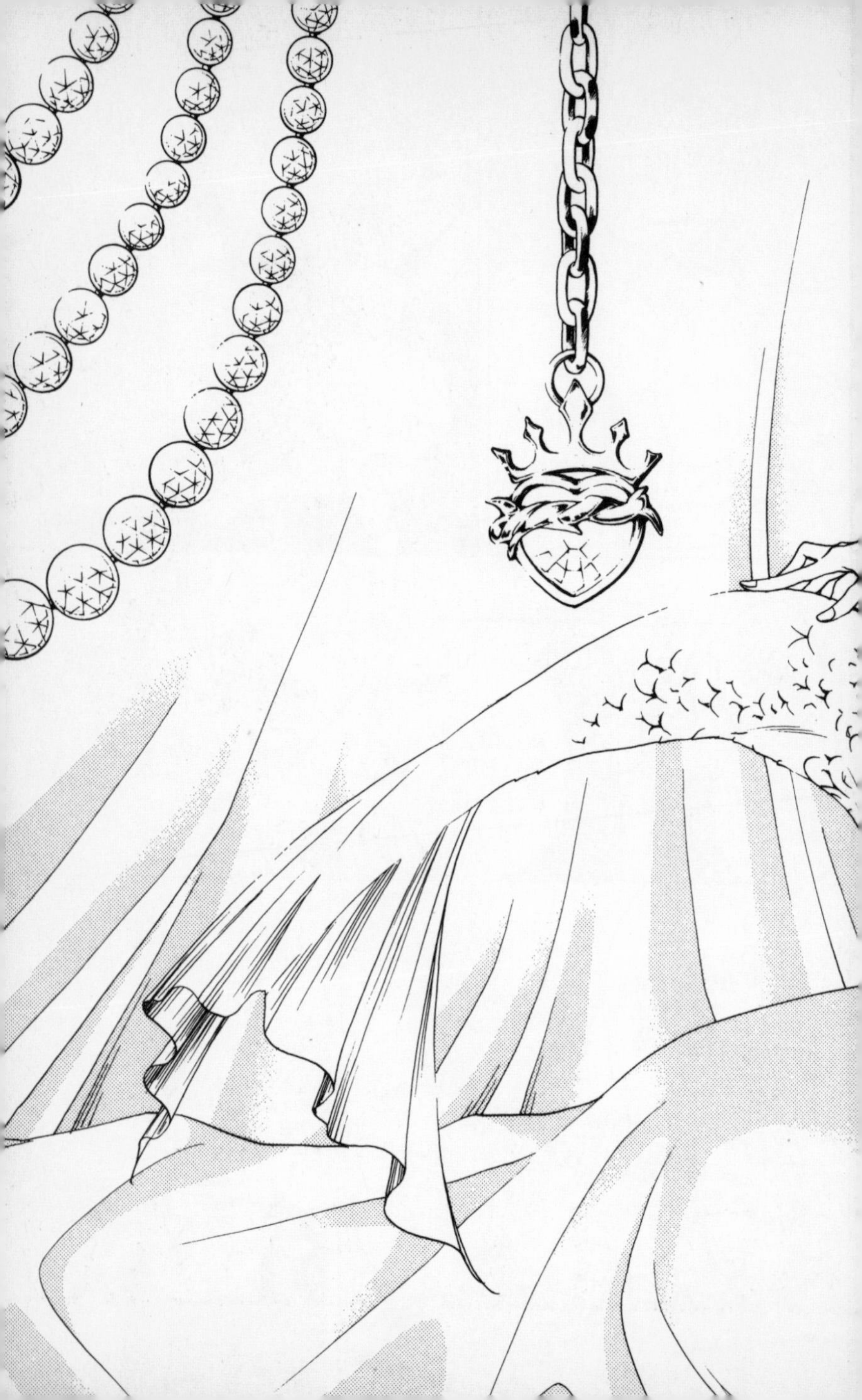

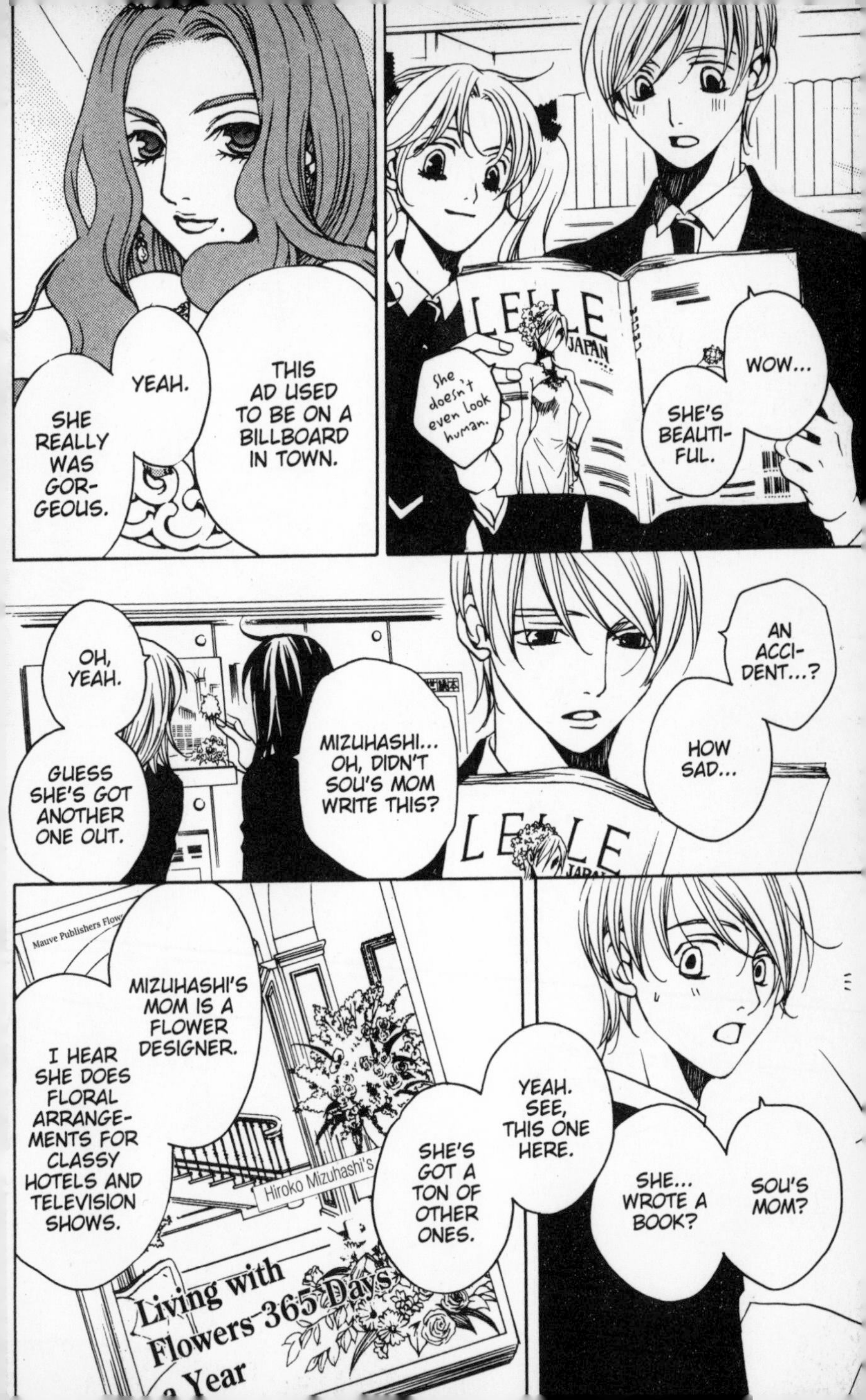
LELLE JAPAN
WOW... SHE'S BEAUTIFUL.
She doesn't even look human.
THIS AD USED TO BE ON A BILLBOARD IN TOWN.
YEAH. SHE REALLY WAS GORGEOUS.
AN ACCIDENT...? HOW SAD...
LELLE JAPAN
MIZUHASHI... OH, DIDN'T SOU'S MOM WRITE THIS?
OH, YEAH. GUESS SHE'S GOT ANOTHER ONE OUT.
SOU'S MOM? SHE... WROTE A BOOK?
YEAH. SEE, THIS ONE HERE.
SHE'S GOT A TON OF OTHER ONES.
Mauve Publishers Flow
MIZUHASHI'S MOM IS A FLOWER DESIGNER.
I HEAR SHE DOES FLORAL ARRANGEMENTS FOR CLASSY HOTELS AND TELEVISION SHOWS.
Hiroko Mizuhashi's
Living with Flowers-365 Days a Year

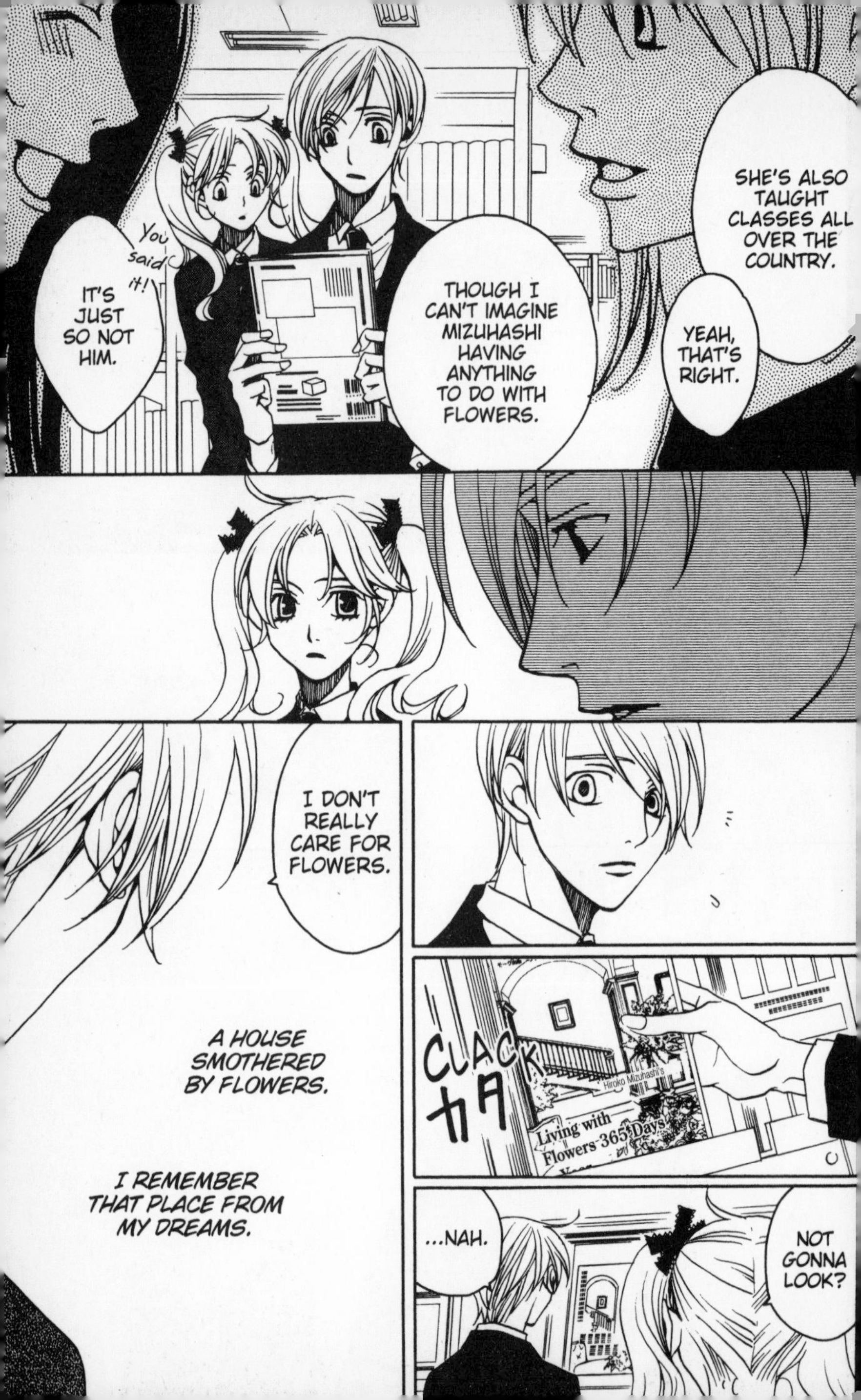
SHE'S ALSO TAUGHT CLASSES ALL OVER THE COUNTRY.
YEAH, THAT'S RIGHT.
THOUGH I CAN'T IMAGINE MIZUHASHI HAVING ANYTHING TO DO WITH FLOWERS.
You said it!
IT'S JUST SO NOT HIM.
CLACK
カチ
Hiroko Mizuhashi's
Living with Flowers-365 Days
NOT GONNA LOOK?
...NAH.
I DON'T REALLY CARE FOR FLOWERS.
A HOUSE SMOTHERED BY FLOWERS.
I REMEMBER THAT PLACE FROM MY DREAMS.

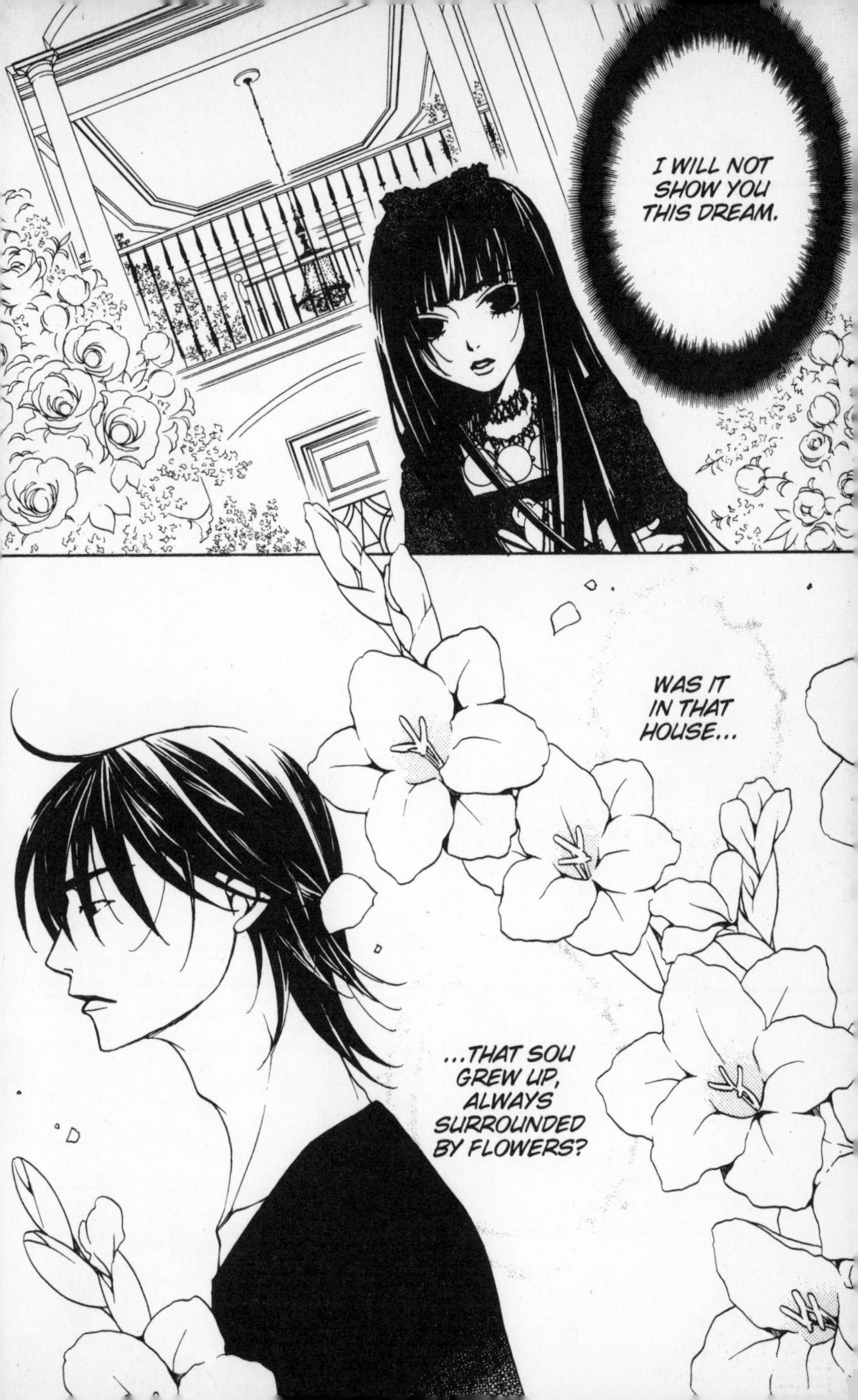
I WILL NOT SHOW YOU THIS DREAM.
WAS IT IN THAT HOUSE...
...THAT SOU GREW UP, ALWAYS SURROUNDED BY FLOWERS?

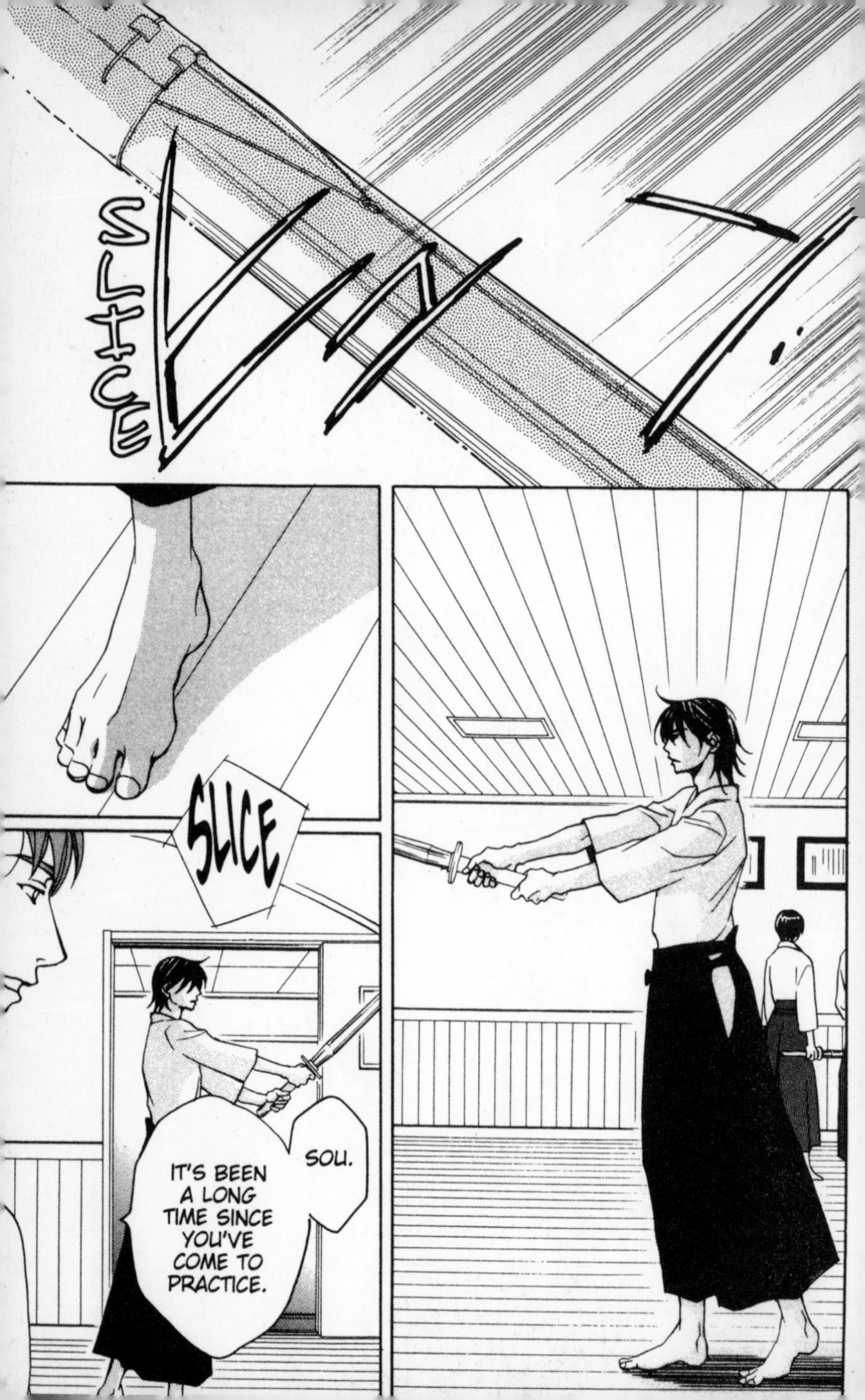
SLICE
SLICE
SOU.
IT'S BEEN A LONG TIME SINCE YOU'VE COME TO PRACTICE.

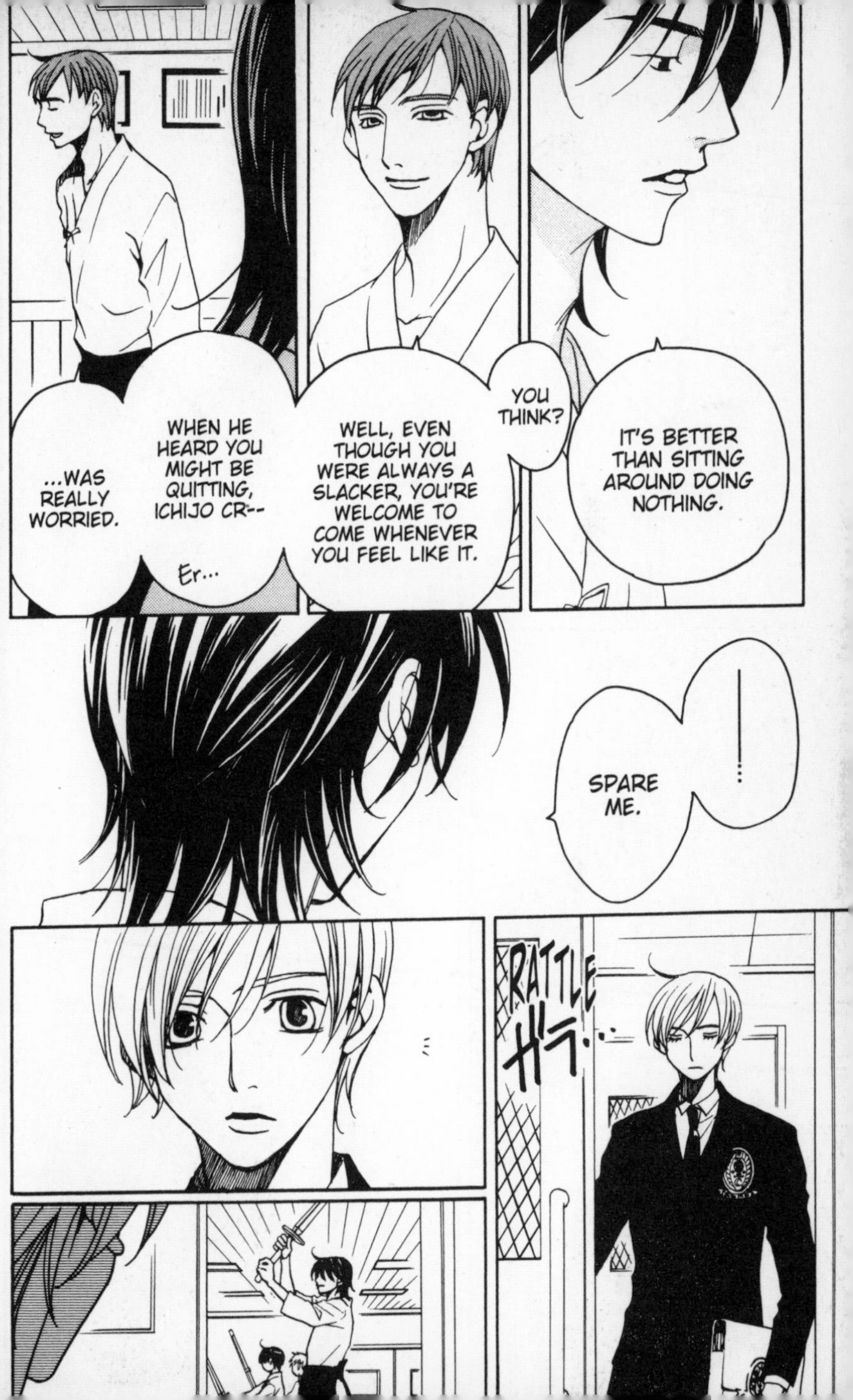
IT'S BETTER THAN SITTING AROUND DOING NOTHING.
YOU THINK?
WELL, EVEN THOUGH YOU WERE ALWAYS A SLACKER, YOU'RE WELCOME TO COME WHENEVER YOU FEEL LIKE IT.
WHEN HE HEARD YOU MIGHT BE QUITTING, ICHIJO CR--
Er...
...WAS REALLY WORRIED.
SPARE ME.
RATTLE
ガラ

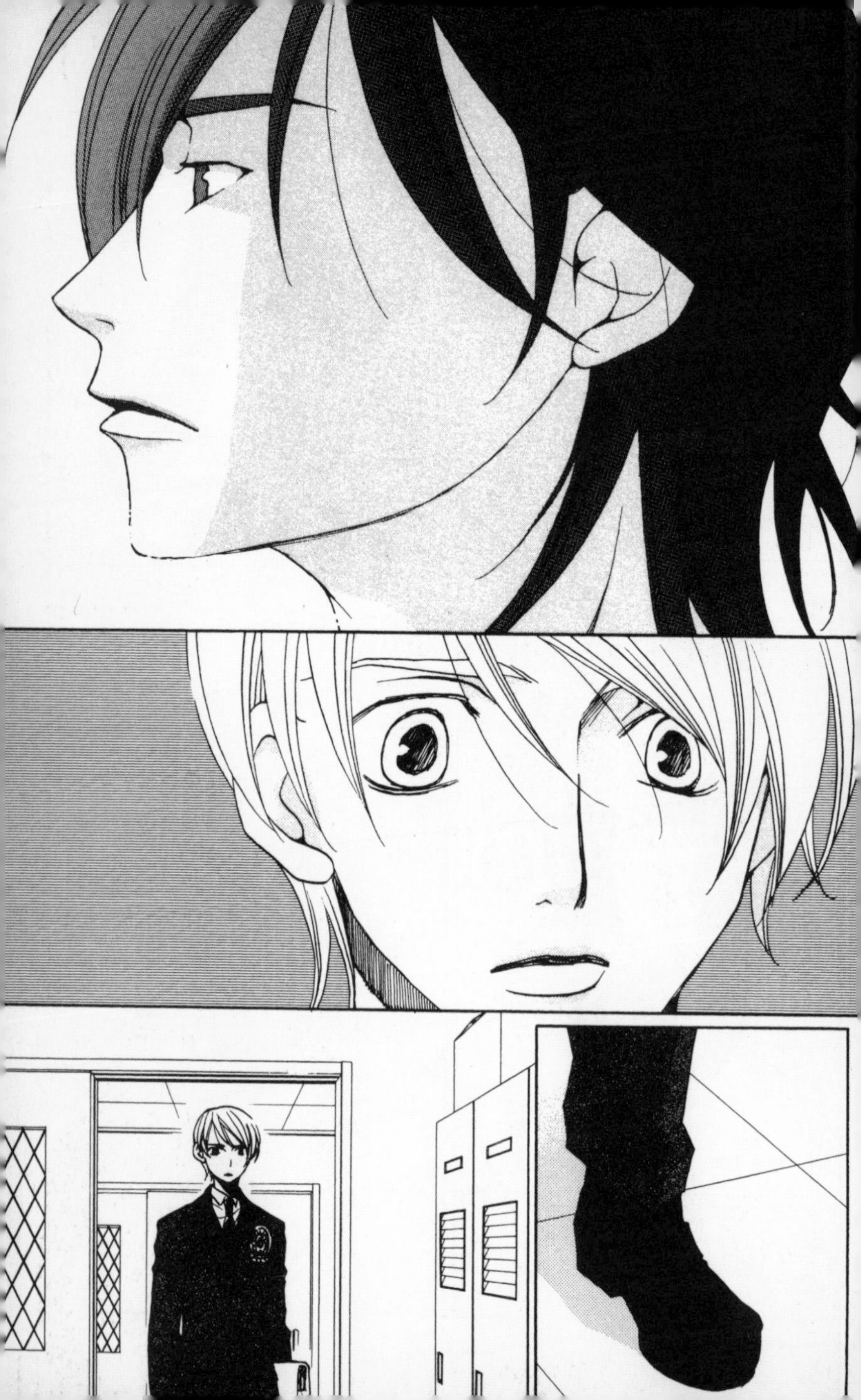

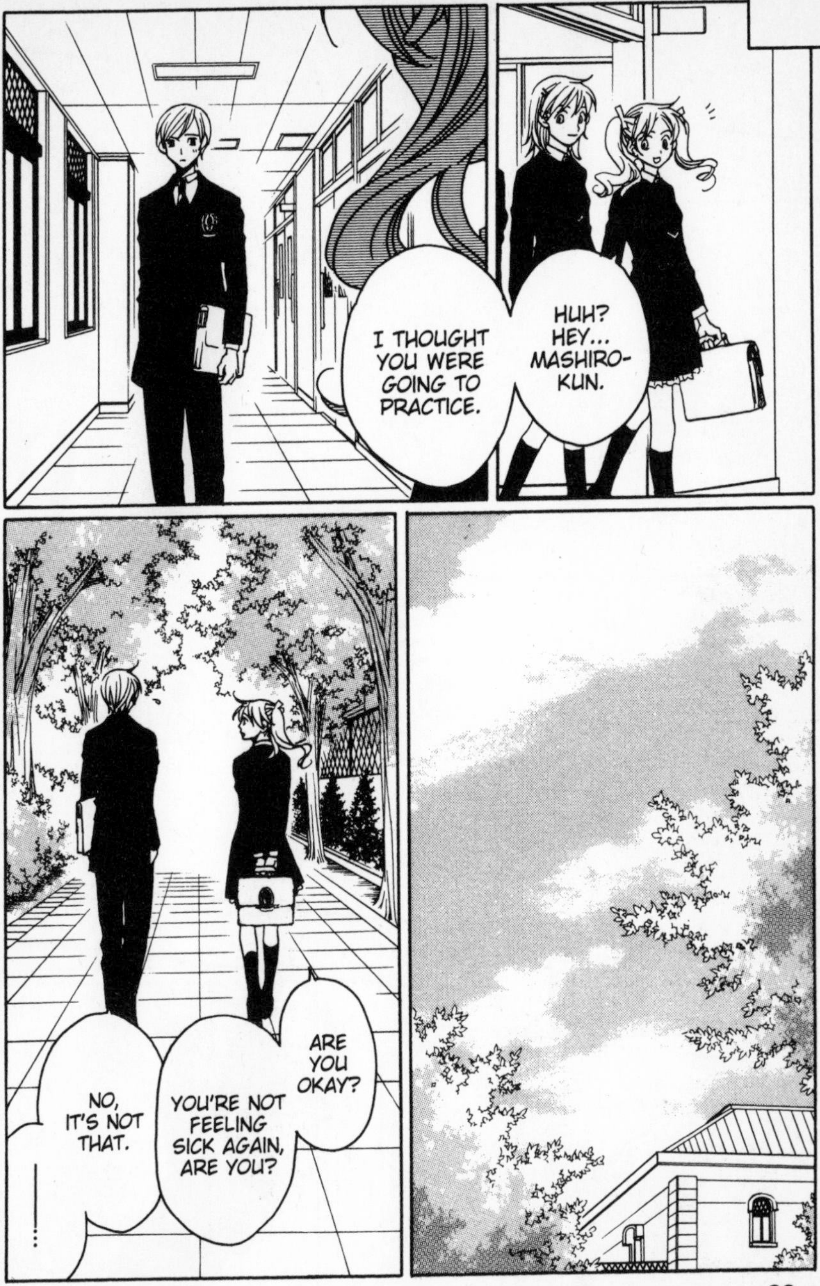
HUH? HEY... MASHIRO-KUN.
I THOUGHT YOU WERE GOING TO PRACTICE.
ARE YOU OKAY?
YOU'RE NOT FEELING SICK AGAIN, ARE YOU?
NO, IT'S NOT THAT.
......

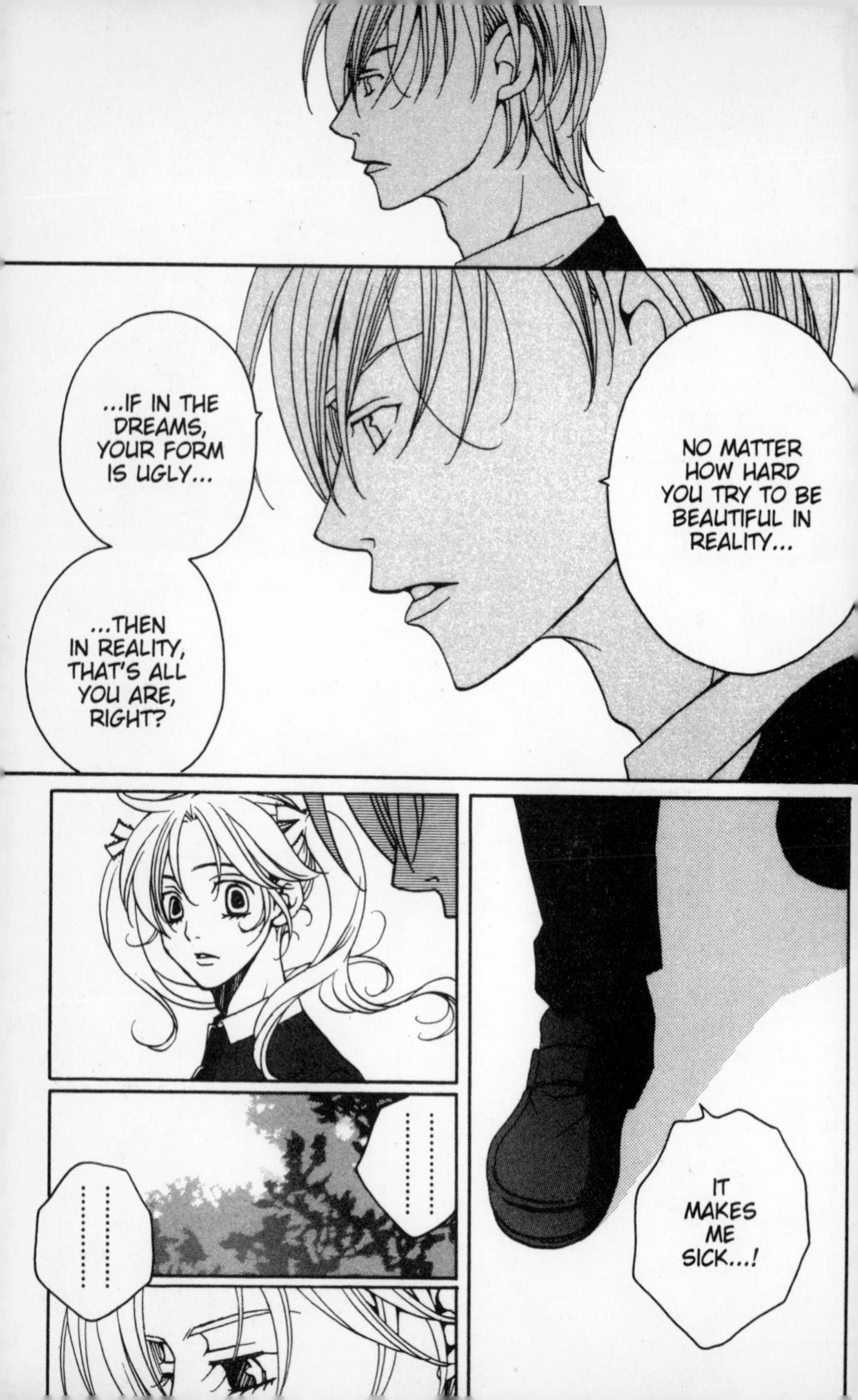
NO MATTER HOW HARD YOU TRY TO BE BEAUTIFUL IN REALITY...
...IF IN THE DREAMS, YOUR FORM IS UGLY...
...THEN IN REALITY, THAT'S ALL YOU ARE, RIGHT?
IT MAKES ME SICK...!
......
......

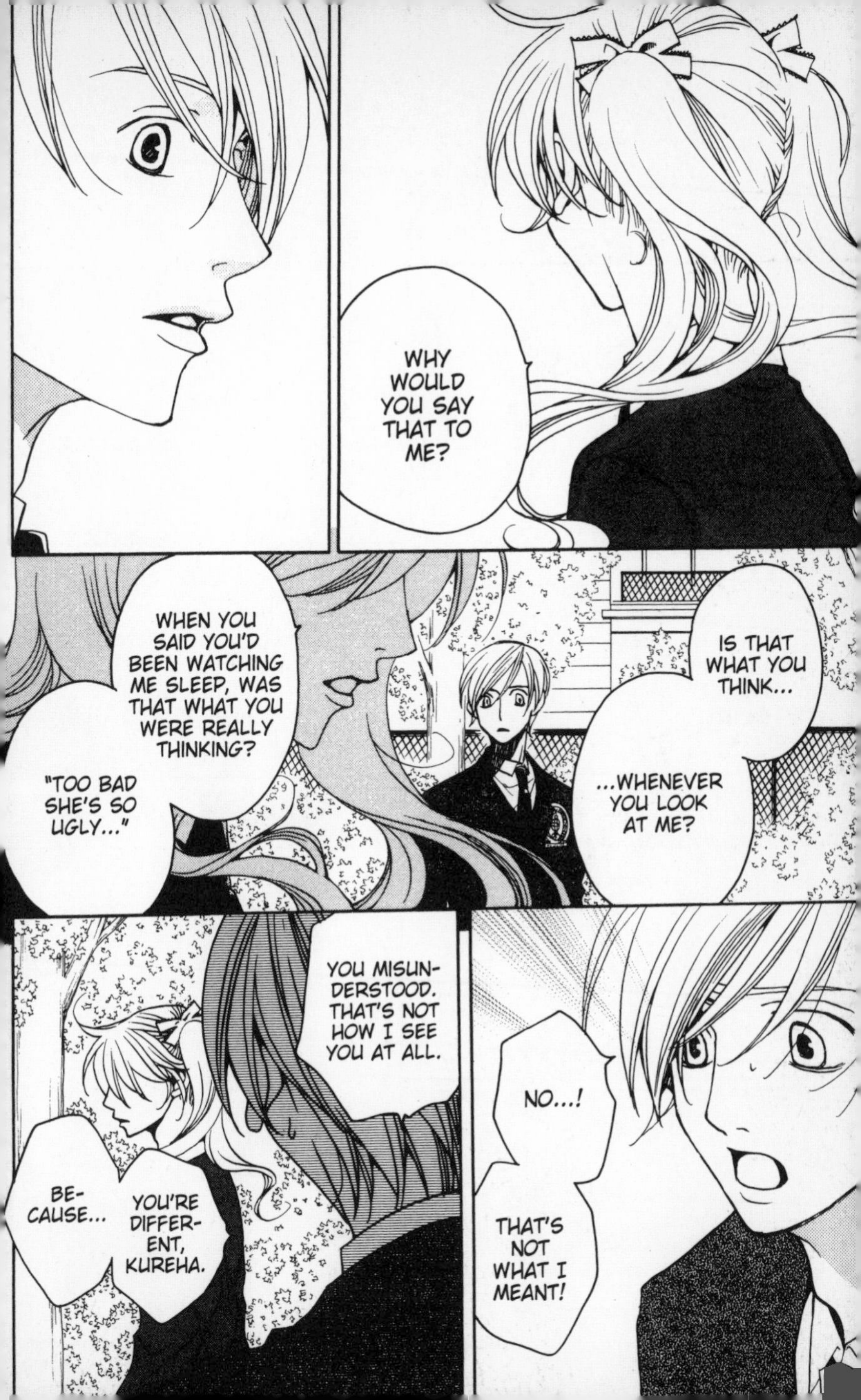
WHY WOULD YOU SAY THAT TO ME?
IS THAT WHAT YOU THINK...
...WHENEVER YOU LOOK AT ME?
WHEN YOU SAID YOU'D BEEN WATCHING ME SLEEP, WAS THAT WHAT YOU WERE REALLY THINKING?
"TOO BAD SHE'S SO UGLY..."
NO...!
THAT'S NOT WHAT I MEANT!
YOU MISUN-DERSTOOD. THAT'S NOT HOW I SEE YOU AT ALL.
BE-CAUSE...
YOU'RE DIFFER-ENT, KUREHA.

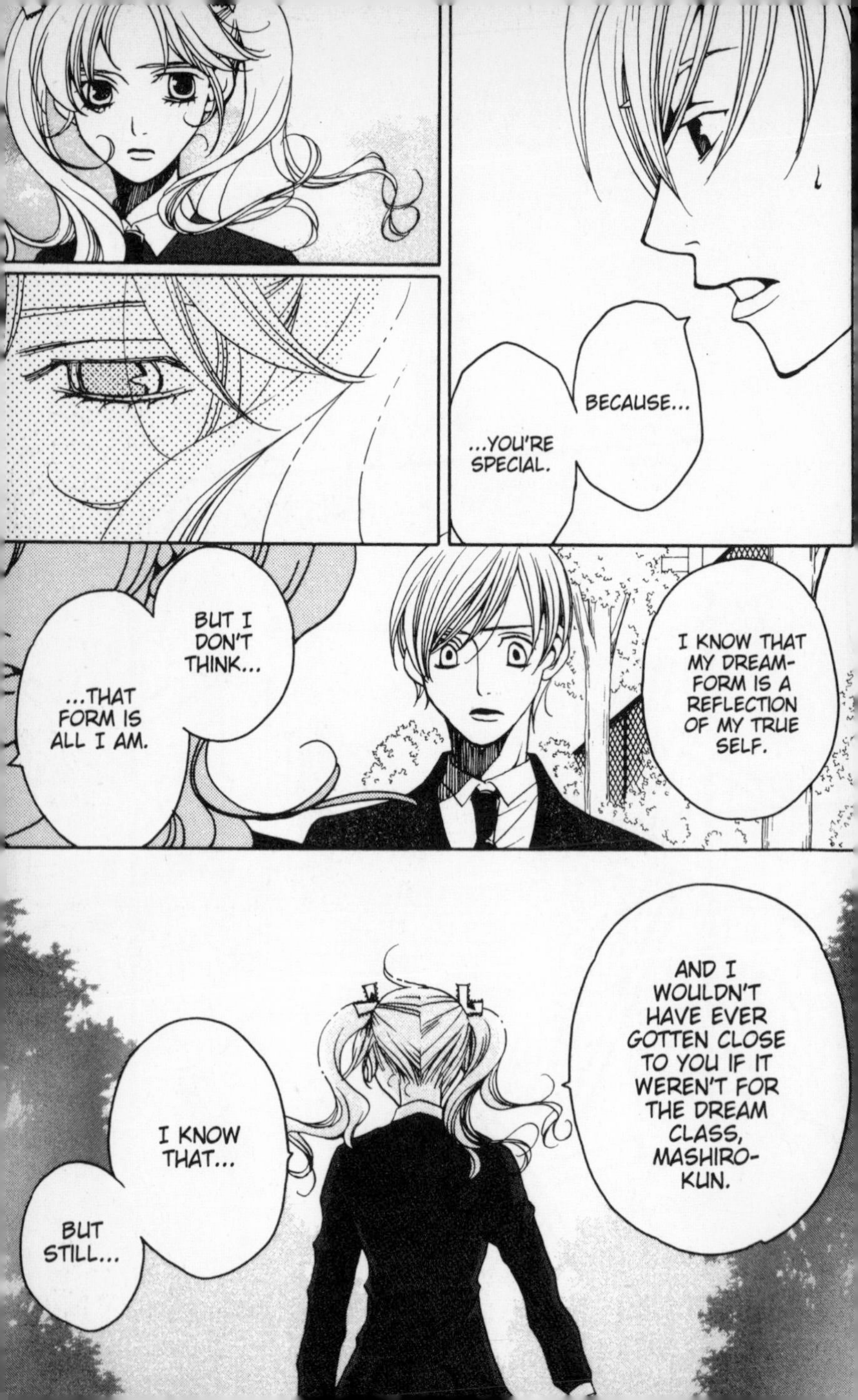
BECAUSE...
...YOU'RE SPECIAL.
I KNOW THAT MY DREAM-FORM IS A REFLECTION OF MY TRUE SELF.
BUT I DON'T THINK...
...THAT FORM IS ALL I AM.
AND I WOULDN'T HAVE EVER GOTTEN CLOSE TO YOU IF IT WEREN'T FOR THE DREAM CLASS, MASHIRO-KUN.
I KNOW THAT...
BUT STILL...

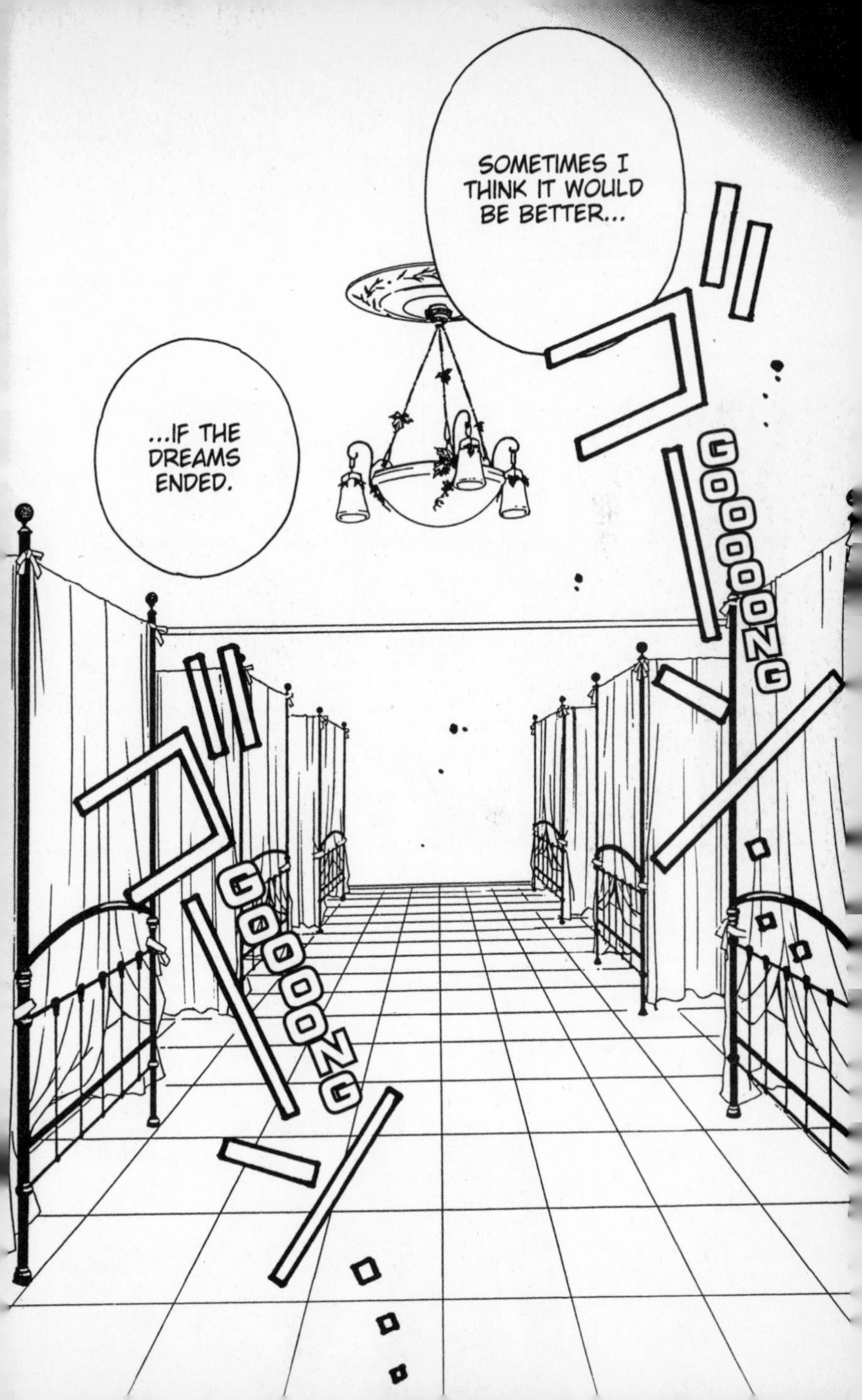
SOMETIMES I THINK IT WOULD BE BETTER...
...IF THE DREAMS ENDED.
GOOOOONG
GOOOOONG

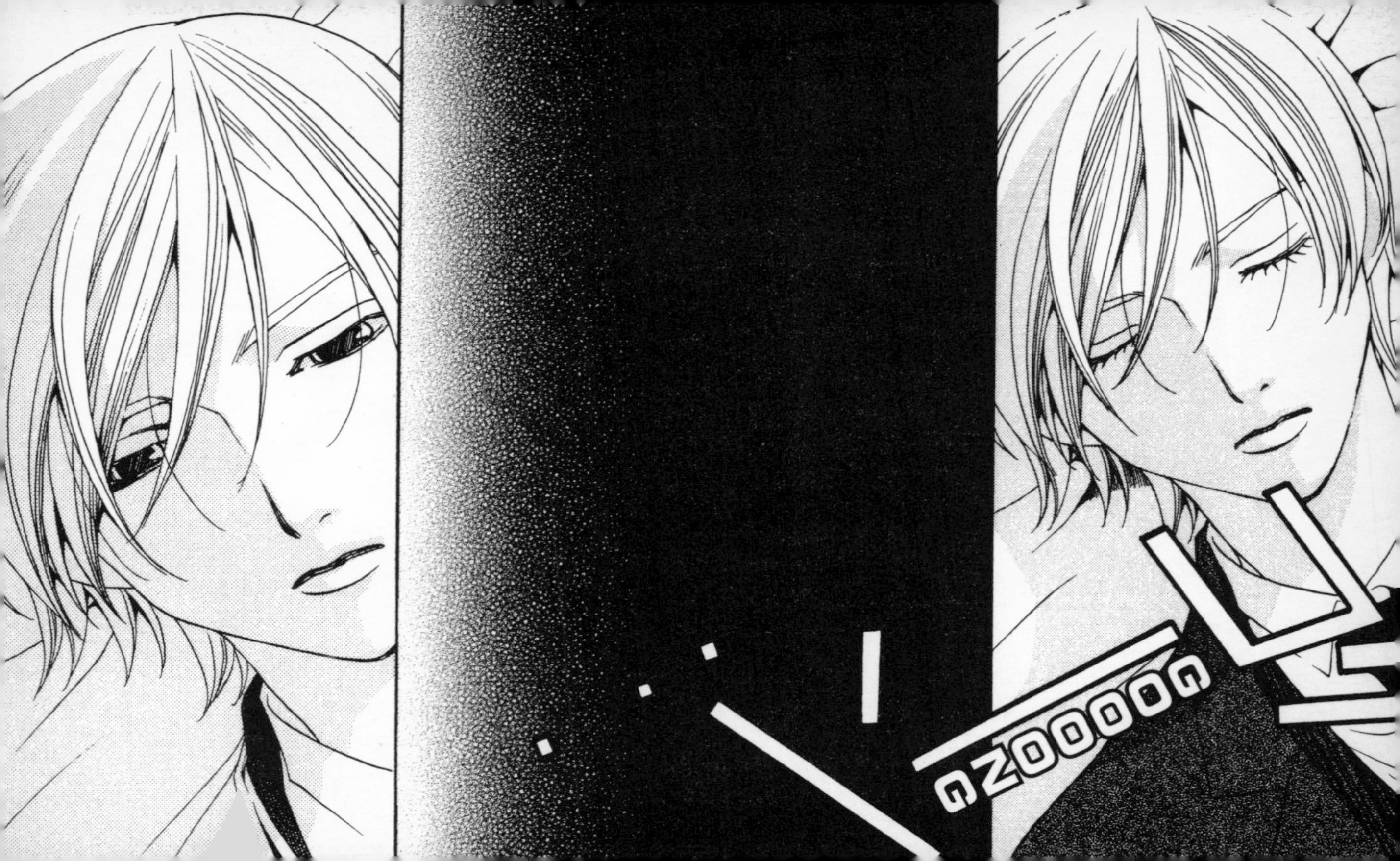
GOOOONG
...

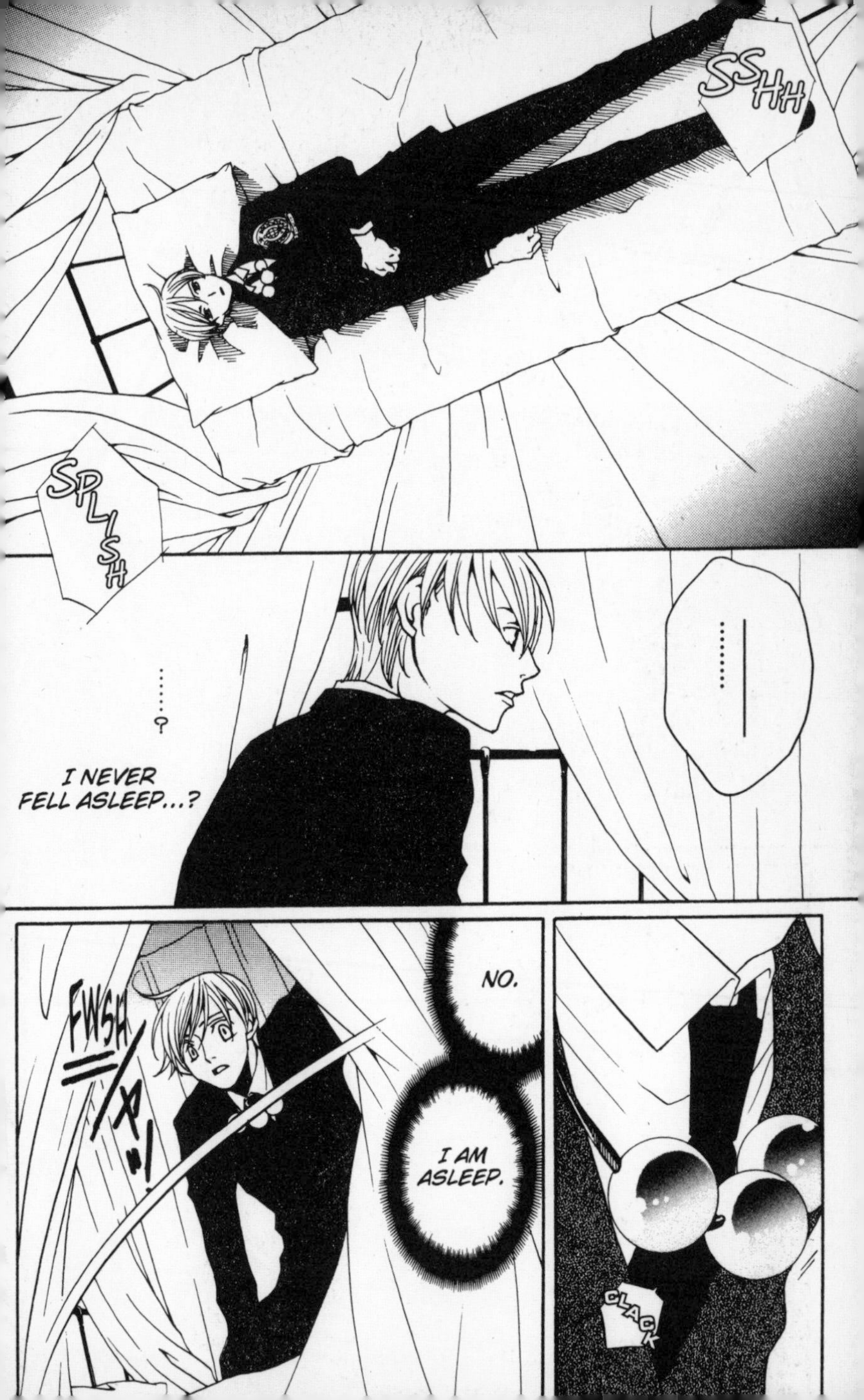
SSHH
SPLISH
......!
......?
I NEVER FELL ASLEEP...?
CLACK
NO.
I AM ASLEEP.
FWSH

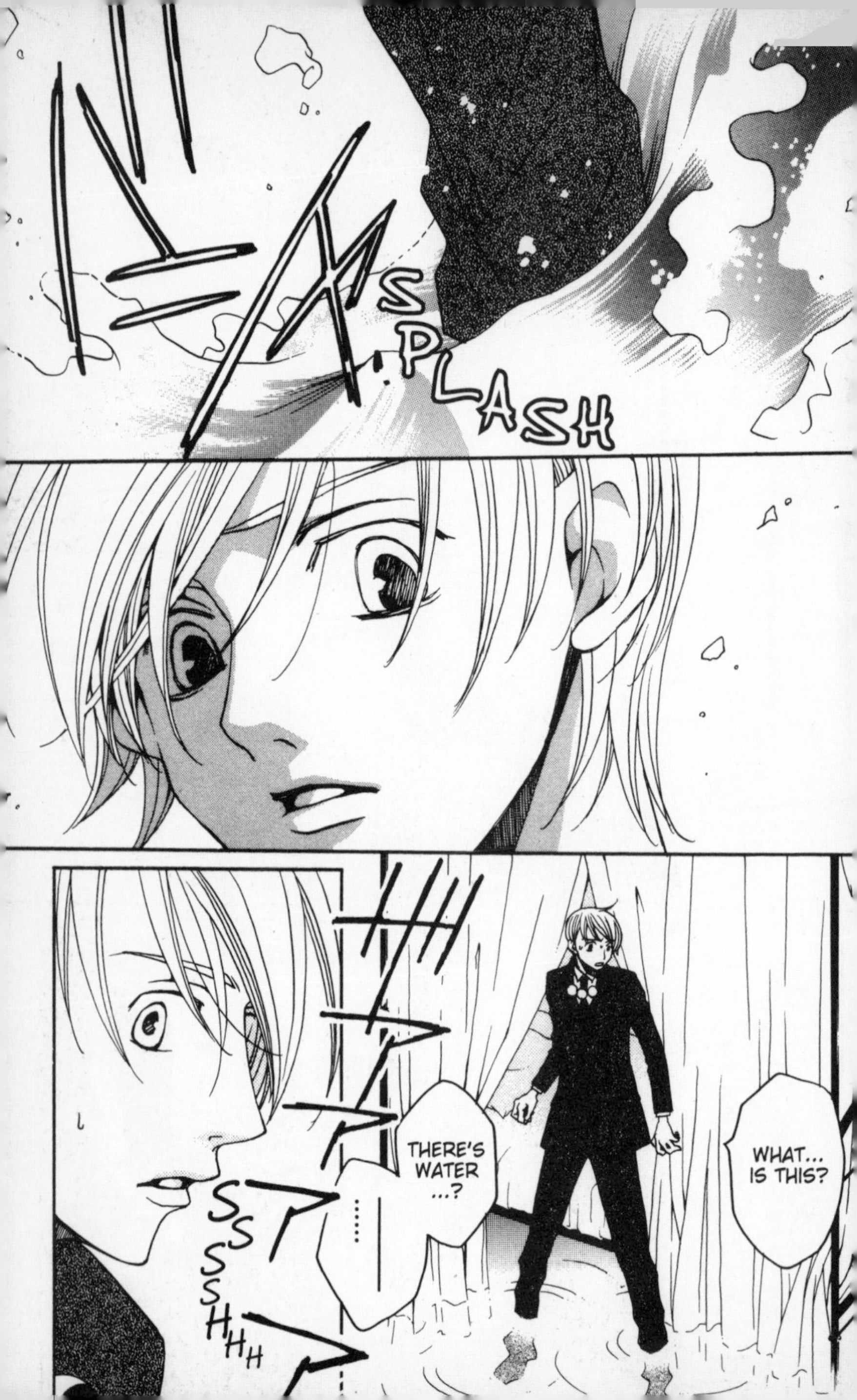
SPLASH
WHAT... IS THIS?
THERE'S WATER ...?
......
SSSSHHH

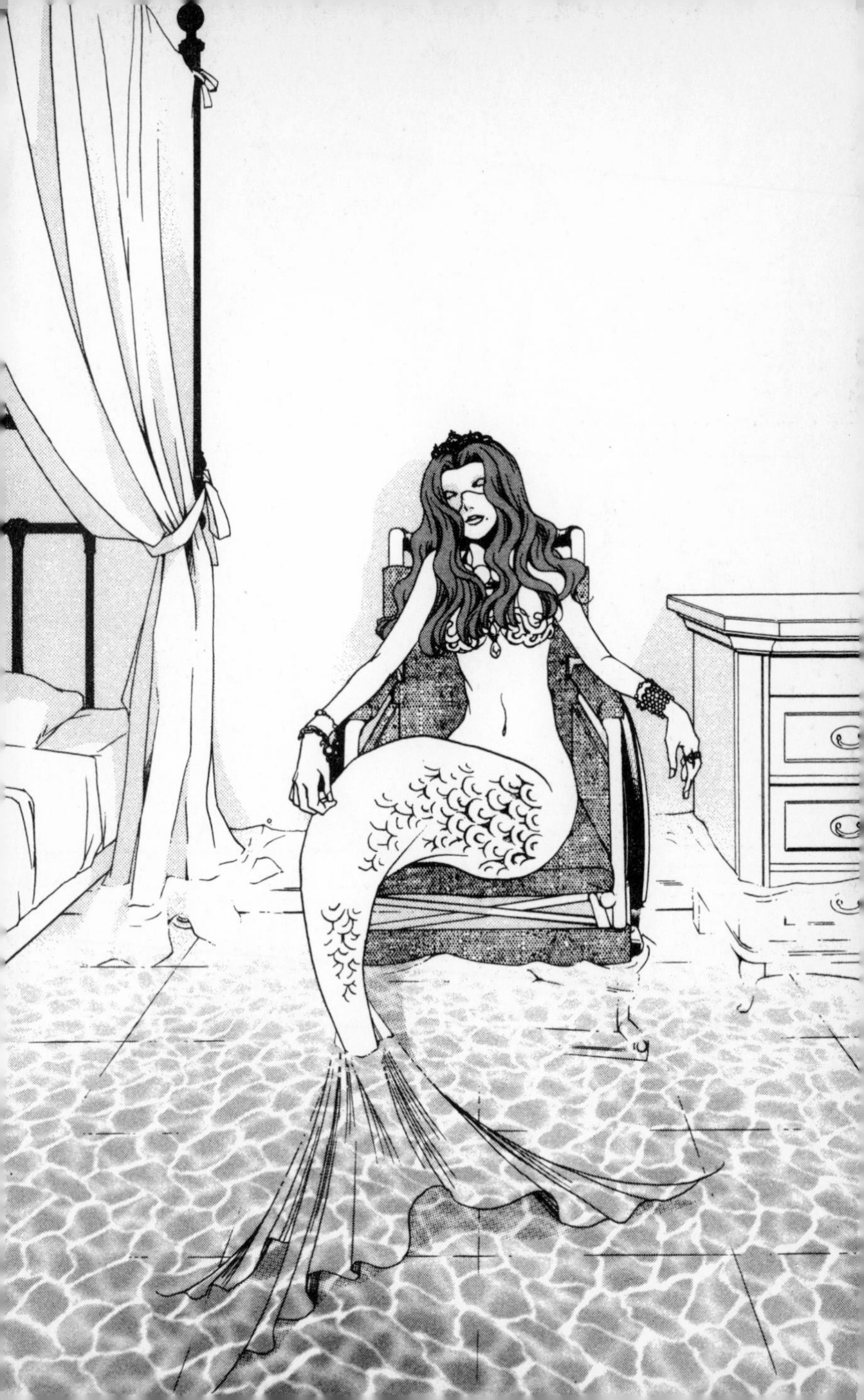

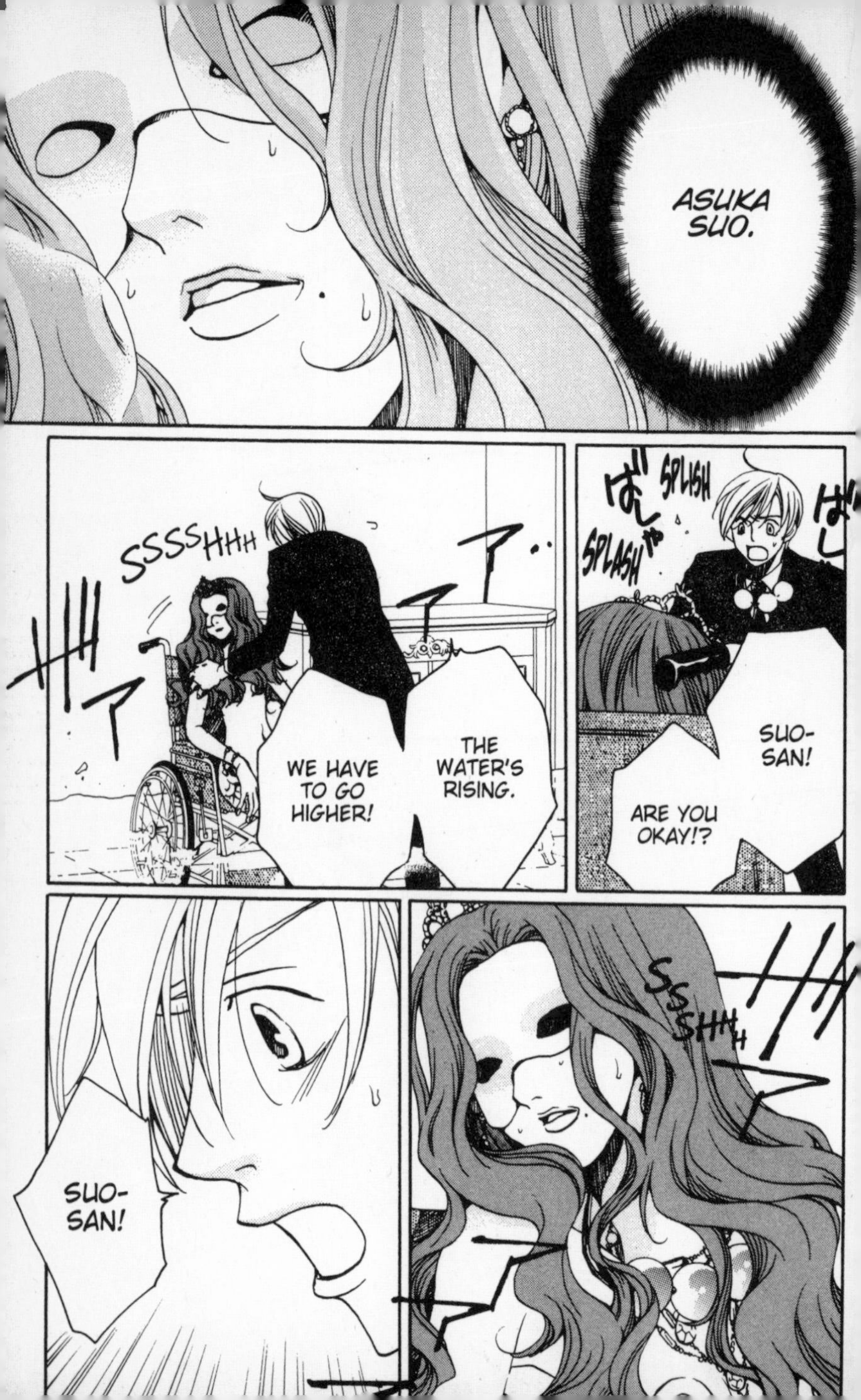
ASUKA SUO.
SPLISH
SPLASH
SUO-SAN!
ARE YOU OKAY!?
SSSSHHH
THE WATER'S RISING.
WE HAVE TO GO HIGHER!
SSSHHH
SUO-SAN!

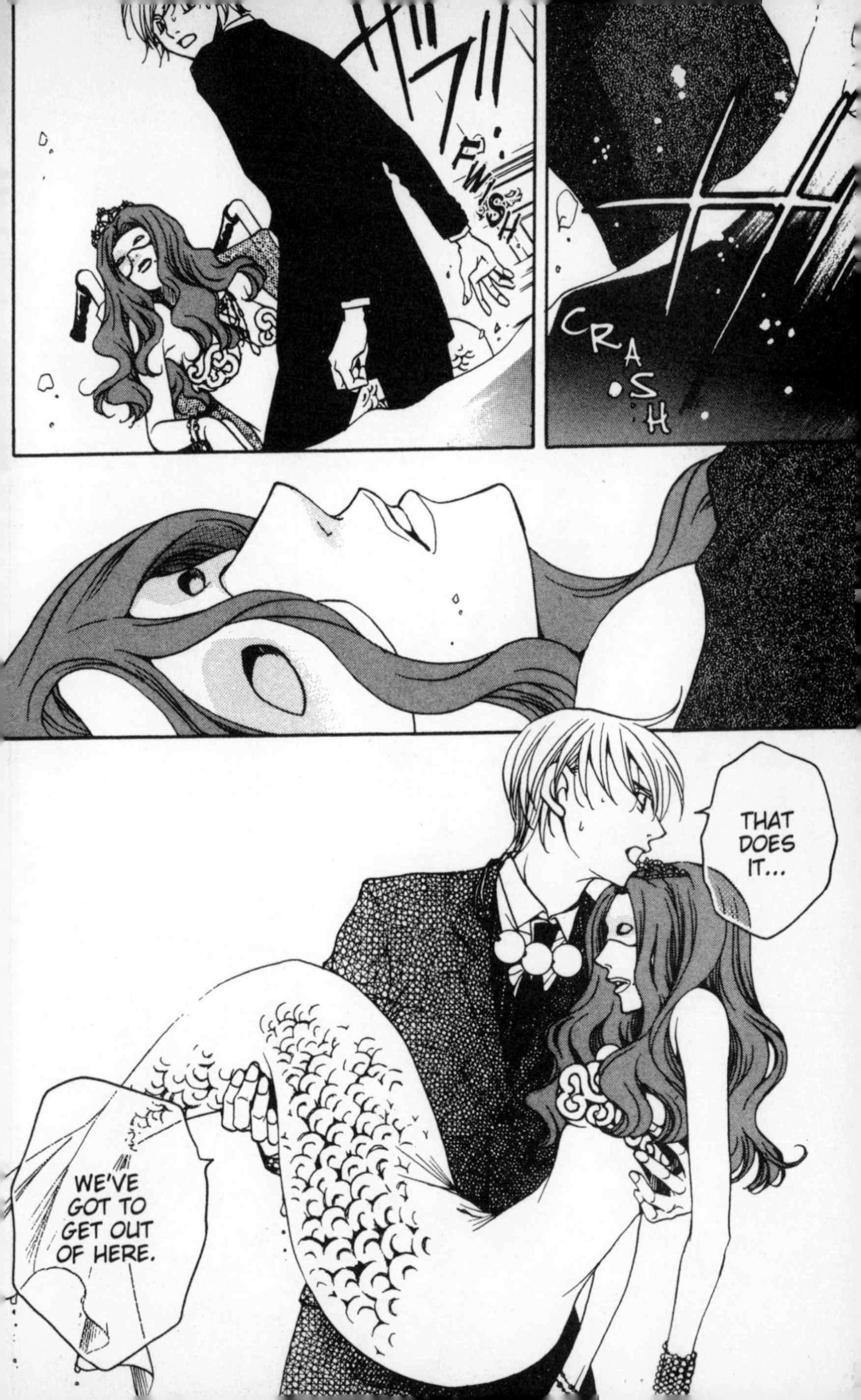
CRASH
FWISH
THAT DOES IT...
WE'VE GOT TO GET OUT OF HERE.

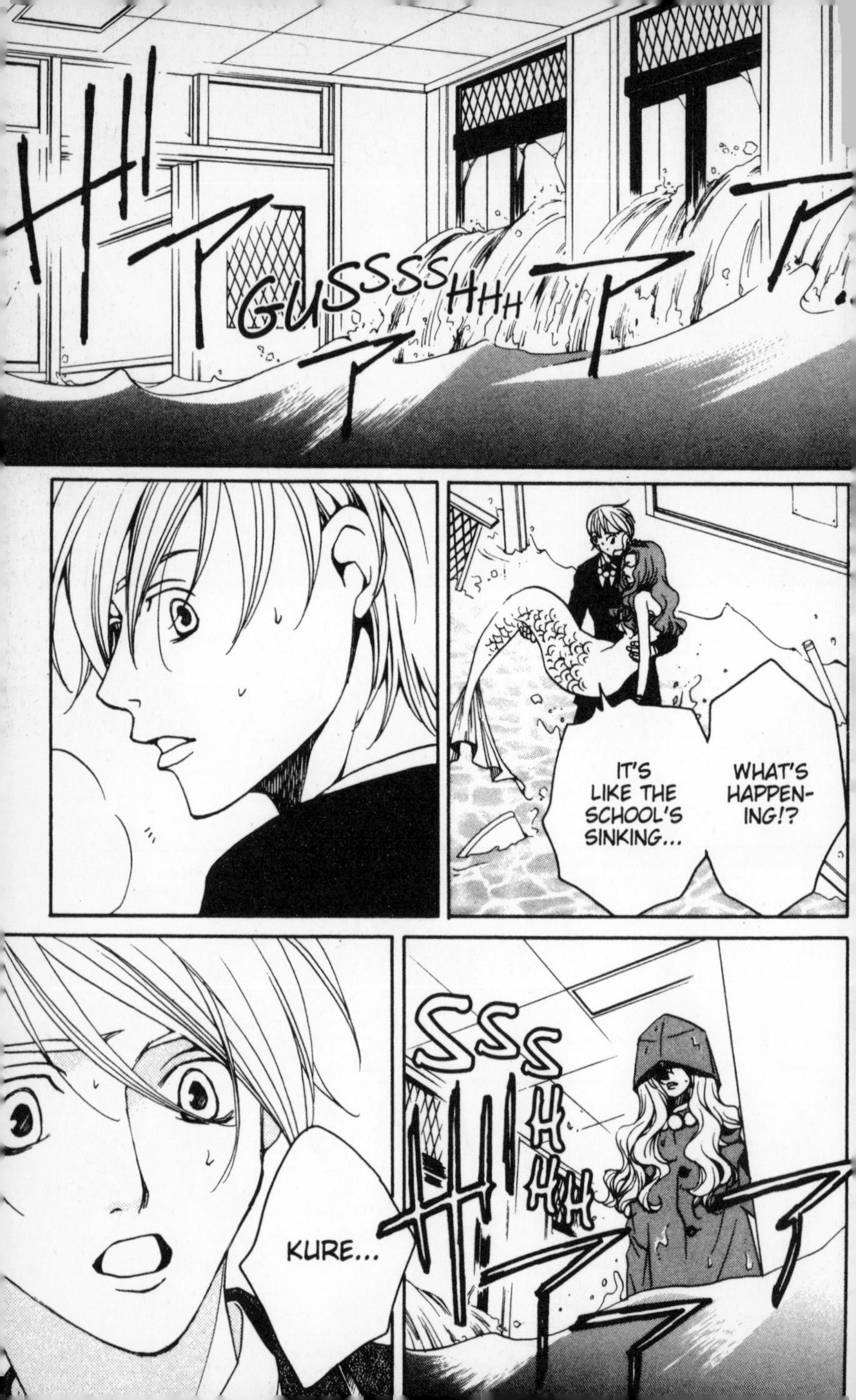
GUSSSSHHH
WHAT'S HAPPEN-ING!?
IT'S LIKE THE SCHOOL'S SINKING...
KURE...

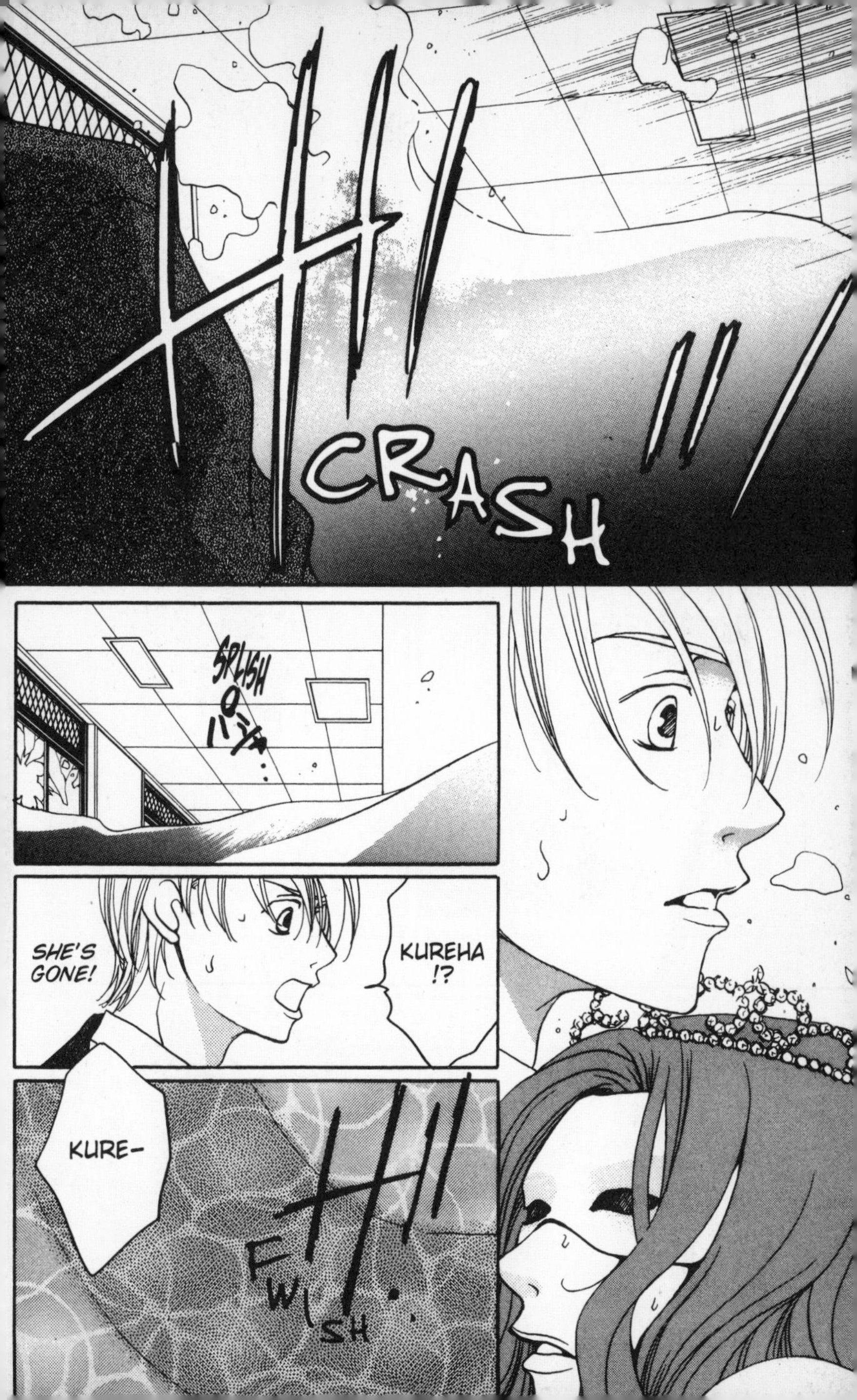
CRASH
SPLISH
パシャ…
KUREHA !?
SHE'S GONE!
KURE-
FWISH

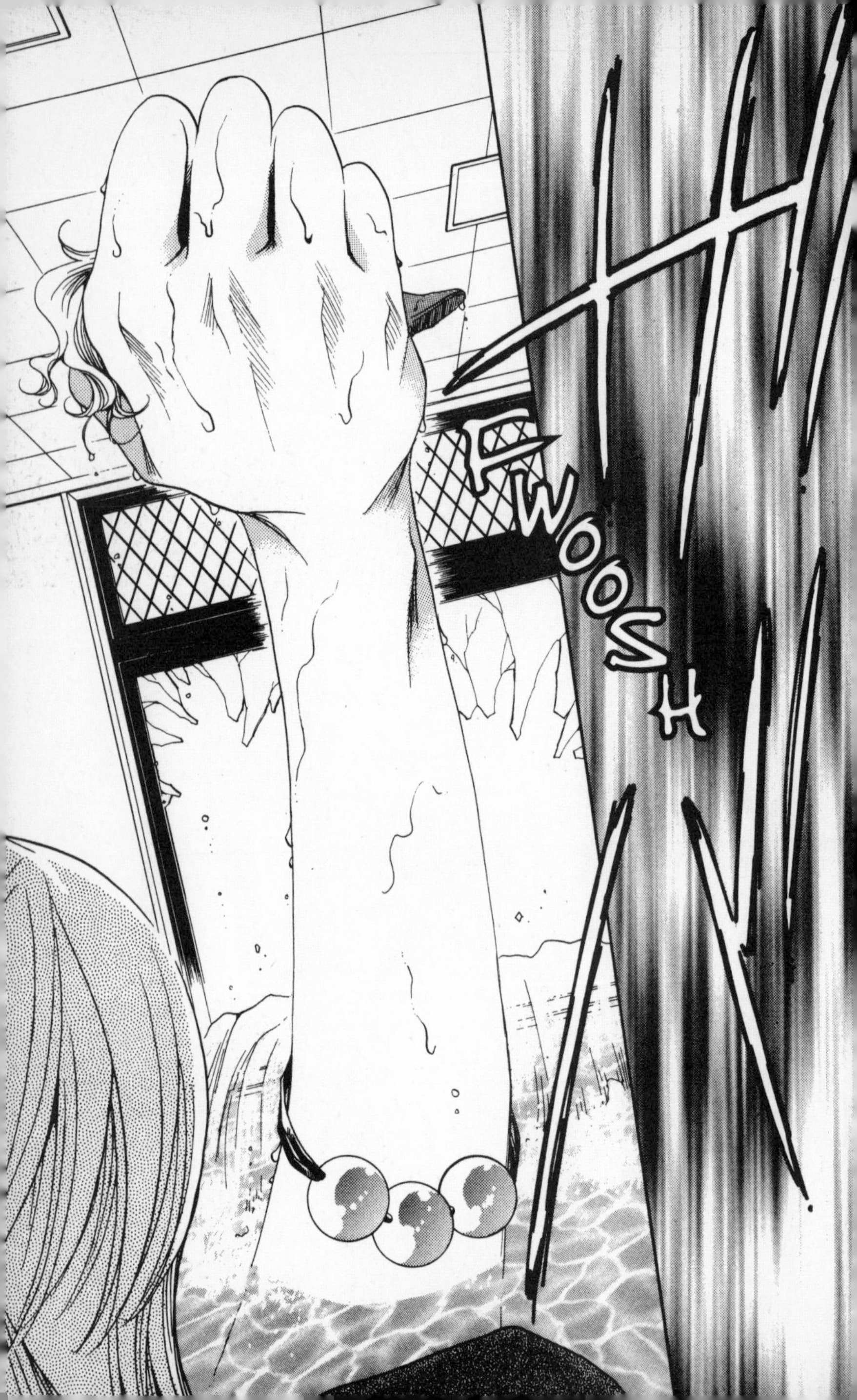
FWOOSH

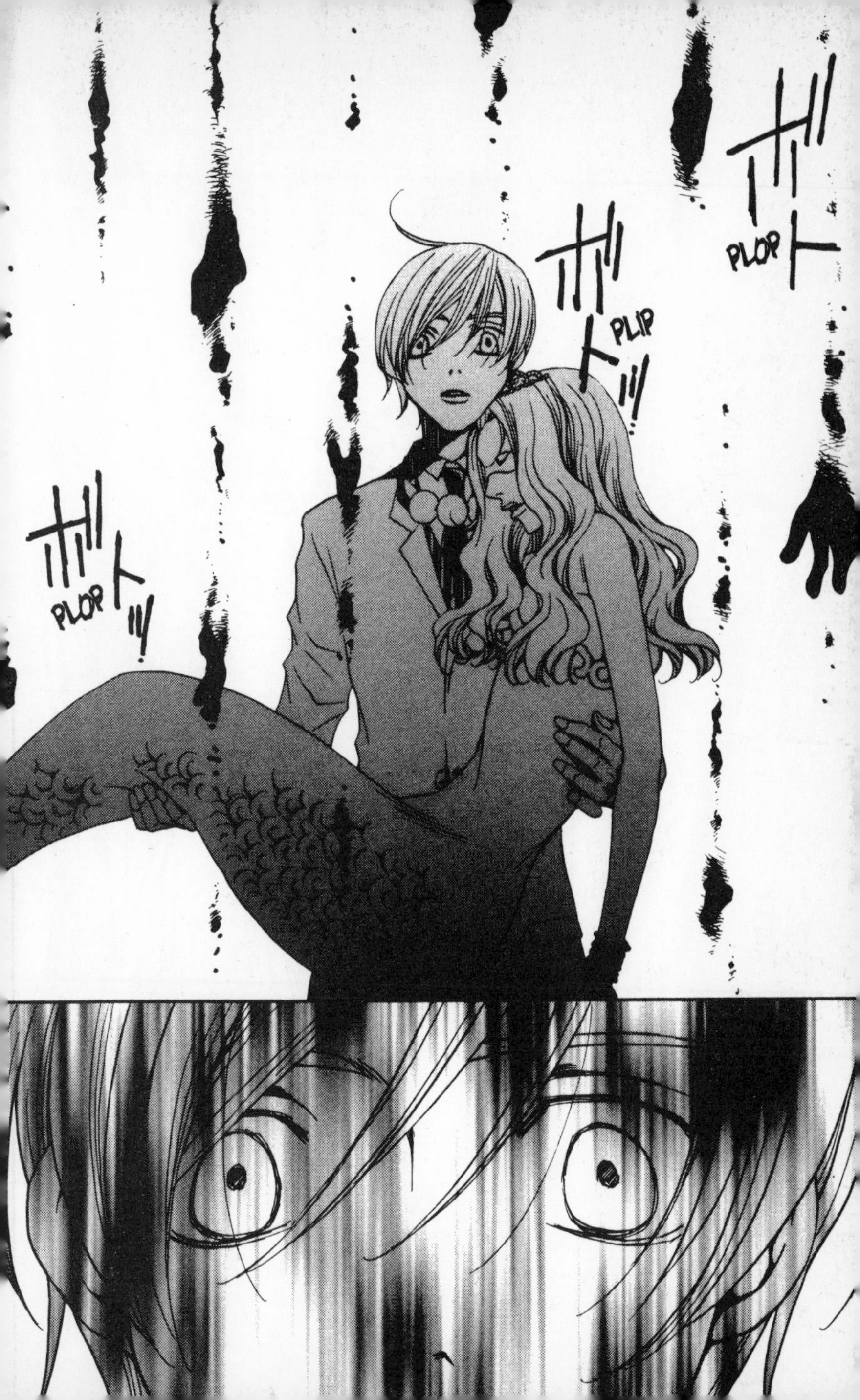
PLOP
PLIP
PLOP

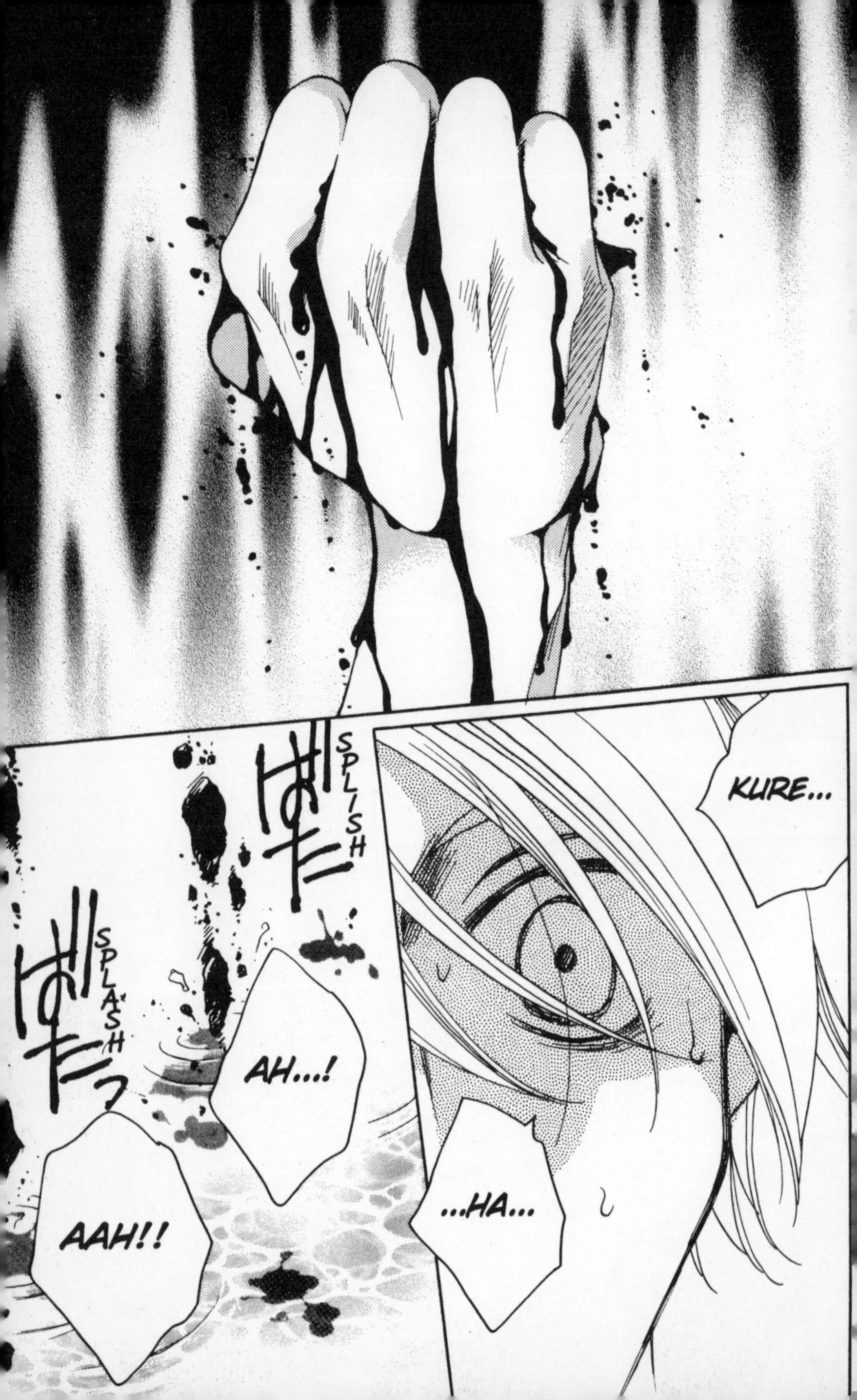
KURE...
...HA...
ぱた
SPLISH
ぱたっ
SPLASH
AH...!
AAH!!

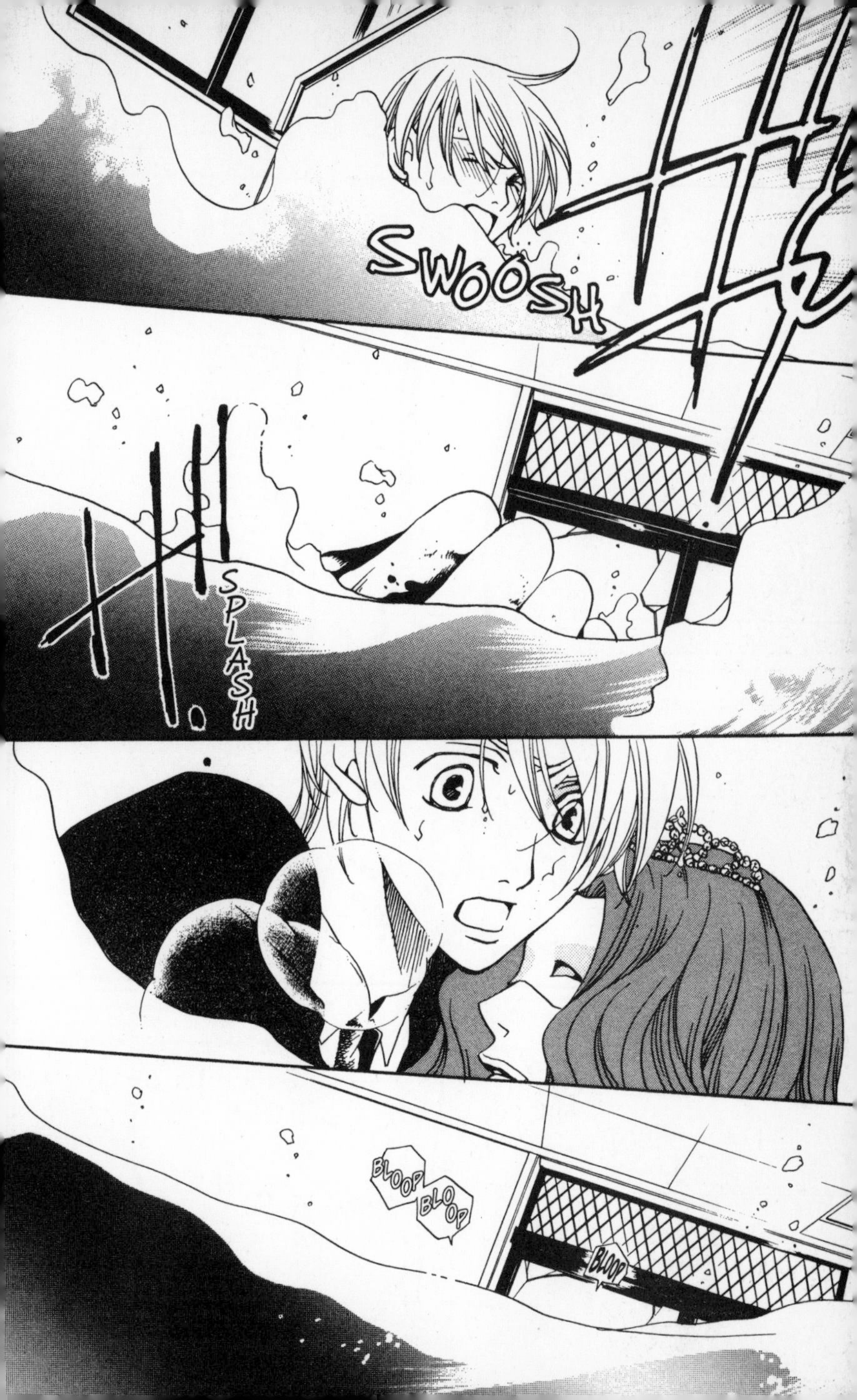
SWOOSH
SPLASH
BLOOP BLOOP
BLOOP

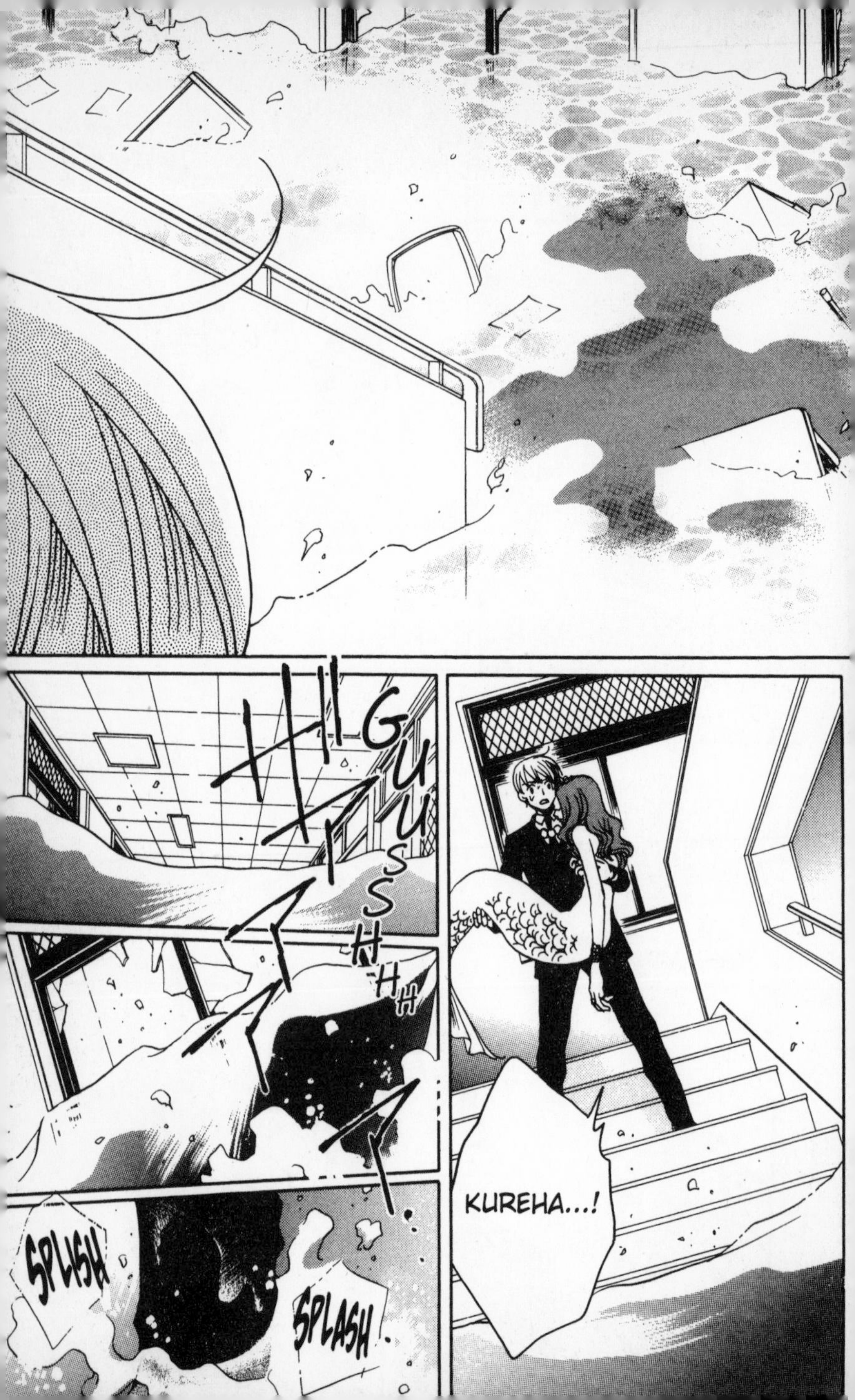
GUUSSHHH
KUREHA...!
SPLASH
SPLISH

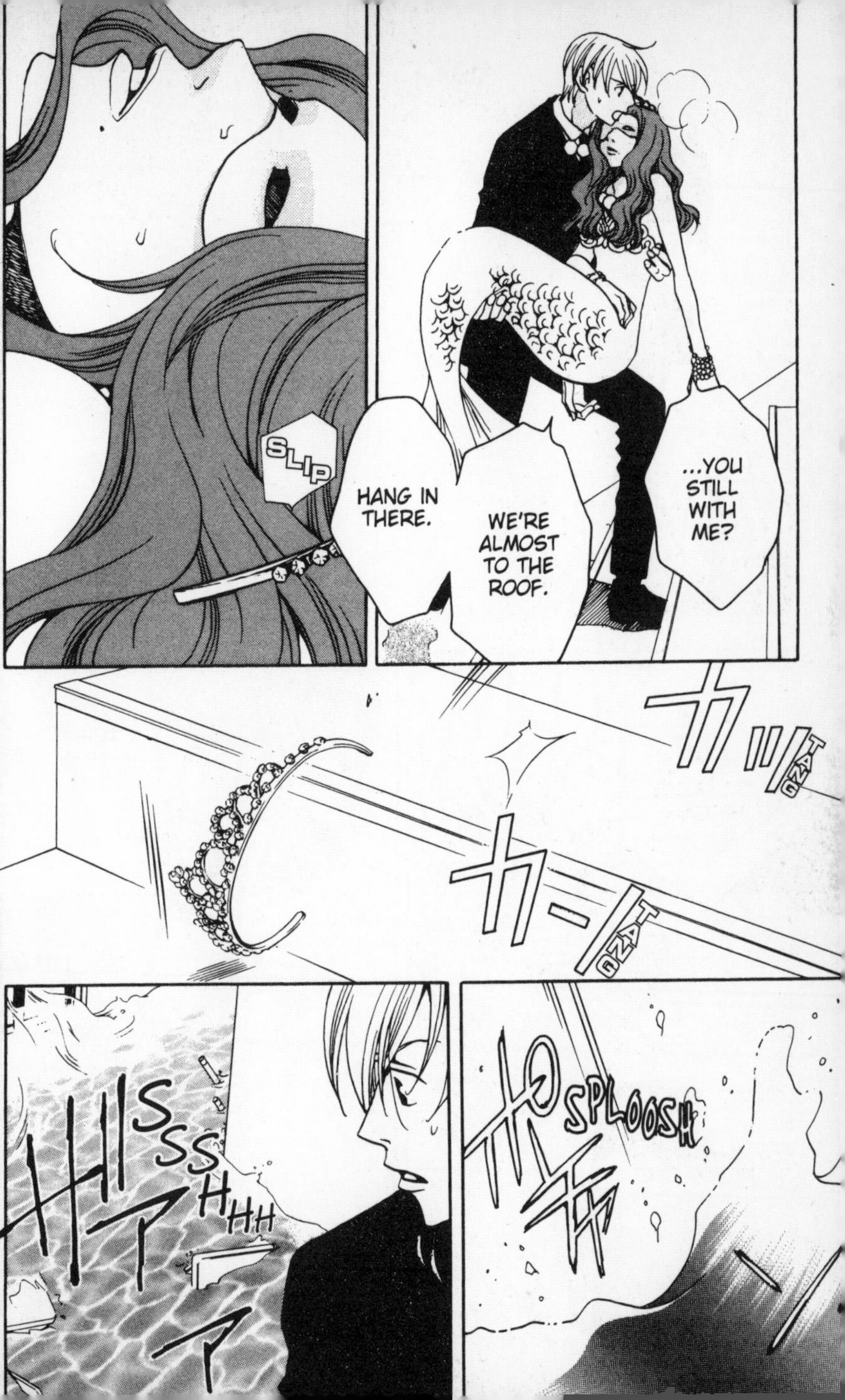
...YOU STILL WITH ME?
WE'RE ALMOST TO THE ROOF.
HANG IN THERE.
SLIP
TANG
TANG
SPLOOSH
SSSHHHH

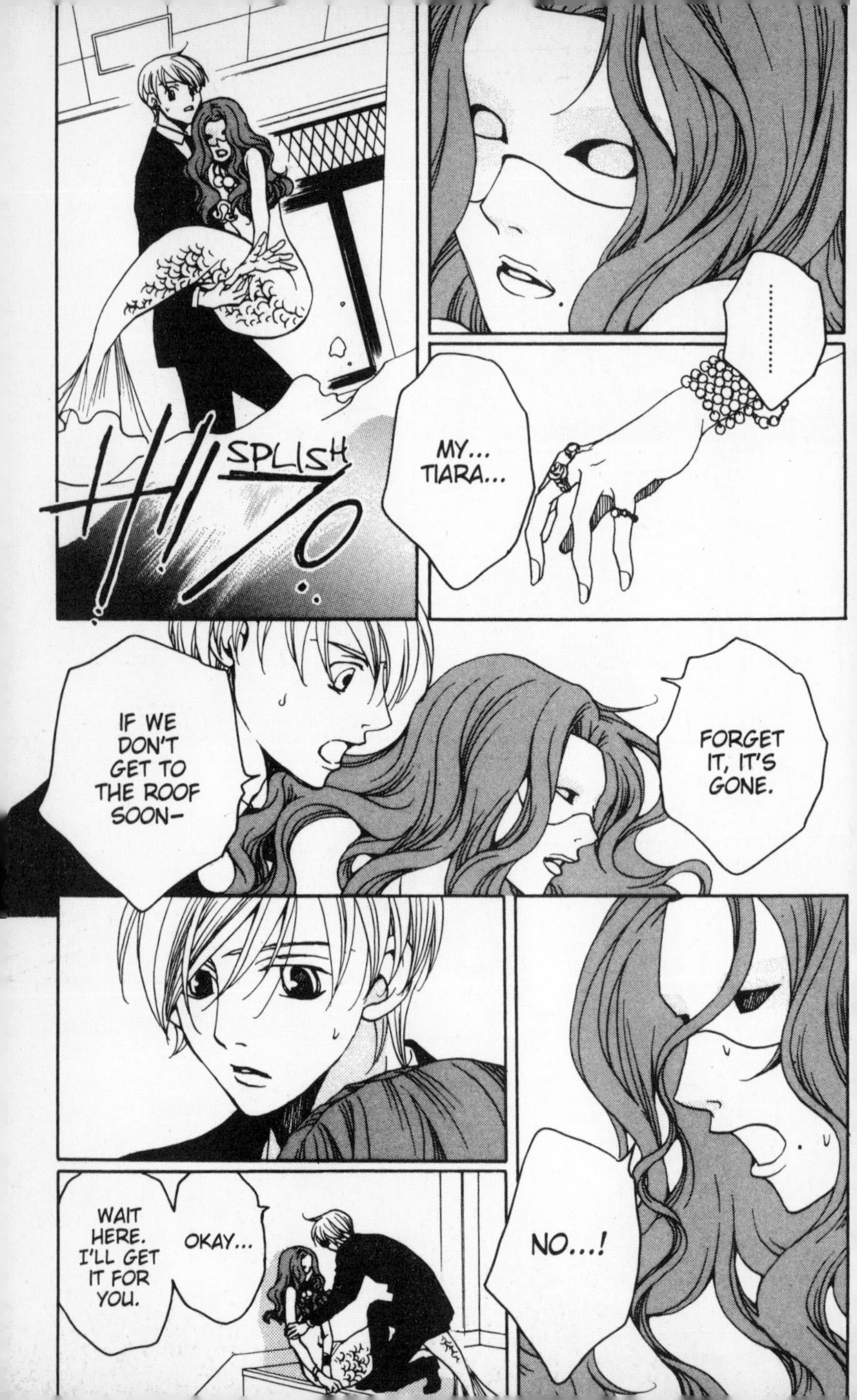
......
MY... TIARA...
SPLISH
FORGET IT, IT'S GONE.
IF WE DON'T GET TO THE ROOF SOON-
NO...!
OKAY...
WAIT HERE. I'LL GET IT FOR YOU.

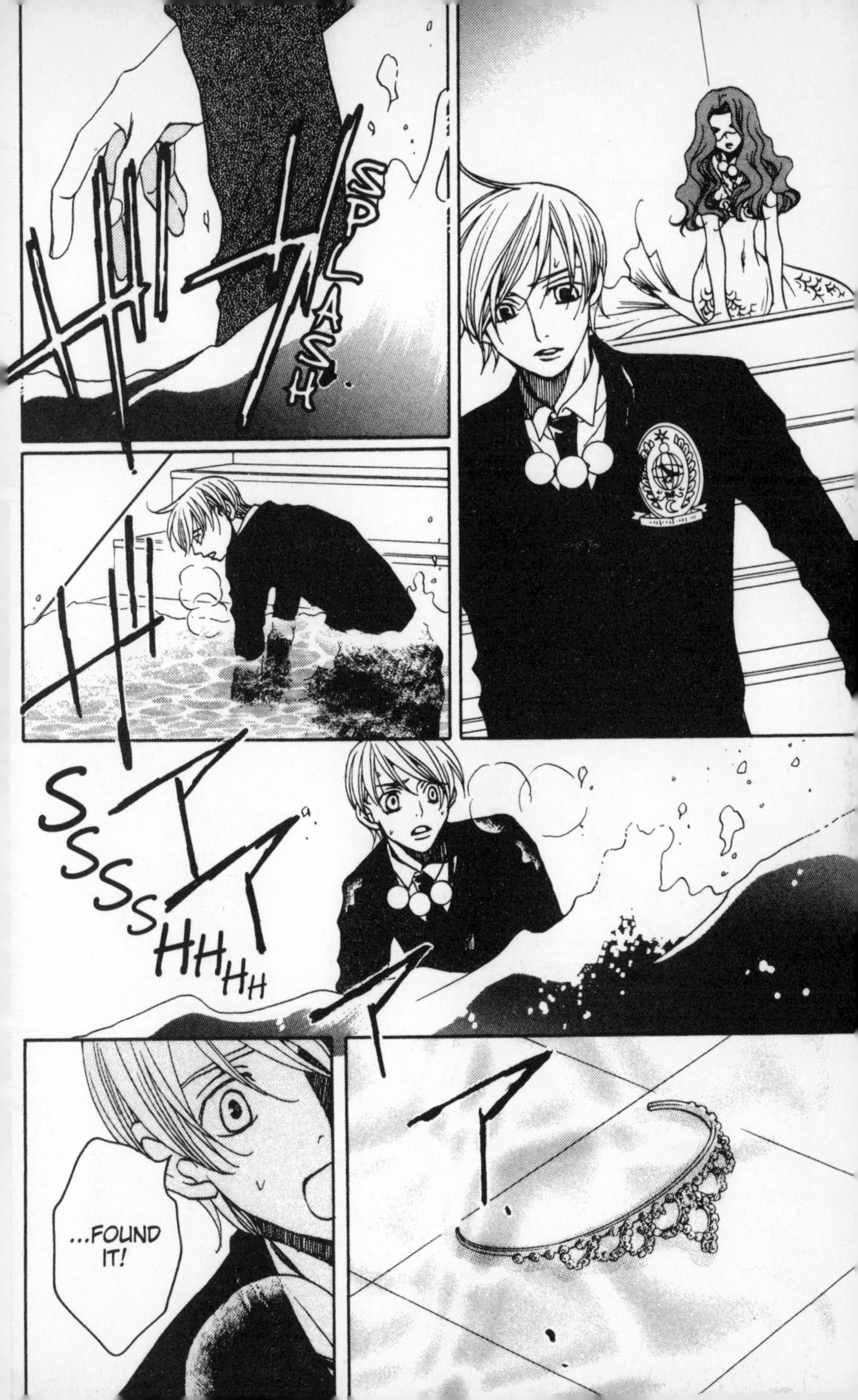
SPLASH
SSSSHHHH
...FOUND IT!

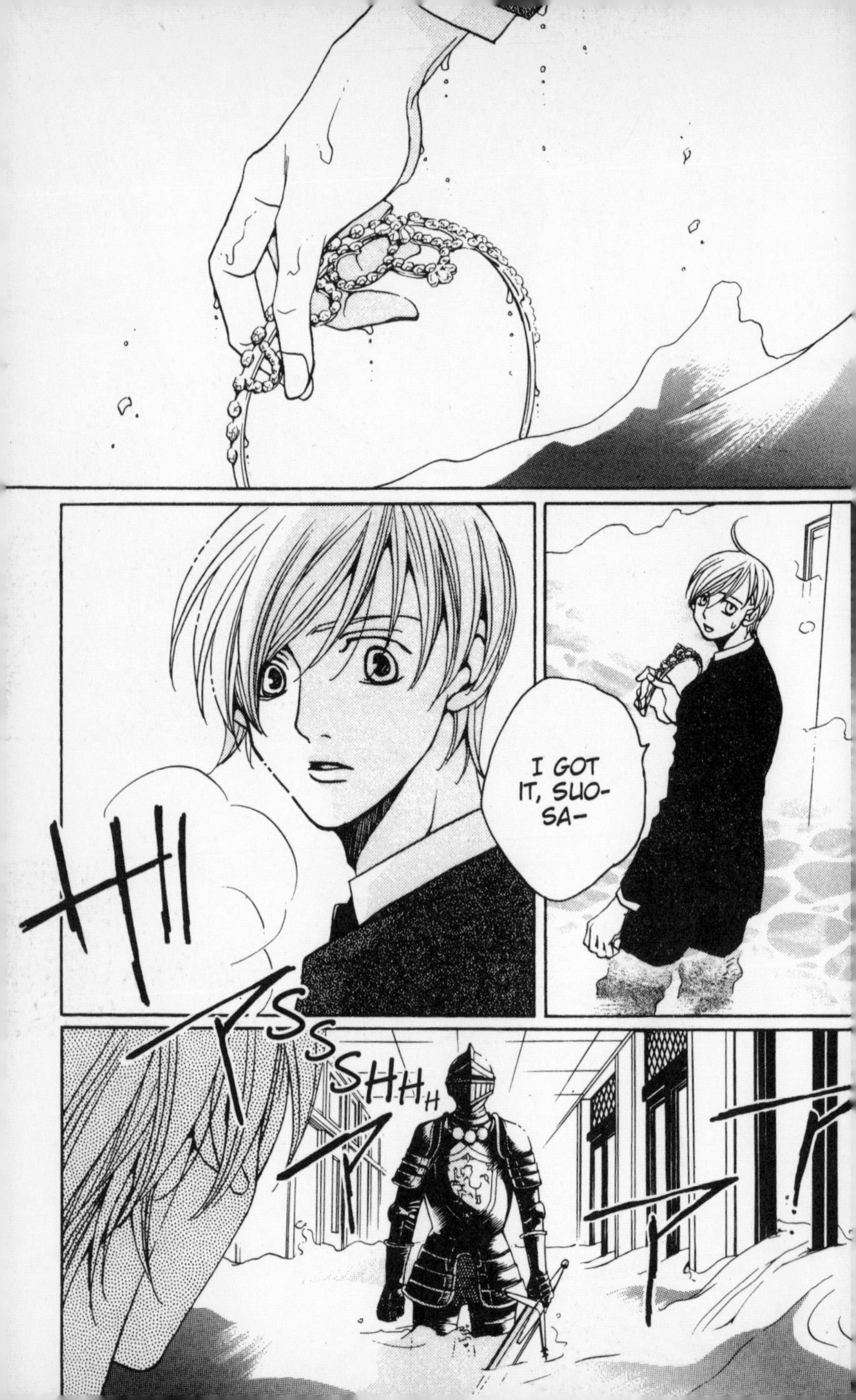
I GOT IT, SUO-SA-
SSSHHH

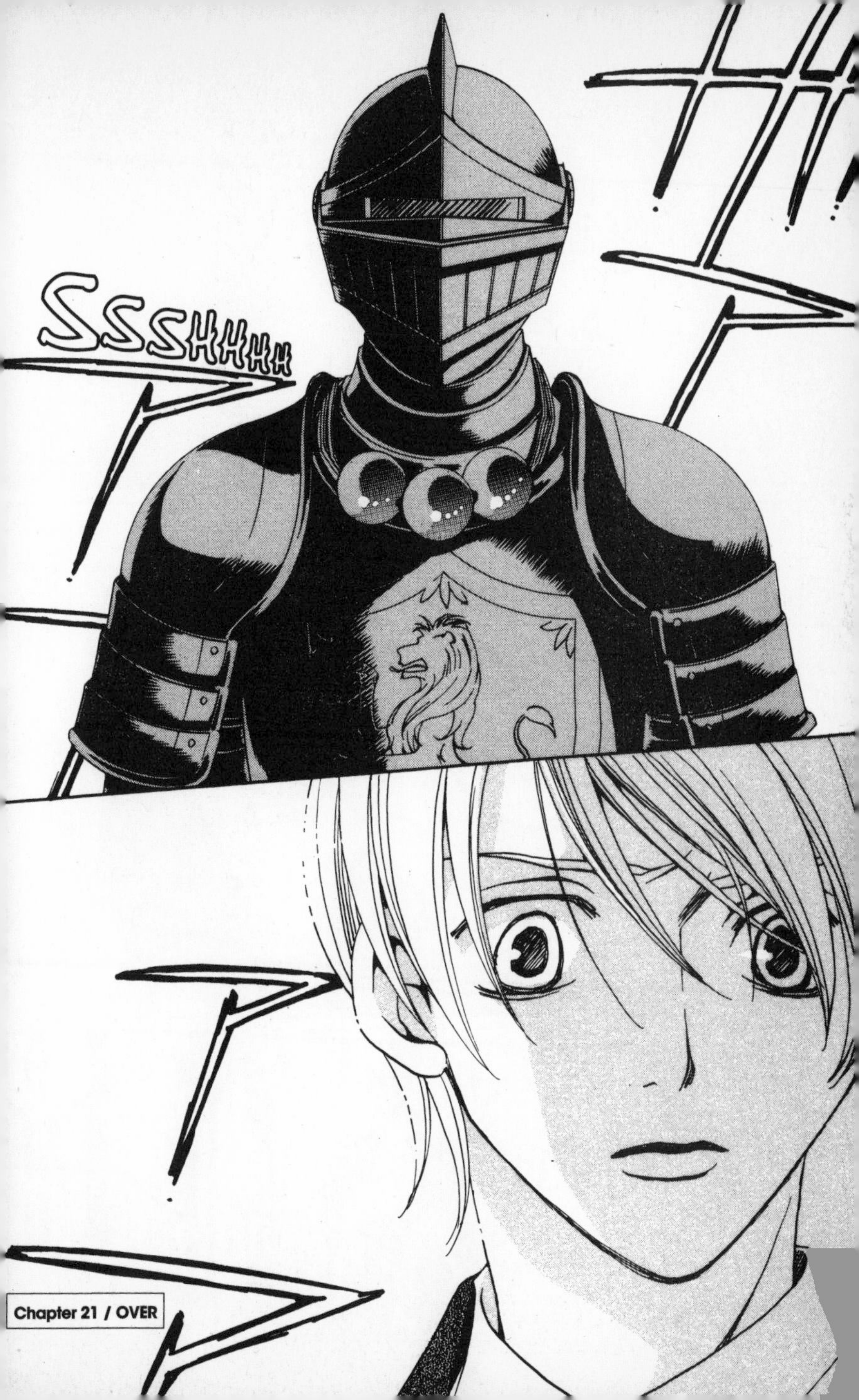
SSSHHHH

Chapter 21 / OVER

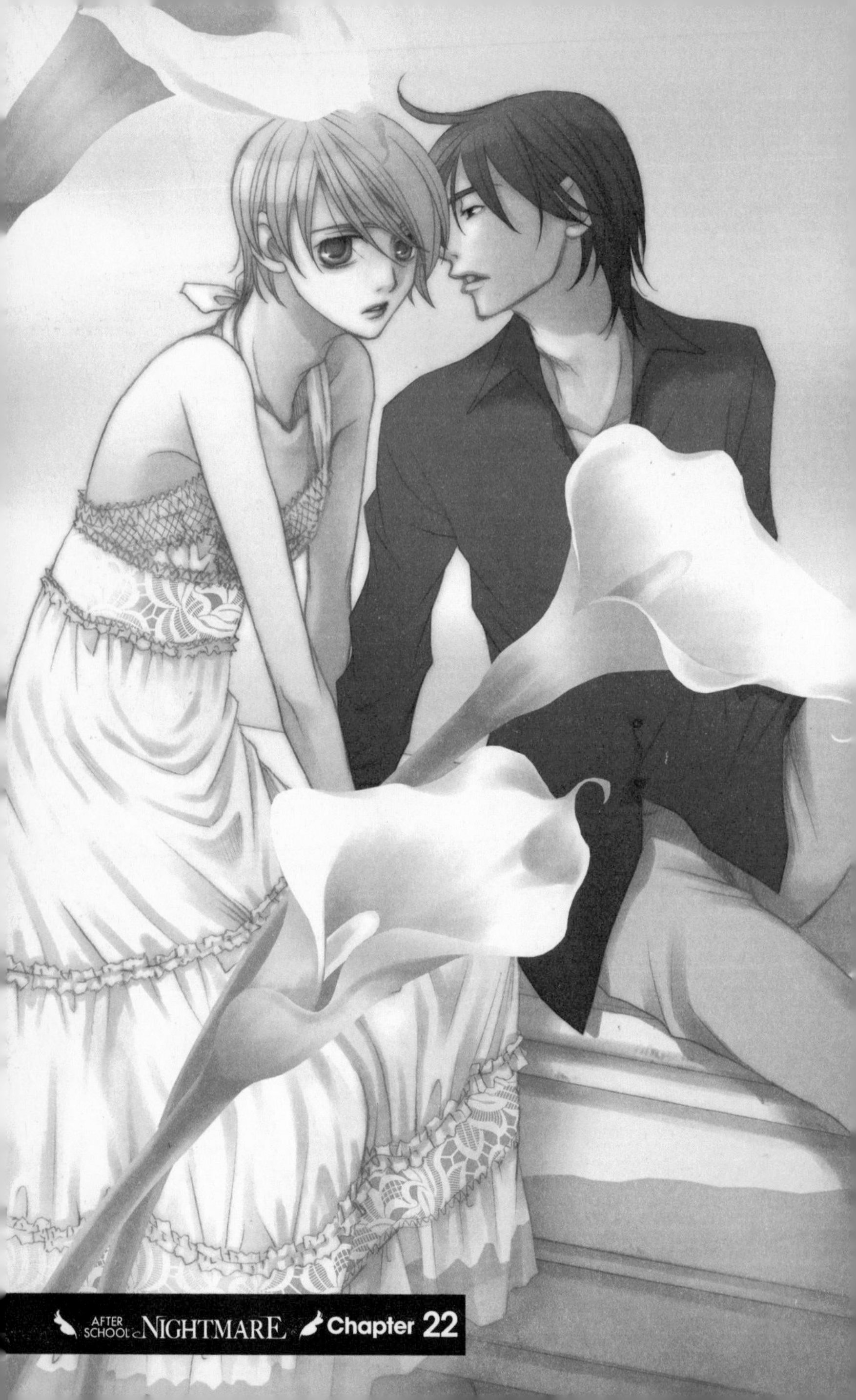

AFTER SCHOOL NIGHTMARE Chapter 22

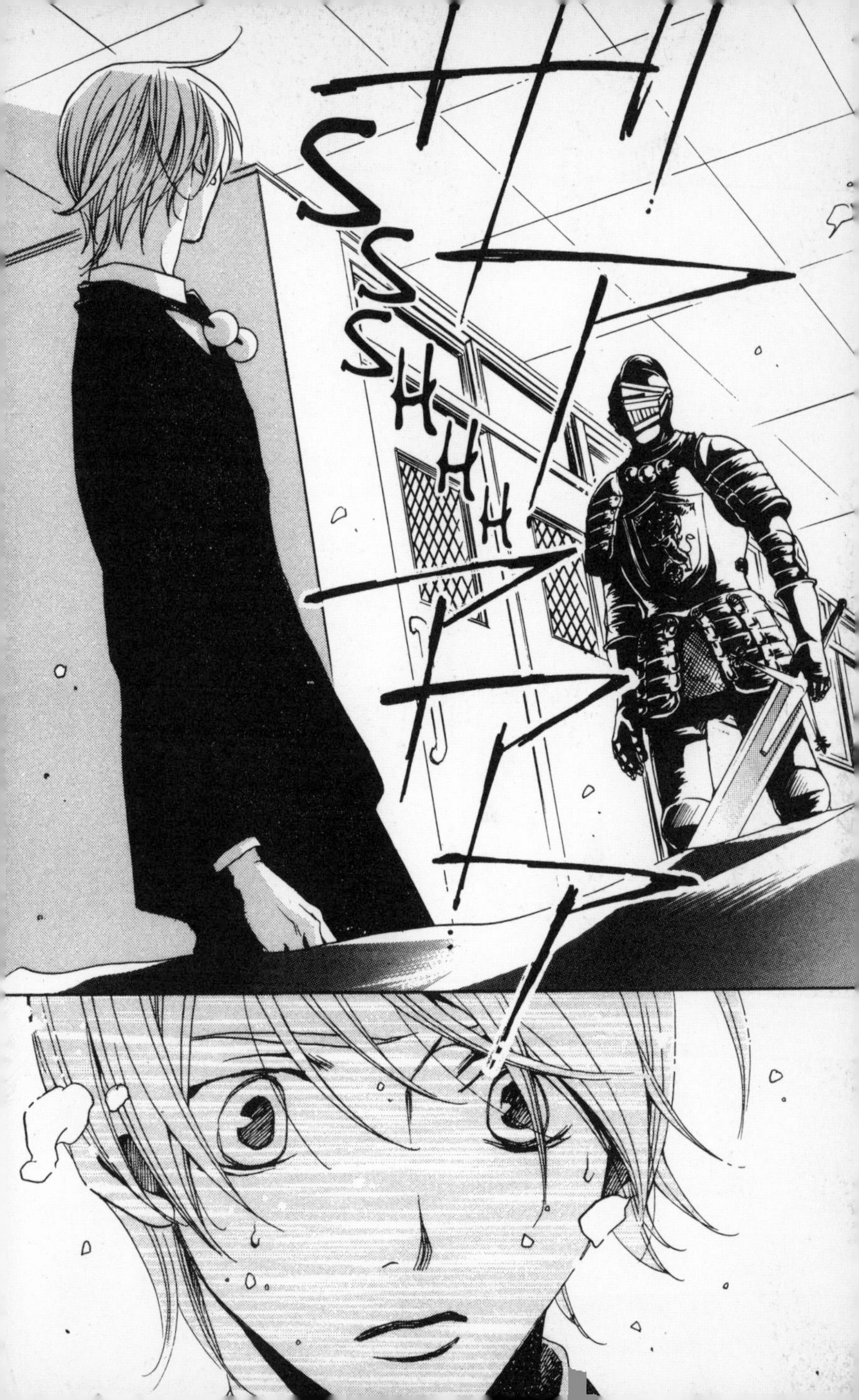
SSSSHHHH

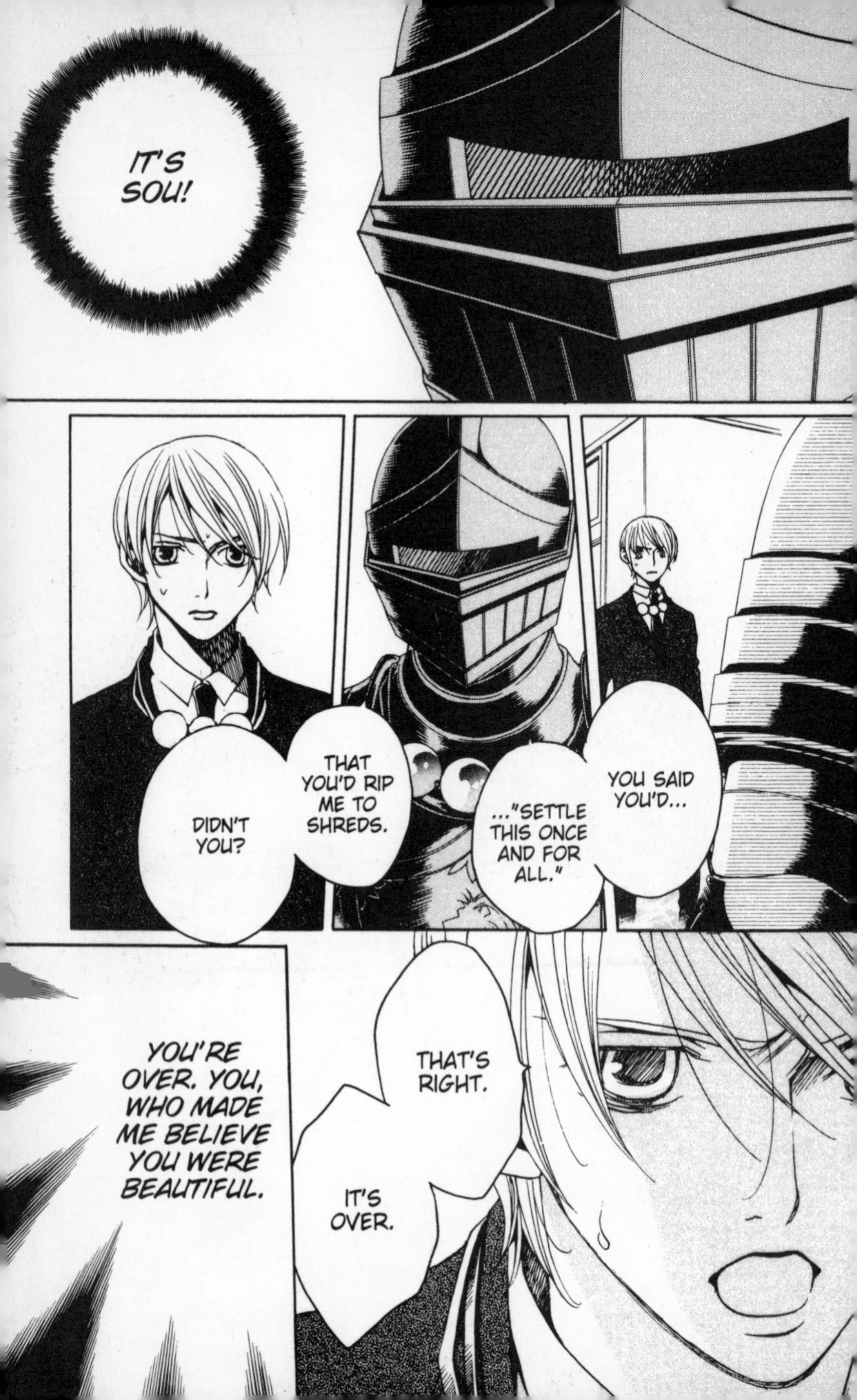
IT'S SOU!
YOU SAID YOU'D...
..."SETTLE THIS ONCE AND FOR ALL."
THAT YOU'D RIP ME TO SHREDS.
DIDN'T YOU?
THAT'S RIGHT.
IT'S OVER.
YOU'RE OVER. YOU, WHO MADE ME BELIEVE YOU WERE BEAUTIFUL.

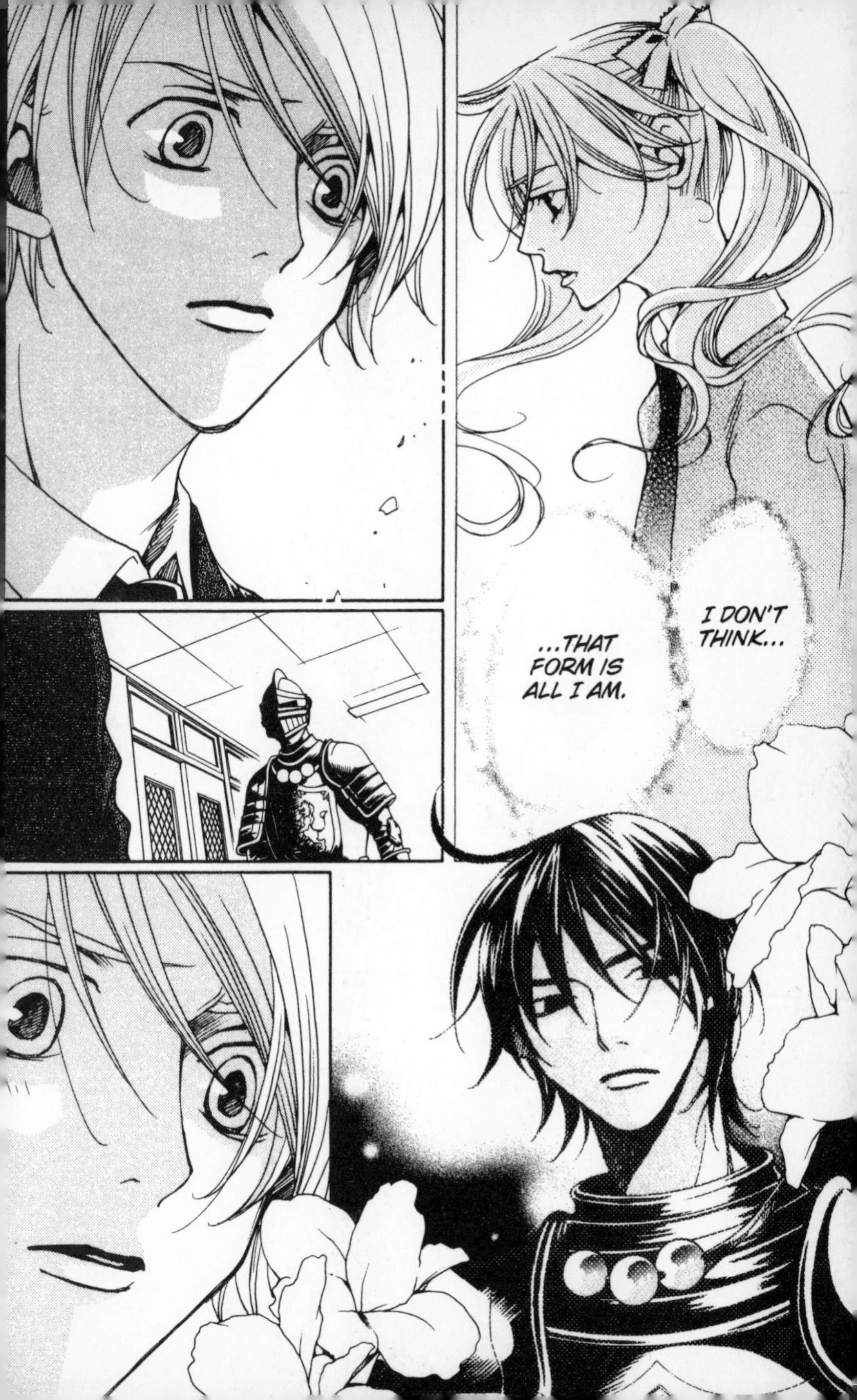
I DON'T THINK...
...THAT FORM IS ALL I AM.

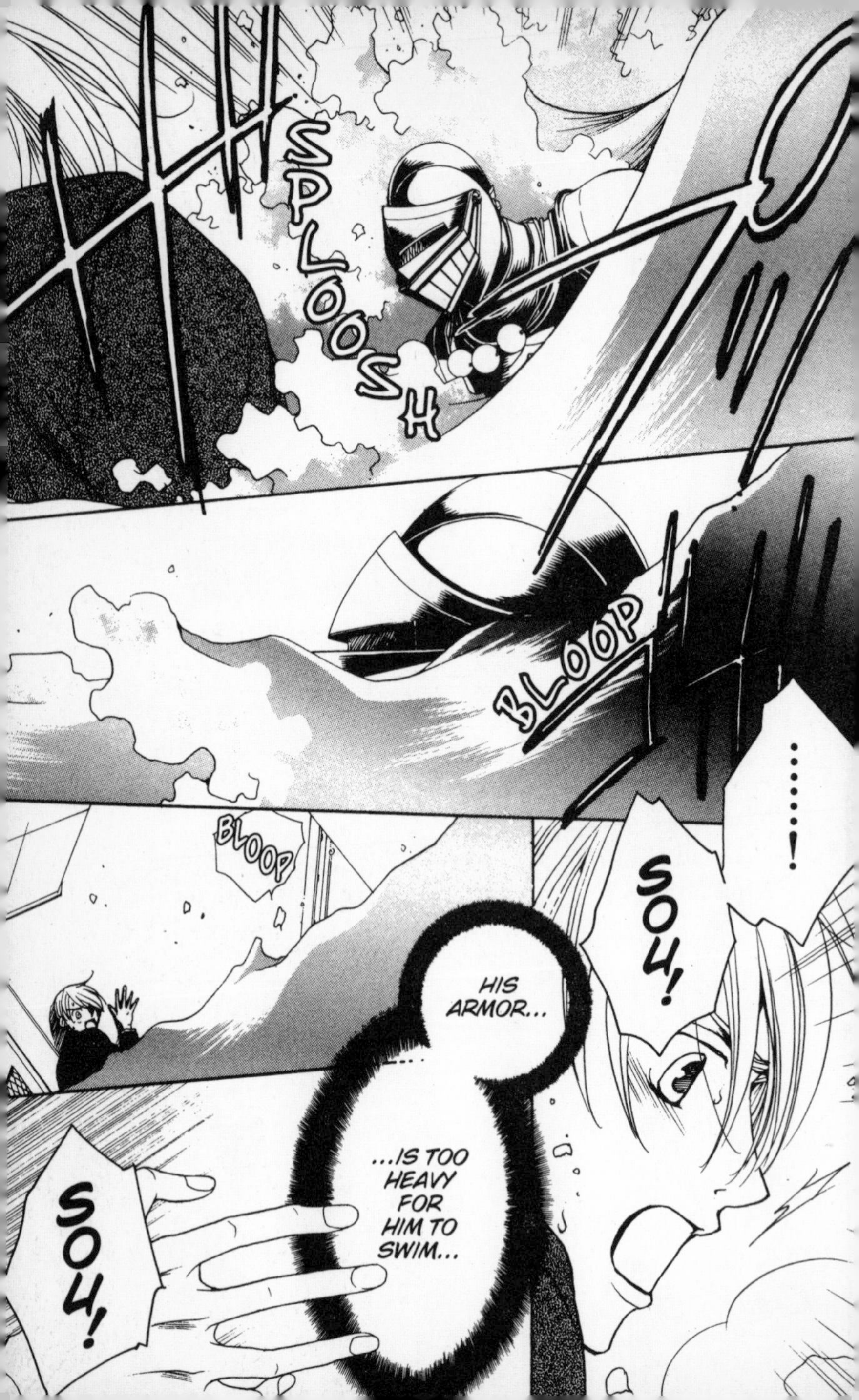
SPLOOSH
BLOOP
......!
SOU!
HIS ARMOR...
...IS TOO HEAVY FOR HIM TO SWIM...
BLOOP
SOU!

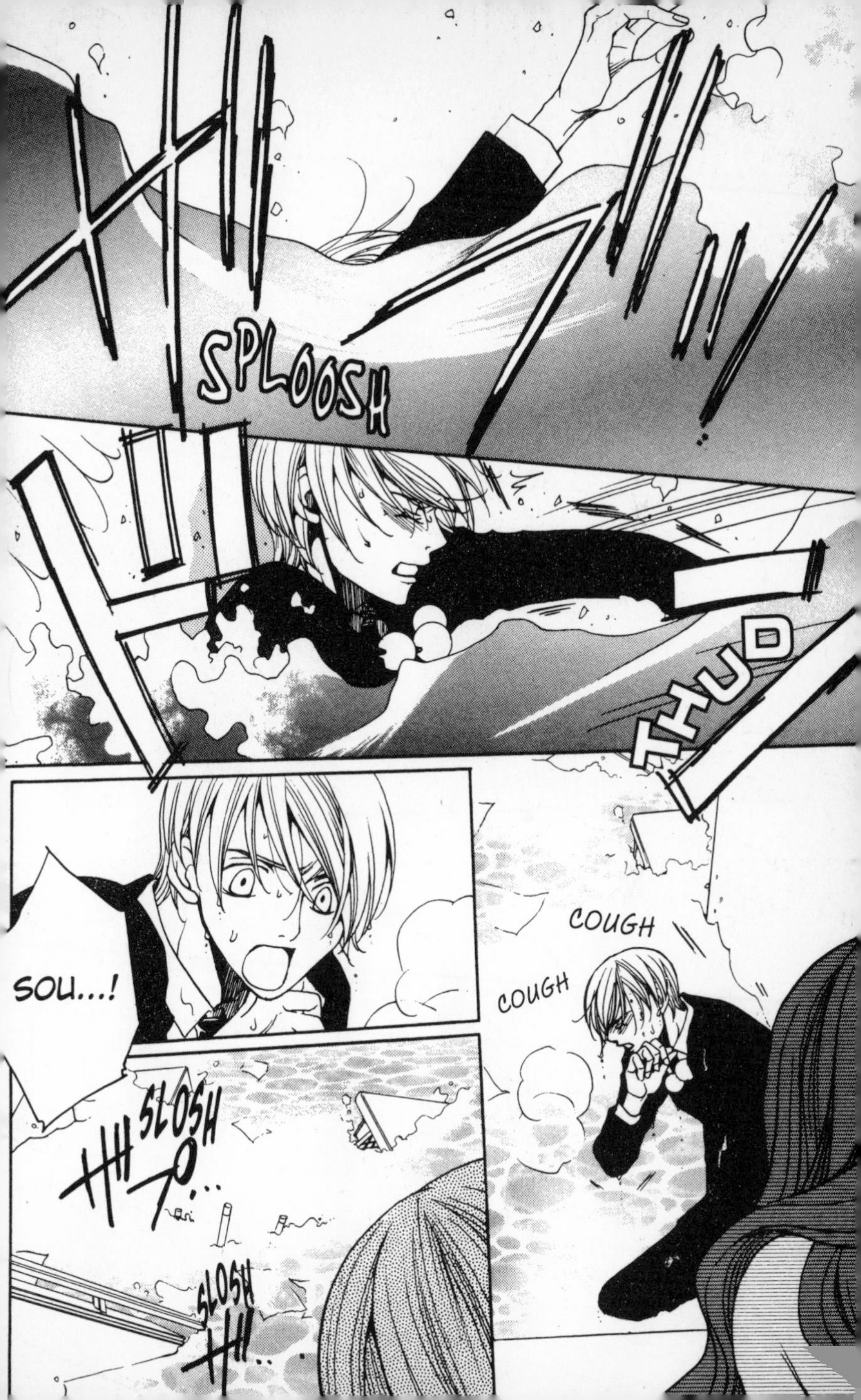
SPLOOSH
THUD
COUGH
COUGH
SOU...!
SLOSH
SLOSH

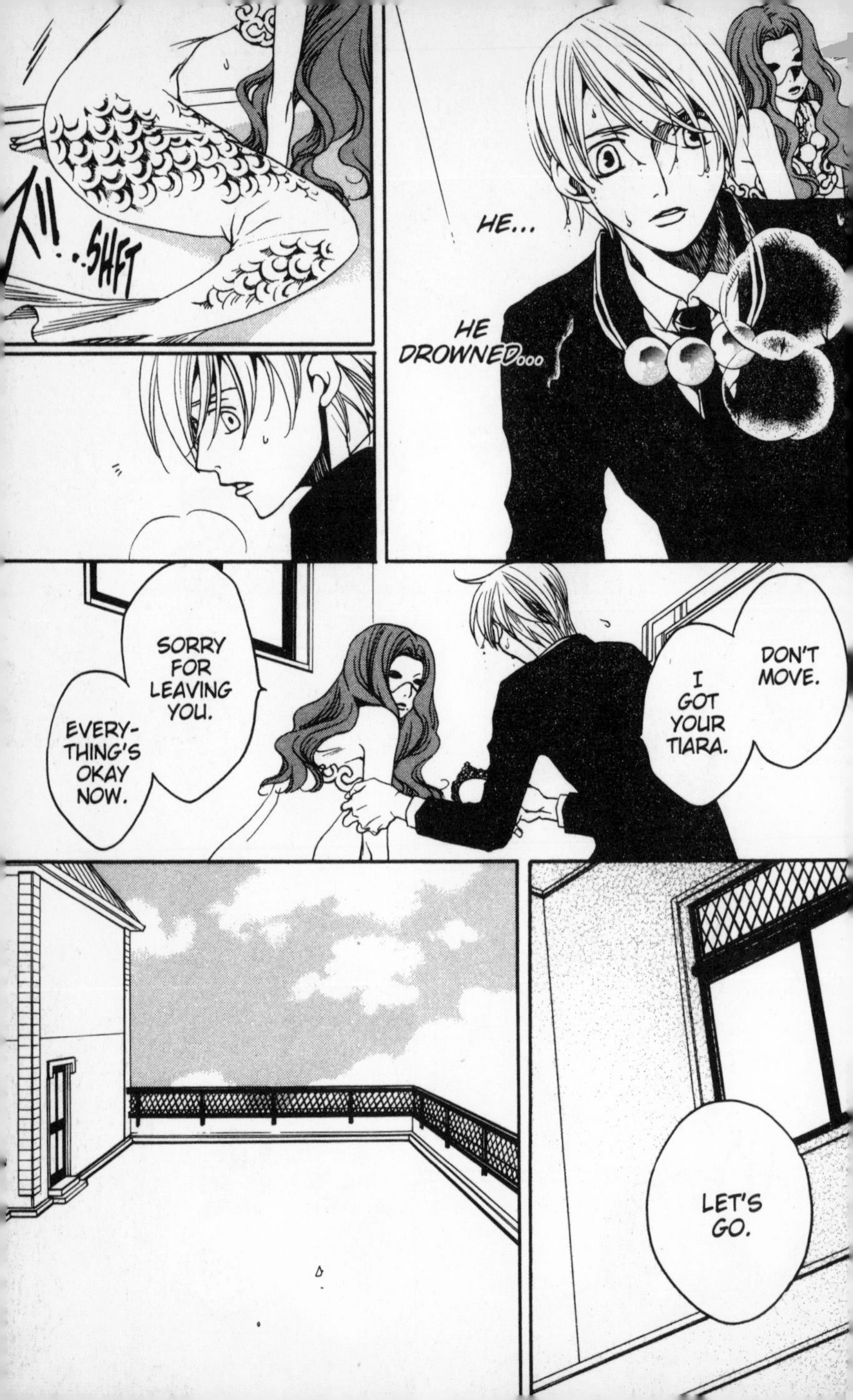
HE...
HE DROWNED...
ズ!! ...SHFT
DON'T MOVE.
I GOT YOUR TIARA.
SORRY FOR LEAVING YOU.
EVERYTHING'S OKAY NOW.
LET'S GO.

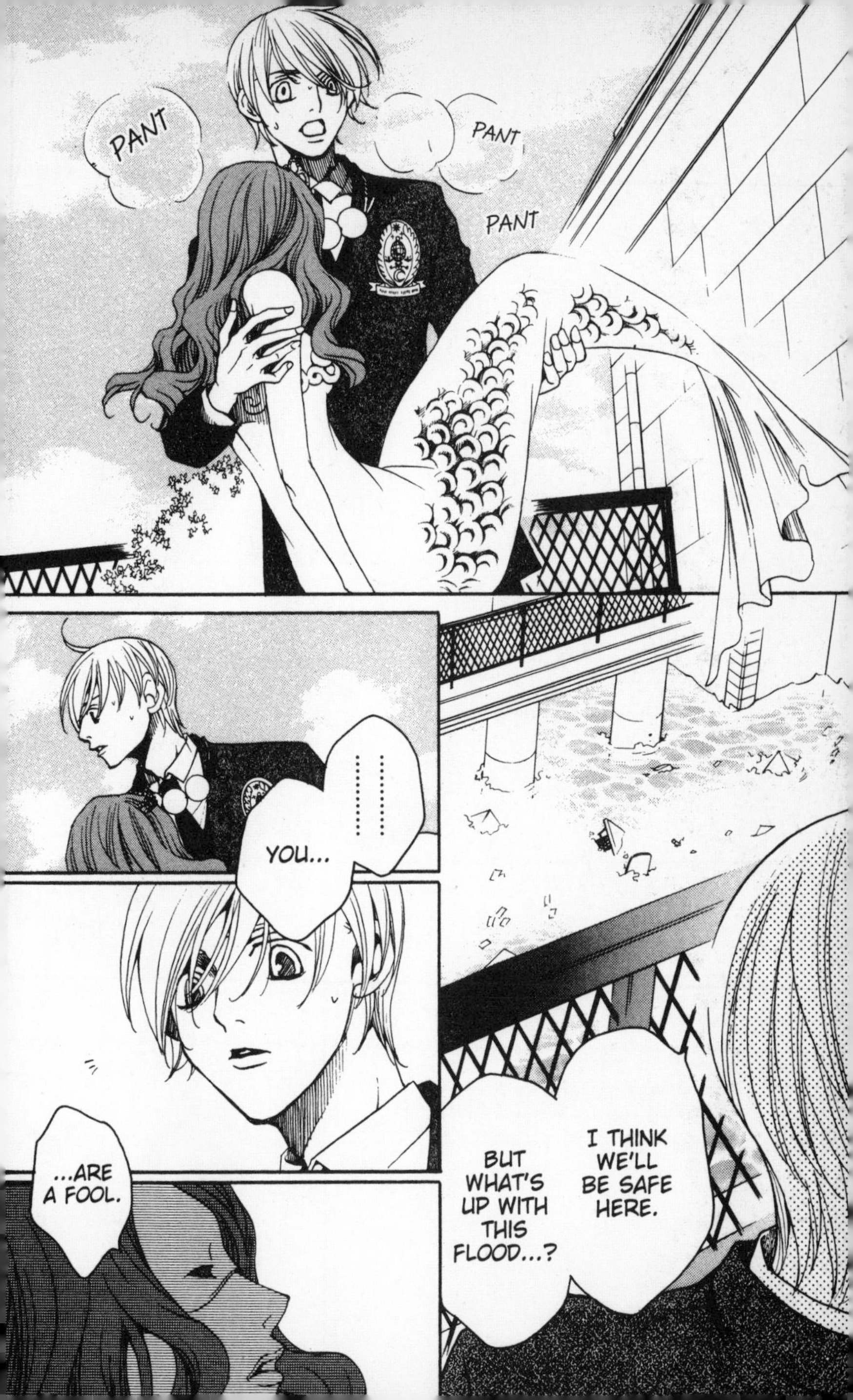
PANT
PANT
PANT
I THINK WE'LL BE SAFE HERE.
BUT WHAT'S UP WITH THIS FLOOD...?
......
YOU...
...ARE A FOOL.

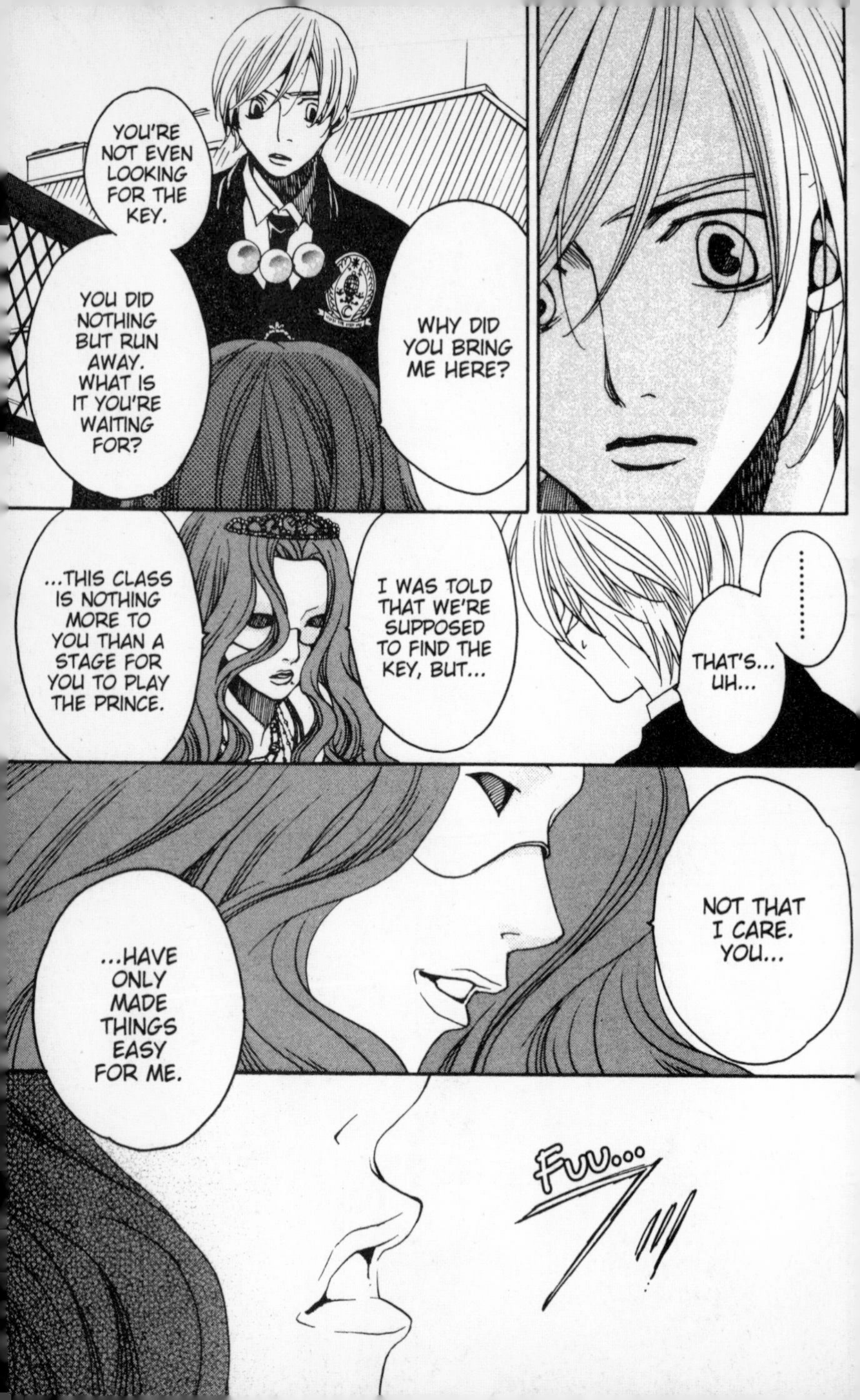
WHY DID YOU BRING ME HERE?
YOU'RE NOT EVEN LOOKING FOR THE KEY.
YOU DID NOTHING BUT RUN AWAY. WHAT IS IT YOU'RE WAITING FOR?
......
THAT'S... UH...
I WAS TOLD THAT WE'RE SUPPOSED TO FIND THE KEY, BUT...
...THIS CLASS IS NOTHING MORE TO YOU THAN A STAGE FOR YOU TO PLAY THE PRINCE.
NOT THAT I CARE. YOU...
...HAVE ONLY MADE THINGS EASY FOR ME.
FUU...

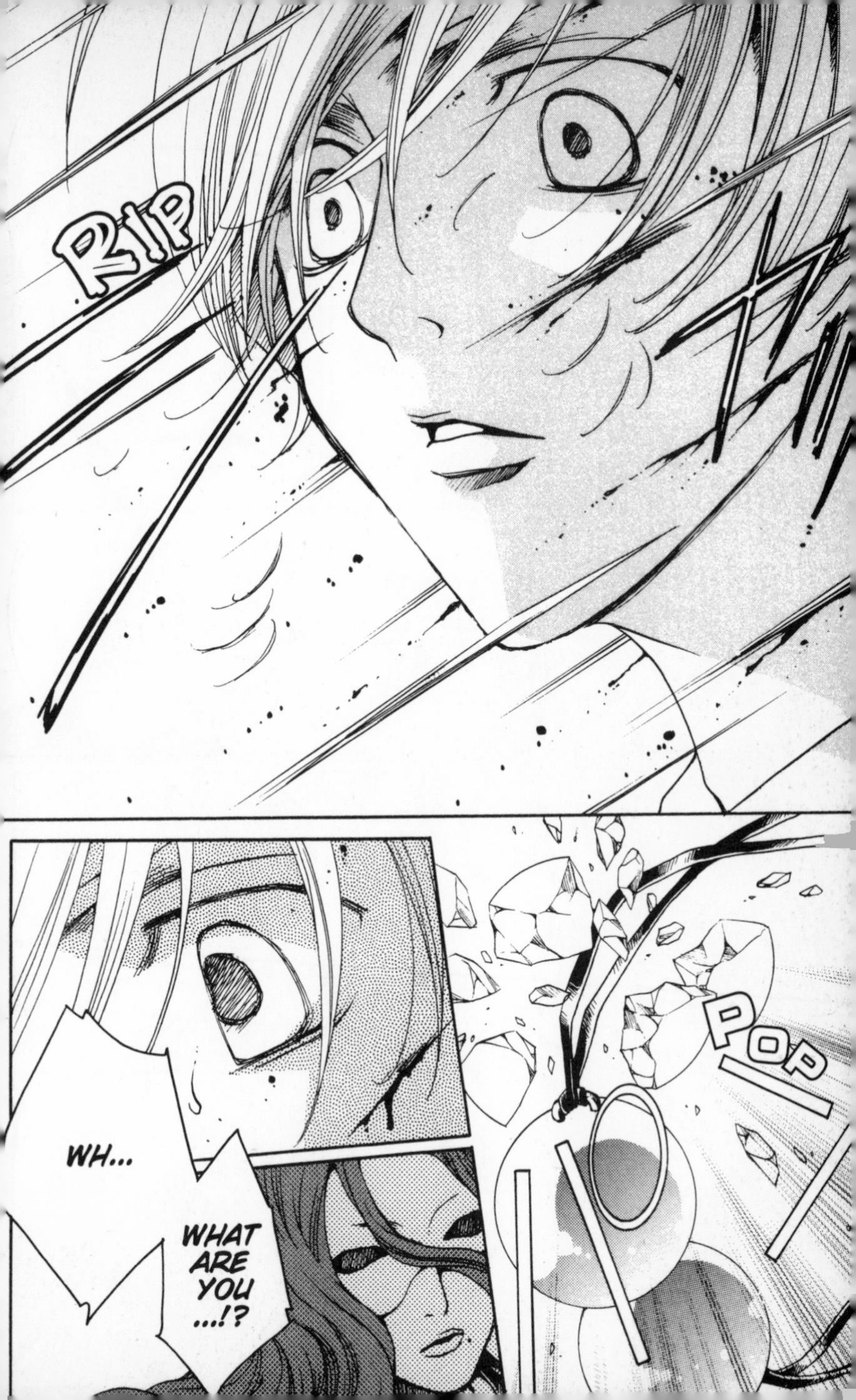
RIP
POP
WH...
WHAT ARE YOU ...!?

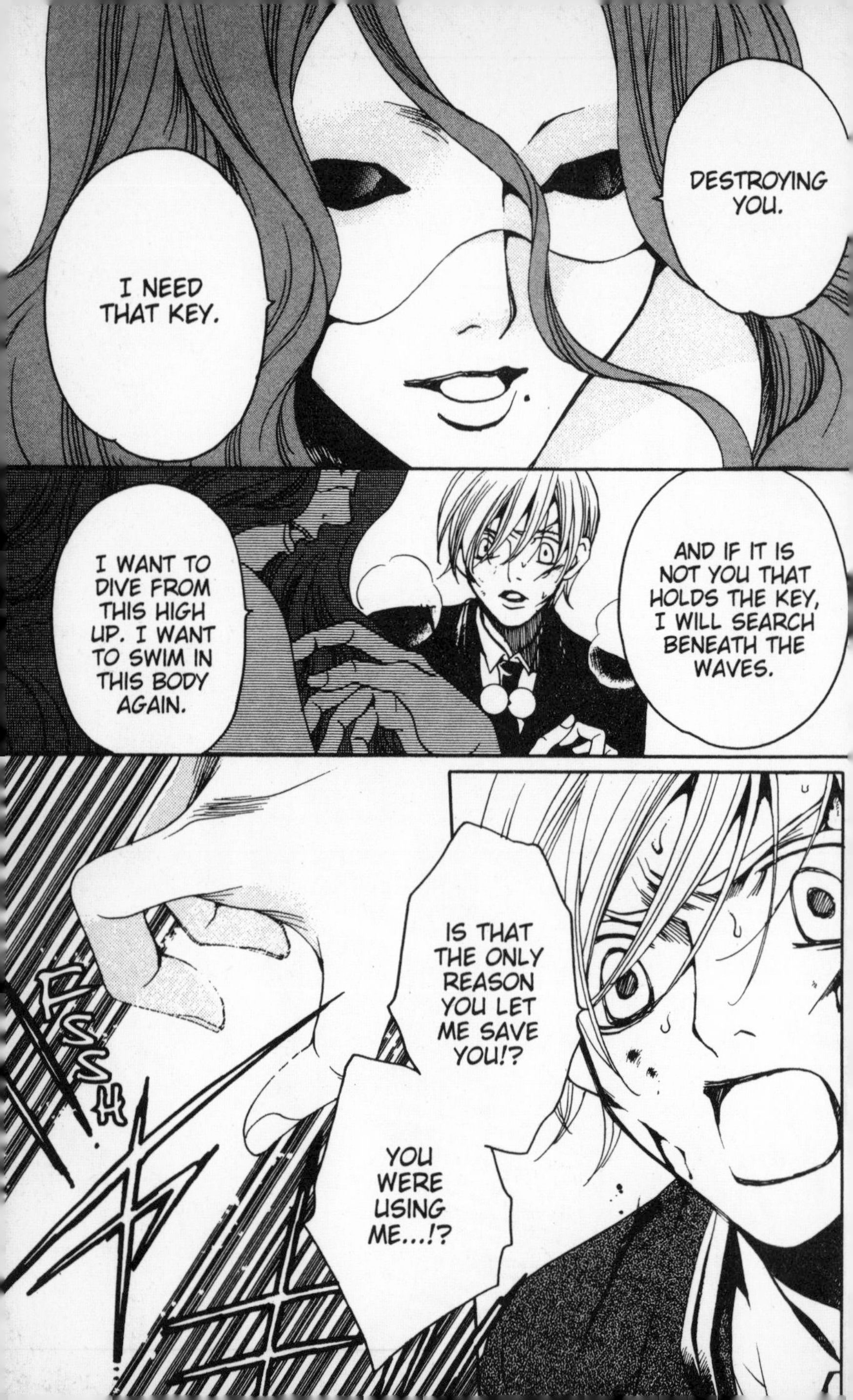
DESTROYING YOU.
I NEED THAT KEY.
AND IF IT IS NOT YOU THAT HOLDS THE KEY, I WILL SEARCH BENEATH THE WAVES.
I WANT TO DIVE FROM THIS HIGH UP. I WANT TO SWIM IN THIS BODY AGAIN.
IS THAT THE ONLY REASON YOU LET ME SAVE YOU!?
YOU WERE USING ME...!?
FSSH

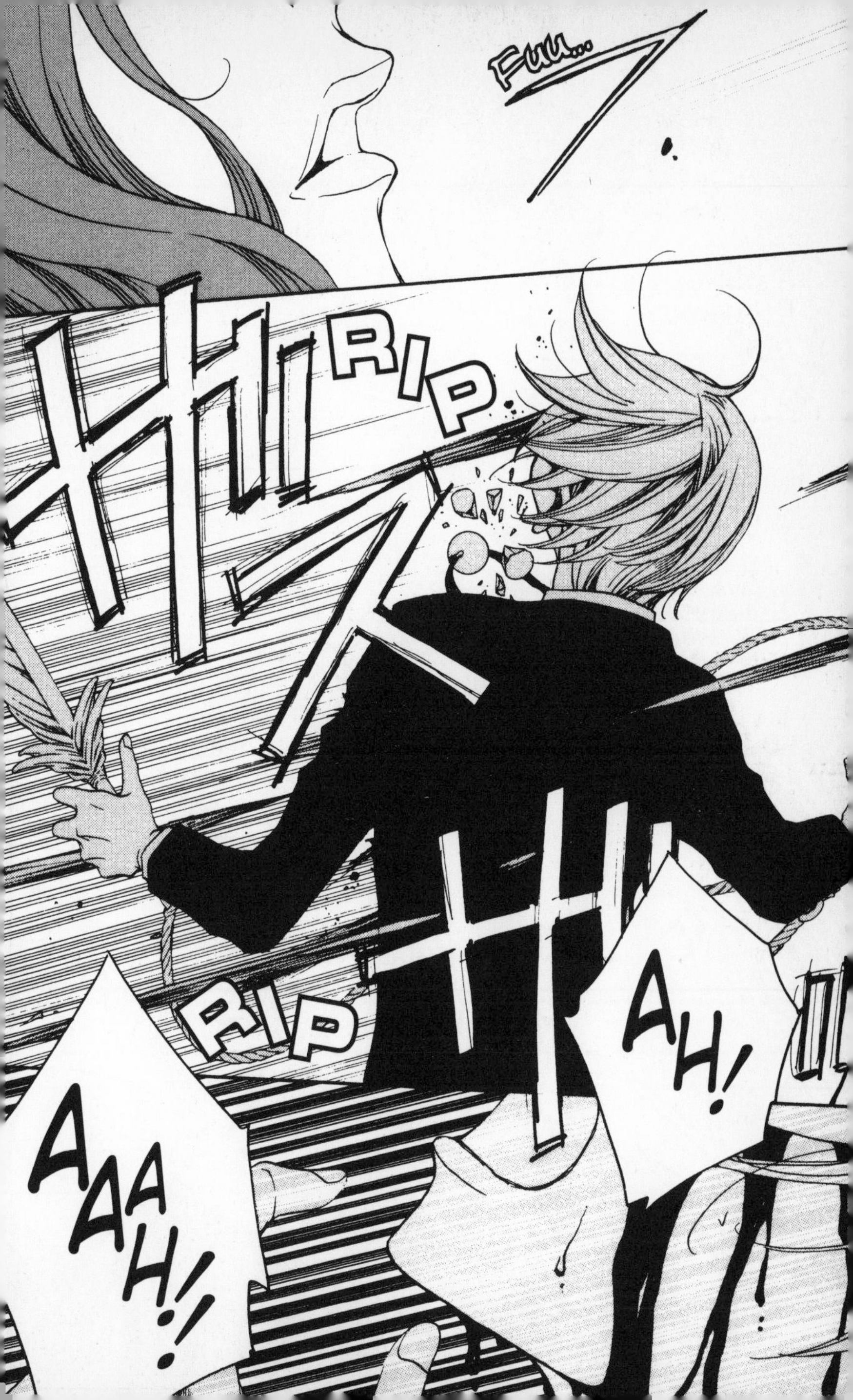
Fuu...
RIP
AH!
RIP
AAAH!!

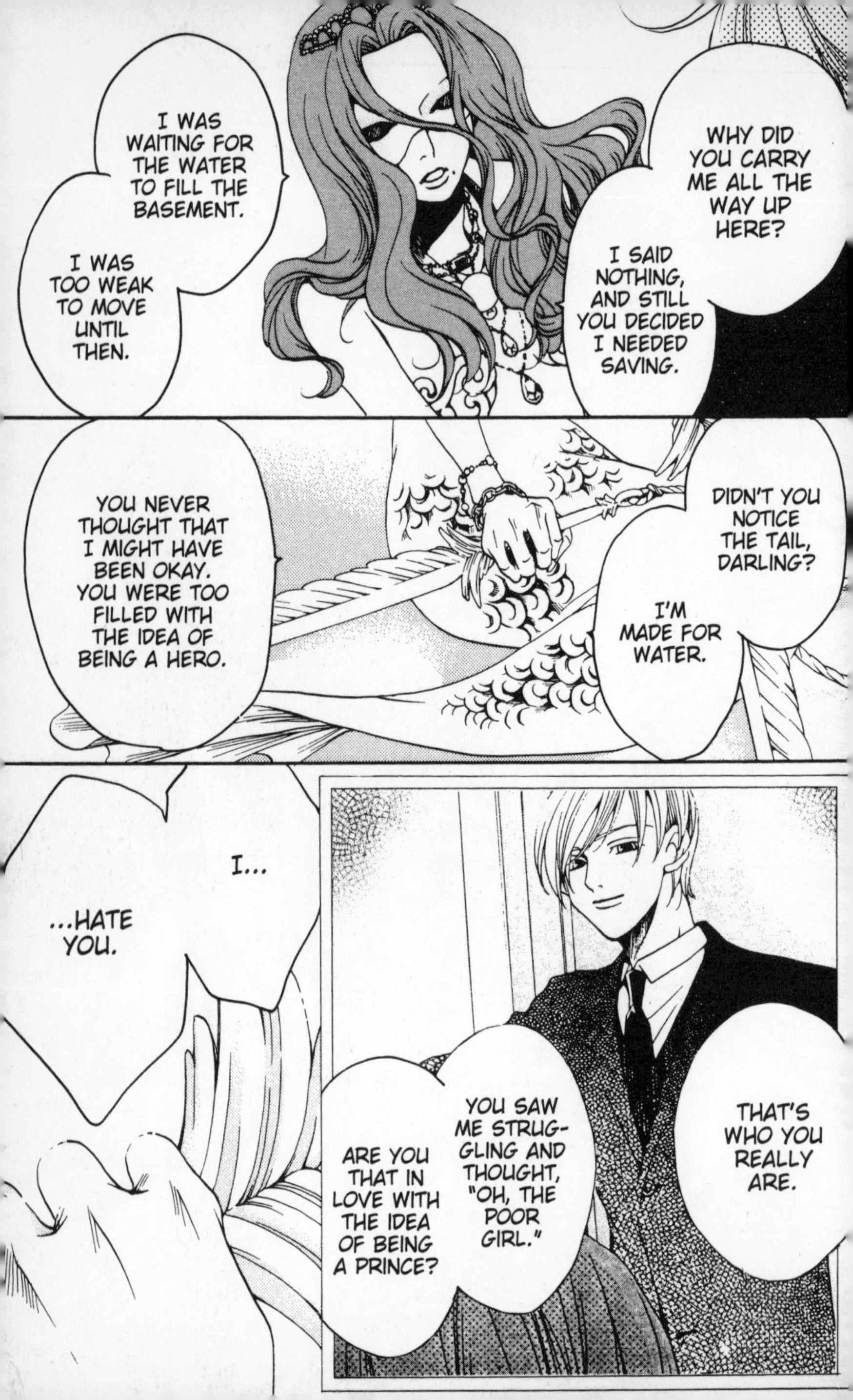
WHY DID YOU CARRY ME ALL THE WAY UP HERE?
I SAID NOTHING, AND STILL YOU DECIDED I NEEDED SAVING.
I WAS WAITING FOR THE WATER TO FILL THE BASEMENT.
I WAS TOO WEAK TO MOVE UNTIL THEN.
DIDN'T YOU NOTICE THE TAIL, DARLING?
I'M MADE FOR WATER.
YOU NEVER THOUGHT THAT I MIGHT HAVE BEEN OKAY. YOU WERE TOO FILLED WITH THE IDEA OF BEING A HERO.
THAT'S WHO YOU REALLY ARE.
YOU SAW ME STRUG-GLING AND THOUGHT, "OH, THE POOR GIRL."
ARE YOU THAT IN LOVE WITH THE IDEA OF BEING A PRINCE?
I...
...HATE YOU.

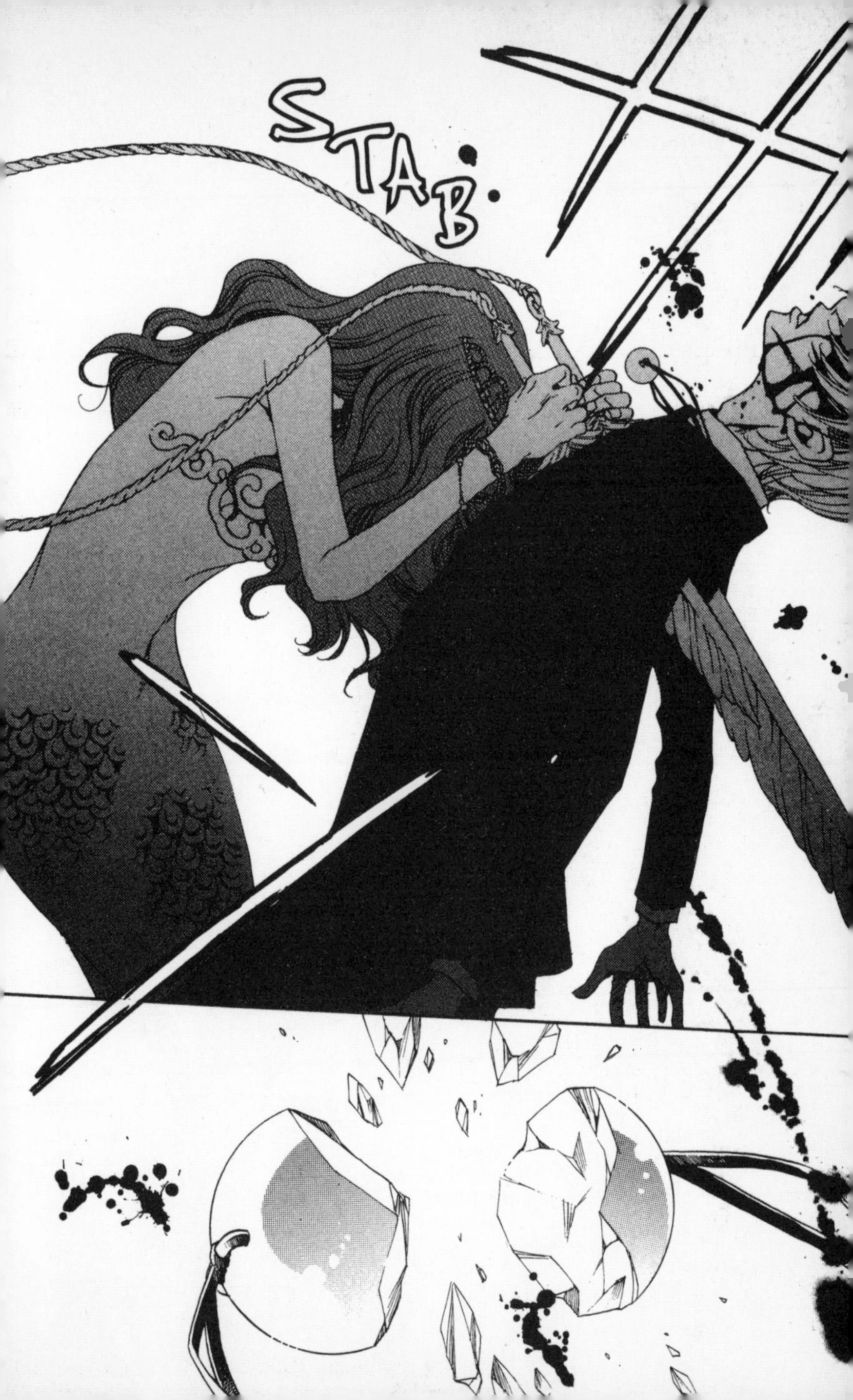
STAB

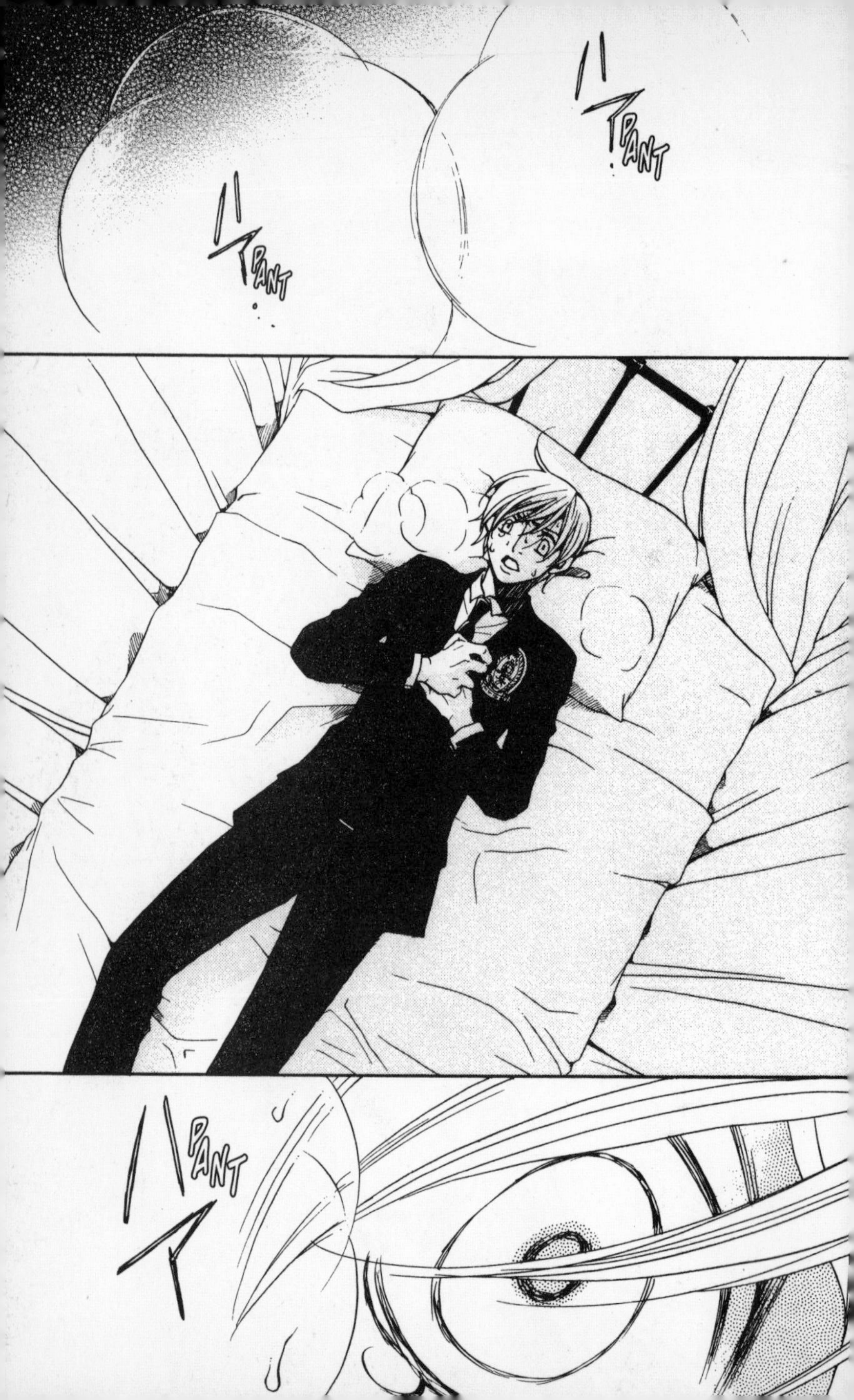

ハァ PANT
ハァ PANT
ハァ PANT

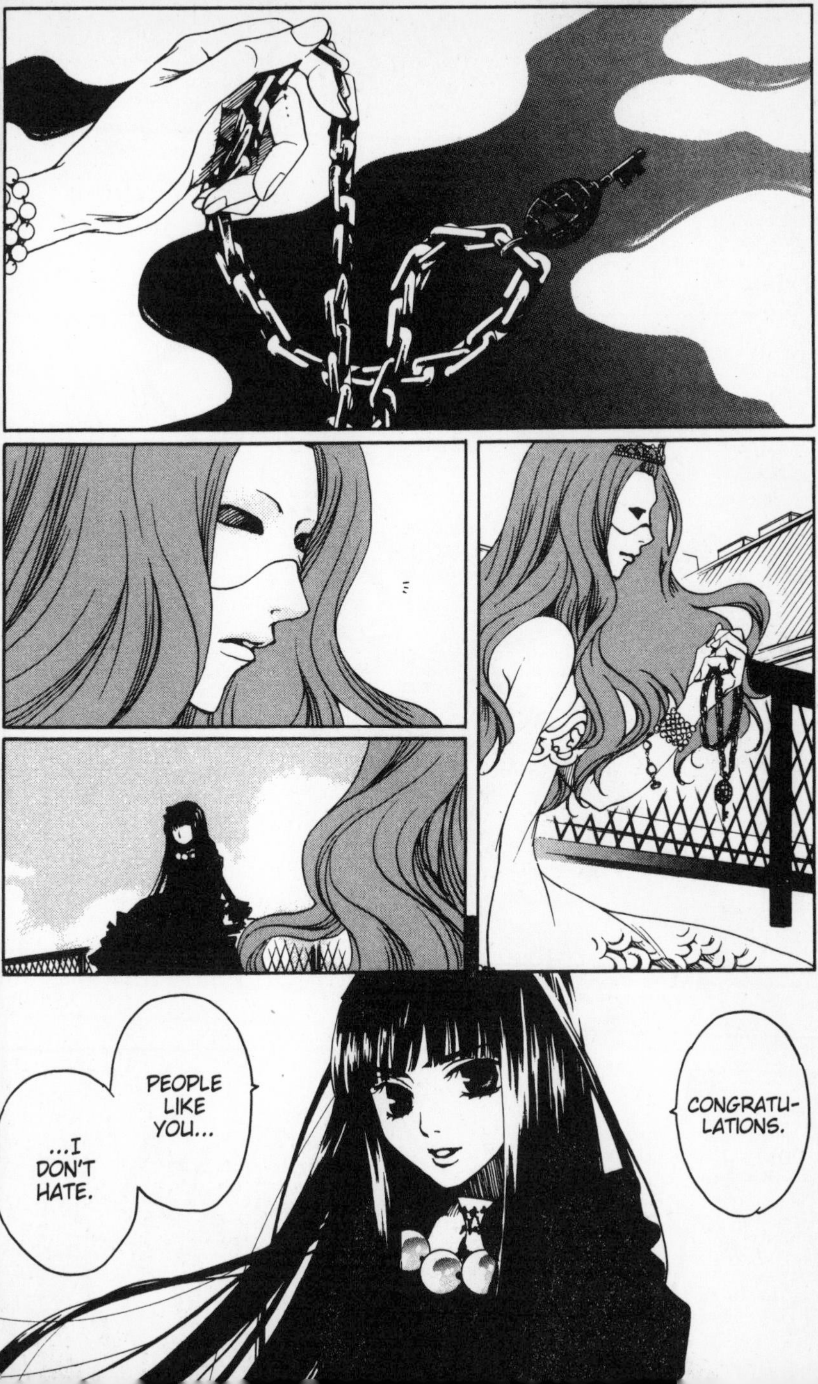
CONGRATU-LATIONS.
PEOPLE LIKE YOU...
...I DON'T HATE.

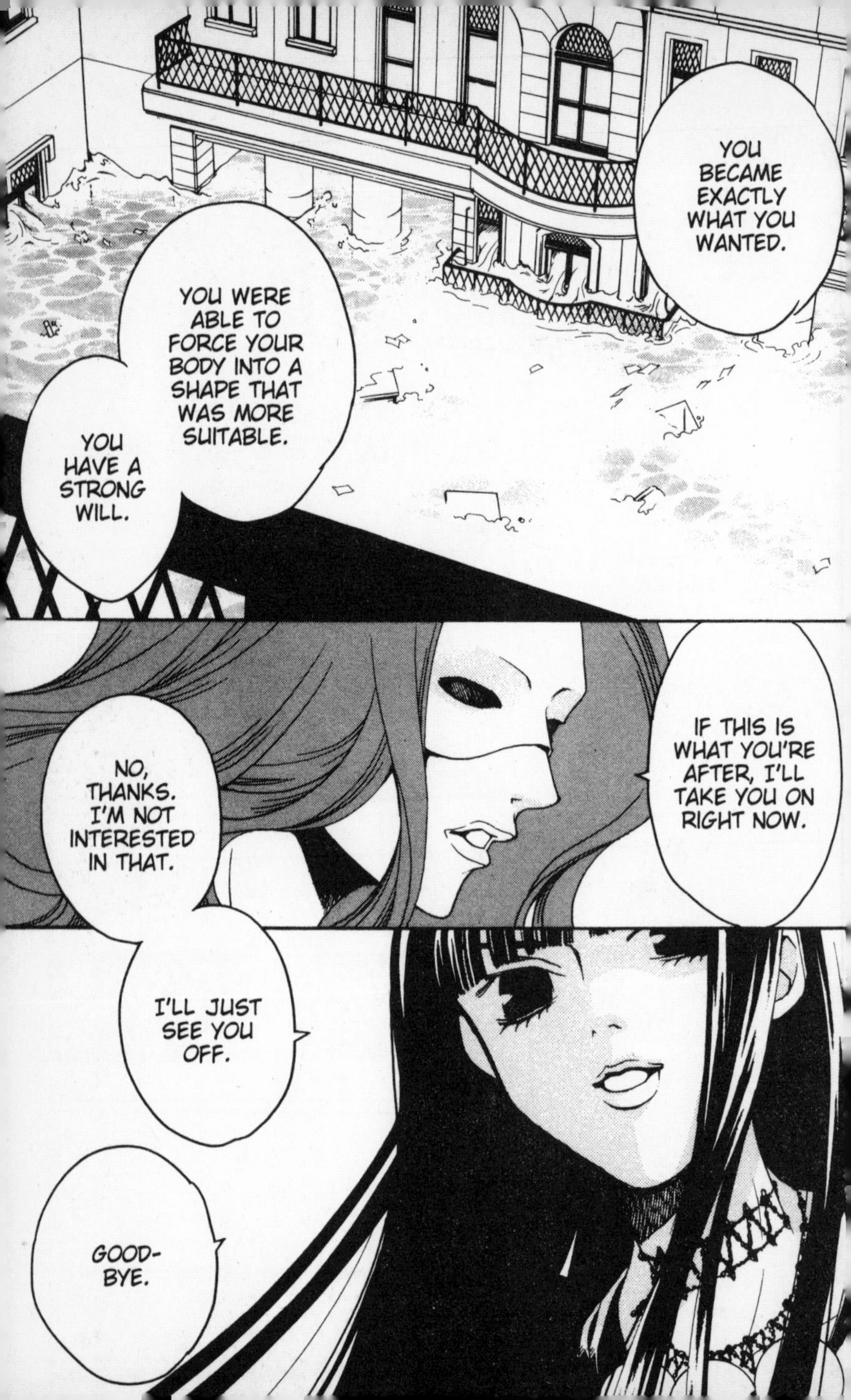
YOU BECAME EXACTLY WHAT YOU WANTED.
YOU WERE ABLE TO FORCE YOUR BODY INTO A SHAPE THAT WAS MORE SUITABLE.
YOU HAVE A STRONG WILL.
IF THIS IS WHAT YOU'RE AFTER, I'LL TAKE YOU ON RIGHT NOW.
NO, THANKS. I'M NOT INTERESTED IN THAT.
I'LL JUST SEE YOU OFF.
GOOD-BYE.

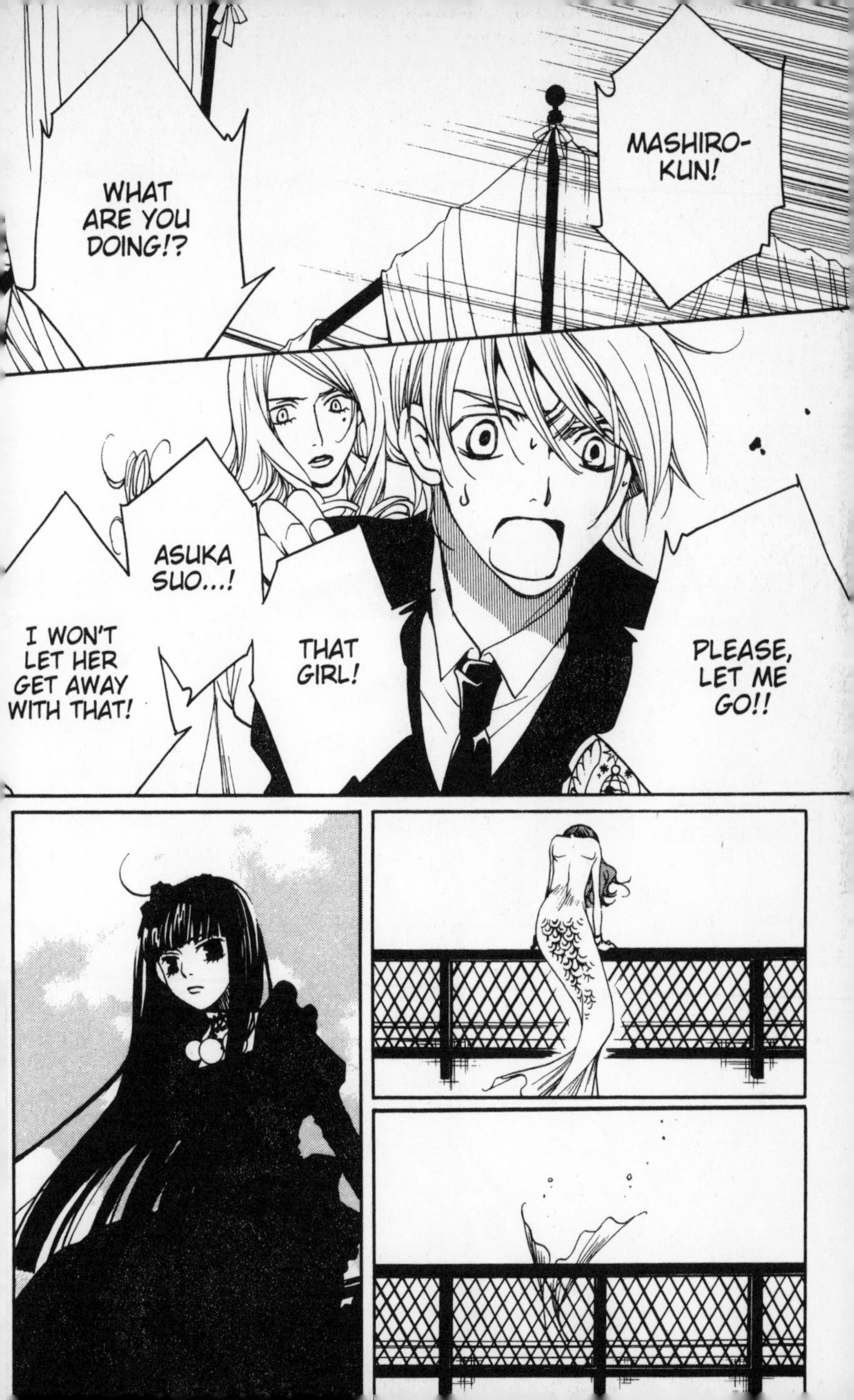
MASHIRO-KUN!
WHAT ARE YOU DOING!?
PLEASE, LET ME GO!!
ASUKA SUO...!
THAT GIRL!
I WON'T LET HER GET AWAY WITH THAT!

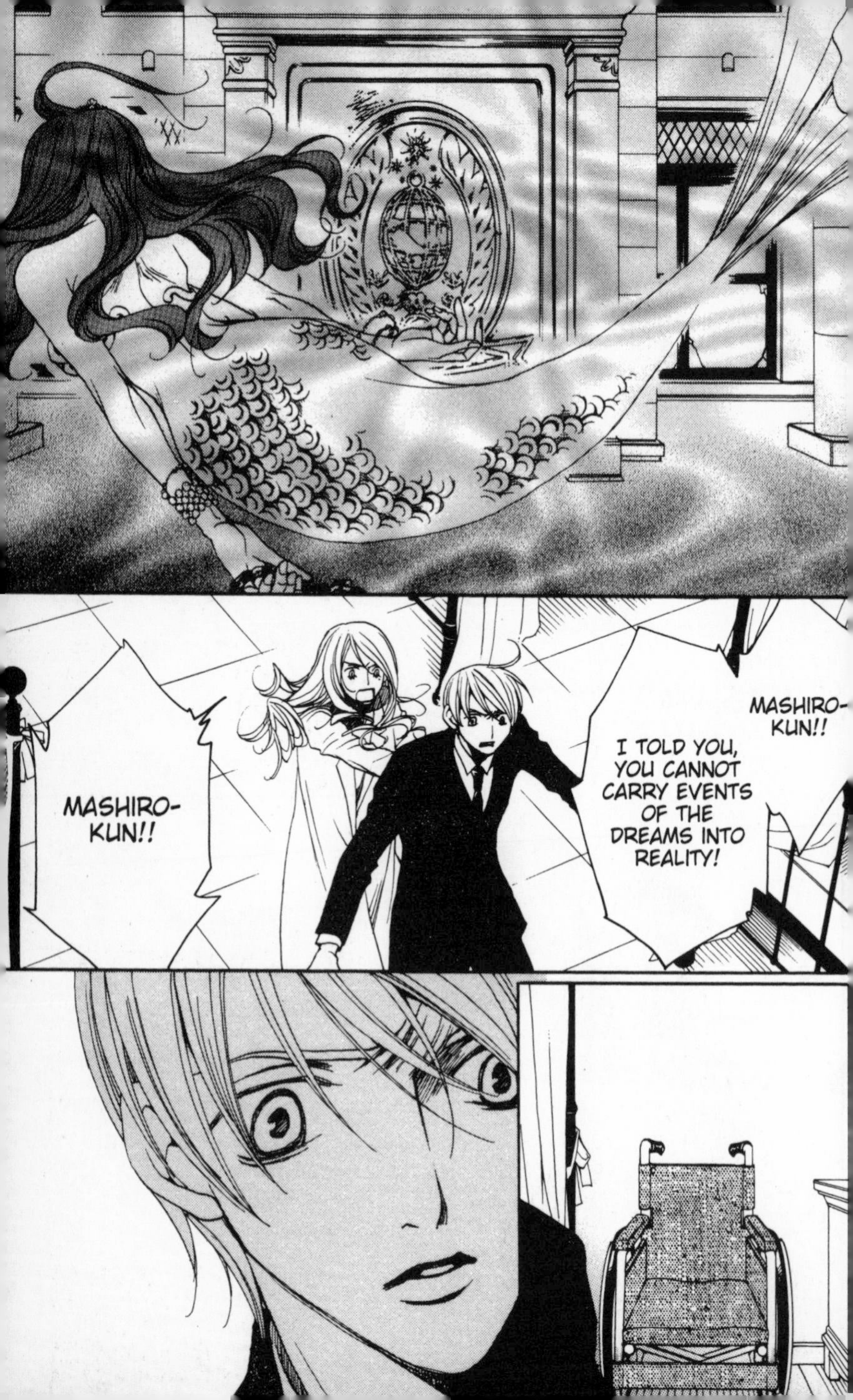
MASHIRO-KUN!!
I TOLD YOU, YOU CANNOT CARRY EVENTS OF THE DREAMS INTO REALITY!
MASHIRO-KUN!!

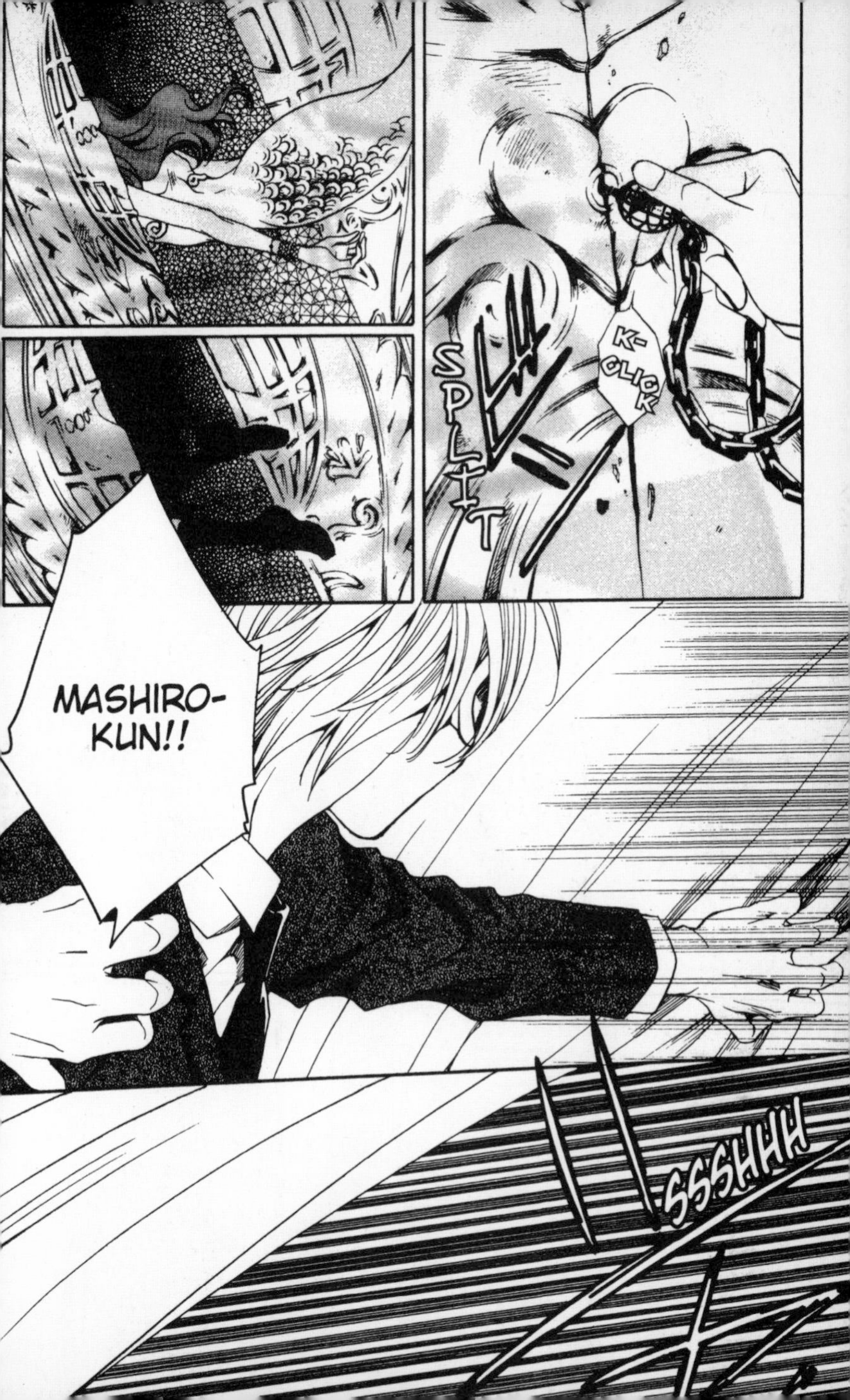
K-CLICK
SPLIT
MASHIRO-KUN!!
SSSHHH

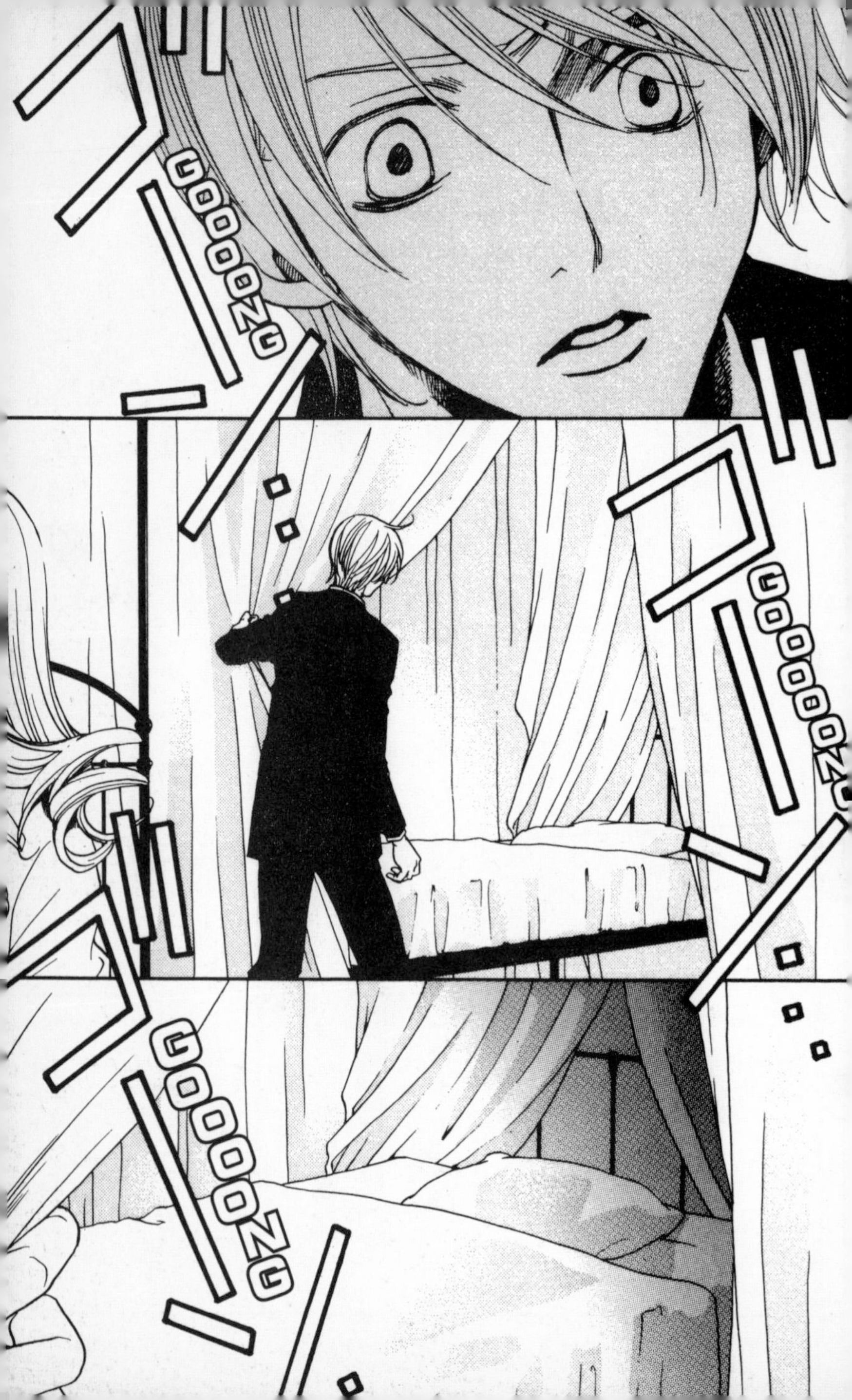
GOOOONG
GOOOOONG
GOOOONG

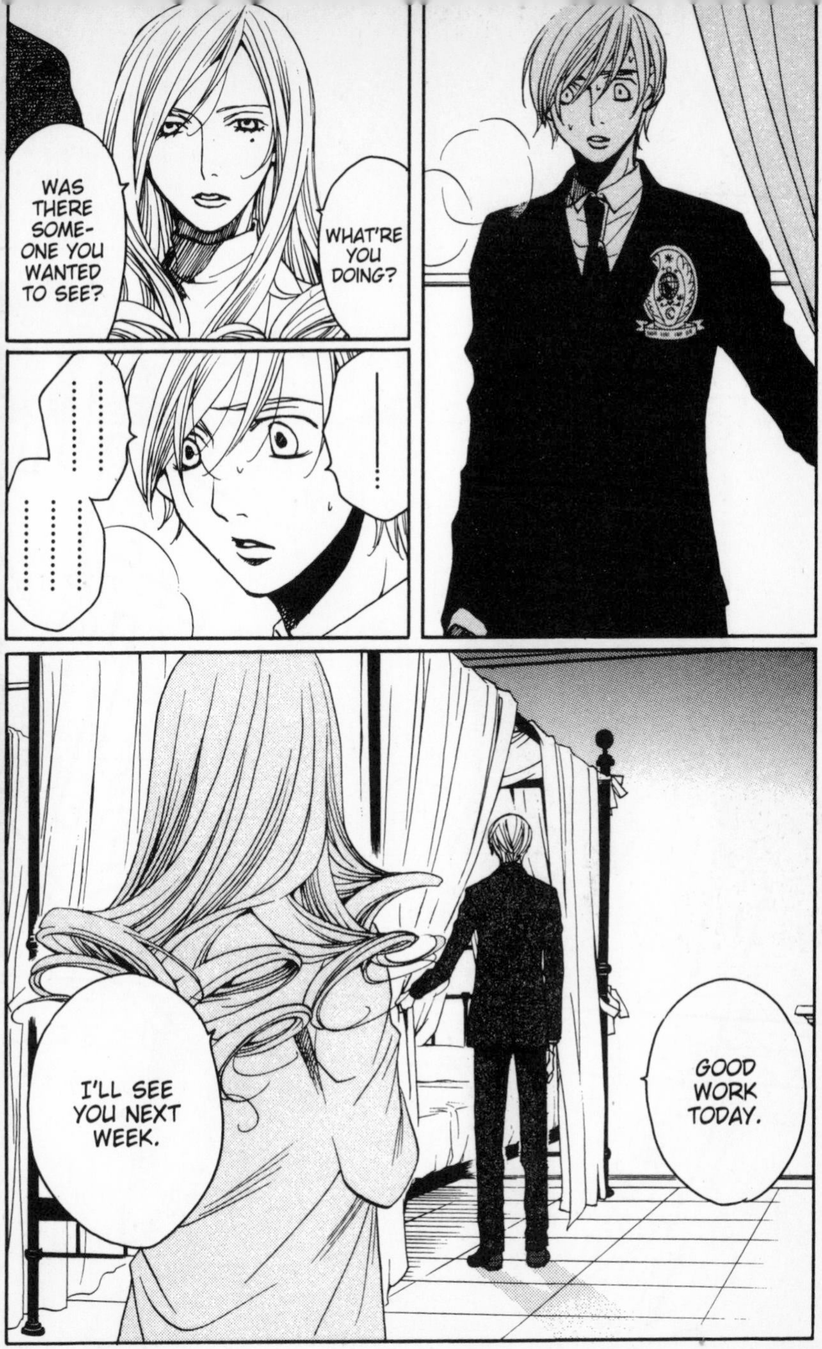
WHAT'RE YOU DOING?
WAS THERE SOME-ONE YOU WANTED TO SEE?
......!
......
GOOD WORK TODAY.
I'LL SEE YOU NEXT WEEK.

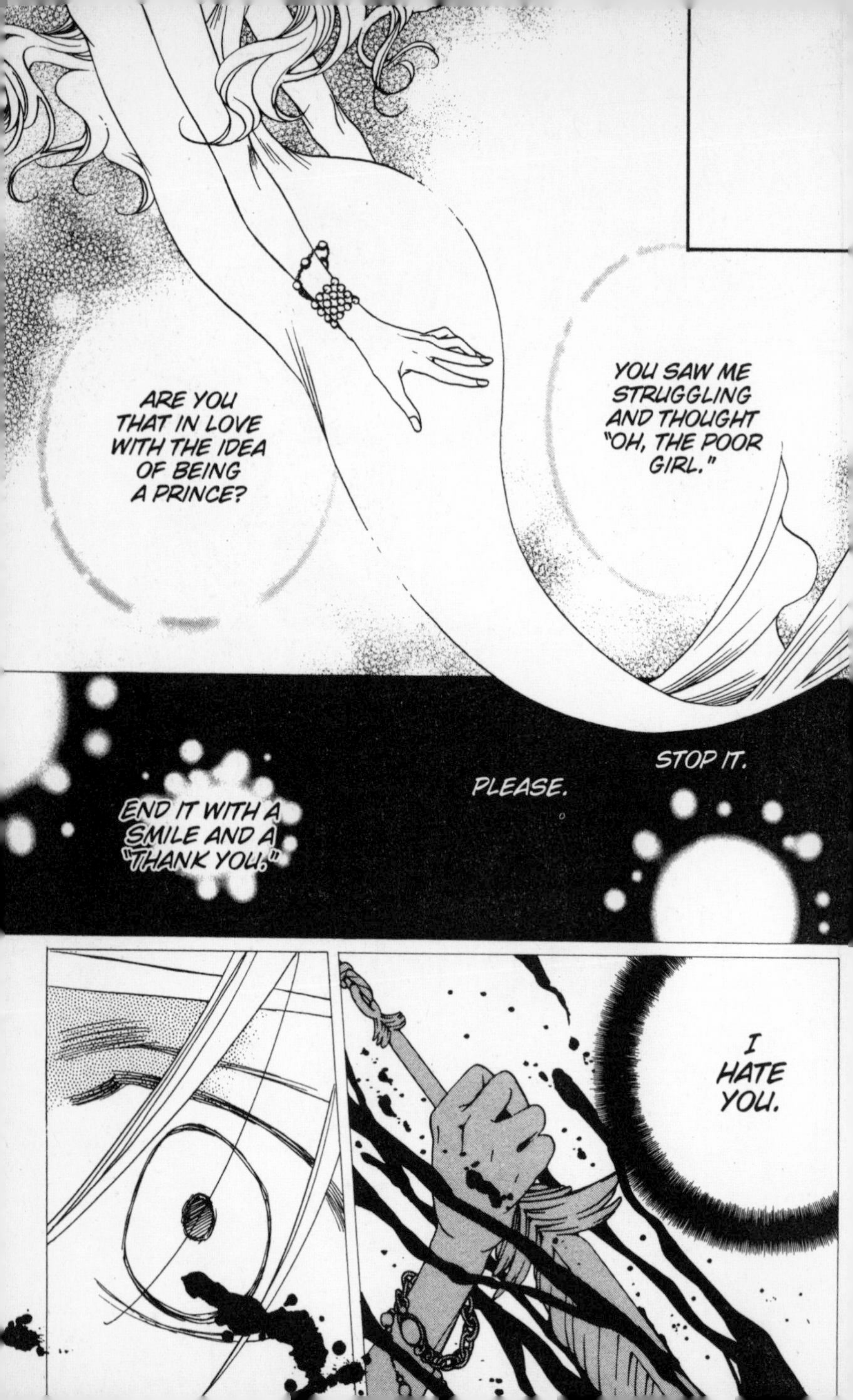
YOU SAW ME STRUGGLING AND THOUGHT "OH, THE POOR GIRL."
ARE YOU THAT IN LOVE WITH THE IDEA OF BEING A PRINCE?
STOP IT.
PLEASE.
END IT WITH A SMILE AND A "THANK YOU."
I HATE YOU.

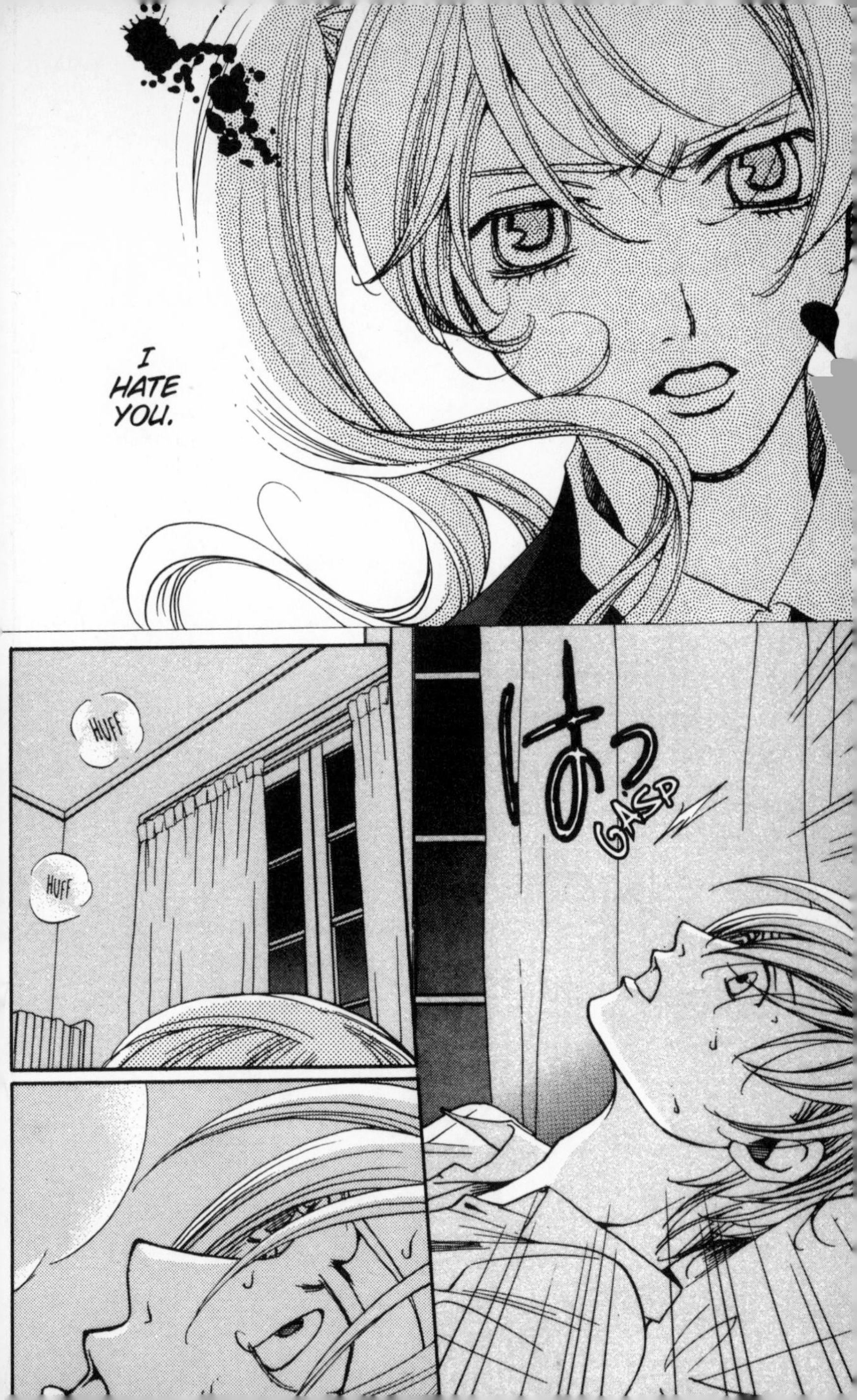
I HATE YOU.
はっ
GASP
HUFF
HUFF

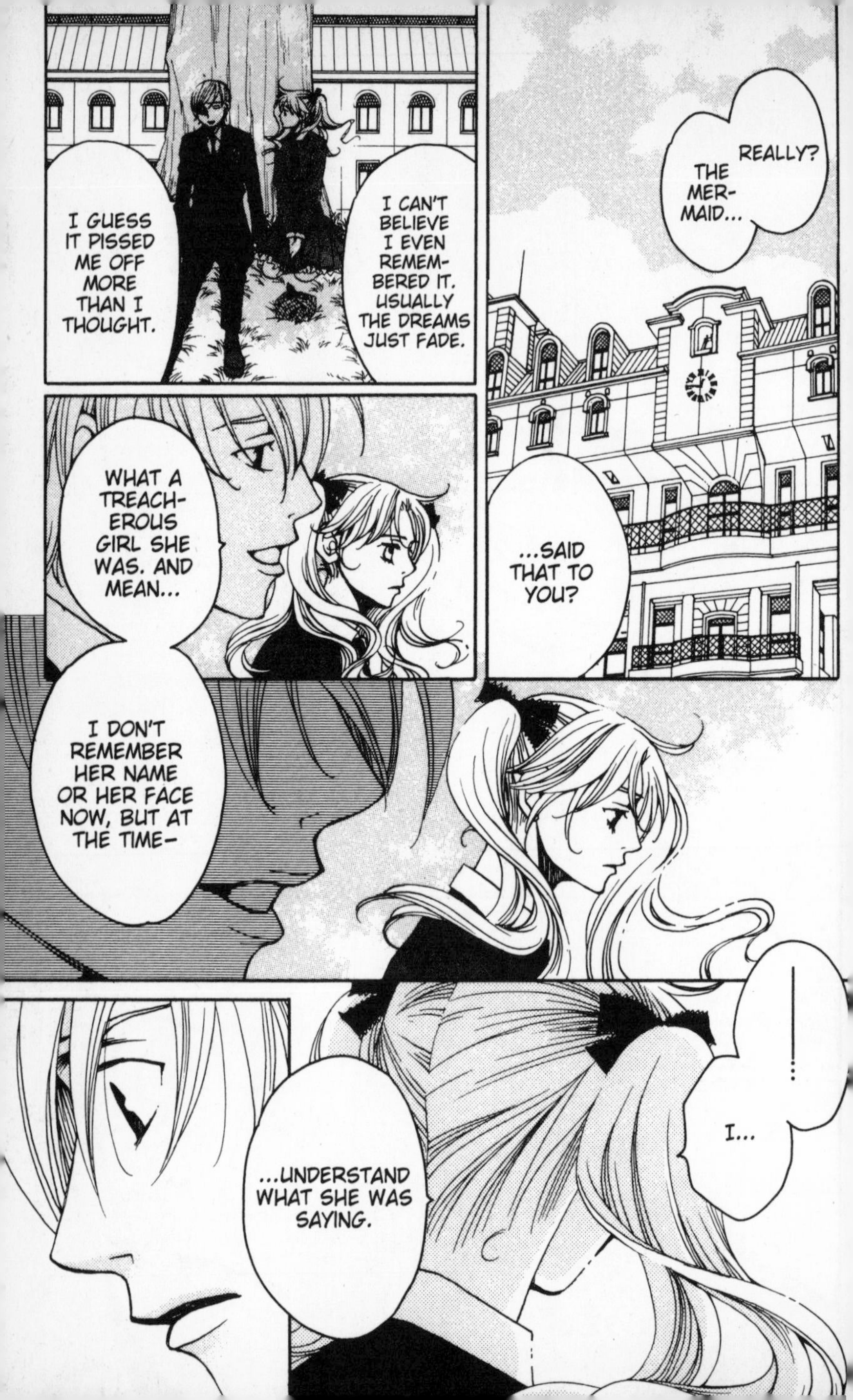
REALLY? THE MERMAID...
...SAID THAT TO YOU?
I CAN'T BELIEVE I EVEN REMEMBERED IT. USUALLY THE DREAMS JUST FADE.
I GUESS IT PISSED ME OFF MORE THAN I THOUGHT.
WHAT A TREACHEROUS GIRL SHE WAS. AND MEAN...
I DON'T REMEMBER HER NAME OR HER FACE NOW, BUT AT THE TIME–
I...
...UNDERSTAND WHAT SHE WAS SAYING.

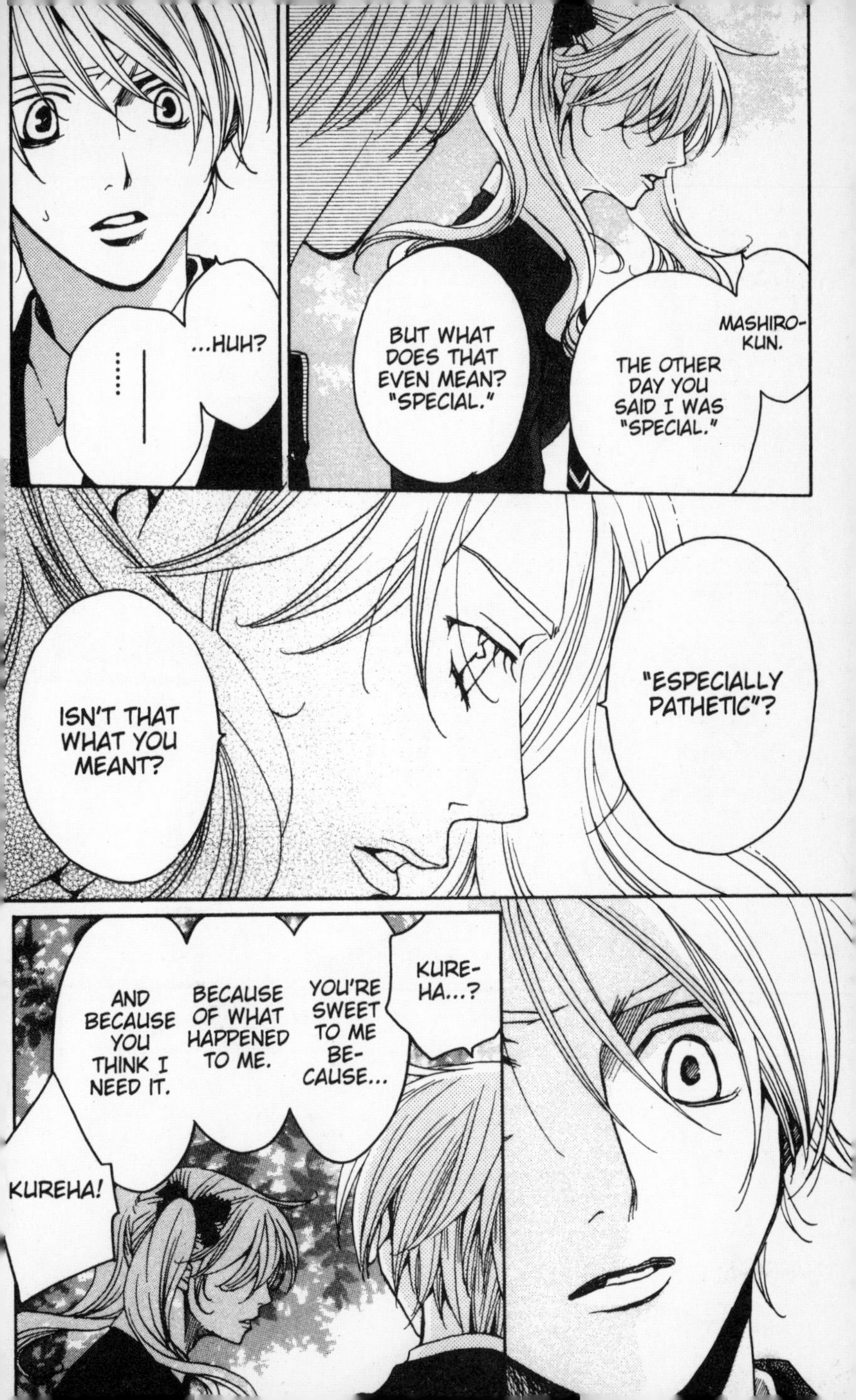
MASHIRO-KUN.
THE OTHER DAY YOU SAID I WAS "SPECIAL."
BUT WHAT DOES THAT EVEN MEAN? "SPECIAL."
...HUH?
"ESPECIALLY PATHETIC"?
ISN'T THAT WHAT YOU MEANT?
KURE-HA...?
YOU'RE SWEET TO ME BE-CAUSE...
BECAUSE OF WHAT HAPPENED TO ME.
AND BECAUSE YOU THINK I NEED IT.
KUREHA!

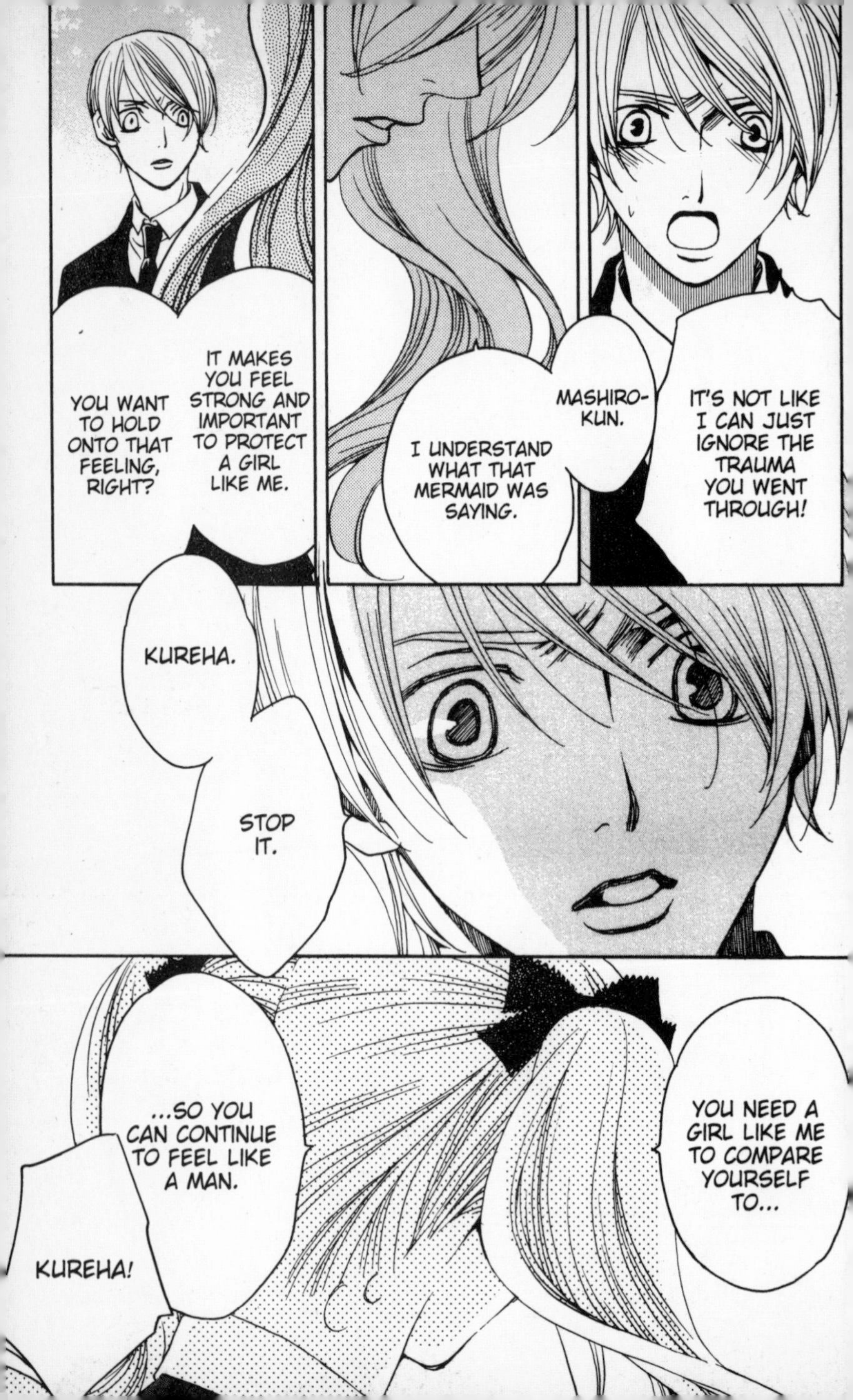
IT'S NOT LIKE I CAN JUST IGNORE THE TRAUMA YOU WENT THROUGH!
MASHIRO-KUN.
I UNDERSTAND WHAT THAT MERMAID WAS SAYING.
IT MAKES YOU FEEL STRONG AND IMPORTANT TO PROTECT A GIRL LIKE ME.
YOU WANT TO HOLD ONTO THAT FEELING, RIGHT?
KUREHA.
STOP IT.
YOU NEED A GIRL LIKE ME TO COMPARE YOURSELF TO...
...SO YOU CAN CONTINUE TO FEEL LIKE A MAN.
KUREHA!

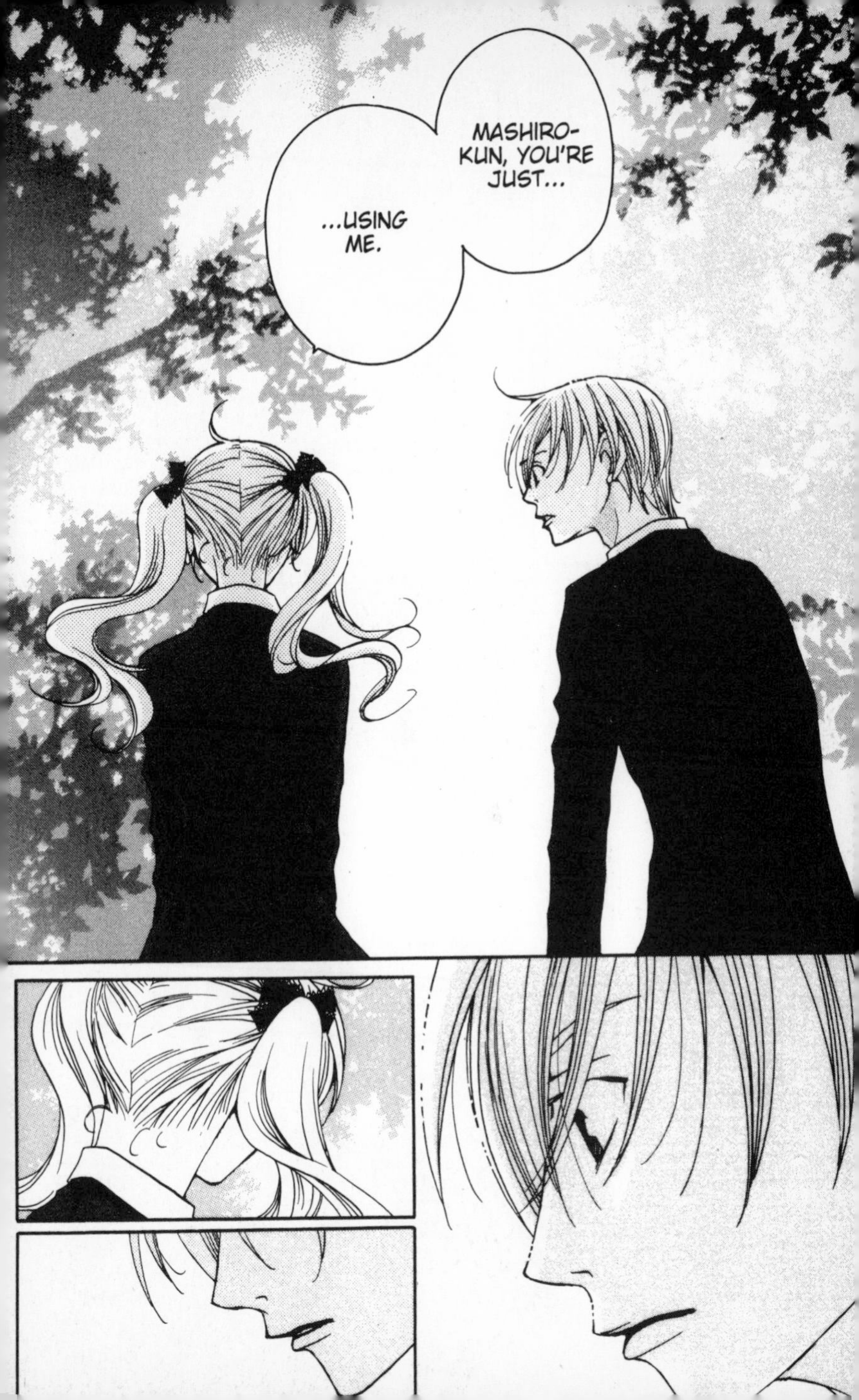
MASHIRO-KUN, YOU'RE JUST...
...USING ME.

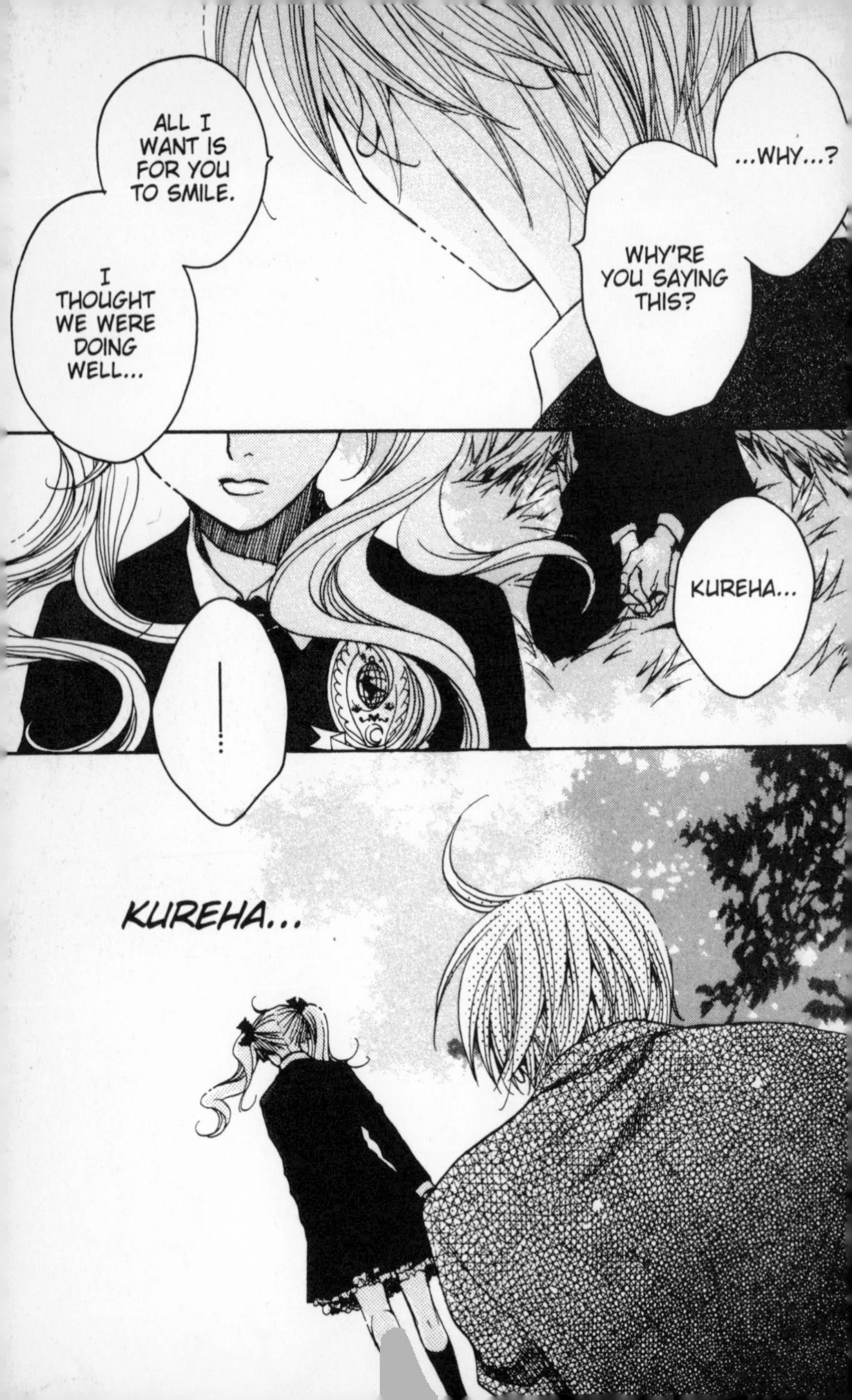
...WHY...?
WHY'RE YOU SAYING THIS?
ALL I WANT IS FOR YOU TO SMILE.
I THOUGHT WE WERE DOING WELL...
KUREHA...
—......
KUREHA...

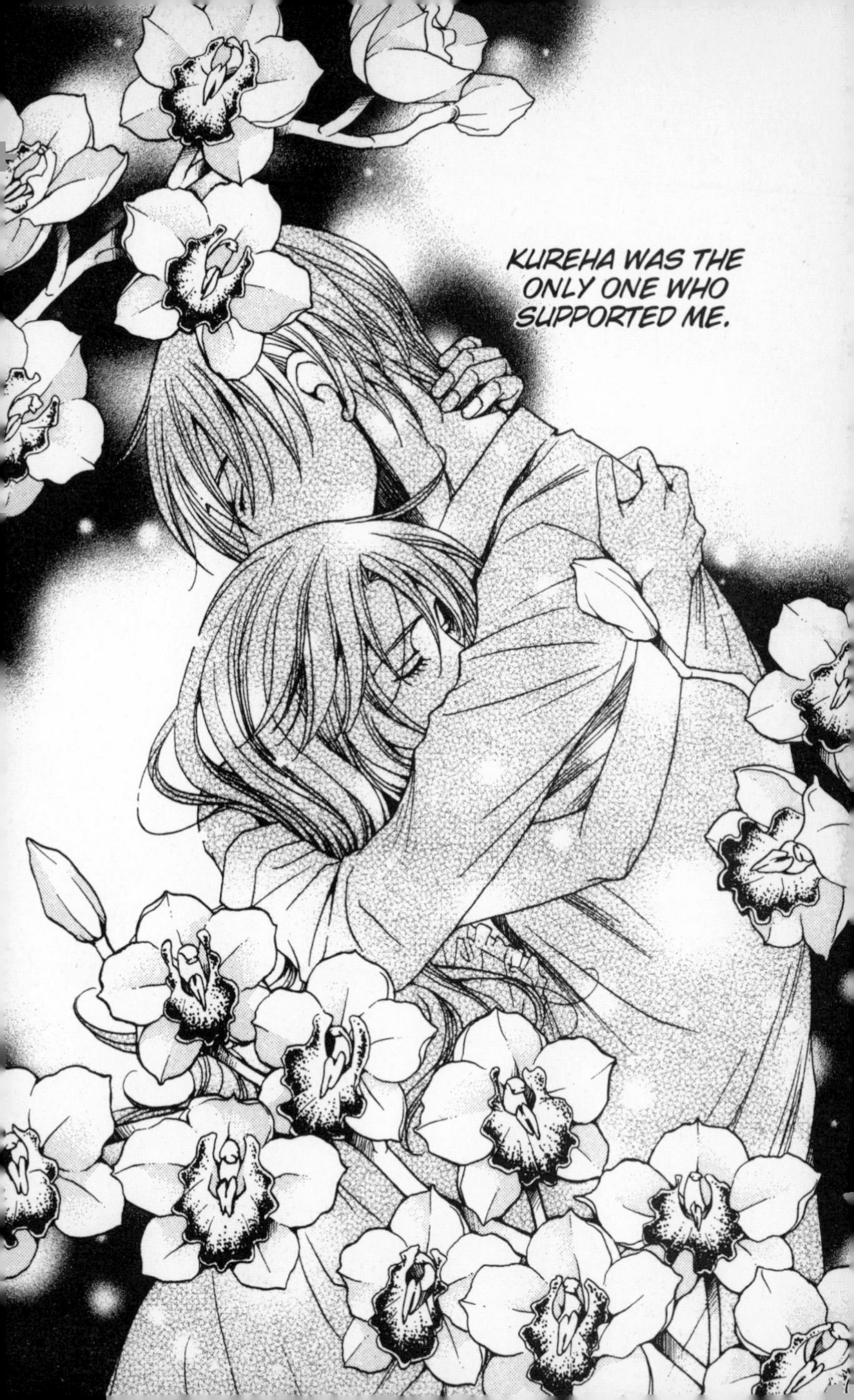
KUREHA WAS THE ONLY ONE WHO SUPPORTED ME.

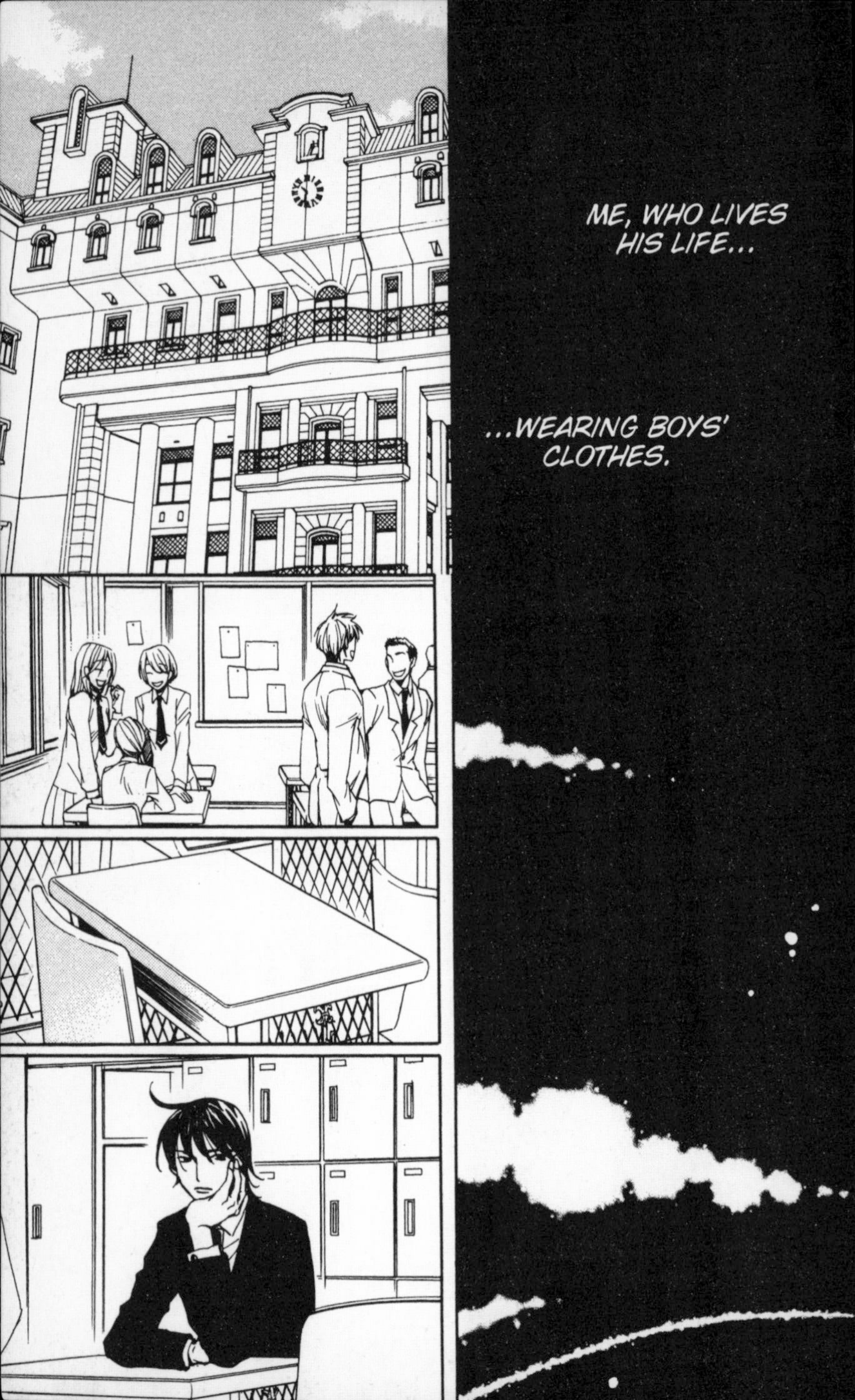
ME, WHO LIVES HIS LIFE...
...WEARING BOYS' CLOTHES.

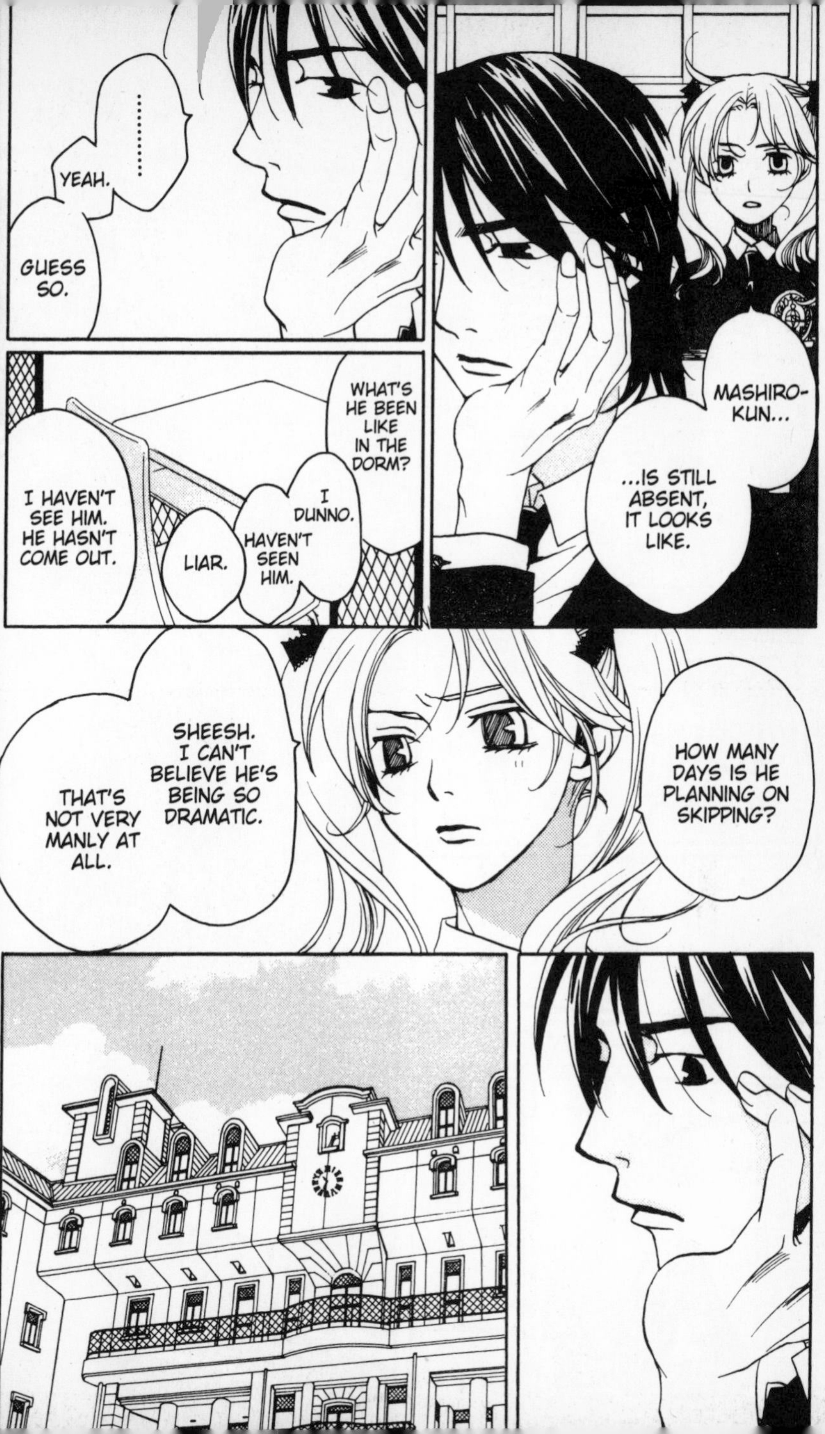
MASHIRO-KUN...
...IS STILL ABSENT, IT LOOKS LIKE.
......
YEAH.
GUESS SO.
WHAT'S HE BEEN LIKE IN THE DORM?
I DUNNO.
HAVEN'T SEEN HIM.
LIAR.
I HAVEN'T SEE HIM. HE HASN'T COME OUT.
HOW MANY DAYS IS HE PLANNING ON SKIPPING?
SHEESH. I CAN'T BELIEVE HE'S BEING SO DRAMATIC.
THAT'S NOT VERY MANLY AT ALL.

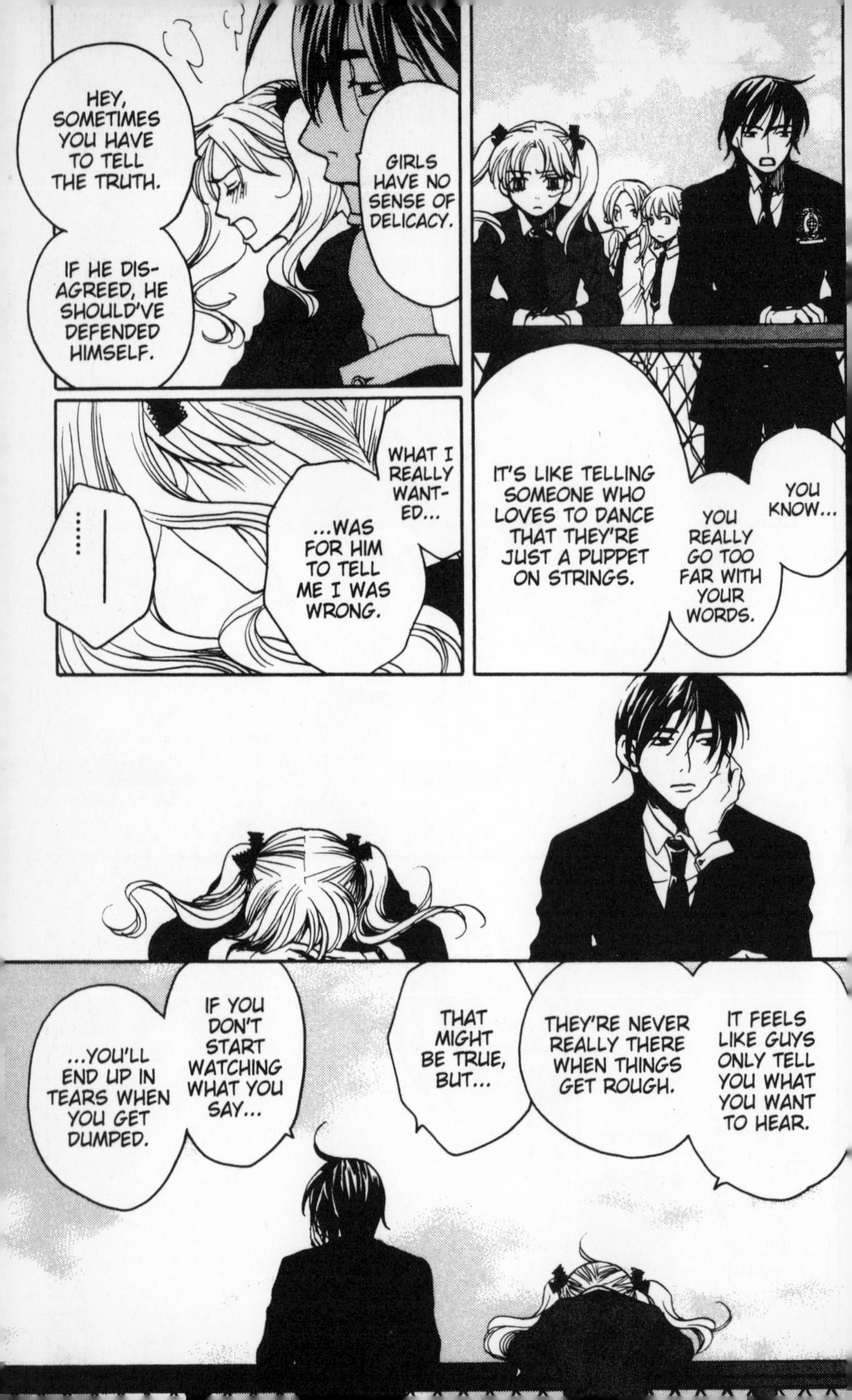
YOU KNOW...
YOU REALLY GO TOO FAR WITH YOUR WORDS.
IT'S LIKE TELLING SOMEONE WHO LOVES TO DANCE THAT THEY'RE JUST A PUPPET ON STRINGS.
GIRLS HAVE NO SENSE OF DELICACY.
HEY, SOMETIMES YOU HAVE TO TELL THE TRUTH.
IF HE DISAGREED, HE SHOULD'VE DEFENDED HIMSELF.
WHAT I REALLY WANTED...
...WAS FOR HIM TO TELL ME I WAS WRONG.
......—
IT FEELS LIKE GUYS ONLY TELL YOU WHAT YOU WANT TO HEAR.
THEY'RE NEVER REALLY THERE WHEN THINGS GET ROUGH.
THAT MIGHT BE TRUE, BUT...
IF YOU DON'T START WATCHING WHAT YOU SAY...
...YOU'LL END UP IN TEARS WHEN YOU GET DUMPED.

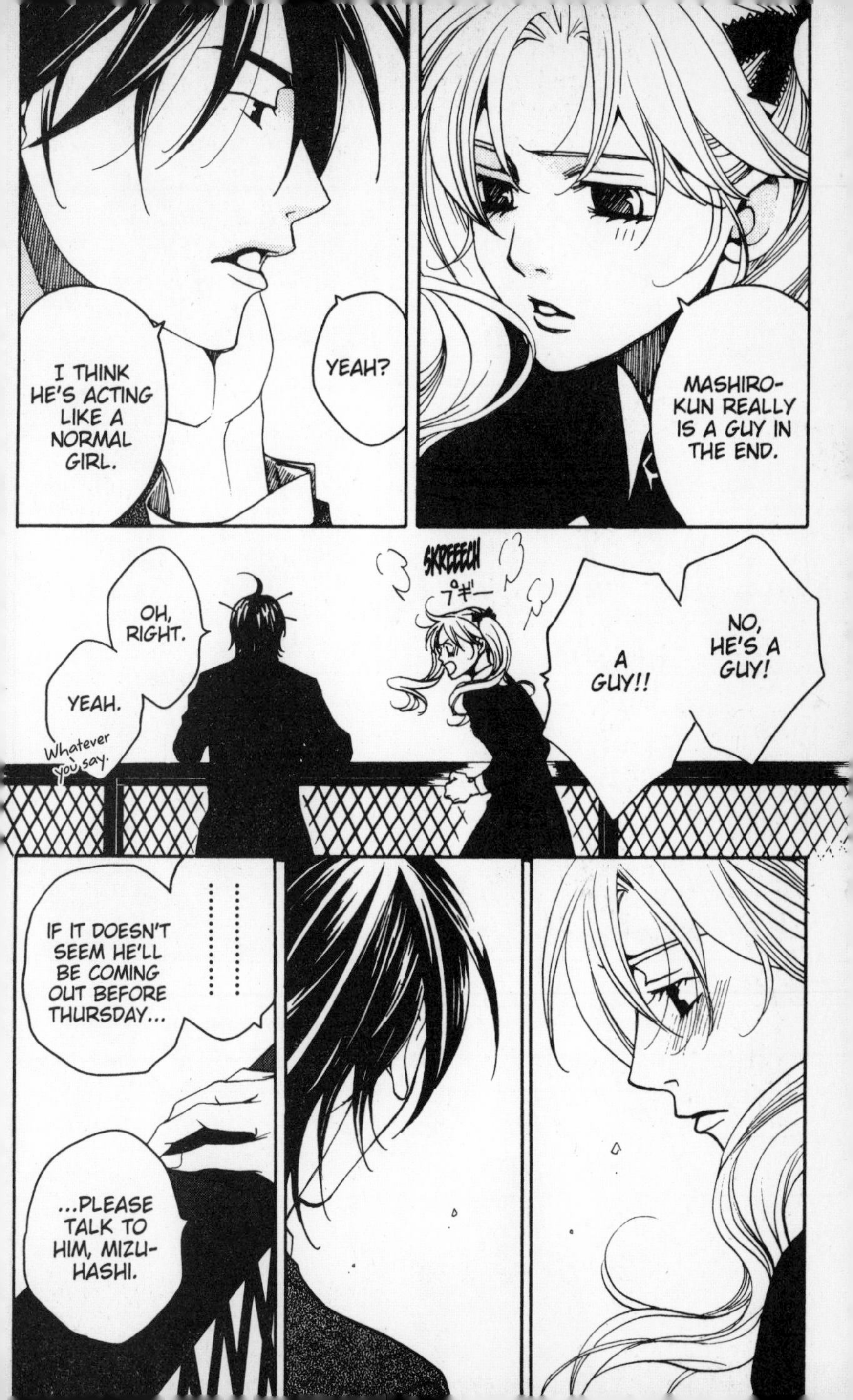
MASHIRO-KUN REALLY IS A GUY IN THE END.
YEAH?
I THINK HE'S ACTING LIKE A NORMAL GIRL.
NO, HE'S A GUY!
A GUY!!
SKREEECH
プギー
OH, RIGHT.
YEAH.
Whatever you say.
......
IF IT DOESN'T SEEM HE'LL BE COMING OUT BEFORE THURSDAY...
...PLEASE TALK TO HIM, MIZU-HASHI.

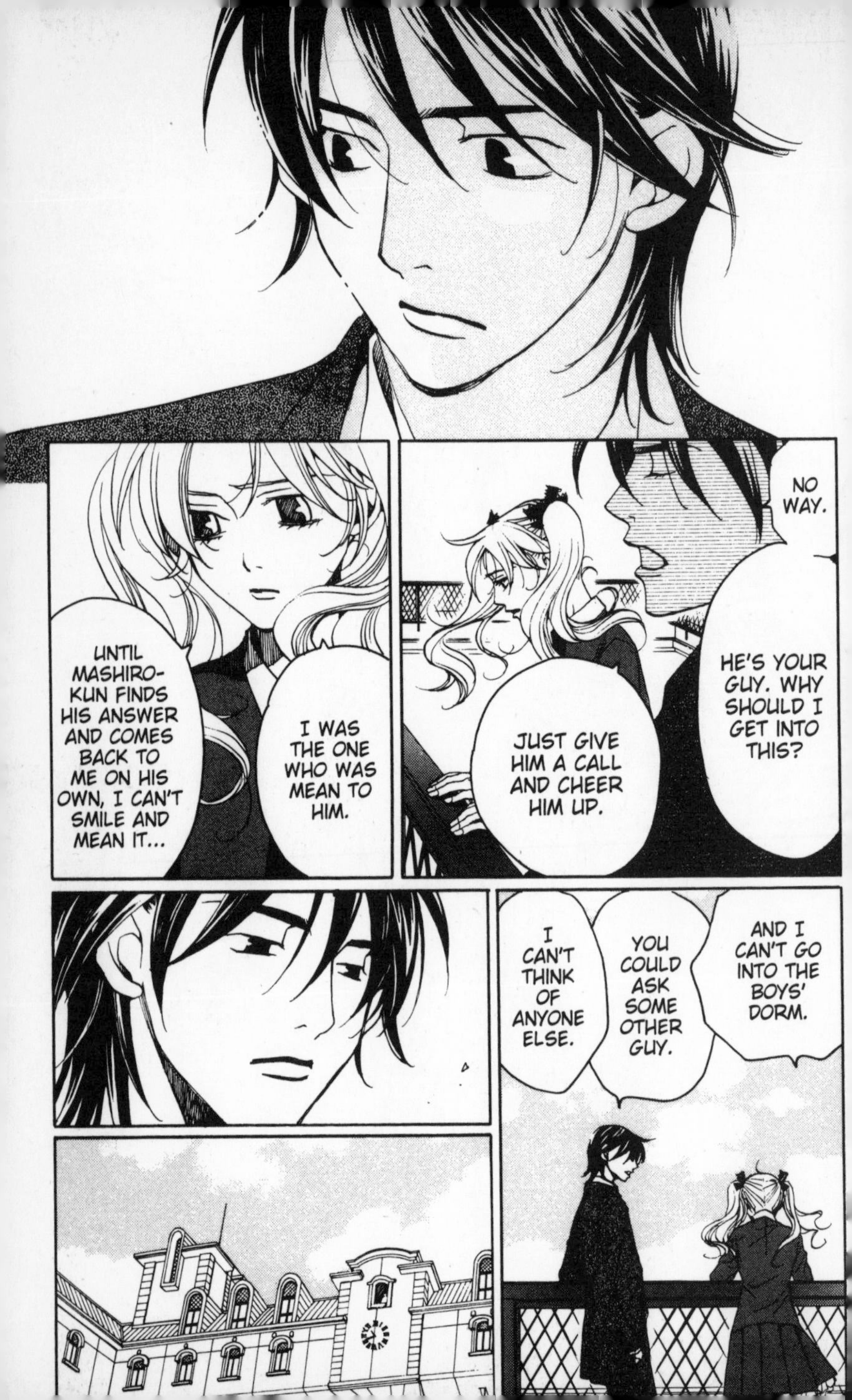
NO WAY.
HE'S YOUR GUY. WHY SHOULD I GET INTO THIS?
JUST GIVE HIM A CALL AND CHEER HIM UP.
I WAS THE ONE WHO WAS MEAN TO HIM.
UNTIL MASHIRO-KUN FINDS HIS ANSWER AND COMES BACK TO ME ON HIS OWN, I CAN'T SMILE AND MEAN IT...
AND I CAN'T GO INTO THE BOYS' DORM.
YOU COULD ASK SOME OTHER GUY.
I CAN'T THINK OF ANYONE ELSE.

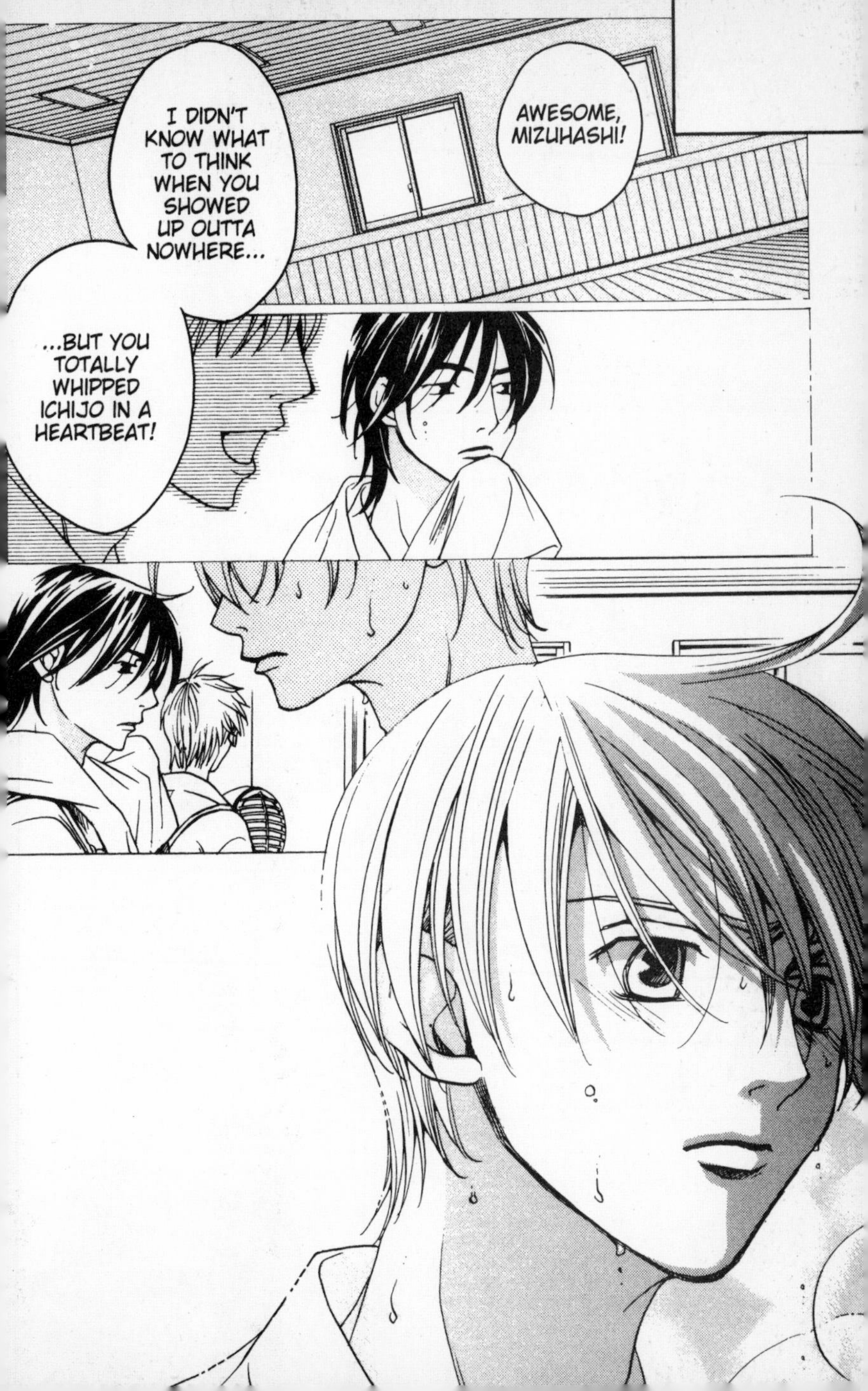
AWESOME, MIZUHASHI!
I DIDN'T KNOW WHAT TO THINK WHEN YOU SHOWED UP OUTTA NOWHERE...
...BUT YOU TOTALLY WHIPPED ICHIJO IN A HEARTBEAT!

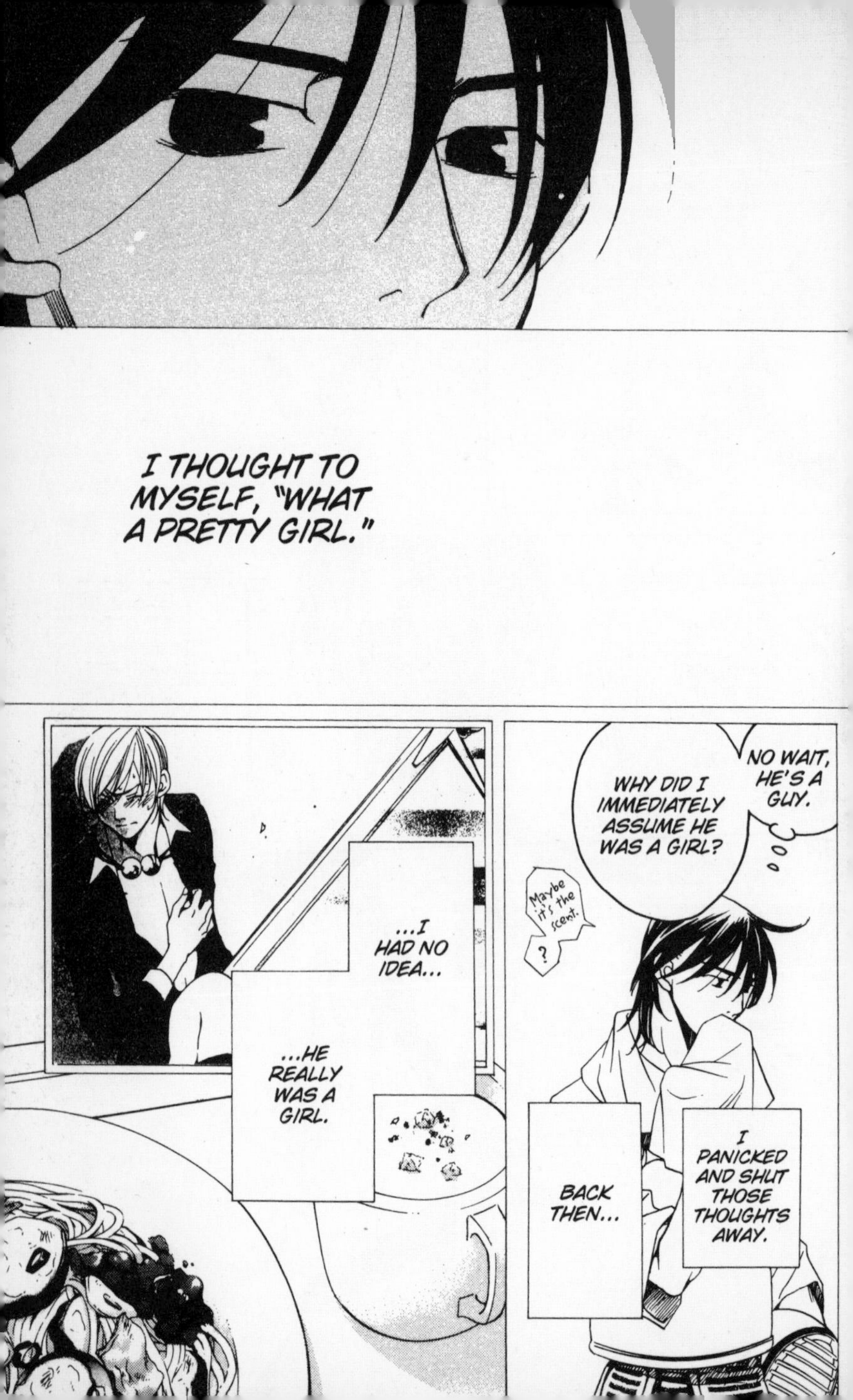
I THOUGHT TO MYSELF, "WHAT A PRETTY GIRL."
NO WAIT, HE'S A GUY.
WHY DID I IMMEDIATELY ASSUME HE WAS A GIRL?
Maybe it's the scent.
?
I PANICKED AND SHUT THOSE THOUGHTS AWAY.
BACK THEN...
...I HAD NO IDEA...
...HE REALLY WAS A GIRL.

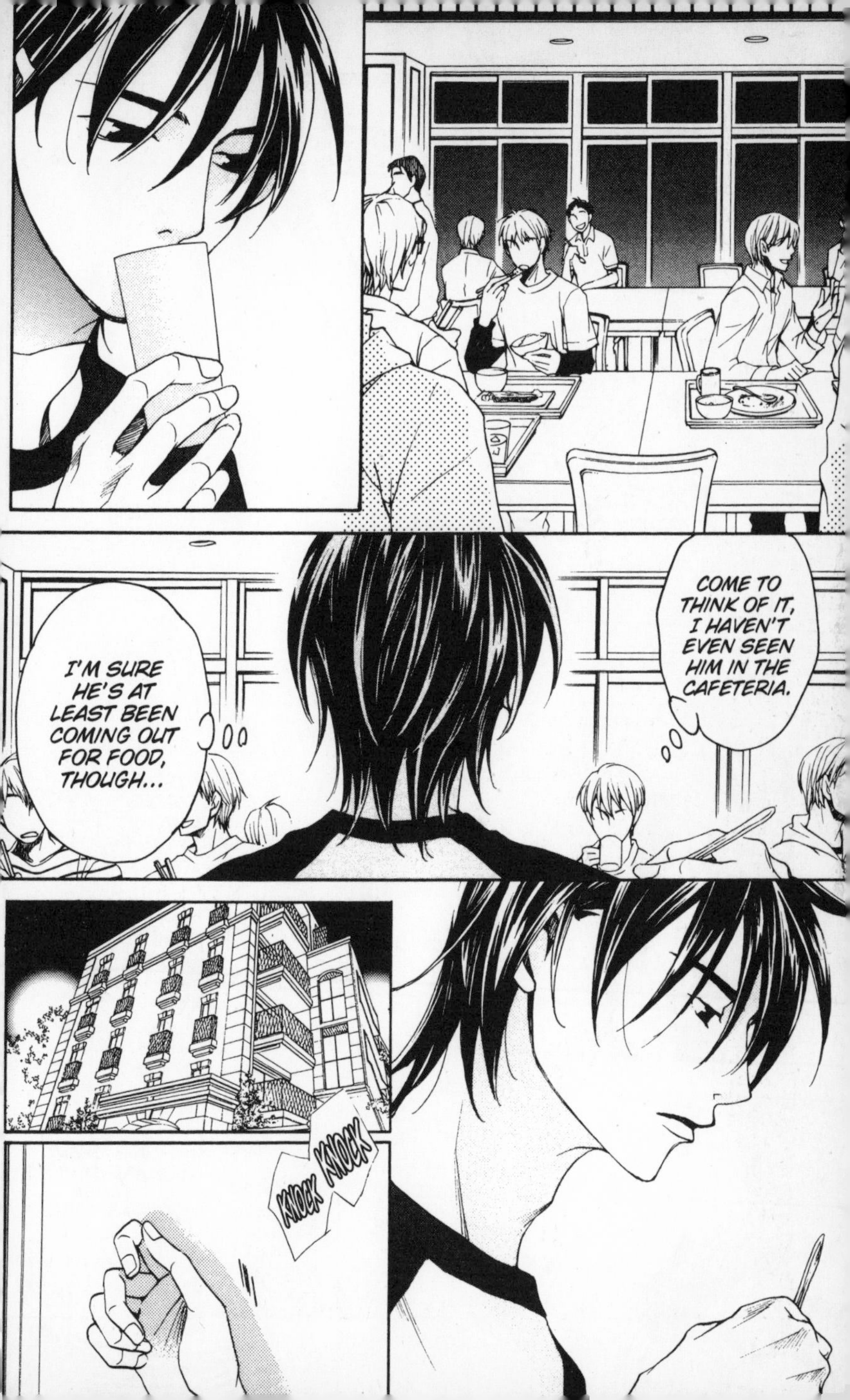
COME TO THINK OF IT, I HAVEN'T EVEN SEEN HIM IN THE CAFETERIA.
I'M SURE HE'S AT LEAST BEEN COMING OUT FOR FOOD, THOUGH...
KNOCK KNOCK

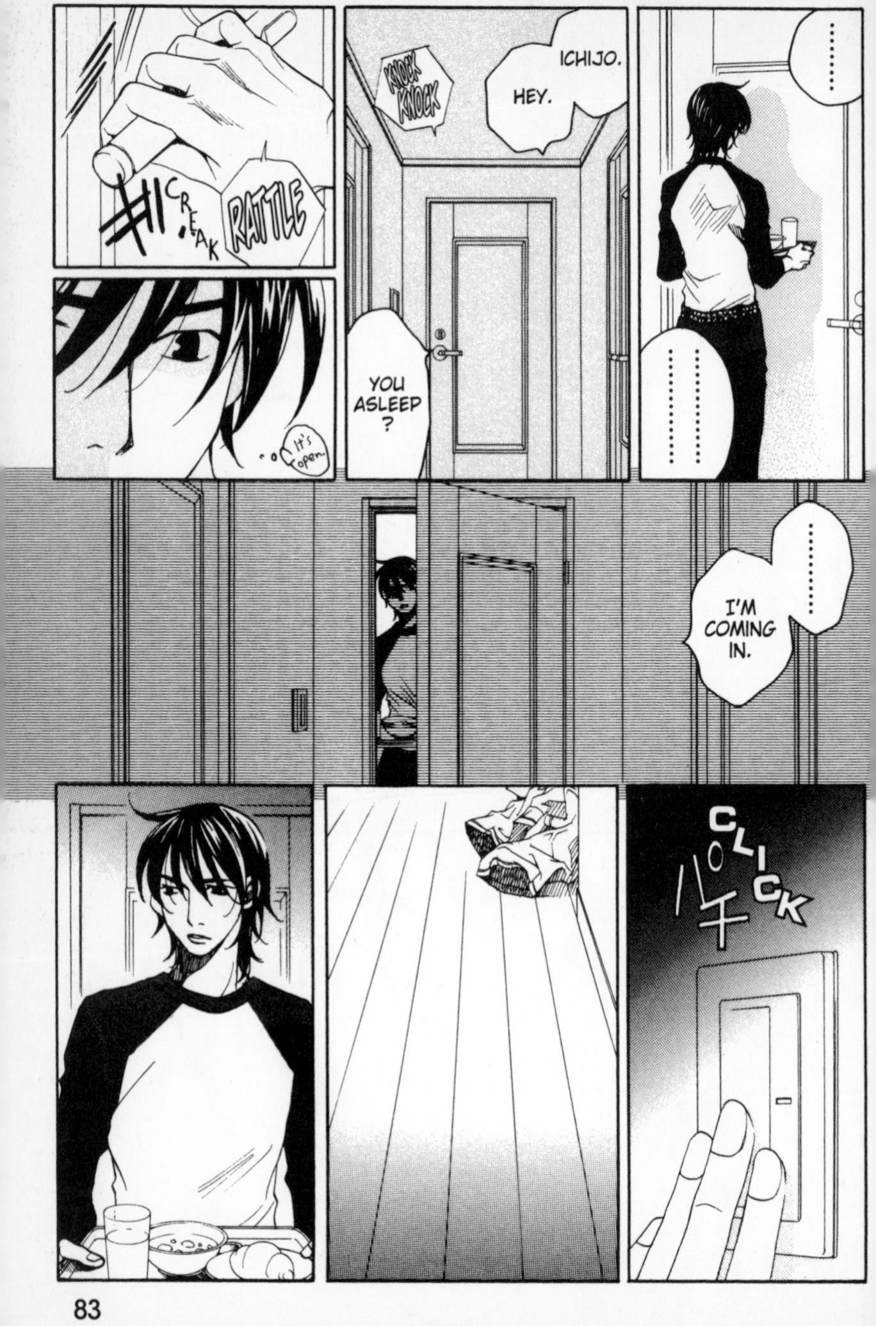
……
……
KNOCK KNOCK
ICHIJO.
HEY.
YOU ASLEEP?
RATTLE
CREAK
It's open..
……
I'M COMING IN.
CLICK
パチ

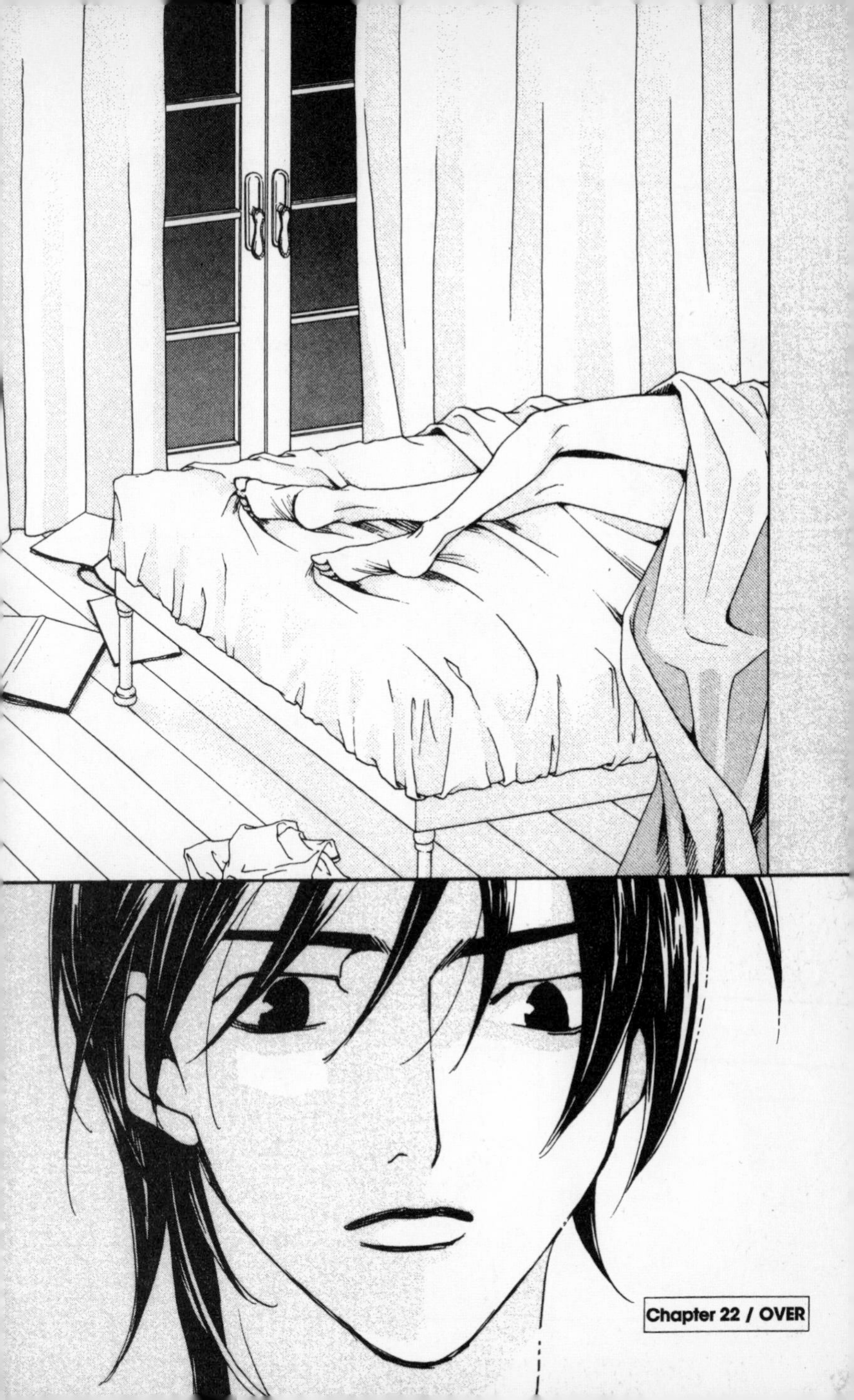
Chapter 22 / OVER

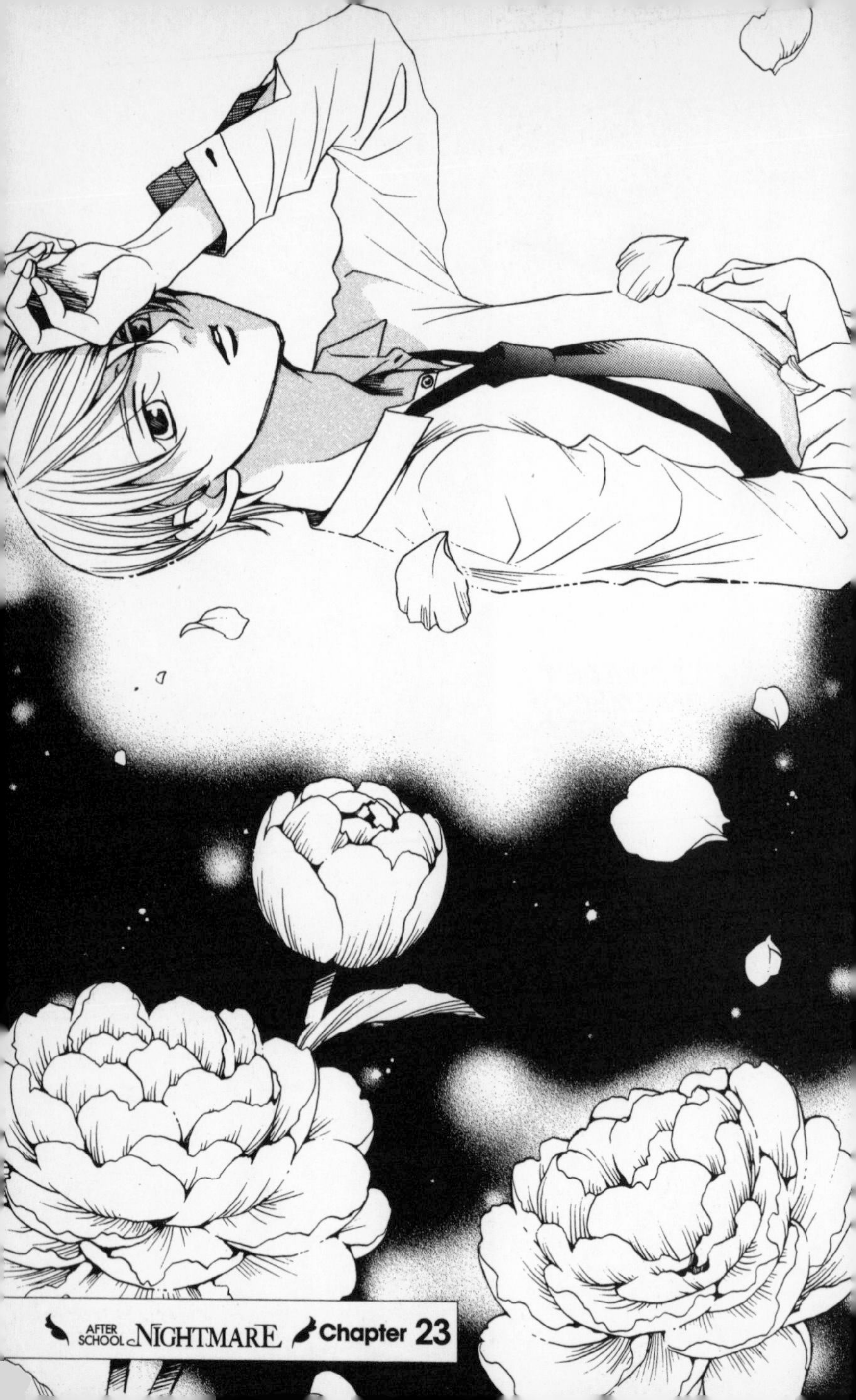
AFTER SCHOOL NIGHTMARE Chapter 23

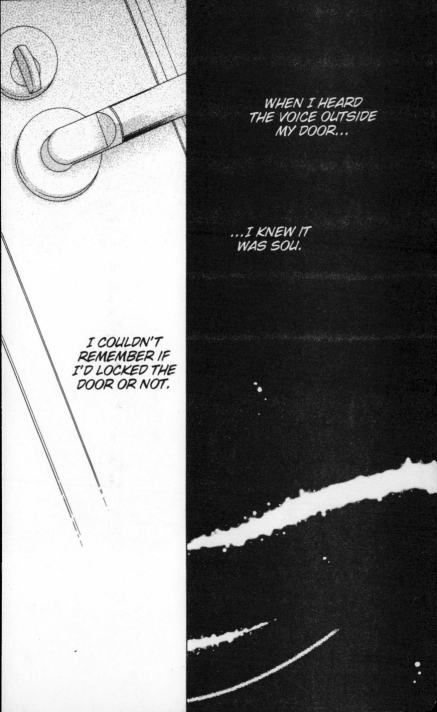

WHEN I HEARD
THE VOICE OUTSIDE
MY DOOR...

...I KNEW IT
WAS SOU.

I COULDN'T
REMEMBER IF
I'D LOCKED THE
DOOR OR NOT.

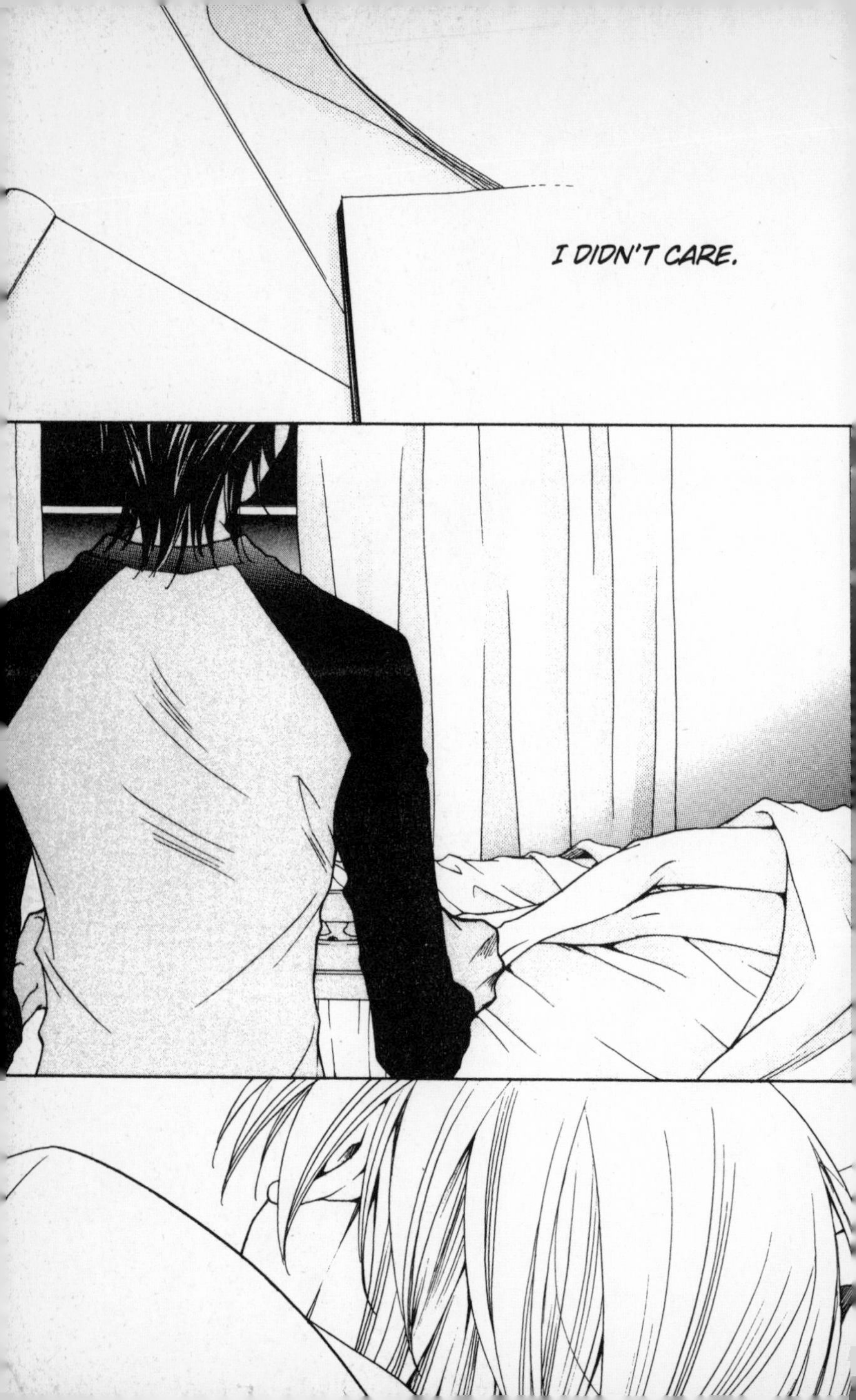
I DIDN'T CARE.

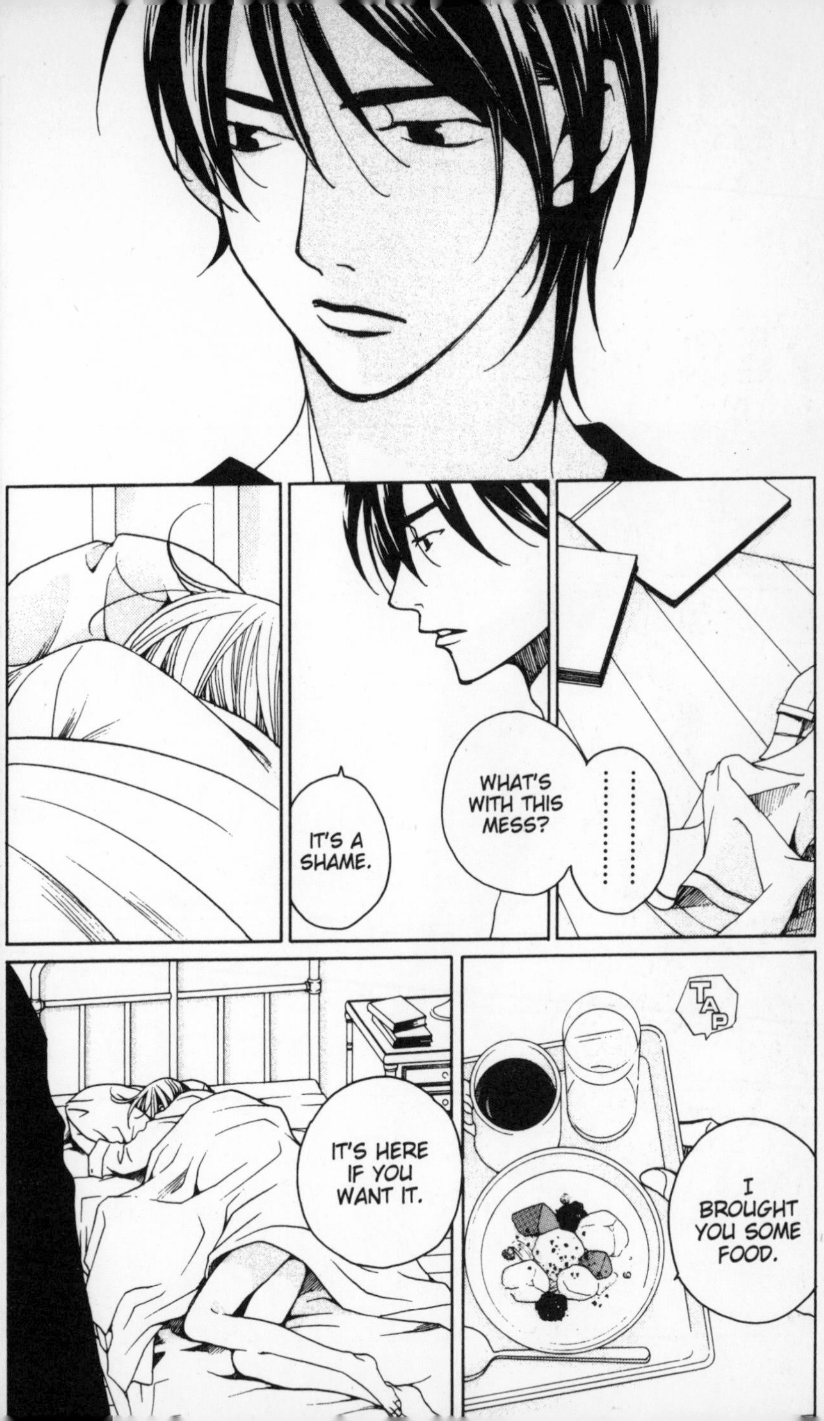
......
WHAT'S WITH THIS MESS?
IT'S A SHAME.
TAP
I BROUGHT YOU SOME FOOD.
IT'S HERE IF YOU WANT IT.

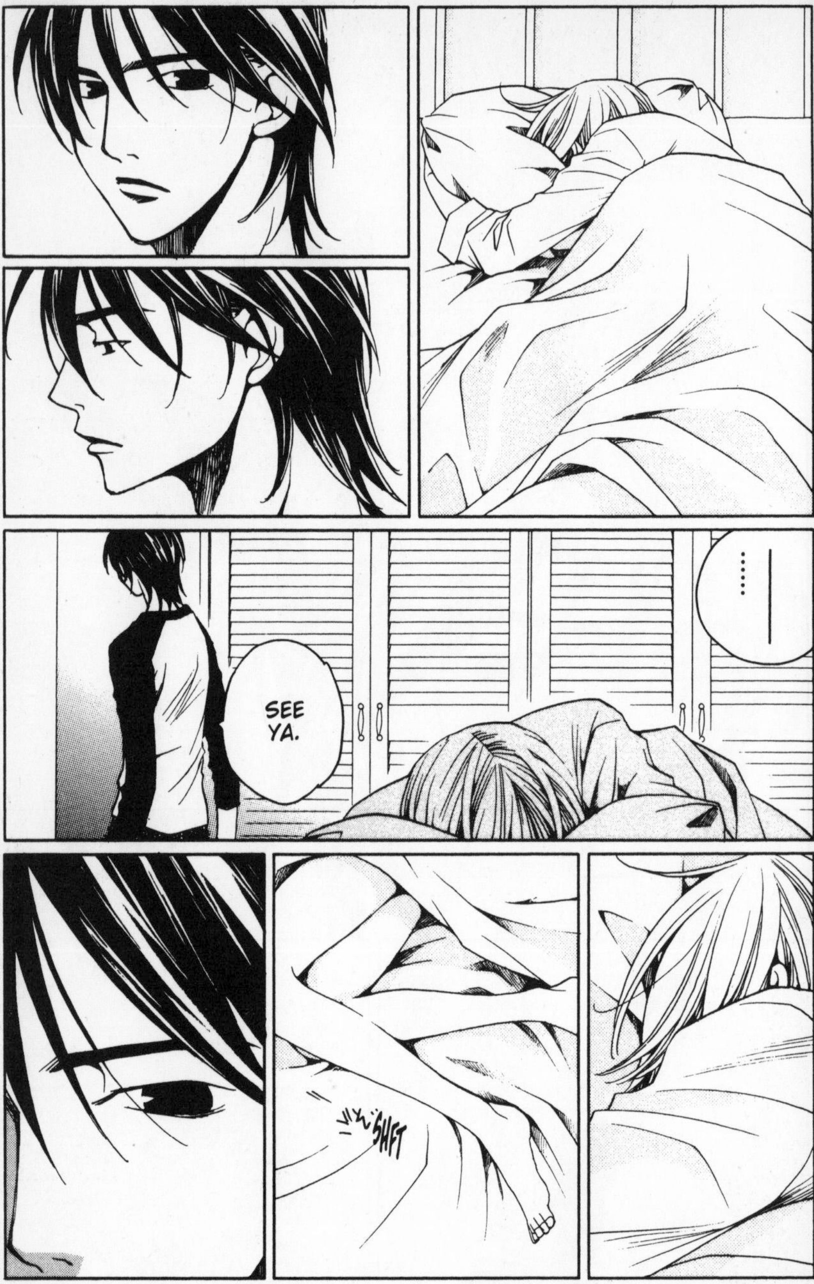
......
SEE YA.
SHFT

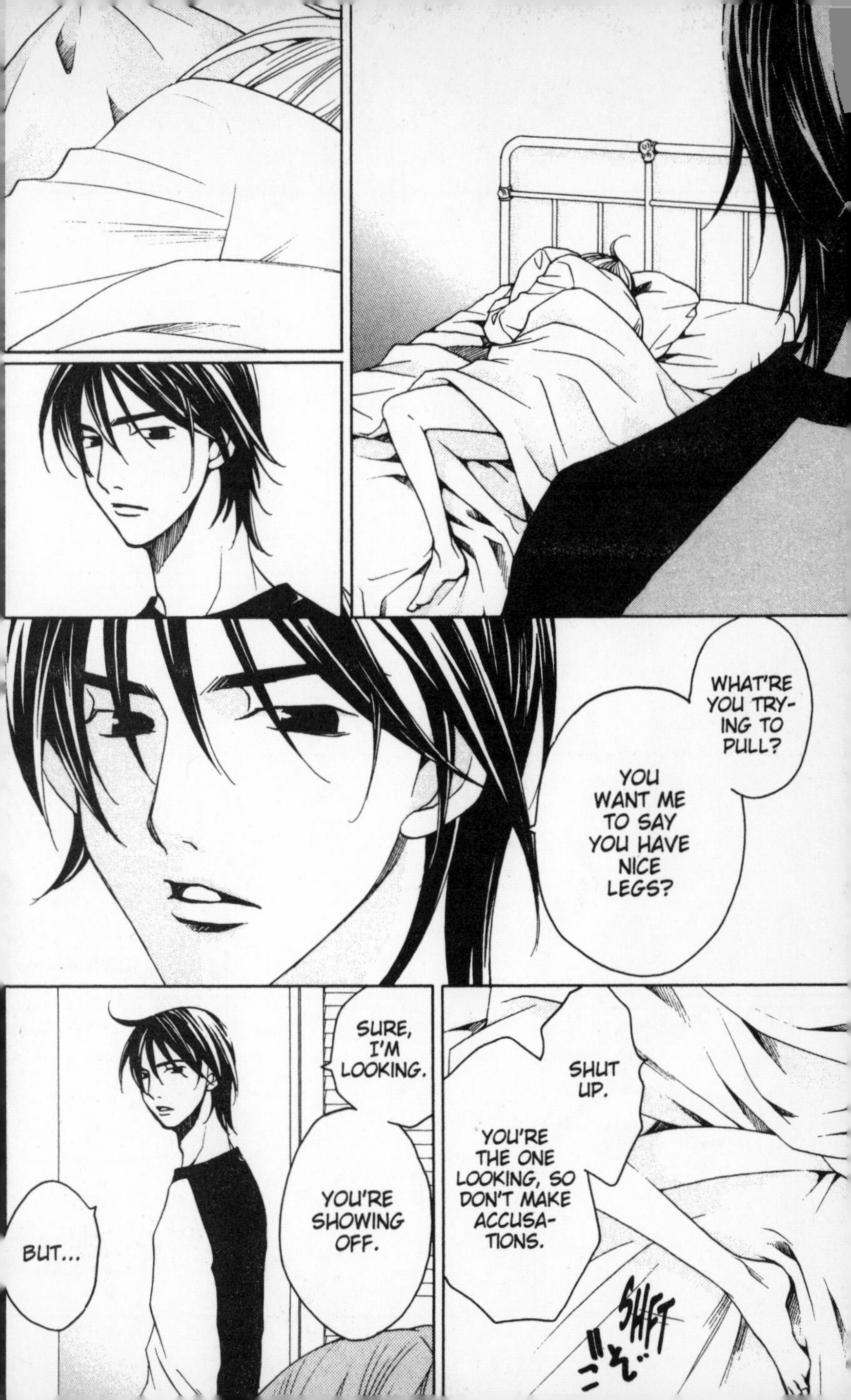
WHAT'RE YOU TRY-ING TO PULL?
YOU WANT ME TO SAY YOU HAVE NICE LEGS?
SHUT UP.
YOU'RE THE ONE LOOKING, SO DON'T MAKE ACCUSA-TIONS.
SHFT
SURE, I'M LOOKING.
YOU'RE SHOWING OFF.
BUT...

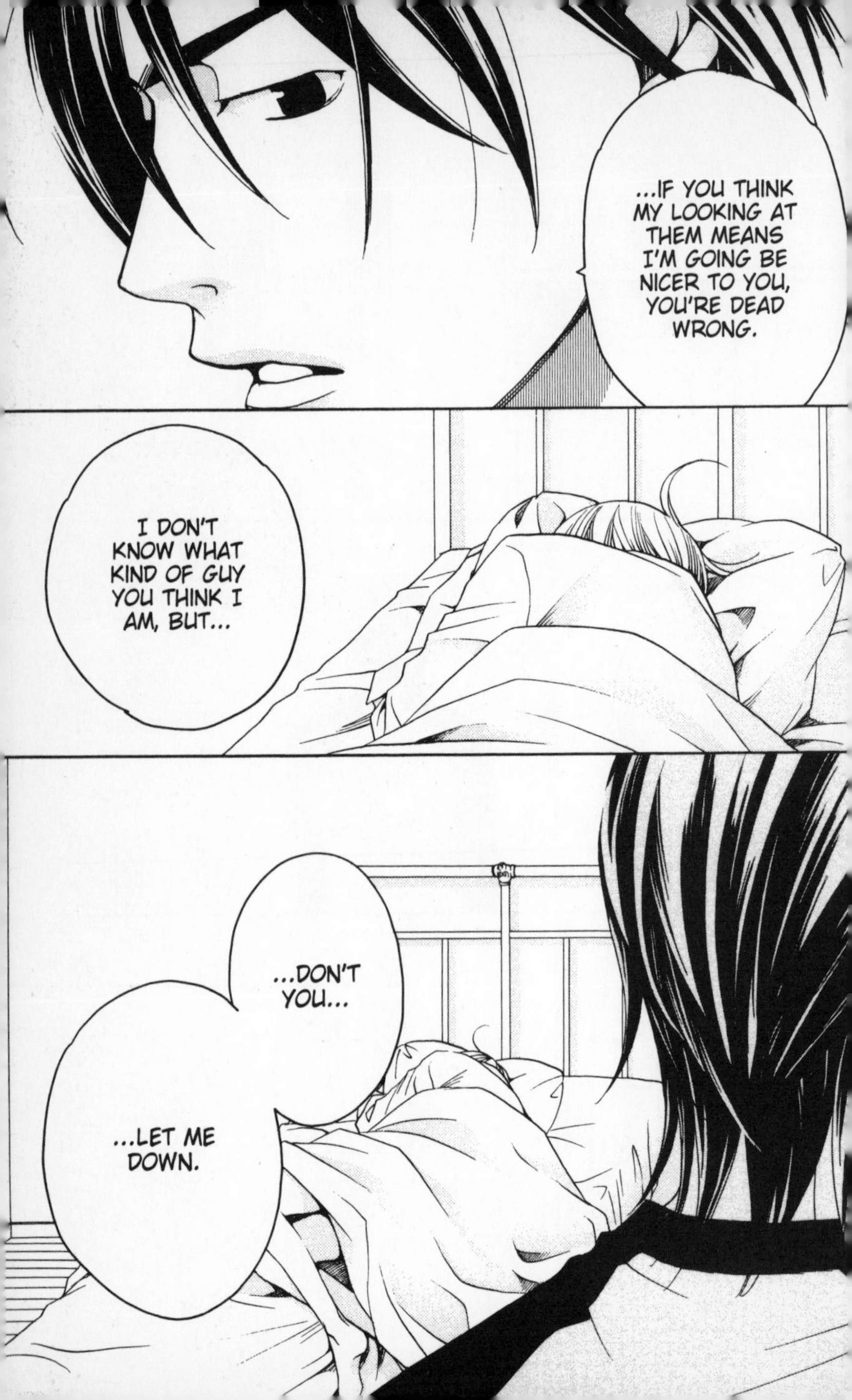
...IF YOU THINK MY LOOKING AT THEM MEANS I'M GOING BE NICER TO YOU, YOU'RE DEAD WRONG.
I DON'T KNOW WHAT KIND OF GUY YOU THINK I AM, BUT...
...DON'T YOU...
...LET ME DOWN.

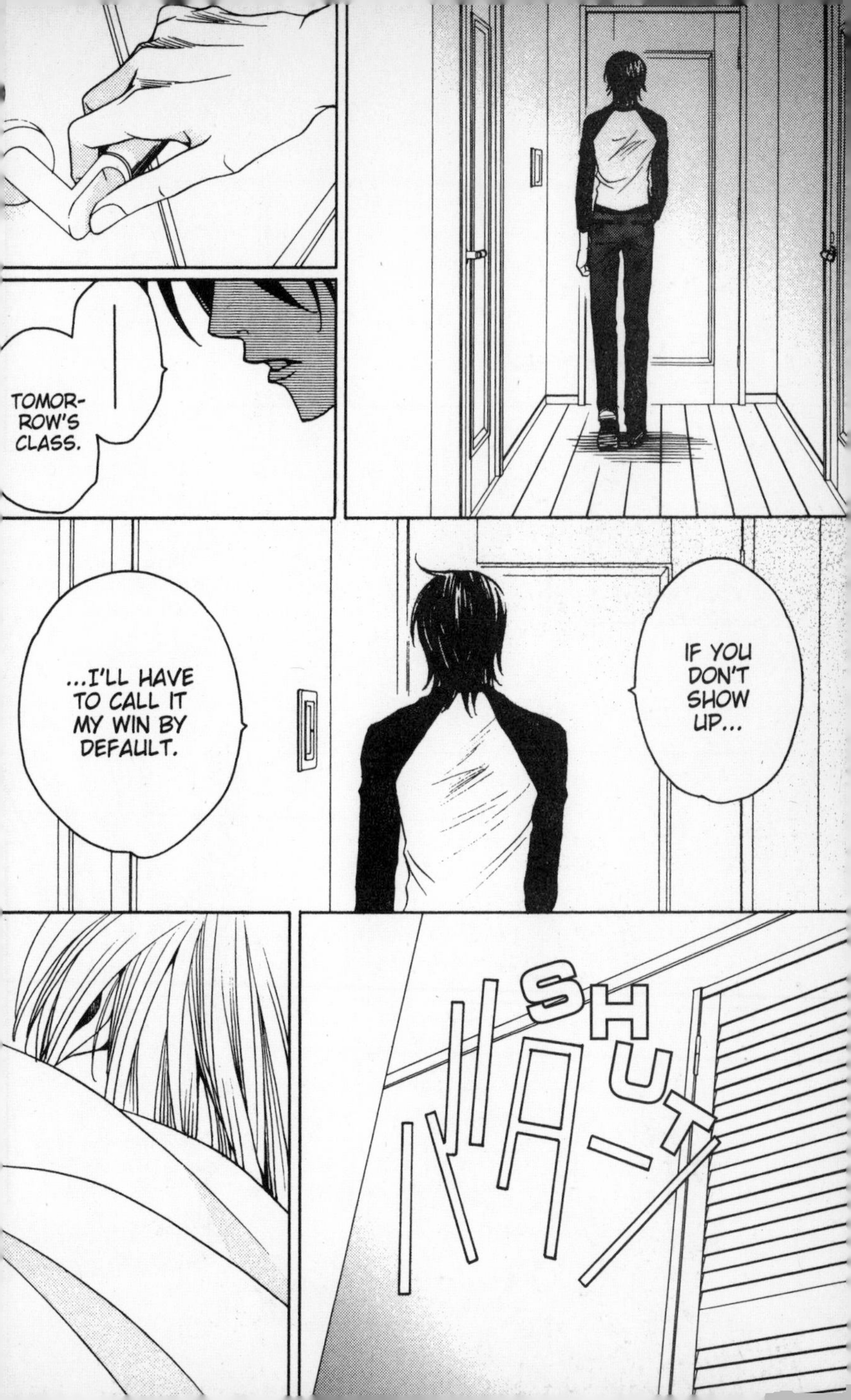
TOMOR-ROW'S CLASS.
IF YOU DON'T SHOW UP...
...I'LL HAVE TO CALL IT MY WIN BY DEFAULT.
SHUT

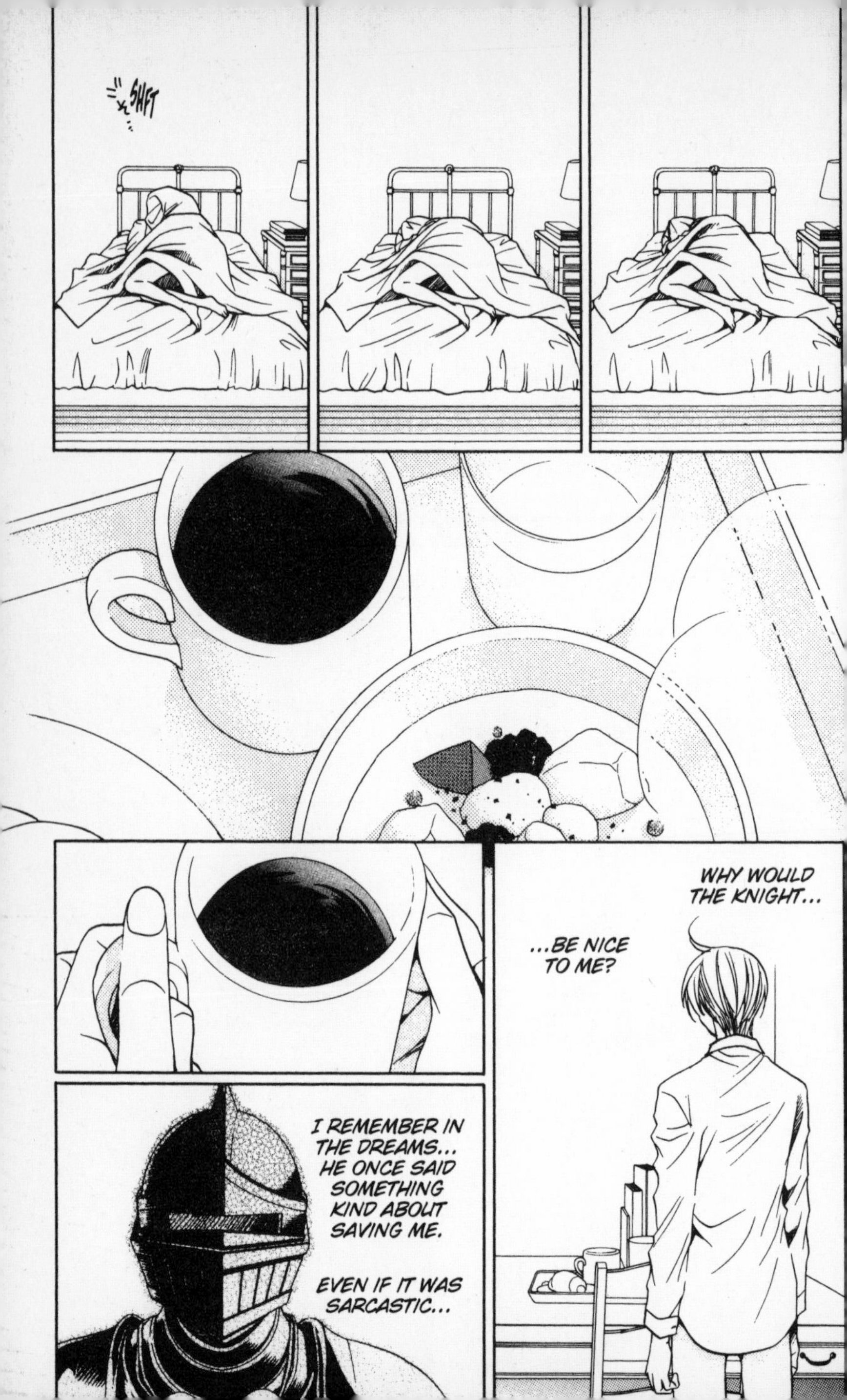
SHFT
WHY WOULD THE KNIGHT...
...BE NICE TO ME?
I REMEMBER IN THE DREAMS... HE ONCE SAID SOMETHING KIND ABOUT SAVING ME.
EVEN IF IT WAS SARCASTIC...

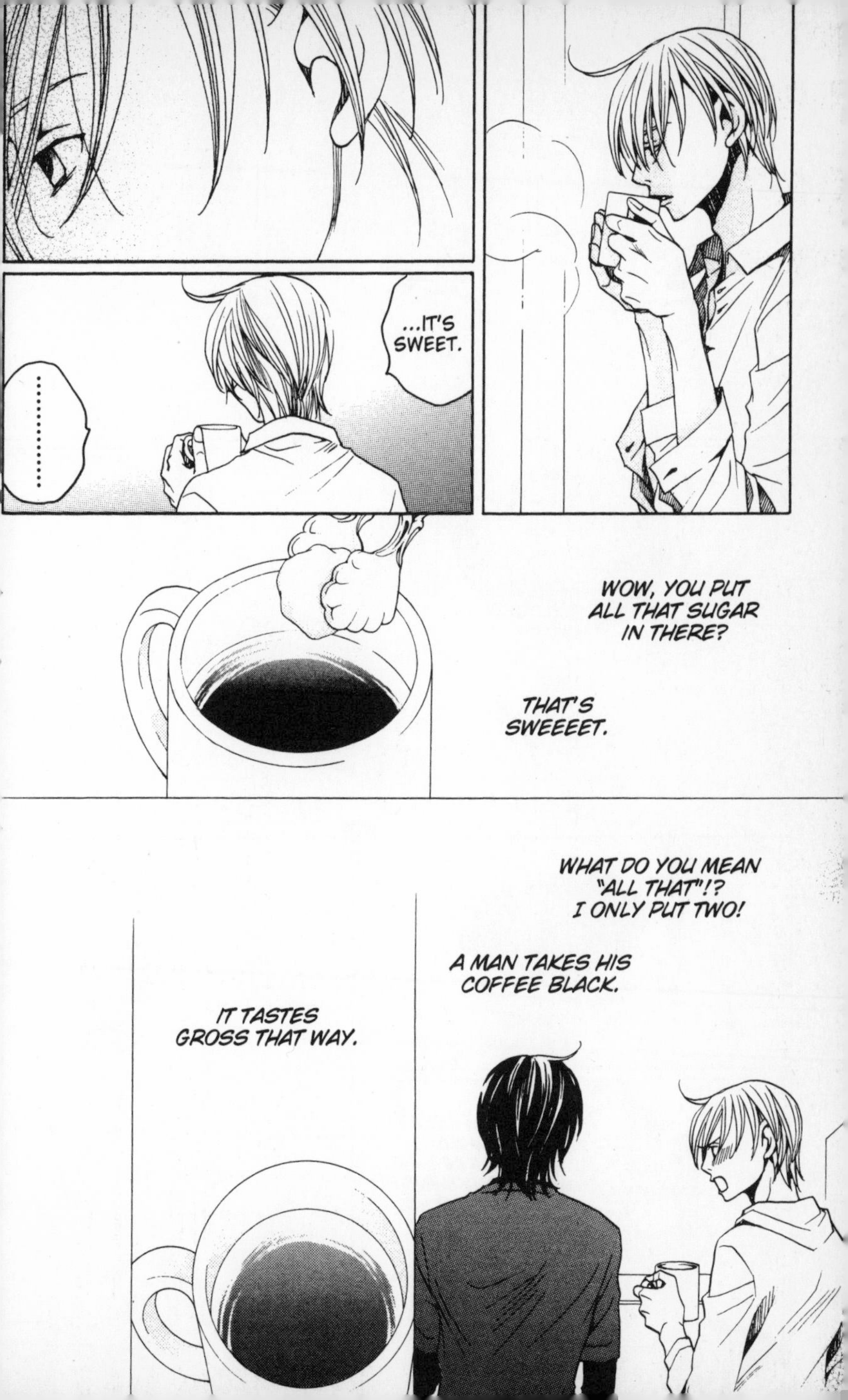
...IT'S SWEET.
......
WOW, YOU PUT ALL THAT SUGAR IN THERE?
THAT'S SWEEEET.
WHAT DO YOU MEAN "ALL THAT"!? I ONLY PUT TWO!
A MAN TAKES HIS COFFEE BLACK.
IT TASTES GROSS THAT WAY.

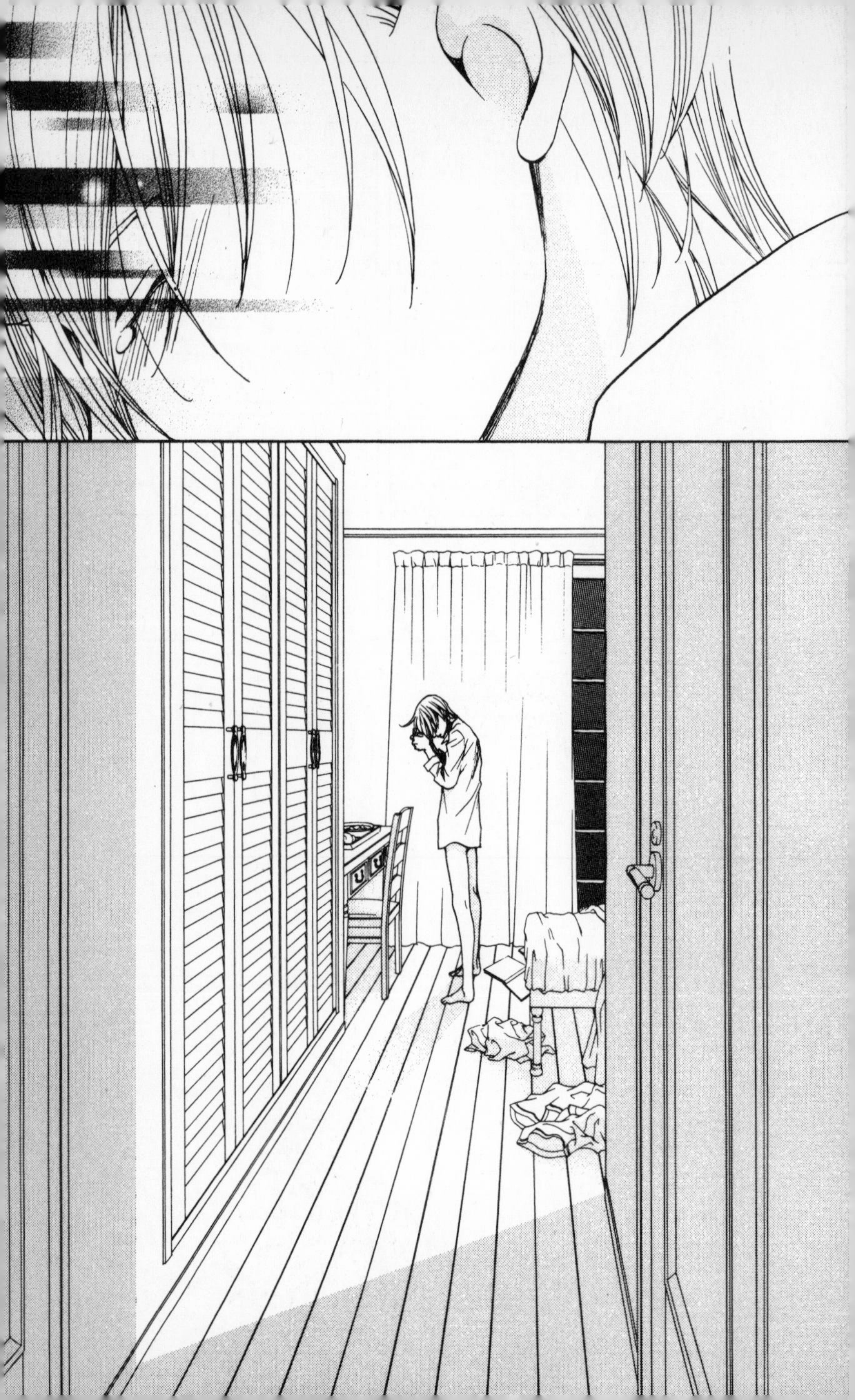

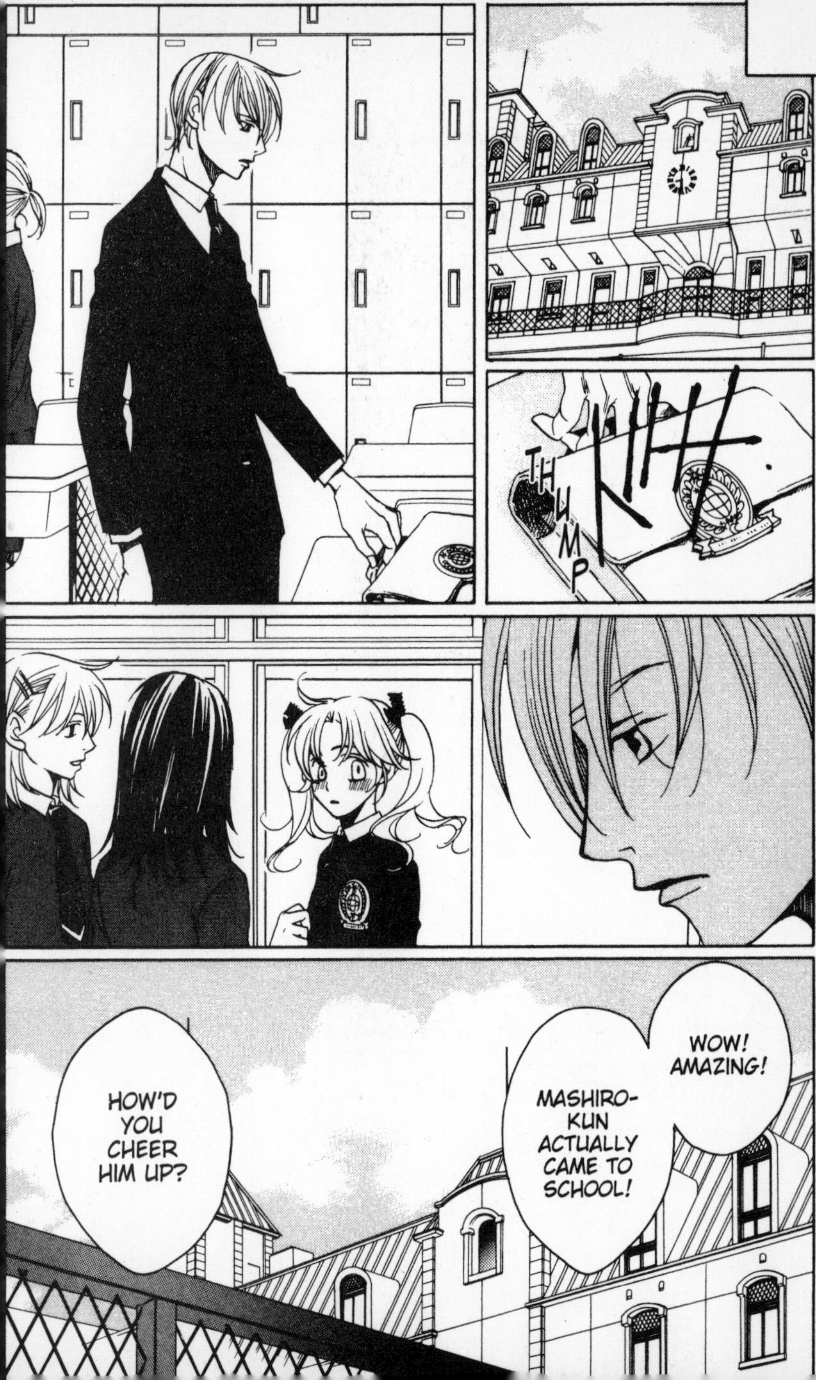
THUMP
WOW! AMAZING!
MASHIRO-KUN ACTUALLY CAME TO SCHOOL!
HOW'D YOU CHEER HIM UP?

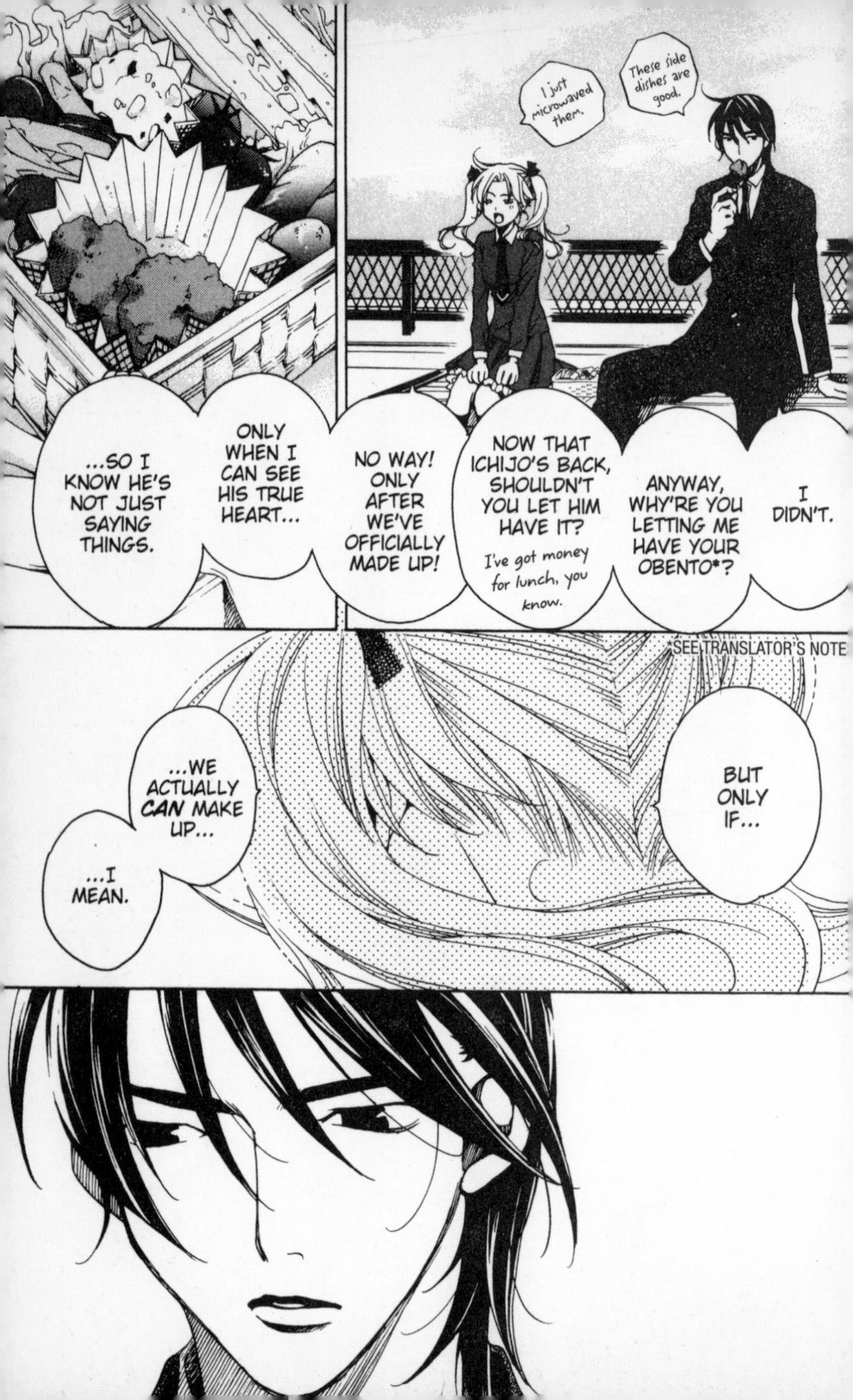
These side dishes are good.
I just microwaved them.
I DIDN'T.
ANYWAY, WHY'RE YOU LETTING ME HAVE YOUR OBENTO*?
NOW THAT ICHIJO'S BACK, SHOULDN'T YOU LET HIM HAVE IT?
I've got money for lunch, you know.
NO WAY! ONLY AFTER WE'VE OFFICIALLY MADE UP!
ONLY WHEN I CAN SEE HIS TRUE HEART...
...SO I KNOW HE'S NOT JUST SAYING THINGS.
*SEE TRANSLATOR'S NOTE
BUT ONLY IF...
...WE ACTUALLY **CAN** MAKE UP...
...I MEAN.

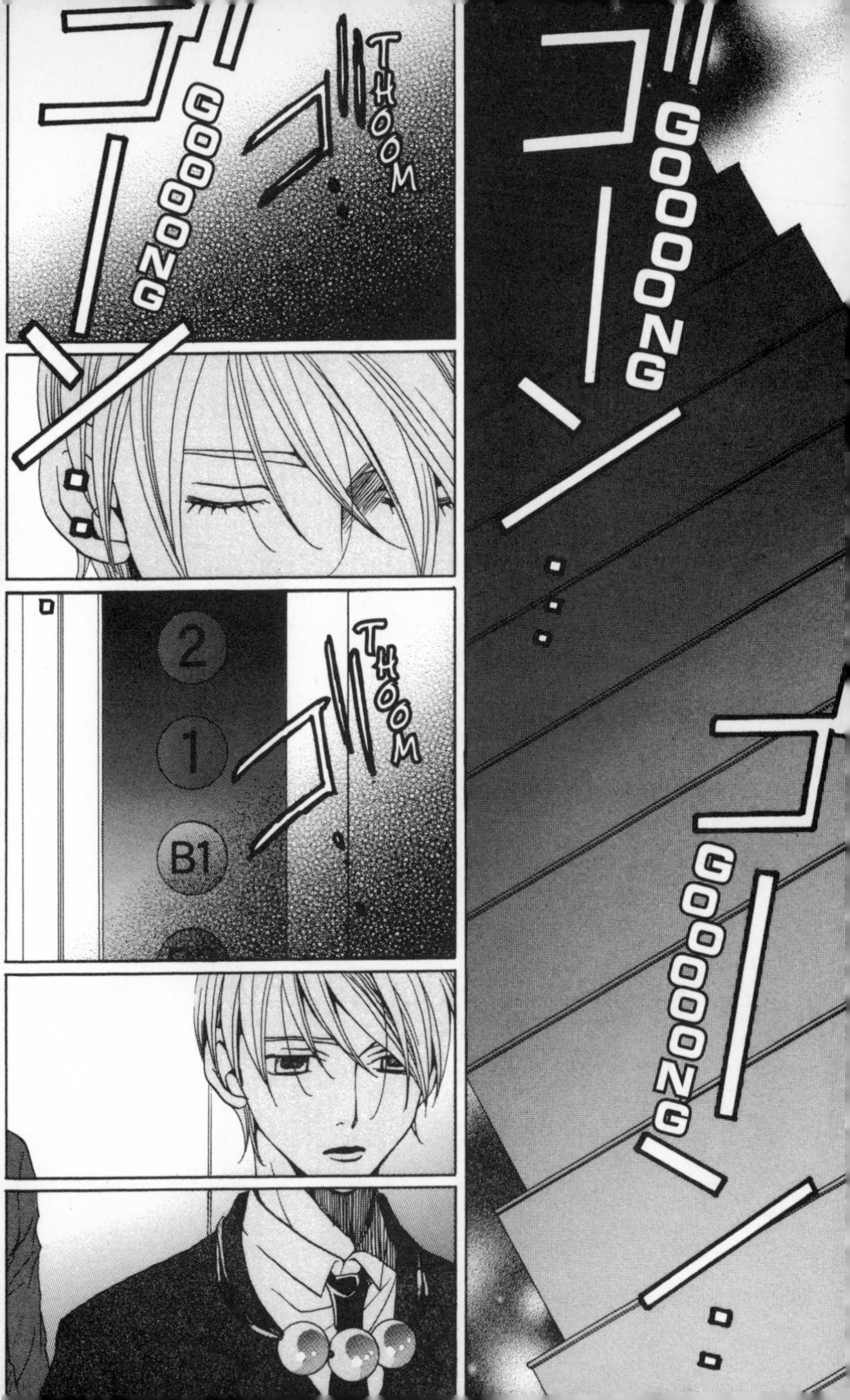
GOOOOONG
GOOOOONG
THOOM
GOOOONG
THOOM

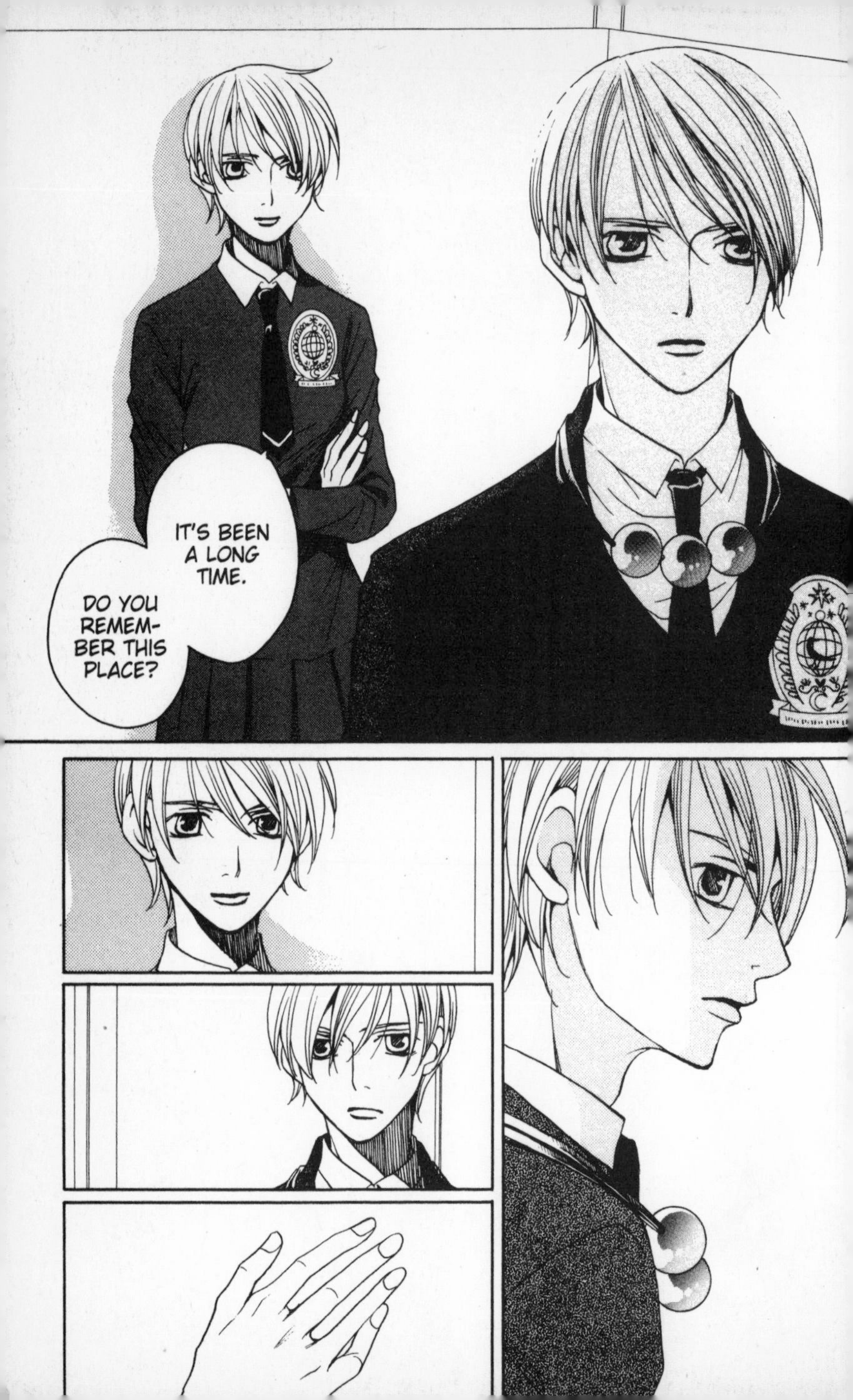

IT'S BEEN A LONG TIME.
DO YOU REMEMBER THIS PLACE?

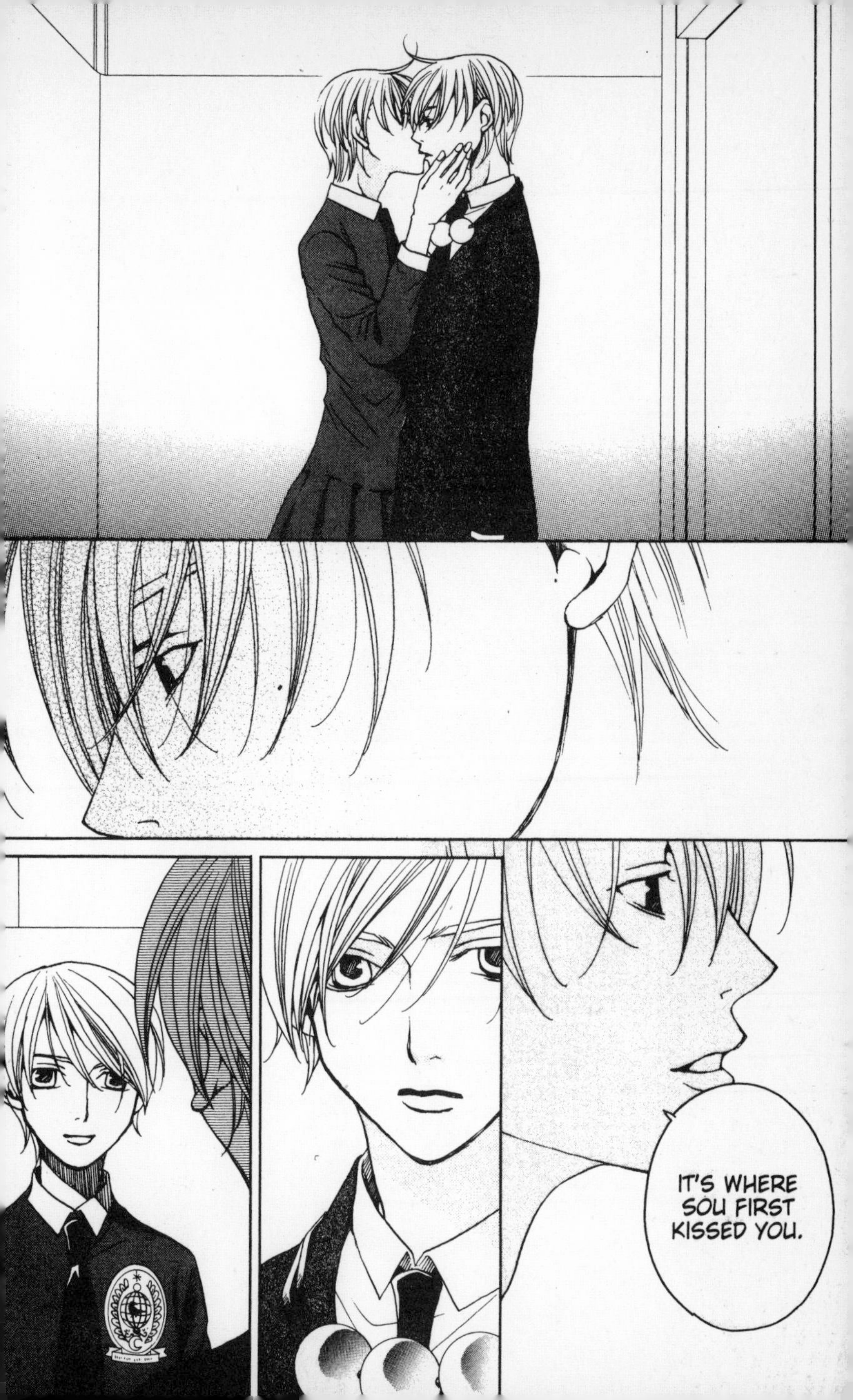
IT'S WHERE SOU FIRST KISSED YOU.

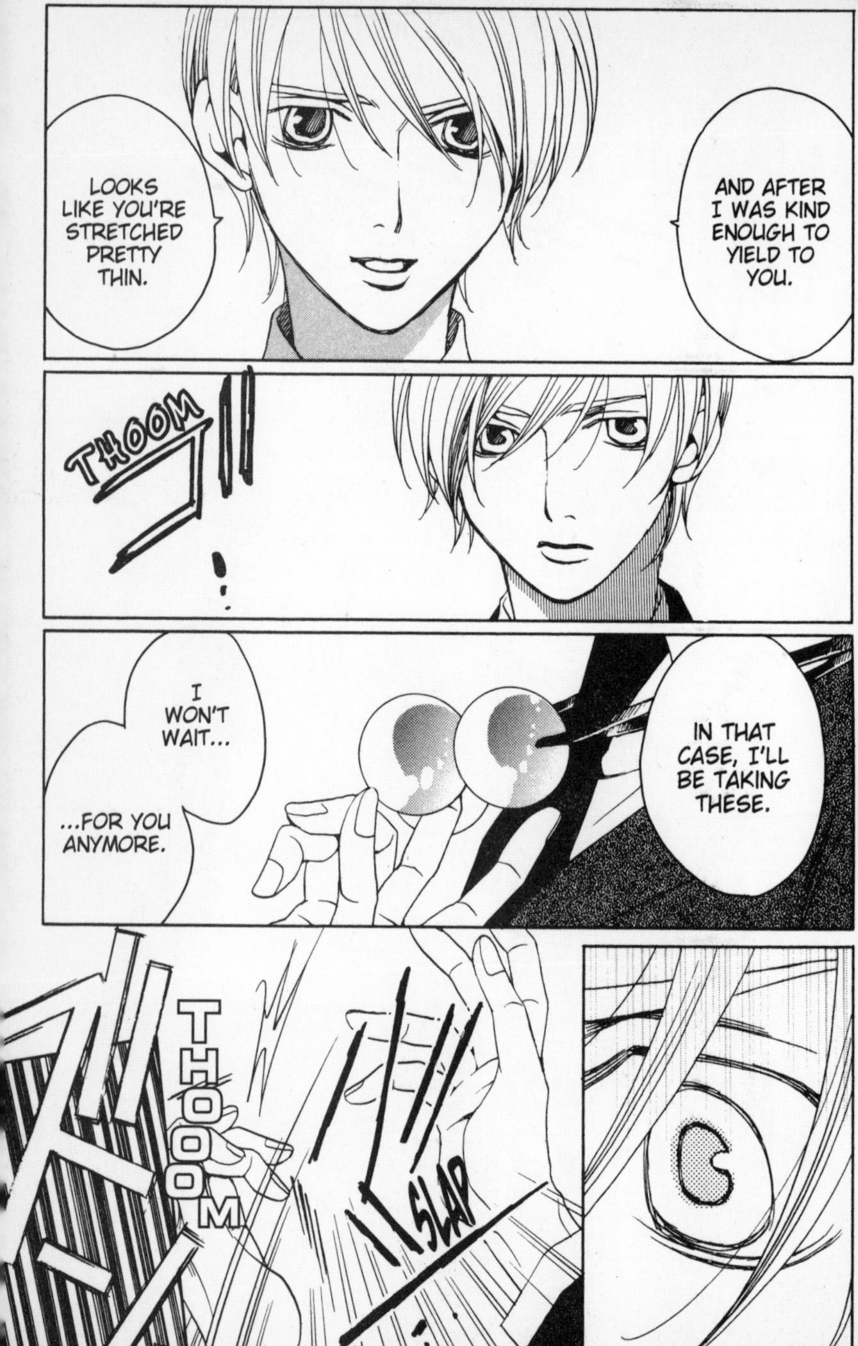
AND AFTER I WAS KIND ENOUGH TO YIELD TO YOU.
LOOKS LIKE YOU'RE STRETCHED PRETTY THIN.
THOOM
IN THAT CASE, I'LL BE TAKING THESE.
I WON'T WAIT...
...FOR YOU ANYMORE.
THOOOM
SLAP

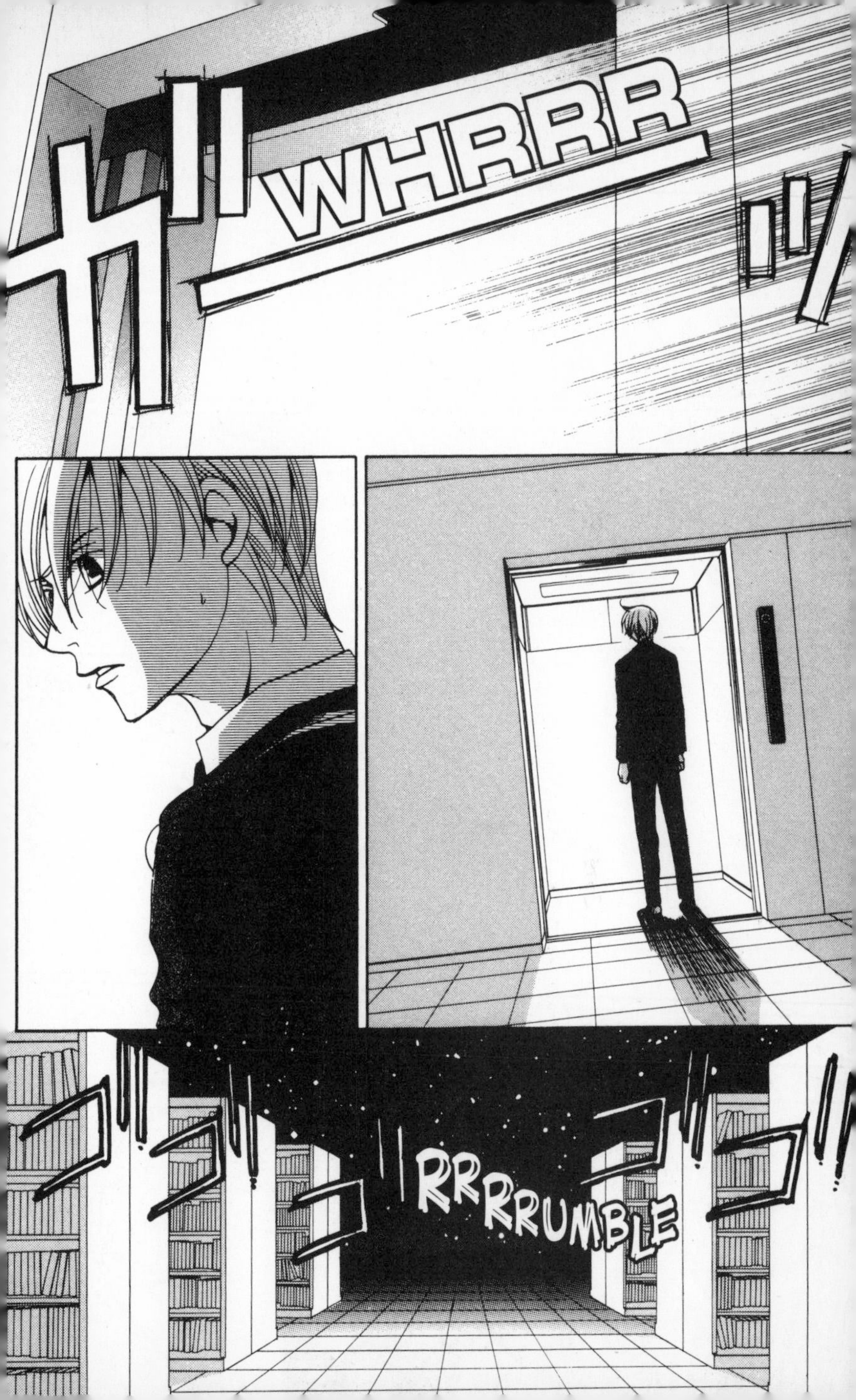
WHRRR
RRRRUMBLE

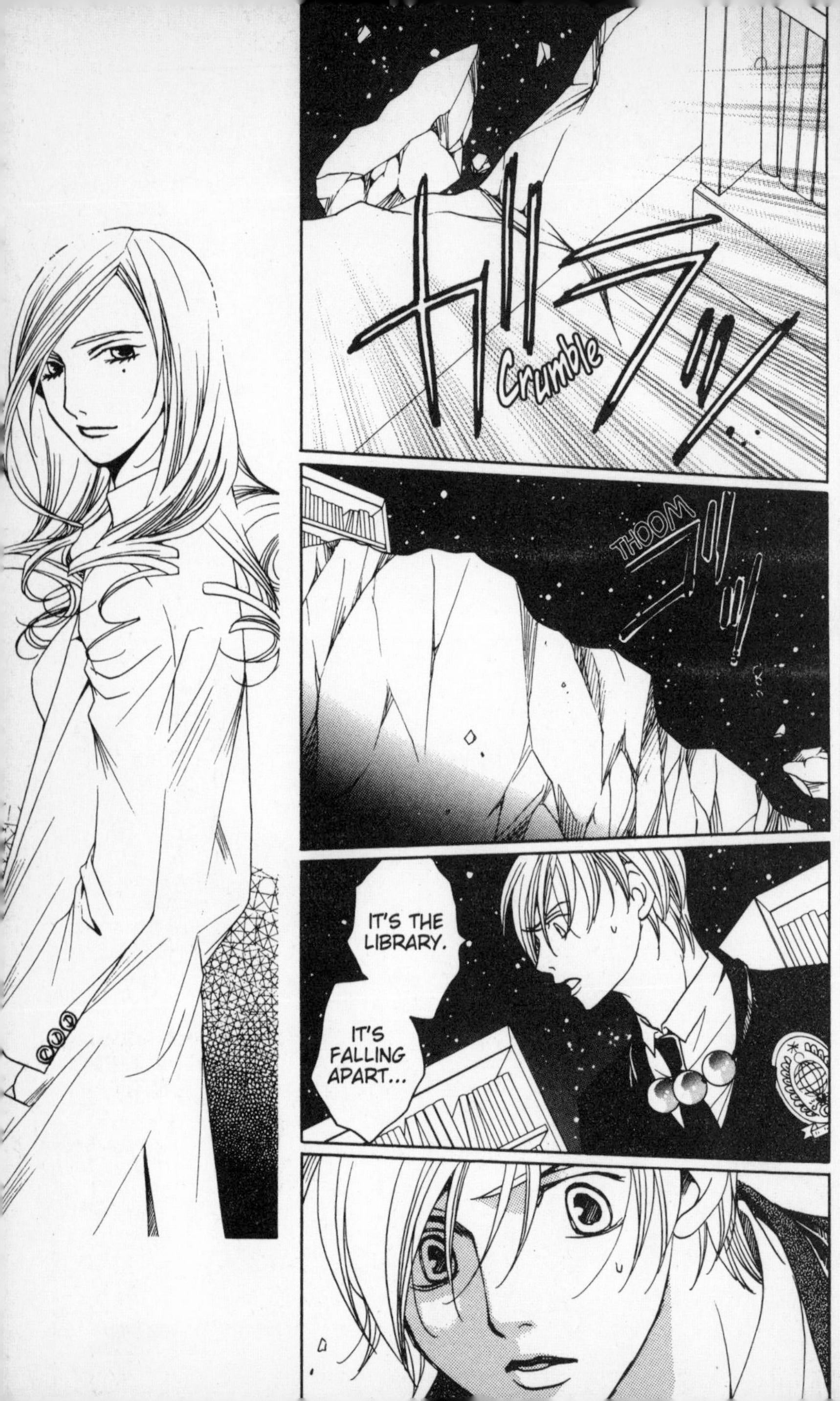
Crumble
THOOM
IT'S THE LIBRARY.
IT'S FALLING APART...

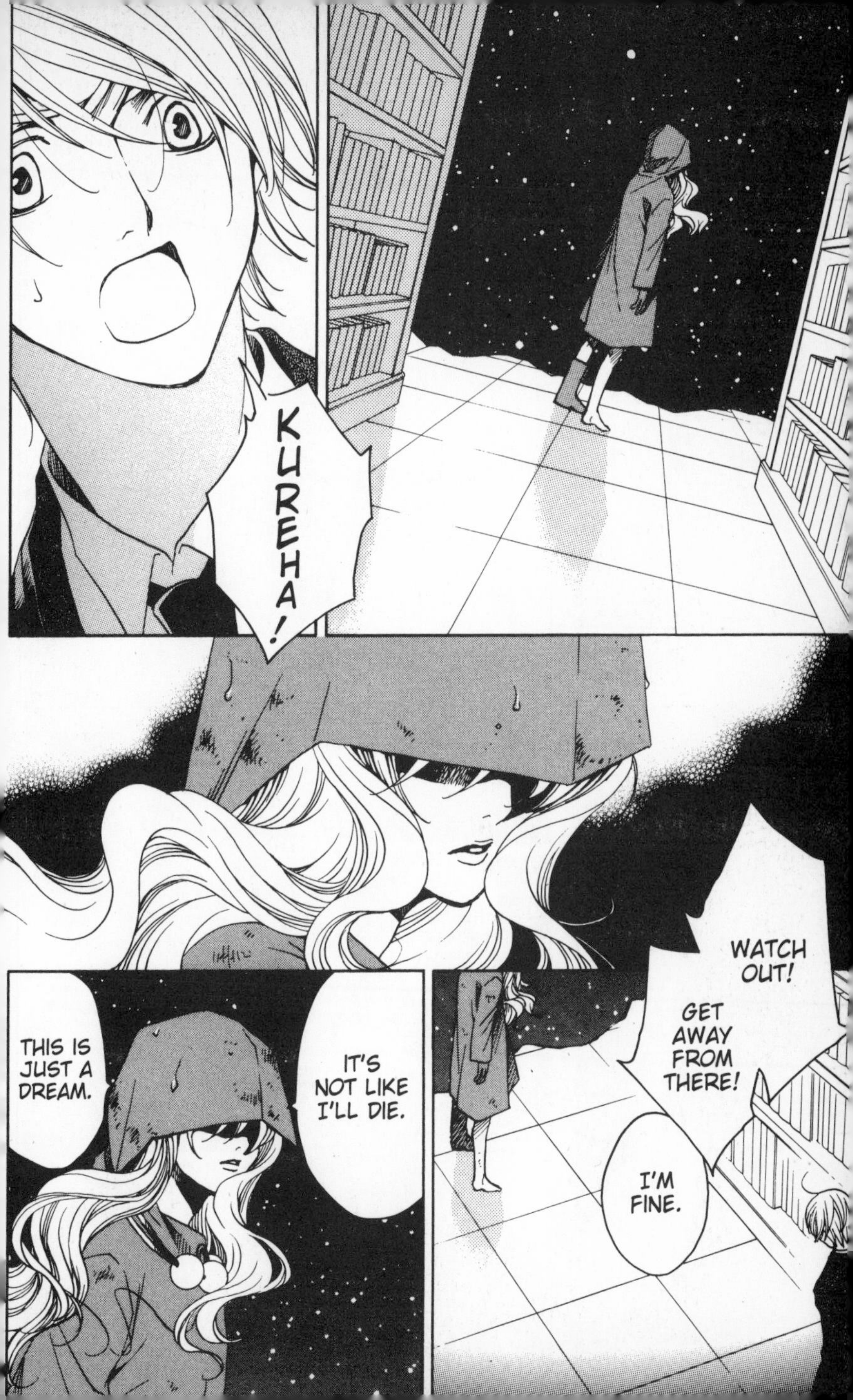
KUREHA!
WATCH OUT!
GET AWAY FROM THERE!
I'M FINE.
IT'S NOT LIKE I'LL DIE.
THIS IS JUST A DREAM.

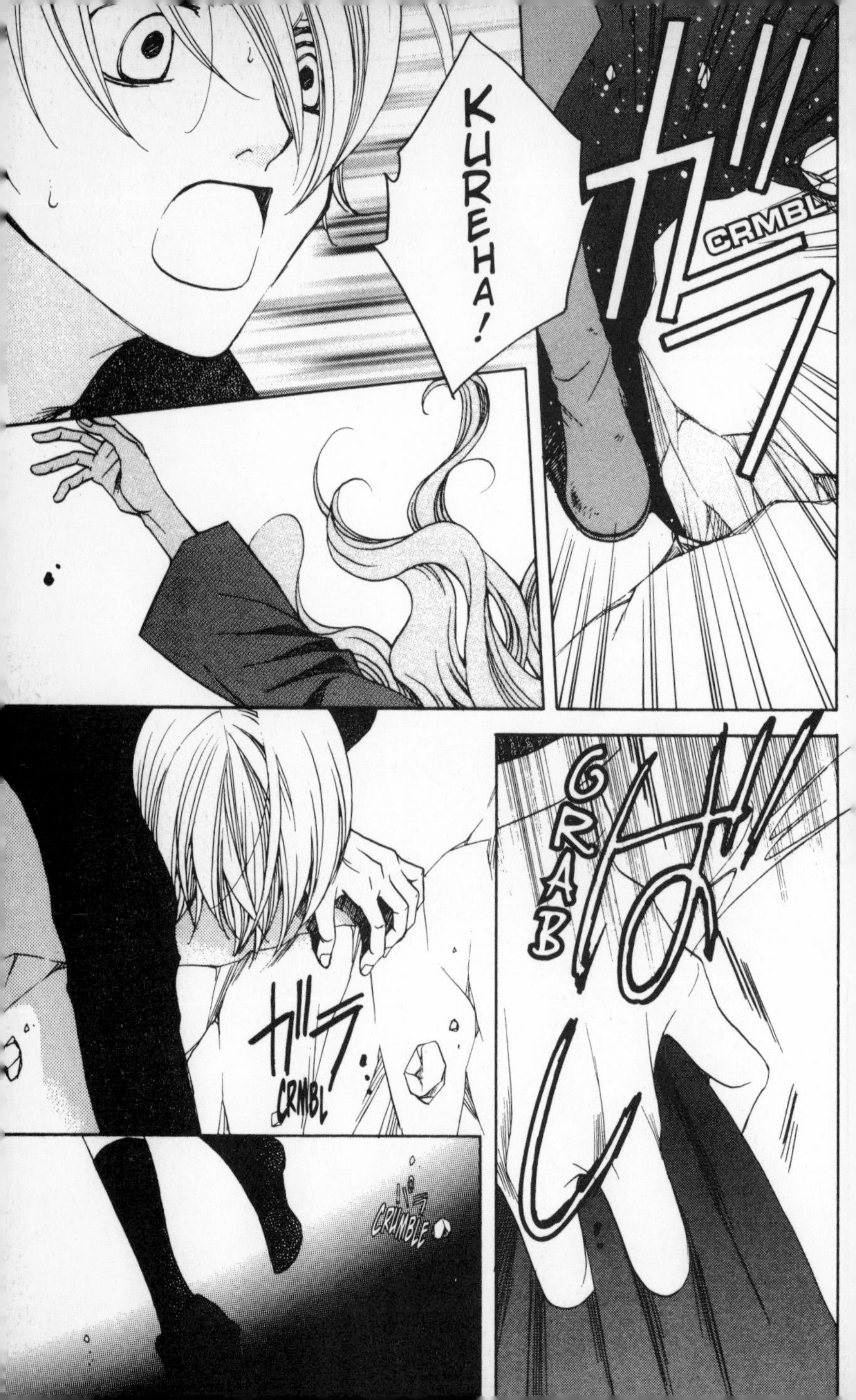
CRMBL
KUREHA!
GRAB
CRMBL
CRUMBLE

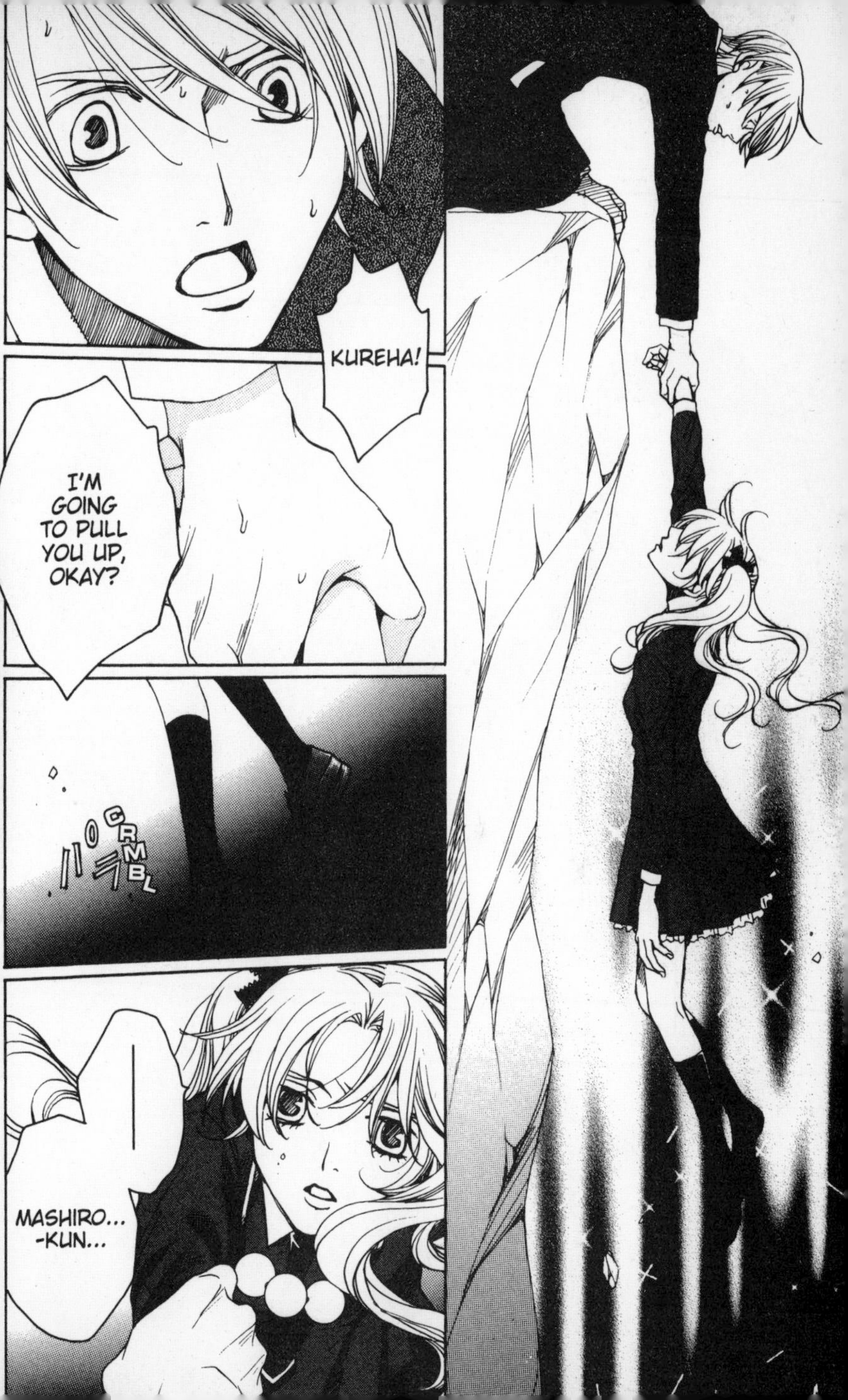
KUREHA!
I'M GOING TO PULL YOU UP, OKAY?
CRMBL
MASHIRO... -KUN...

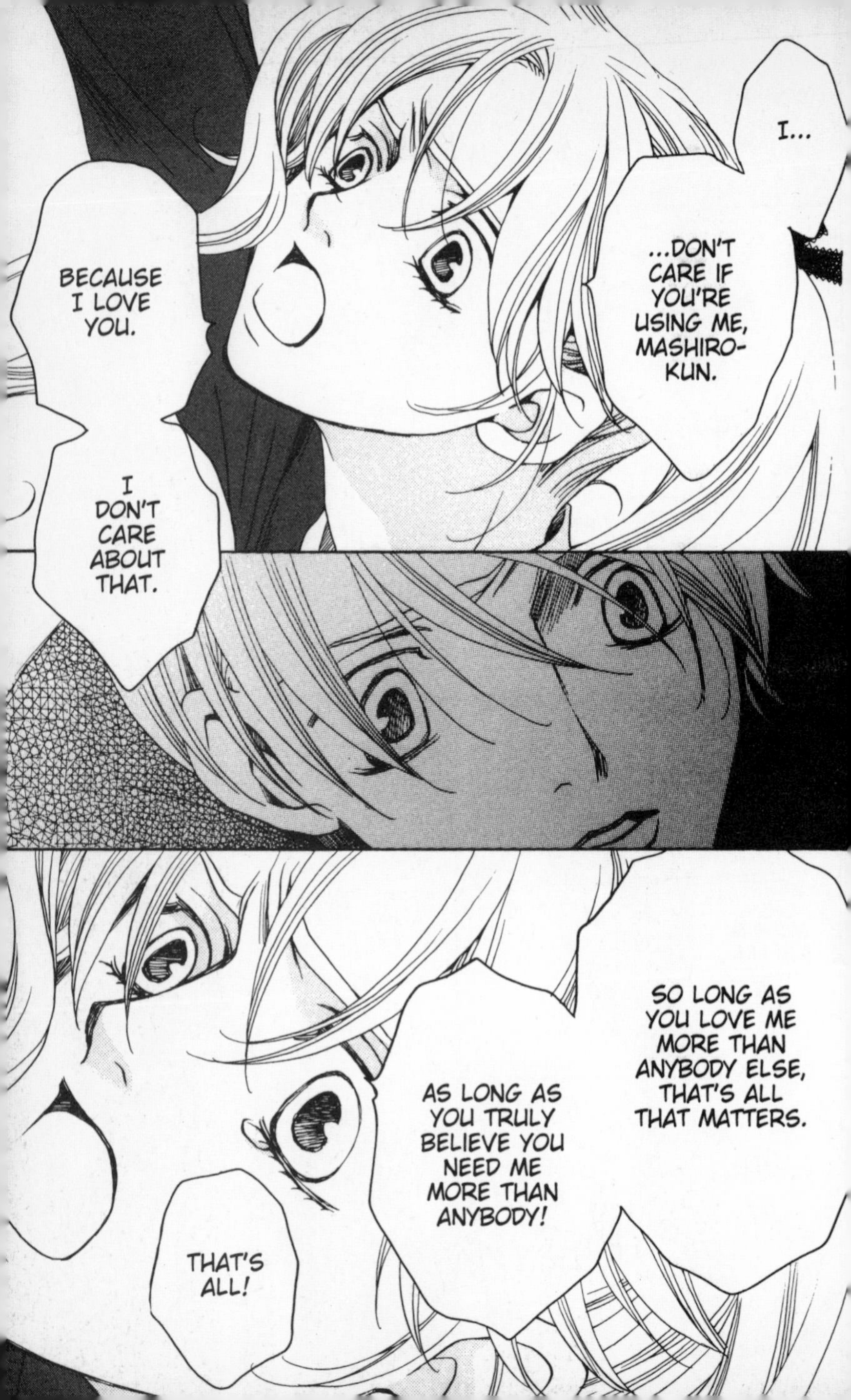
I...
...DON'T CARE IF YOU'RE USING ME, MASHIRO-KUN.
BECAUSE I LOVE YOU.
I DON'T CARE ABOUT THAT.
SO LONG AS YOU LOVE ME MORE THAN ANYBODY ELSE, THAT'S ALL THAT MATTERS.
AS LONG AS YOU TRULY BELIEVE YOU NEED ME MORE THAN ANYBODY!
THAT'S ALL!

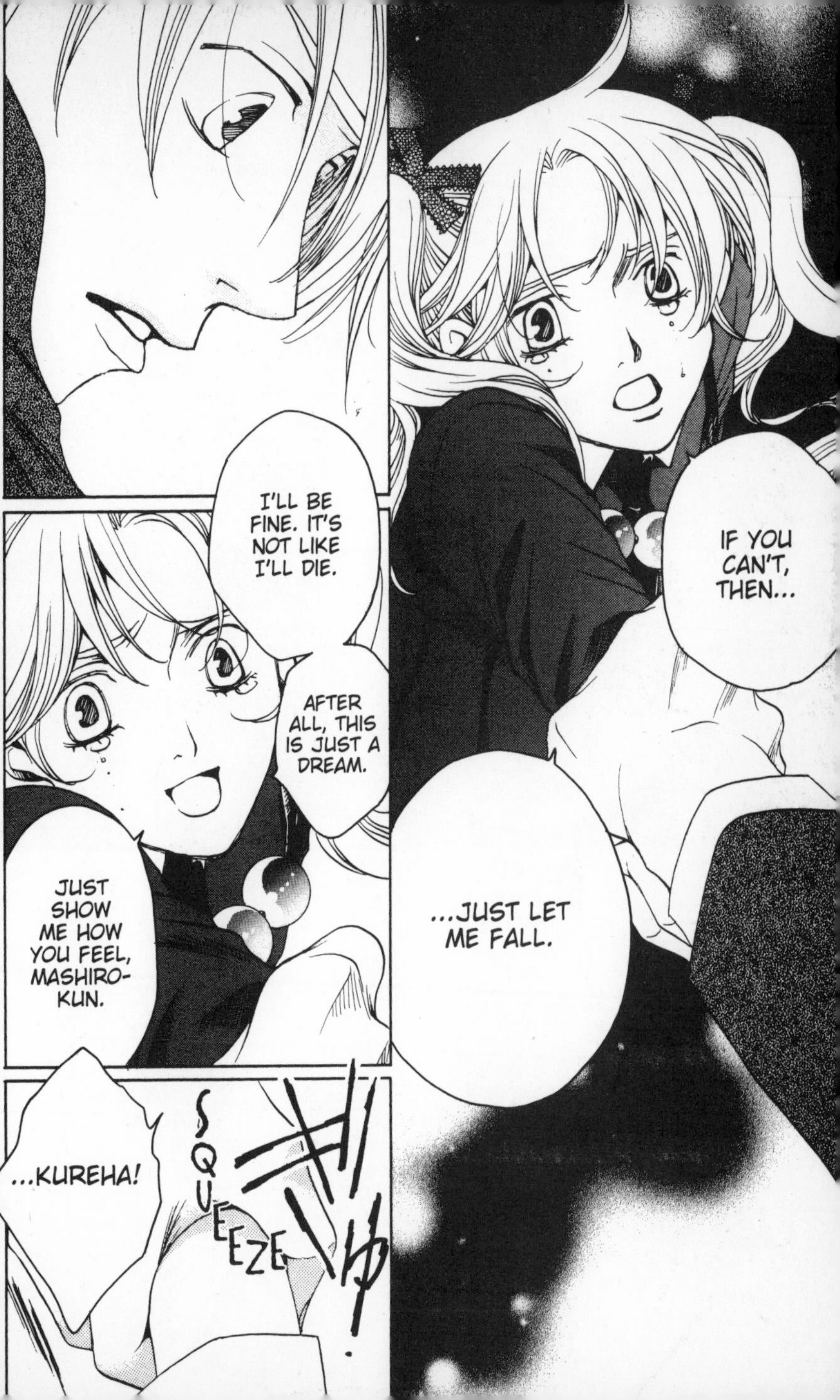
IF YOU CAN'T, THEN...
...JUST LET ME FALL.
I'LL BE FINE. IT'S NOT LIKE I'LL DIE.
AFTER ALL, THIS IS JUST A DREAM.
JUST SHOW ME HOW YOU FEEL, MASHIRO-KUN.
...KUREHA!
SQUEEZE

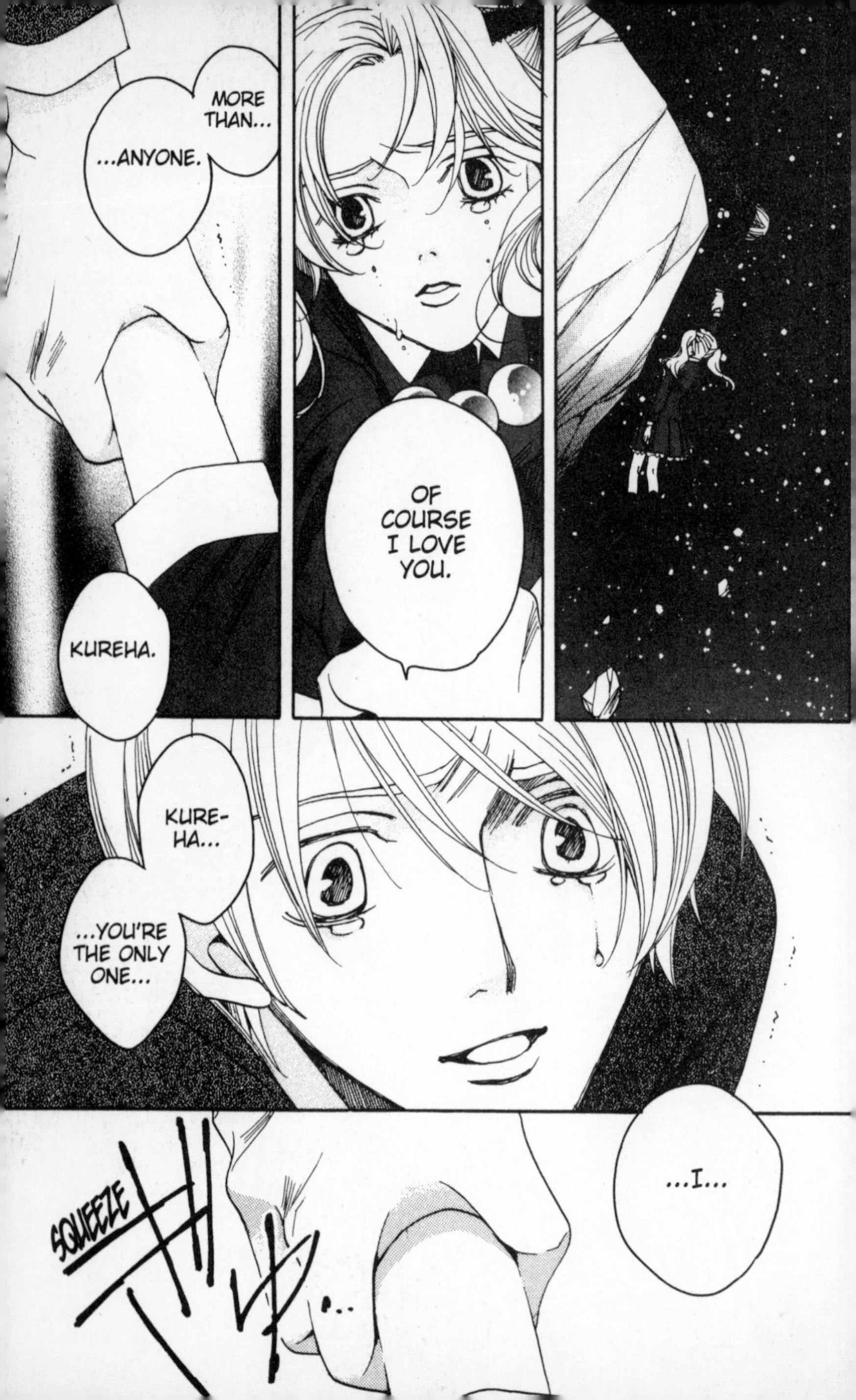
OF COURSE I LOVE YOU.
MORE THAN...
...ANYONE.
KUREHA.
KURE-HA...
...YOU'RE THE ONLY ONE...
...I...
SQUEEZE
...

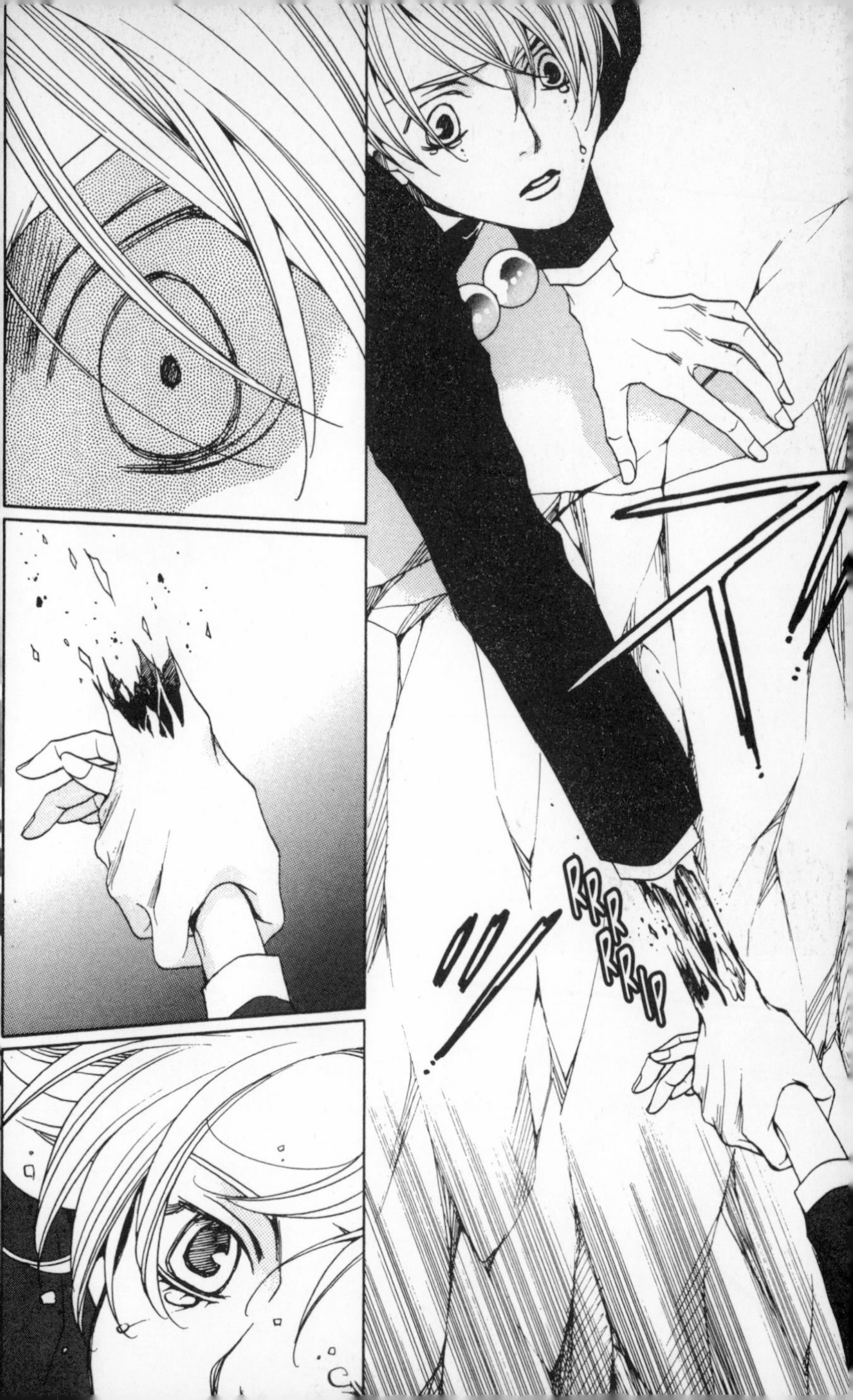
RRRRRRIP

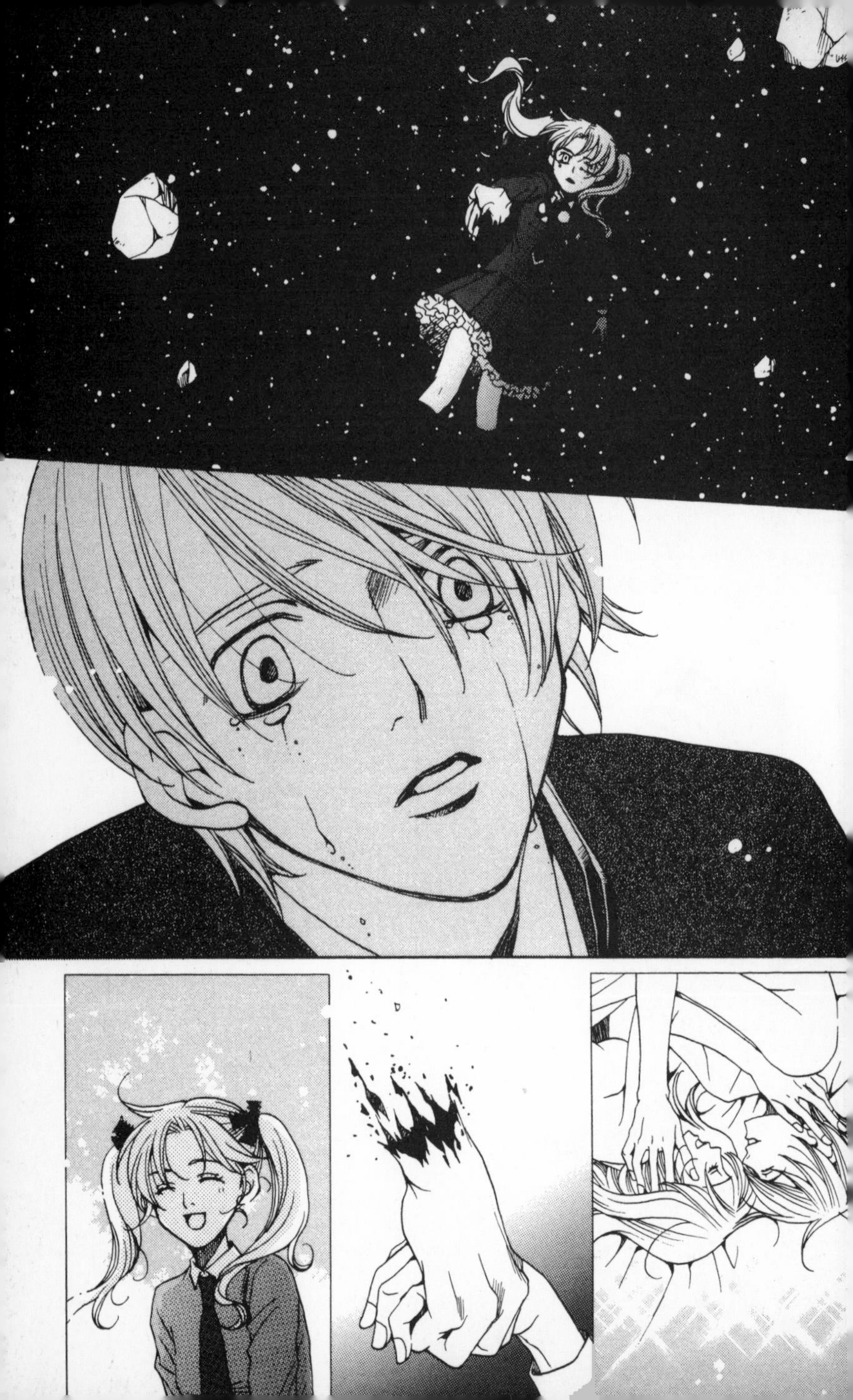

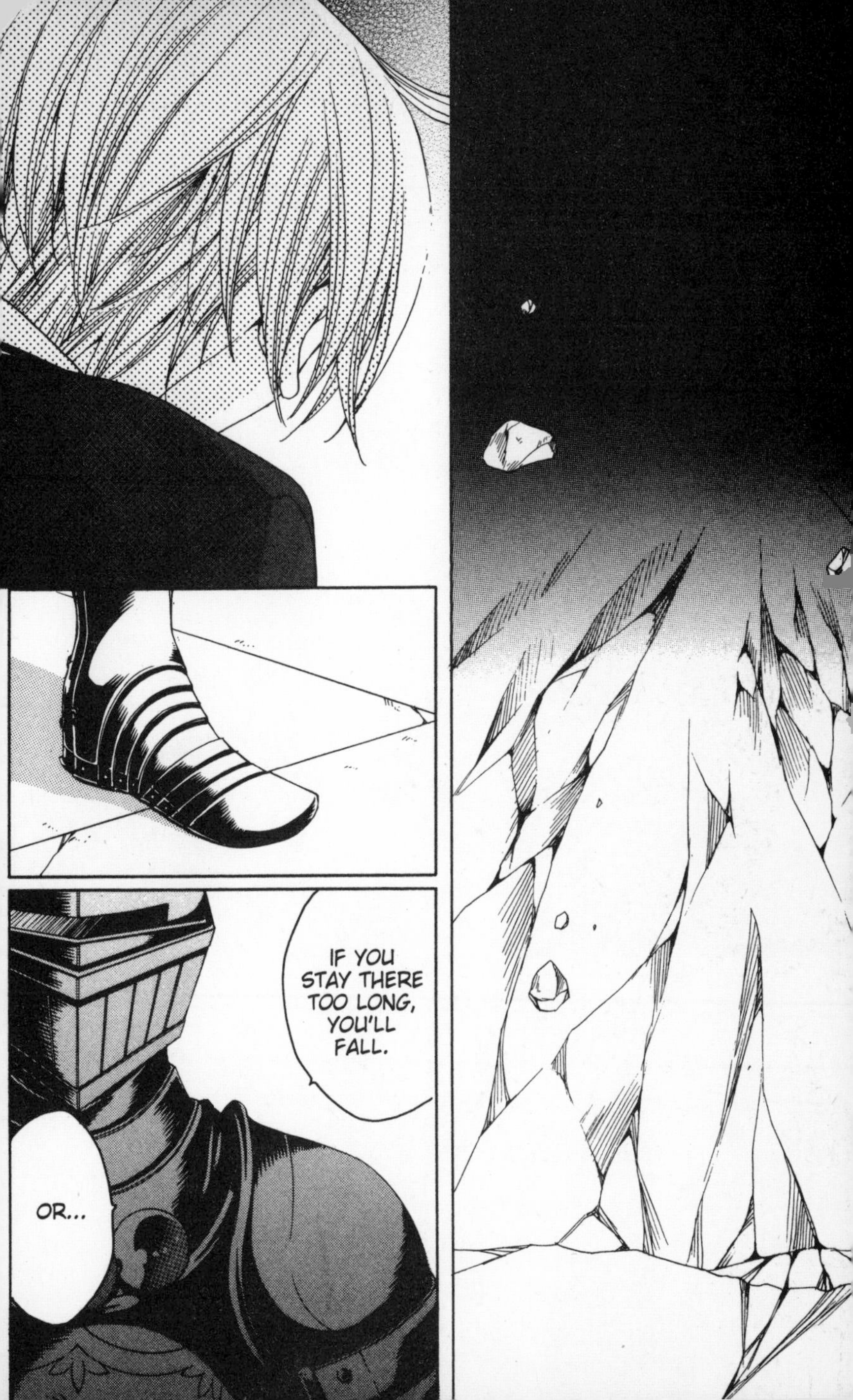
IF YOU STAY THERE TOO LONG, YOU'LL FALL.
OR...

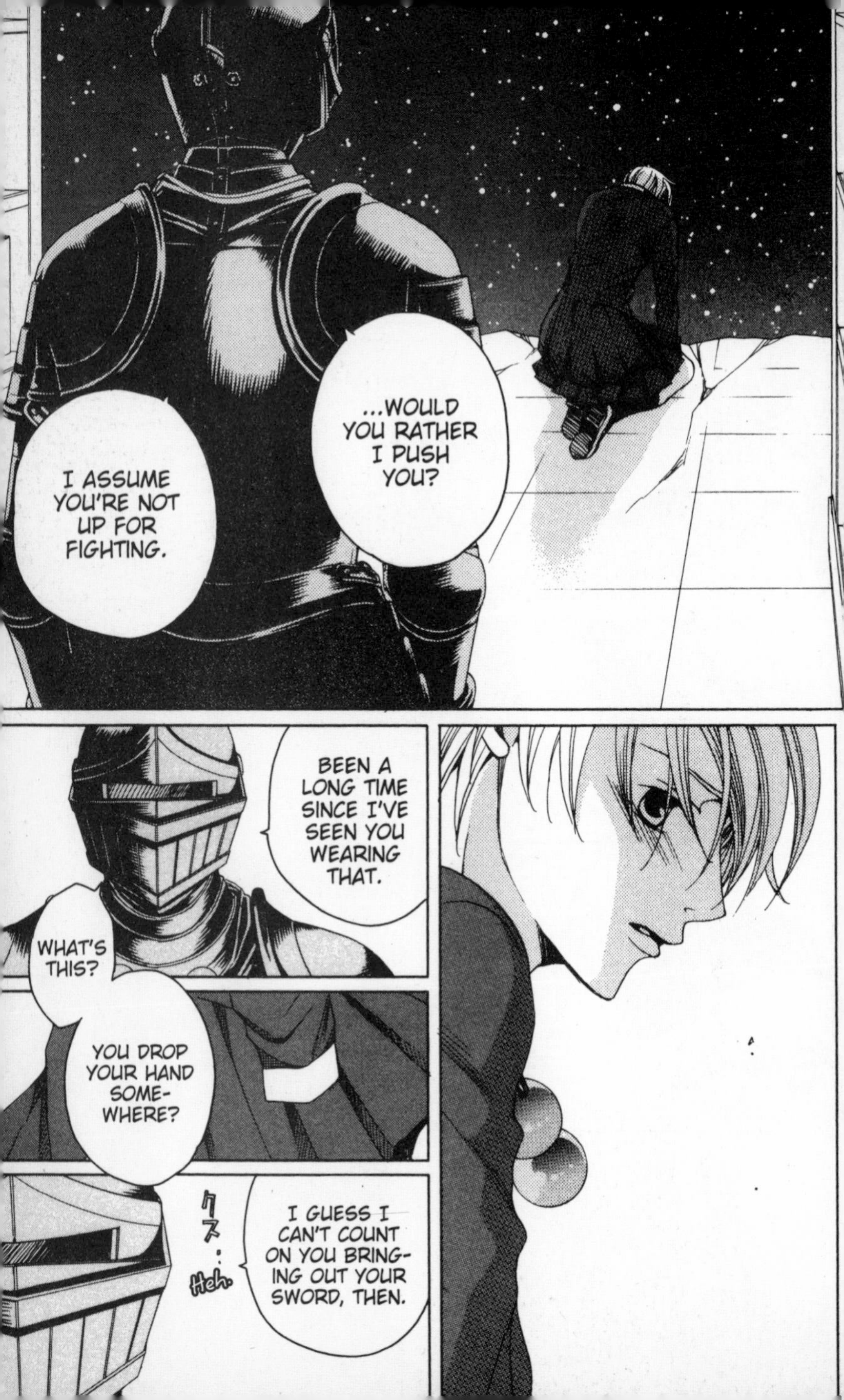
...WOULD YOU RATHER I PUSH YOU?
I ASSUME YOU'RE NOT UP FOR FIGHTING.
BEEN A LONG TIME SINCE I'VE SEEN YOU WEARING THAT.
WHAT'S THIS?
YOU DROP YOUR HAND SOME-WHERE?
I GUESS I CAN'T COUNT ON YOU BRING-ING OUT YOUR SWORD, THEN.
クス・・
Heh.

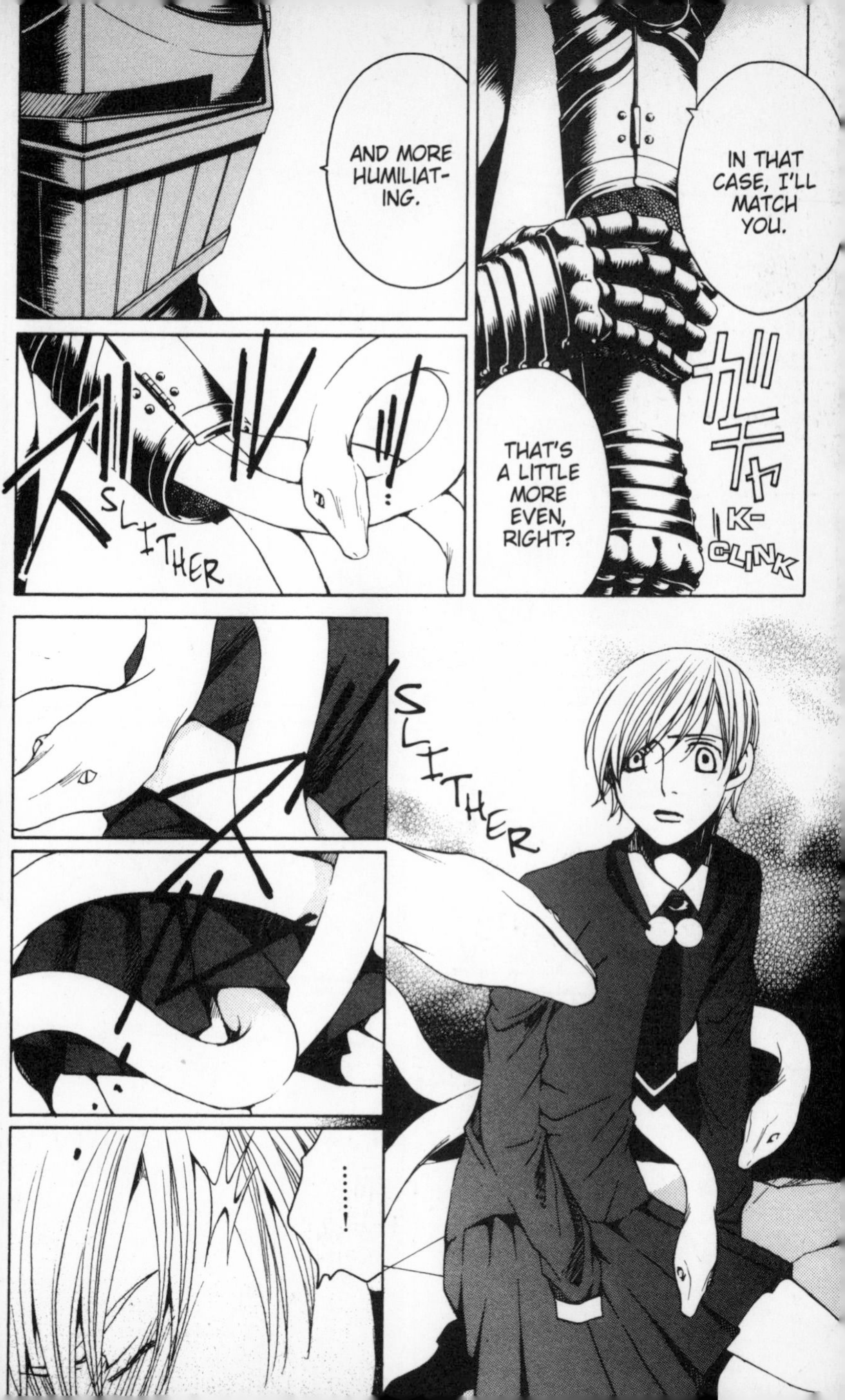
IN THAT CASE, I'LL MATCH YOU.
THAT'S A LITTLE MORE EVEN, RIGHT?
ガチャ
K-CLINK
AND MORE HUMILIAT-ING.
SLITHER
SLITHER
......!

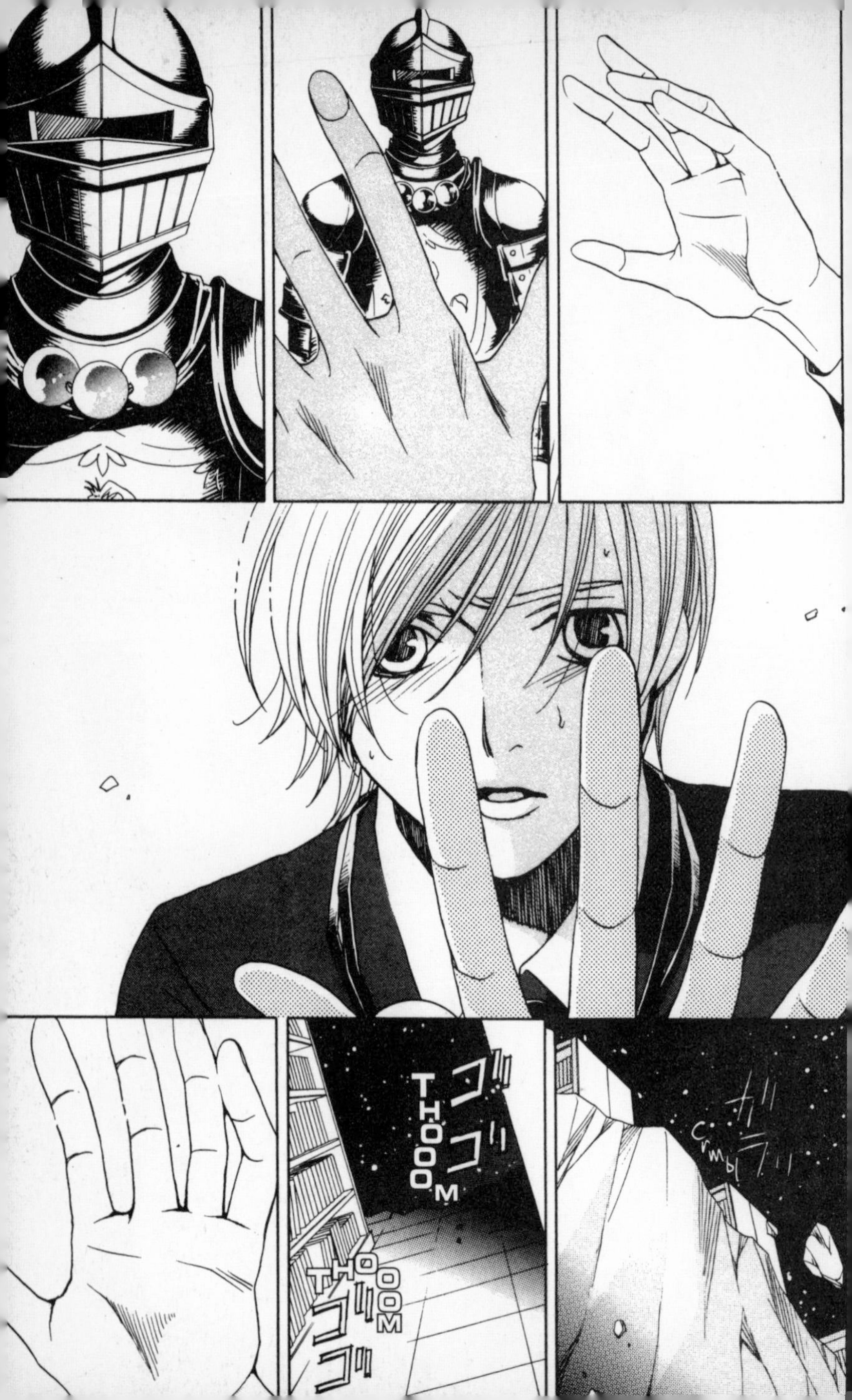
Crmbl
THOOOM
THOOOOM

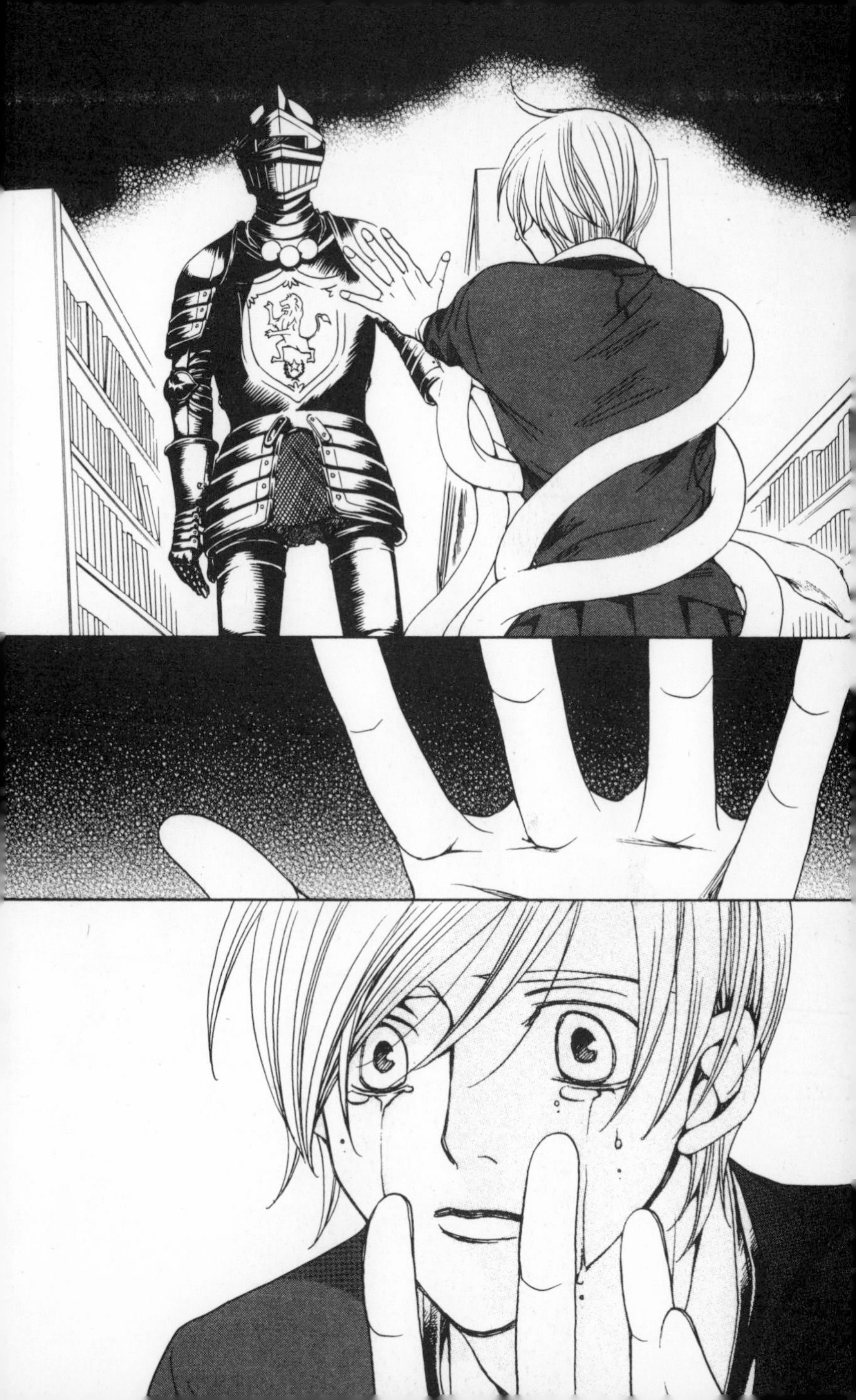

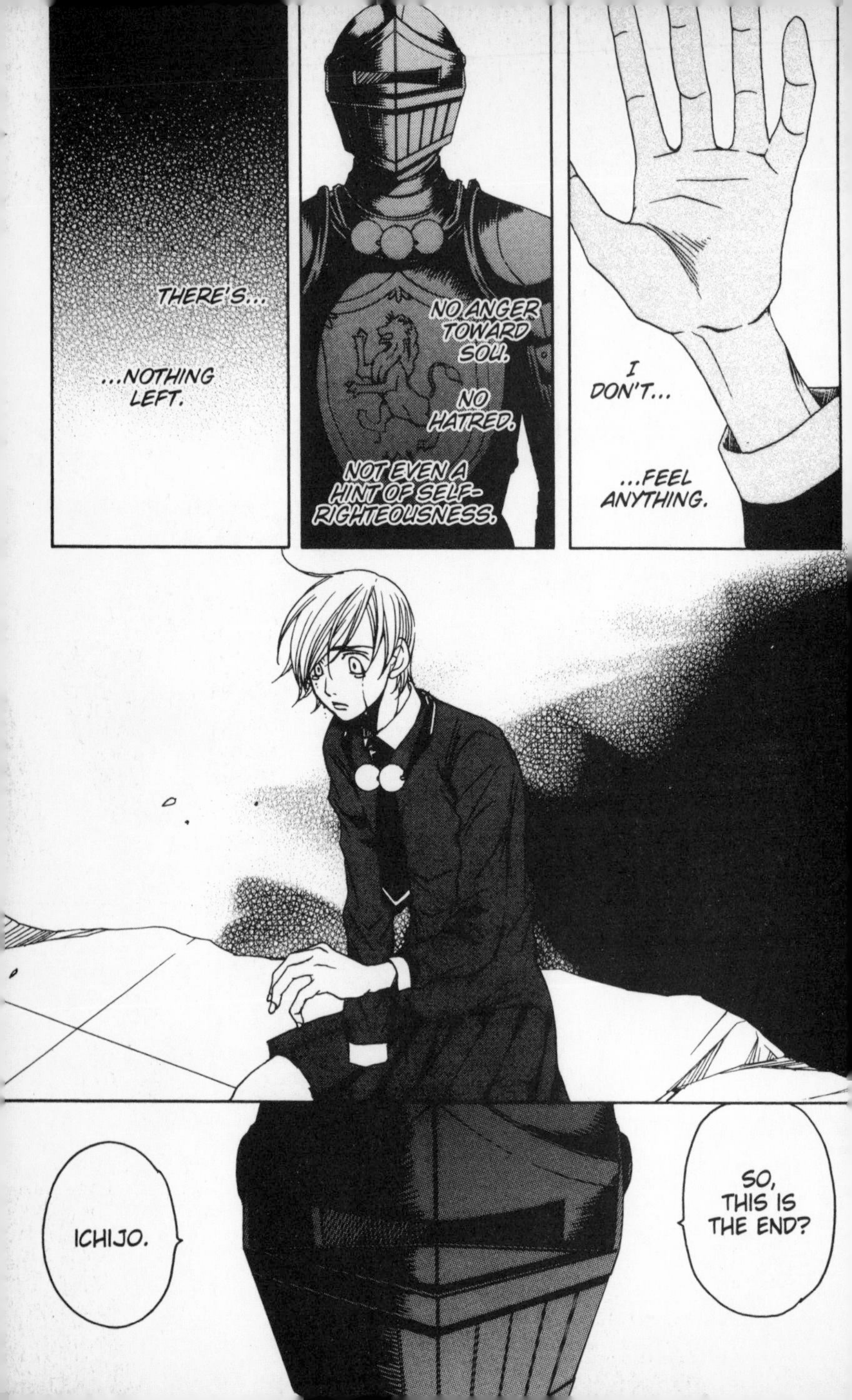
THERE'S...
...NOTHING LEFT.
NO ANGER TOWARD SOU.
NO HATRED.
NOT EVEN A HINT OF SELF-RIGHTEOUSNESS.
I DON'T...
...FEEL ANYTHING.
ICHIJO.
SO, THIS IS THE END?

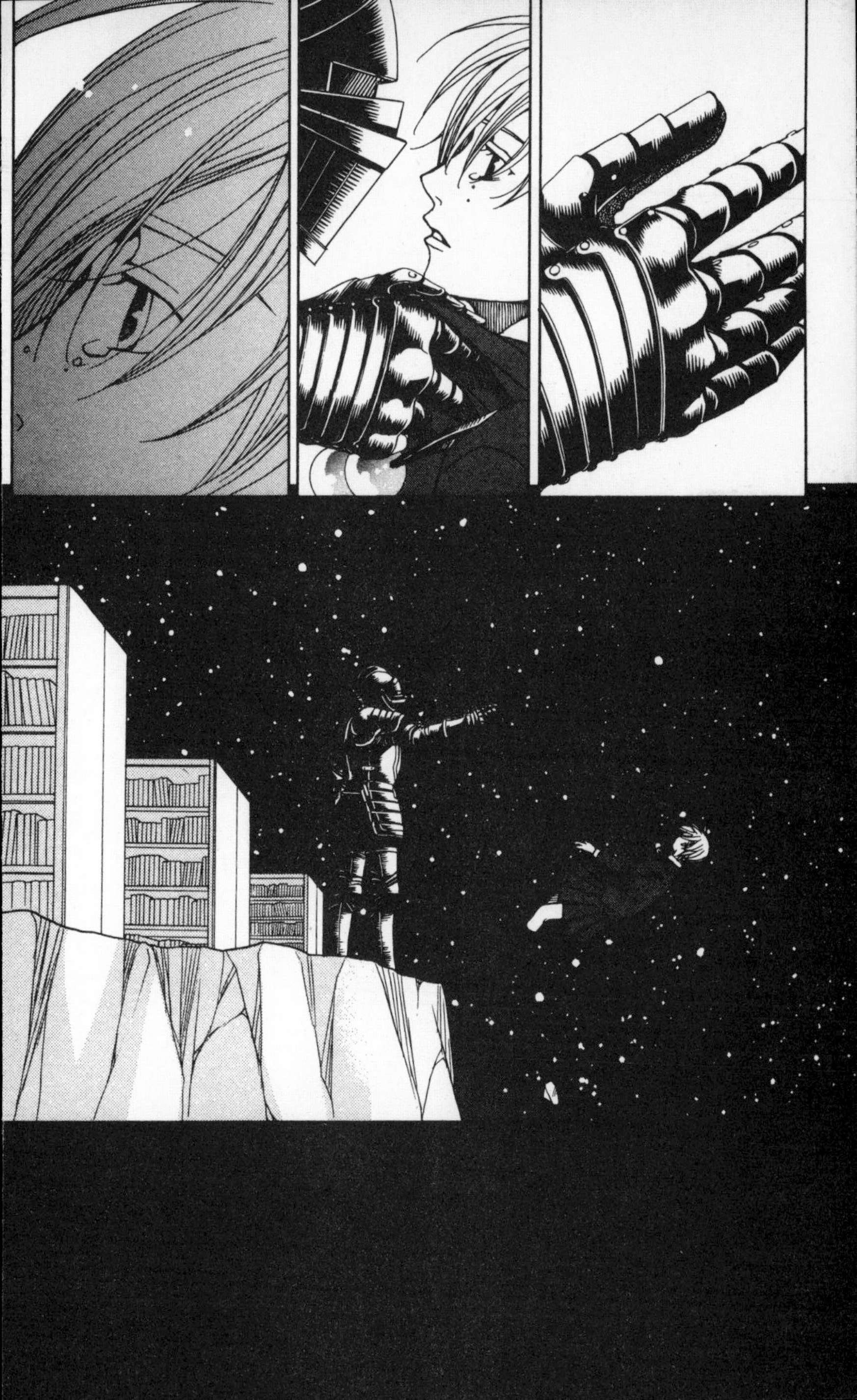

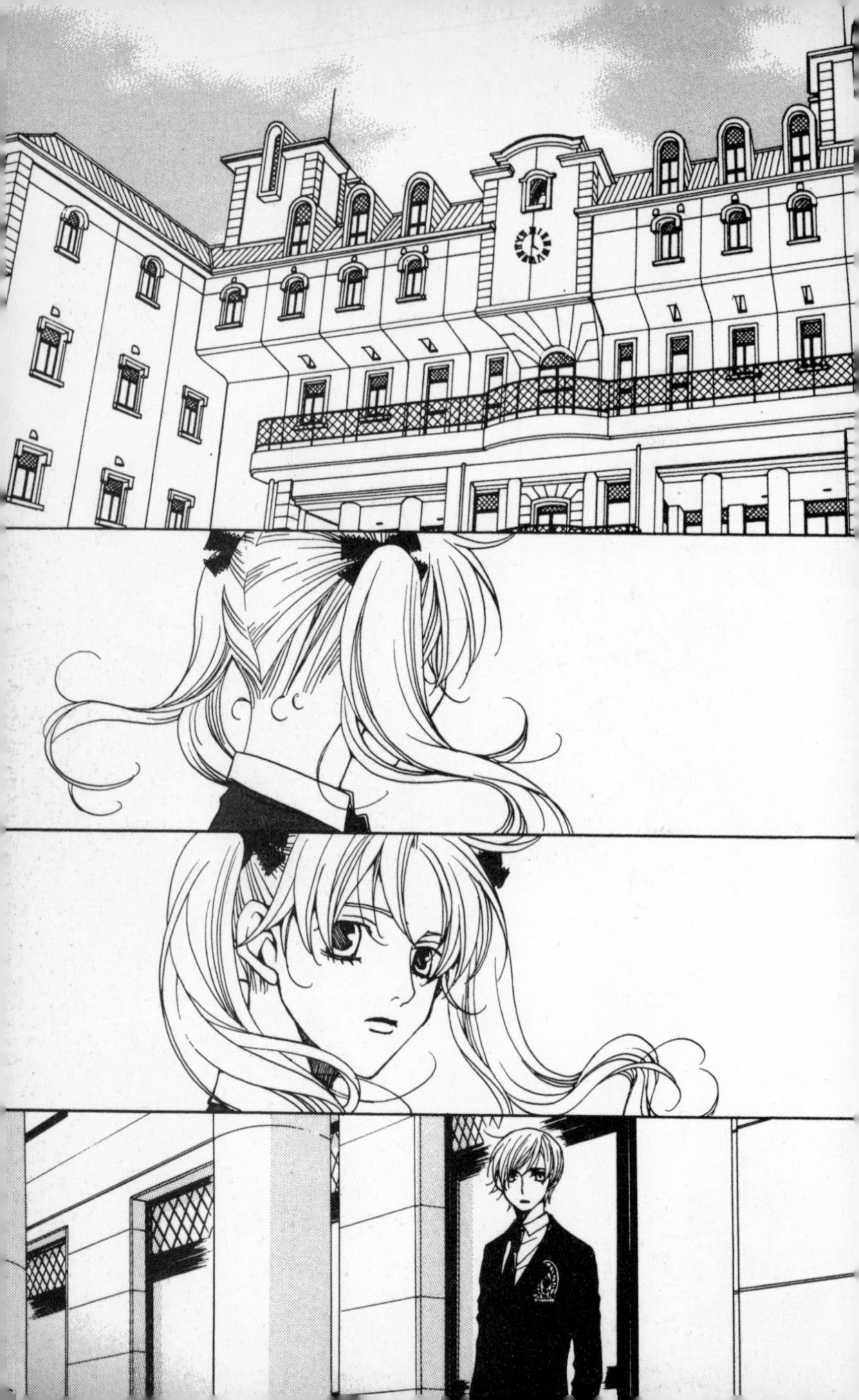

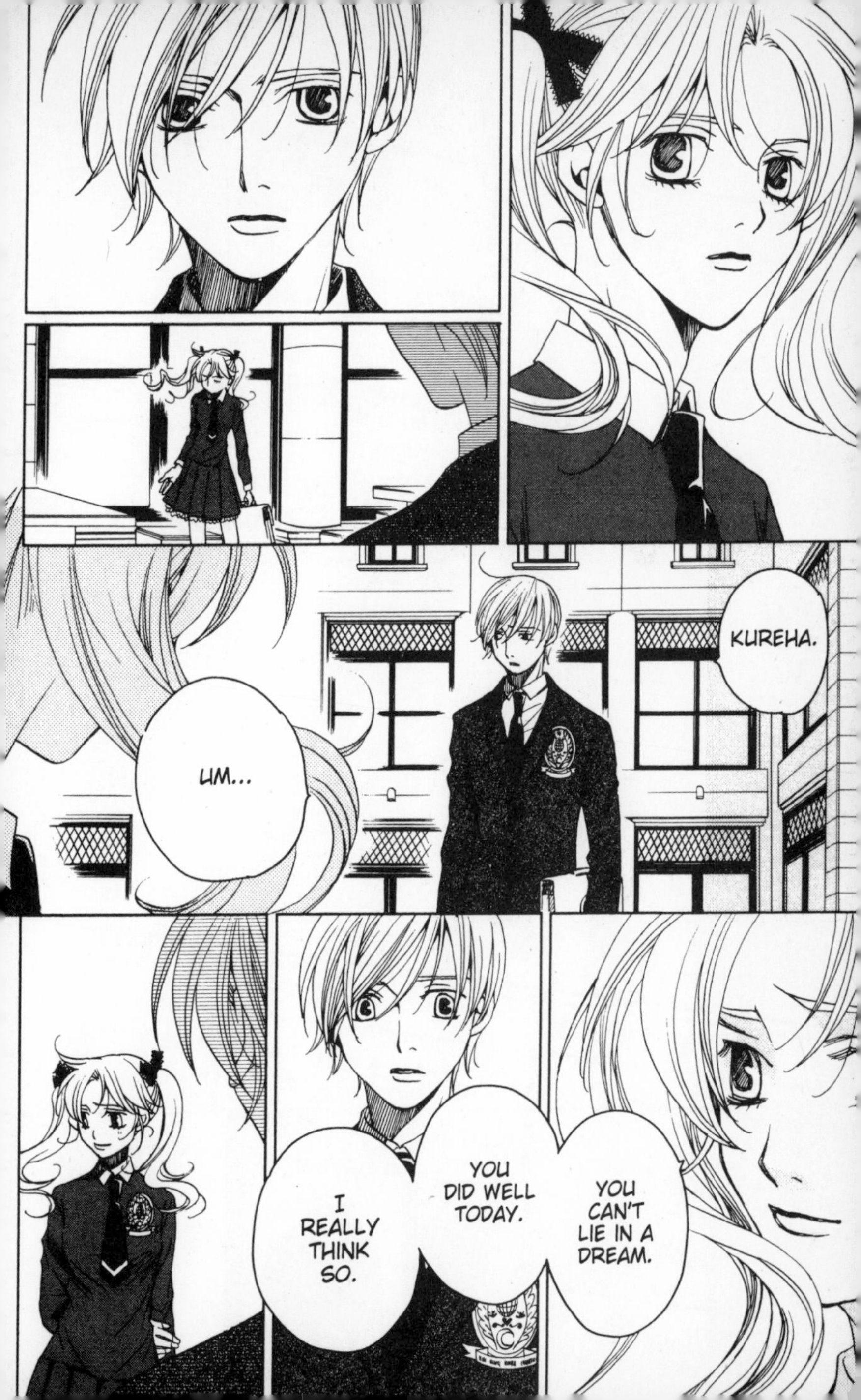
KUREHA.
UM...
YOU CAN'T LIE IN A DREAM.
YOU DID WELL TODAY.
I REALLY THINK SO.

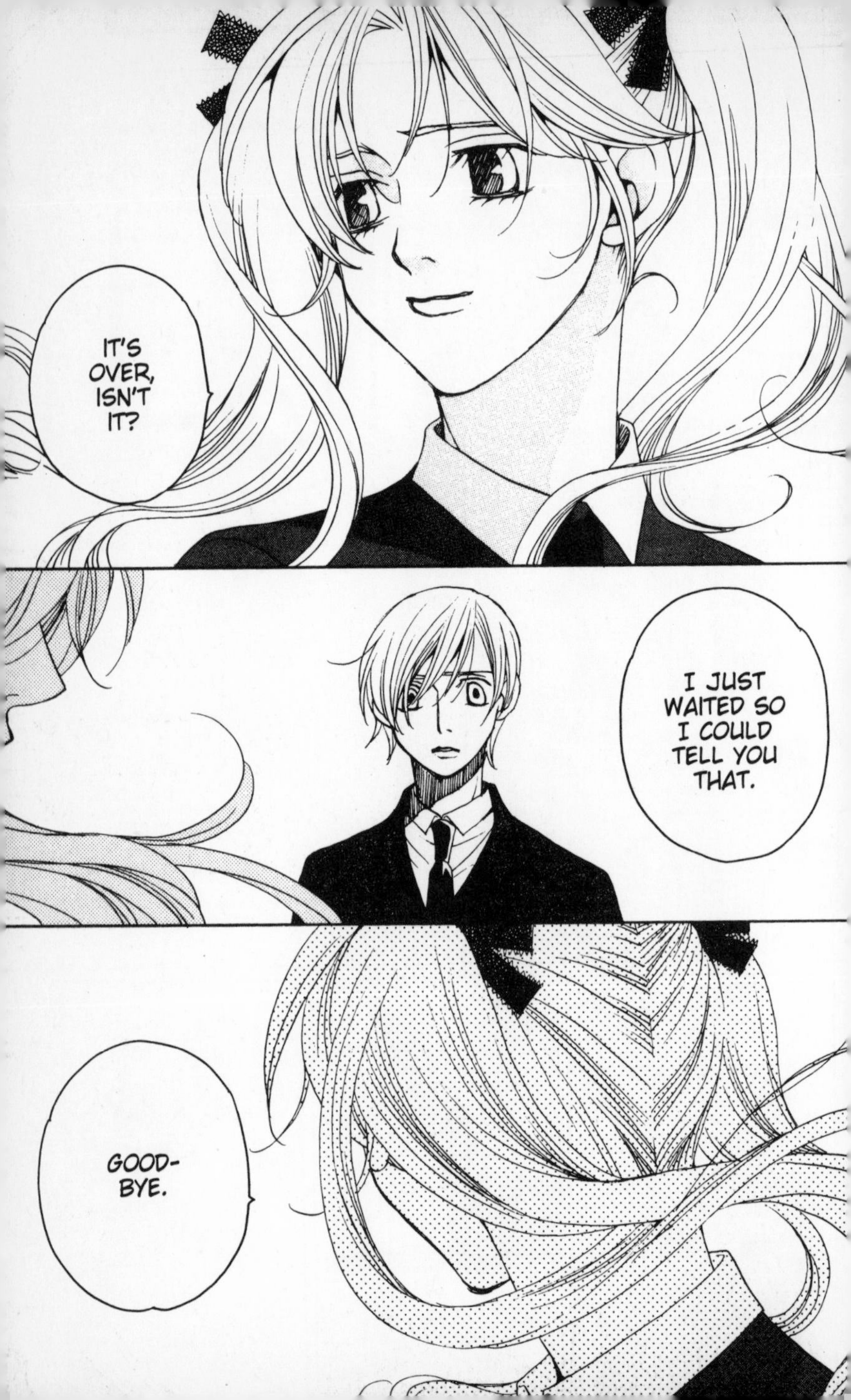
IT'S OVER, ISN'T IT?
I JUST WAITED SO I COULD TELL YOU THAT.
GOOD-BYE.

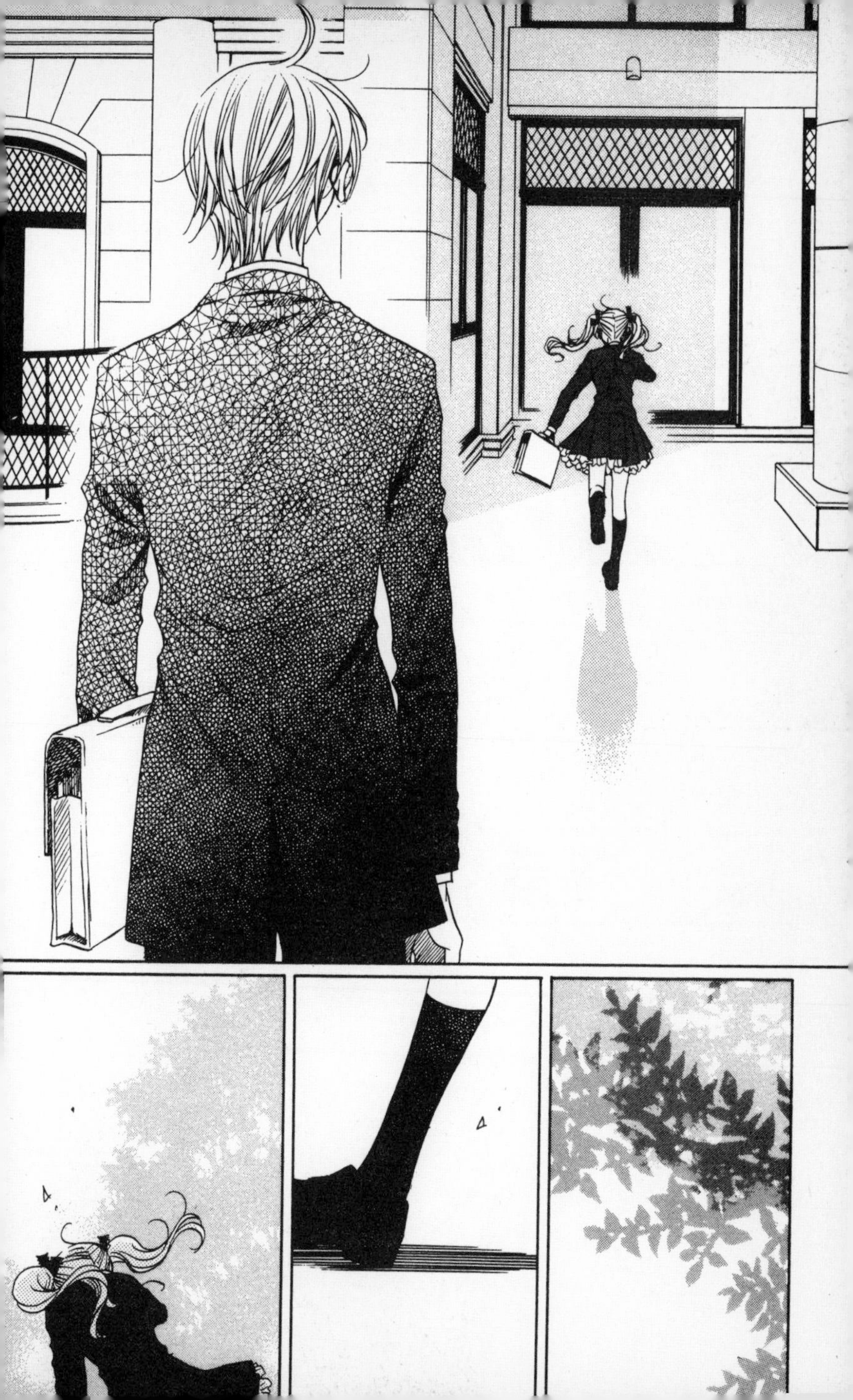

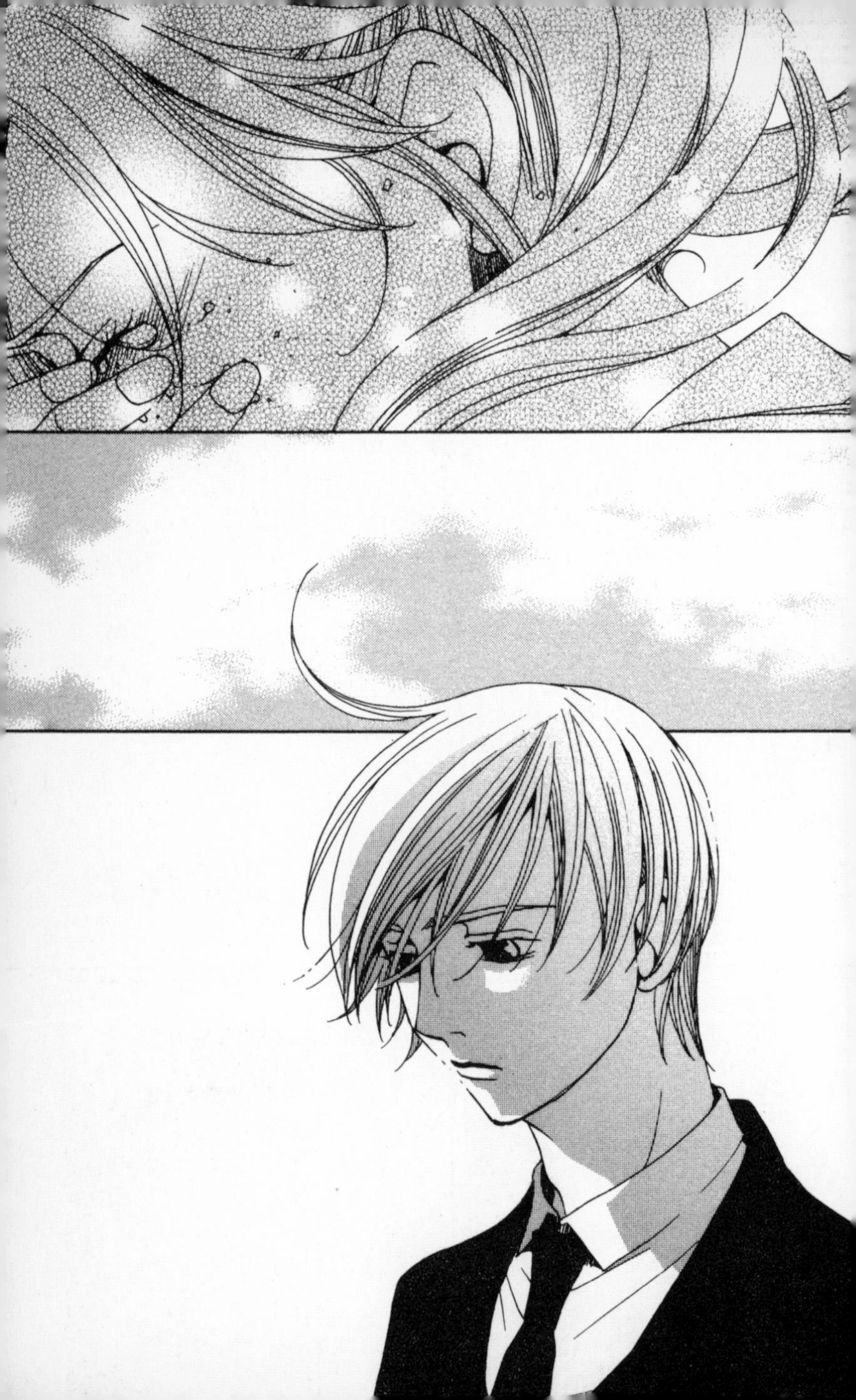

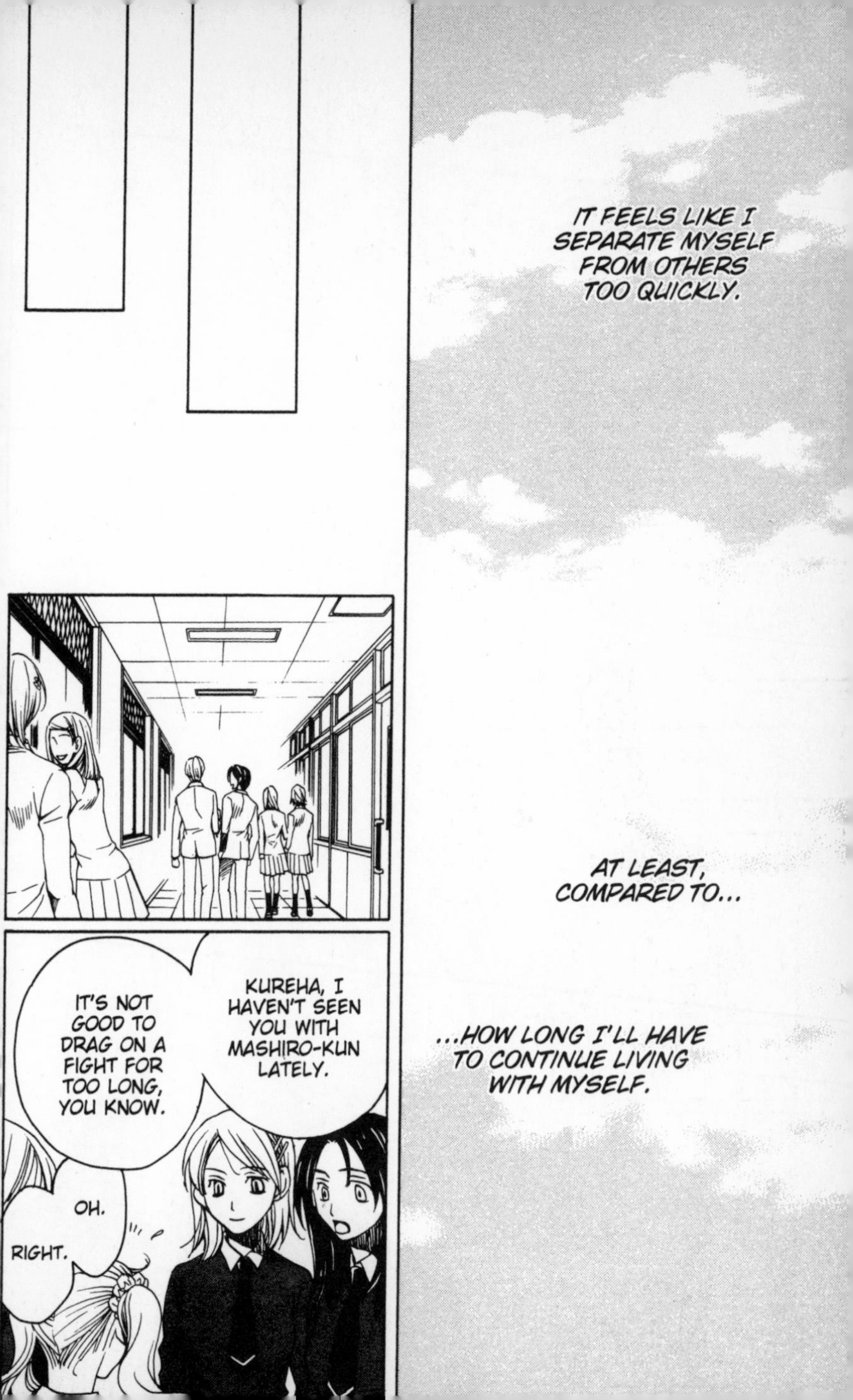
IT FEELS LIKE I SEPARATE MYSELF FROM OTHERS TOO QUICKLY.
AT LEAST, COMPARED TO...
...HOW LONG I'LL HAVE TO CONTINUE LIVING WITH MYSELF.
KUREHA, I HAVEN'T SEEN YOU WITH MASHIRO-KUN LATELY.
IT'S NOT GOOD TO DRAG ON A FIGHT FOR TOO LONG, YOU KNOW.
OH.
RIGHT.

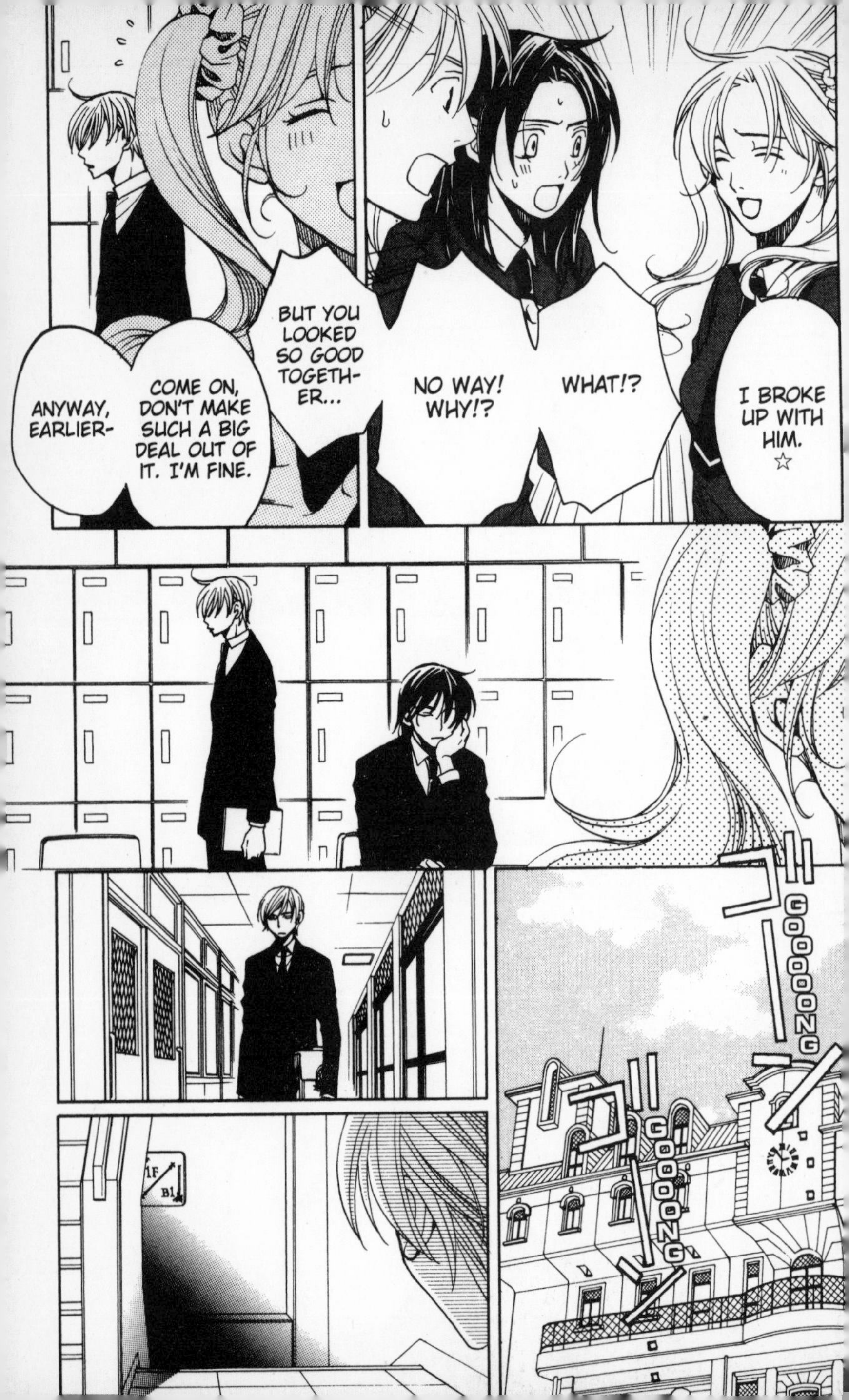
I BROKE UP WITH HIM. ☆
WHAT!?
NO WAY! WHY!?
BUT YOU LOOKED SO GOOD TOGETH-ER...
COME ON, DON'T MAKE SUCH A BIG DEAL OUT OF IT. I'M FINE.
ANYWAY, EARLIER-
GOOOOONG
GOOOONG

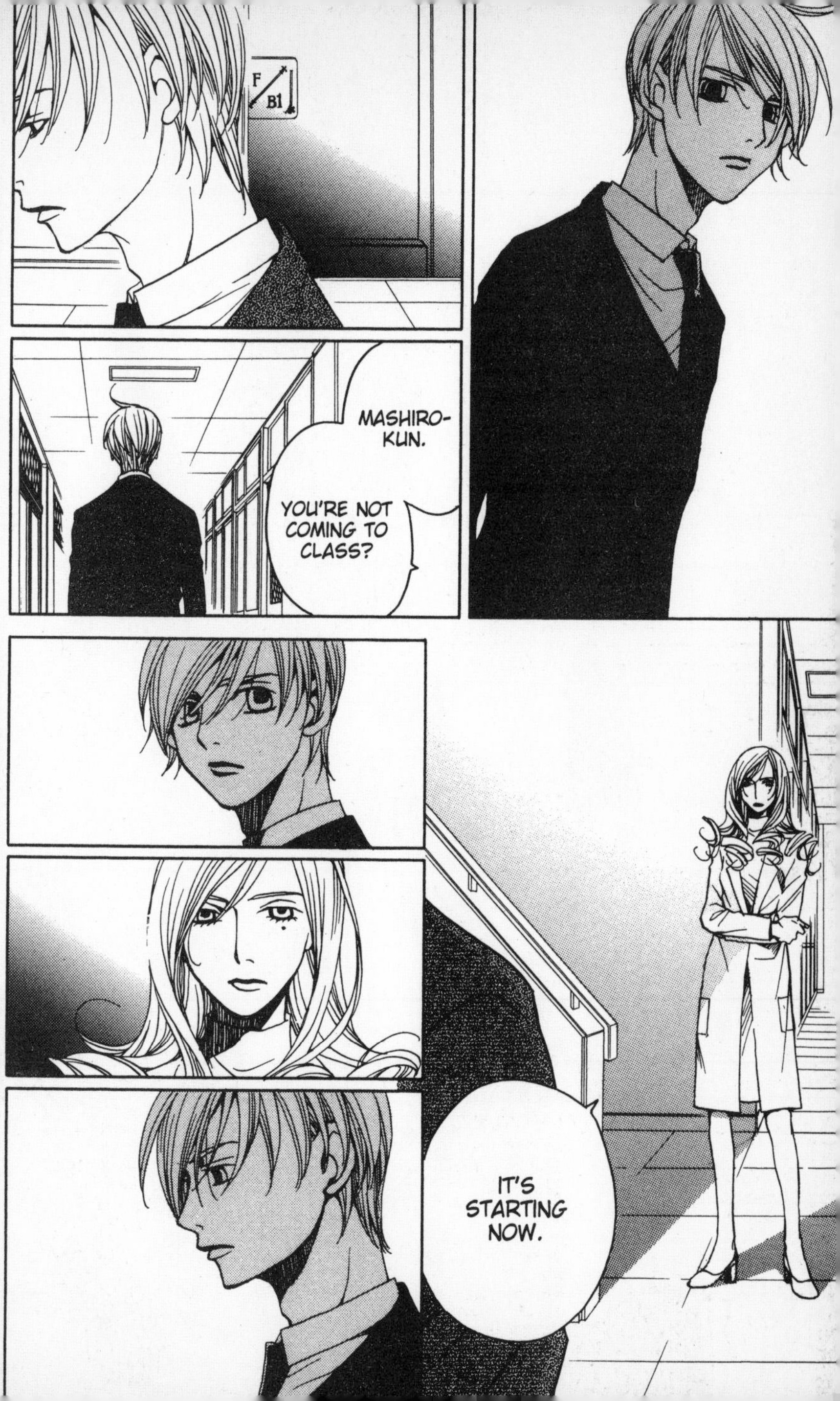
F
B1
MASHIRO-KUN.
YOU'RE NOT COMING TO CLASS?
IT'S STARTING NOW.

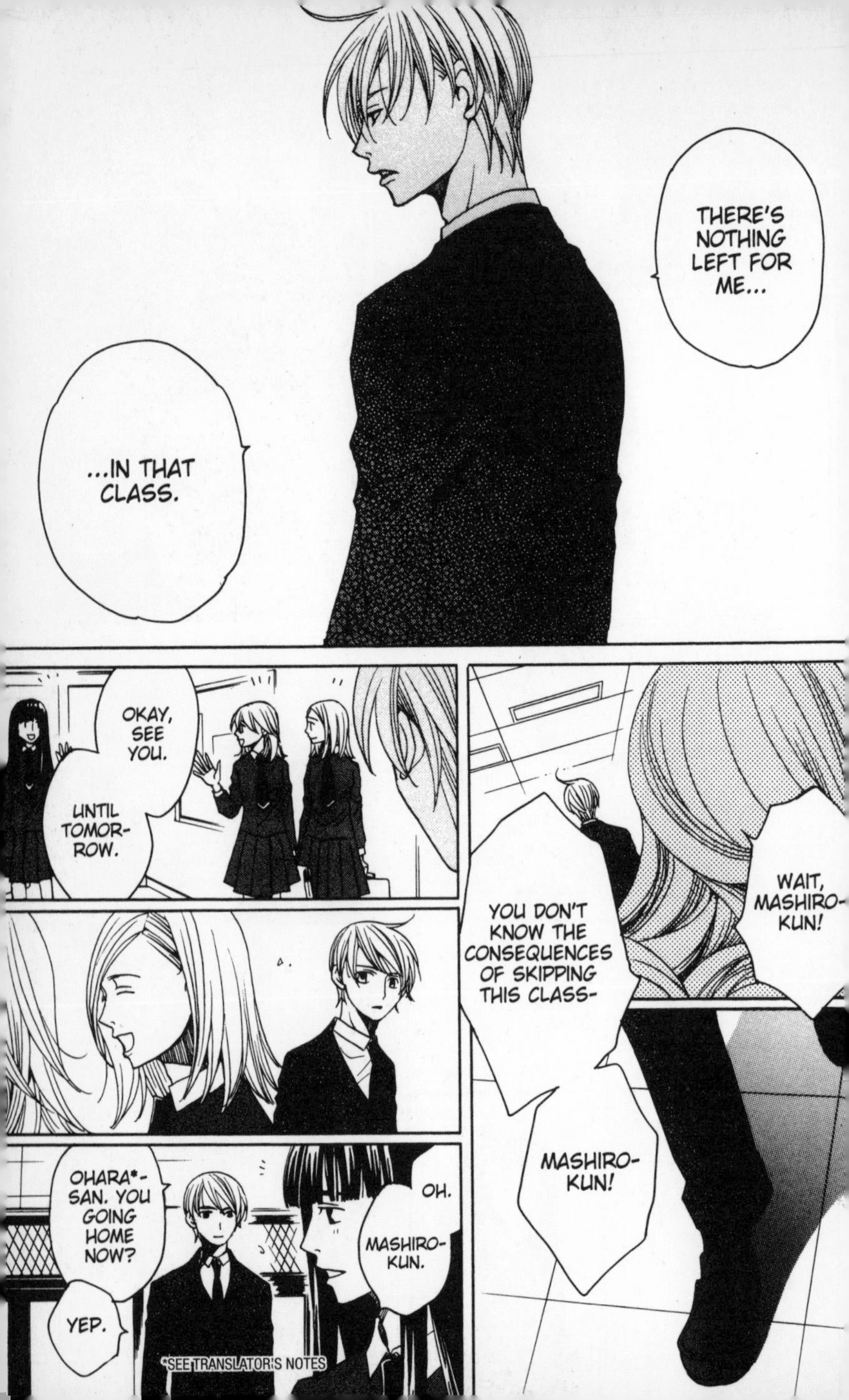
THERE'S NOTHING LEFT FOR ME...
...IN THAT CLASS.
WAIT, MASHIRO-KUN!
YOU DON'T KNOW THE CONSEQUENCES OF SKIPPING THIS CLASS-
MASHIRO-KUN!
OKAY, SEE YOU.
UNTIL TOMOR-ROW.
OH.
MASHIRO-KUN.
OHARA*-SAN. YOU GOING HOME NOW?
YEP.

*SEE TRANSLATOR'S NOTES

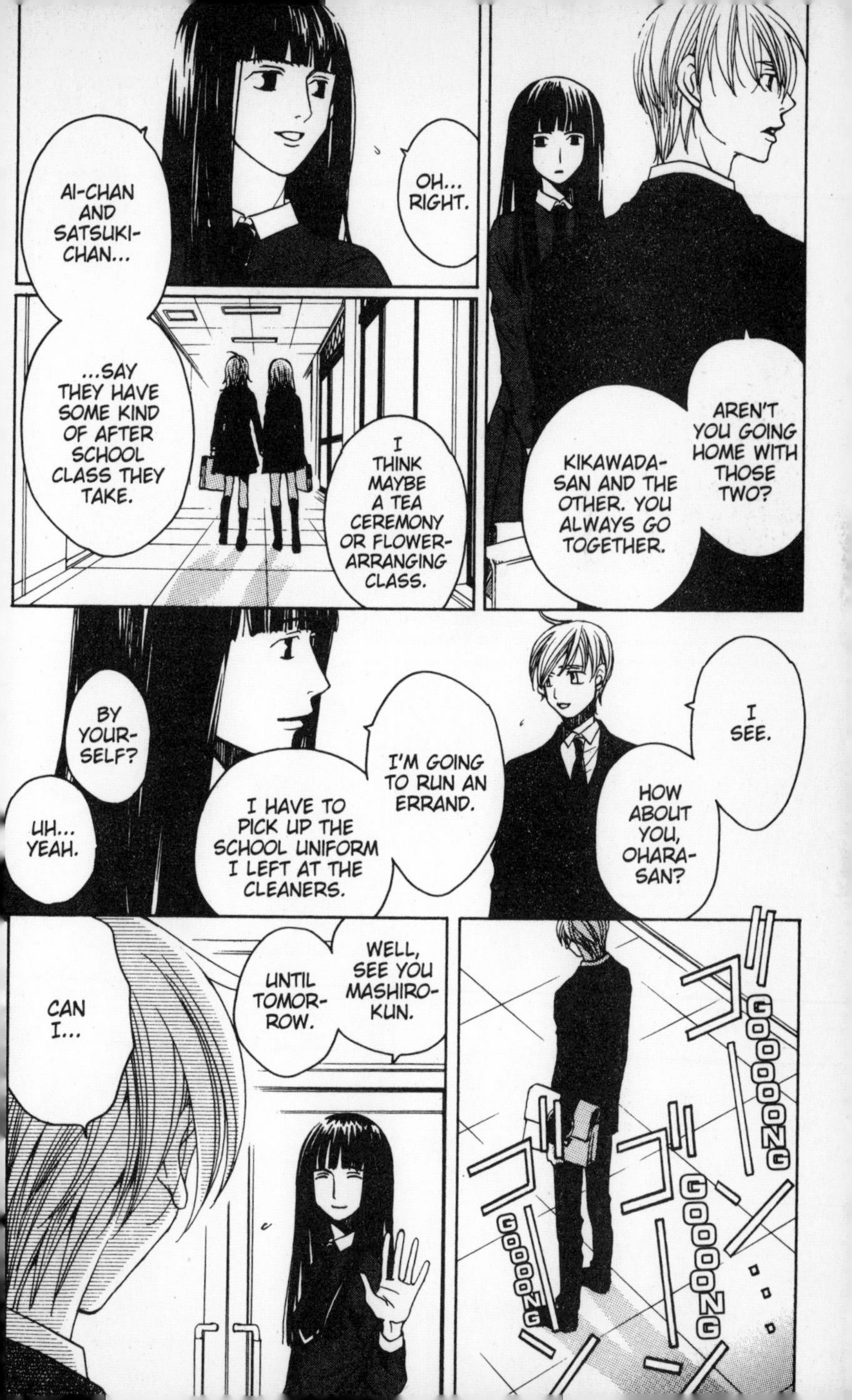
AREN'T YOU GOING HOME WITH THOSE TWO?
KIKAWADA-SAN AND THE OTHER. YOU ALWAYS GO TOGETHER.
OH... RIGHT.
AI-CHAN AND SATSUKI-CHAN...
...SAY THEY HAVE SOME KIND OF AFTER SCHOOL CLASS THEY TAKE.
I THINK MAYBE A TEA CEREMONY OR FLOWER-ARRANGING CLASS.
I SEE.
HOW ABOUT YOU, OHARA-SAN?
I'M GOING TO RUN AN ERRAND.
I HAVE TO PICK UP THE SCHOOL UNIFORM I LEFT AT THE CLEANERS.
BY YOURSELF?
UH... YEAH.
GOOOOONG
GOOOONG
GOOOONG
WELL, SEE YOU MASHIRO-KUN.
UNTIL TOMORROW.
CAN I...

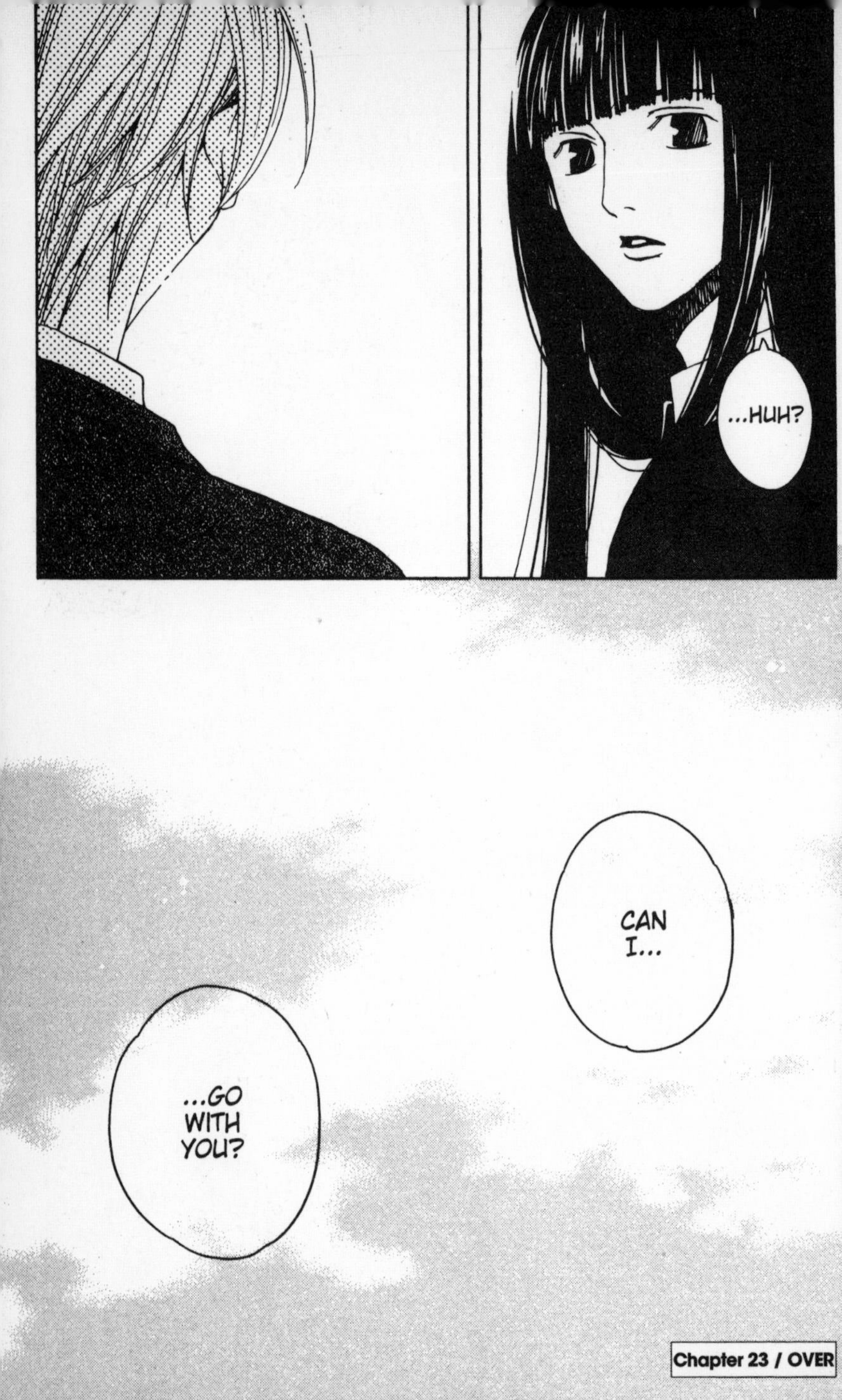
...HUH?
CAN I...
...GO WITH YOU?
Chapter 23 / OVER

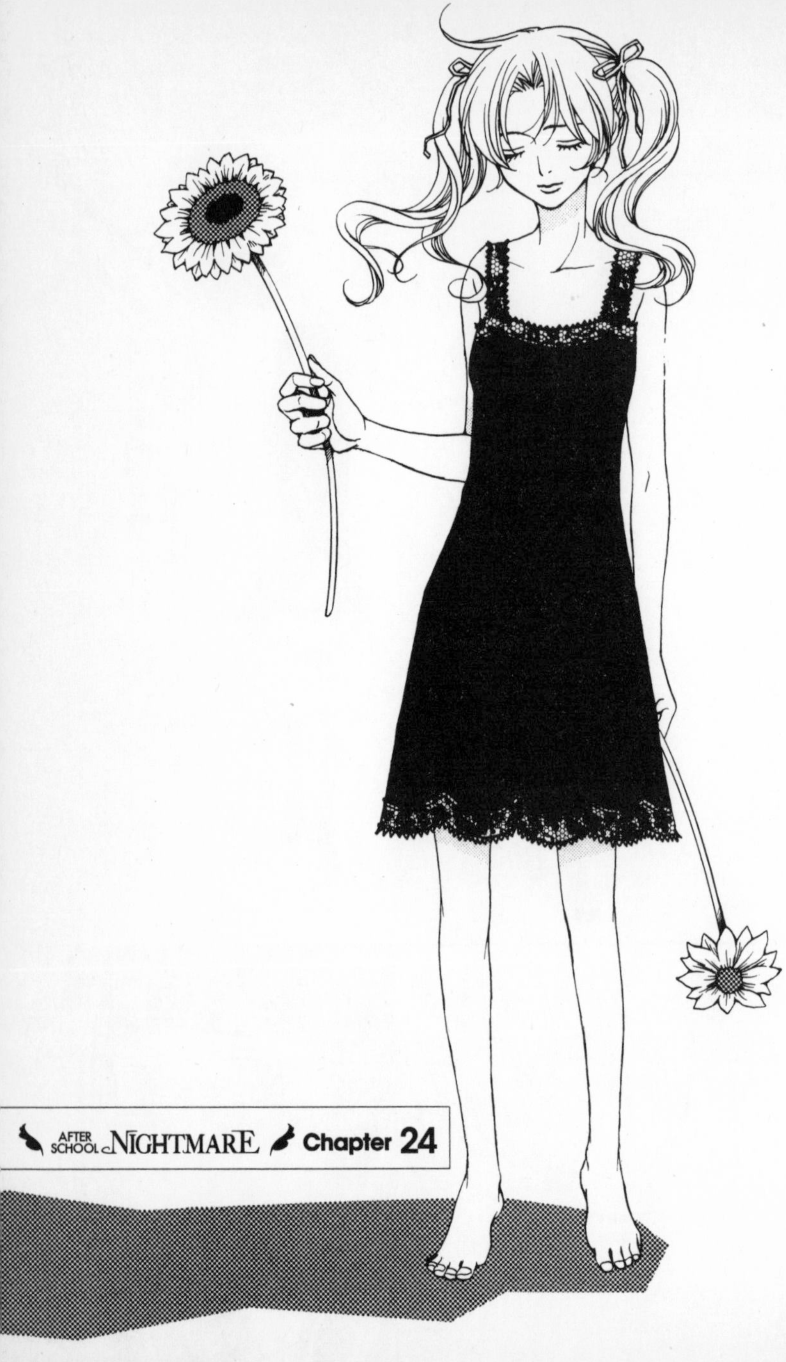

AFTER SCHOOL NIGHTMARE Chapter 24

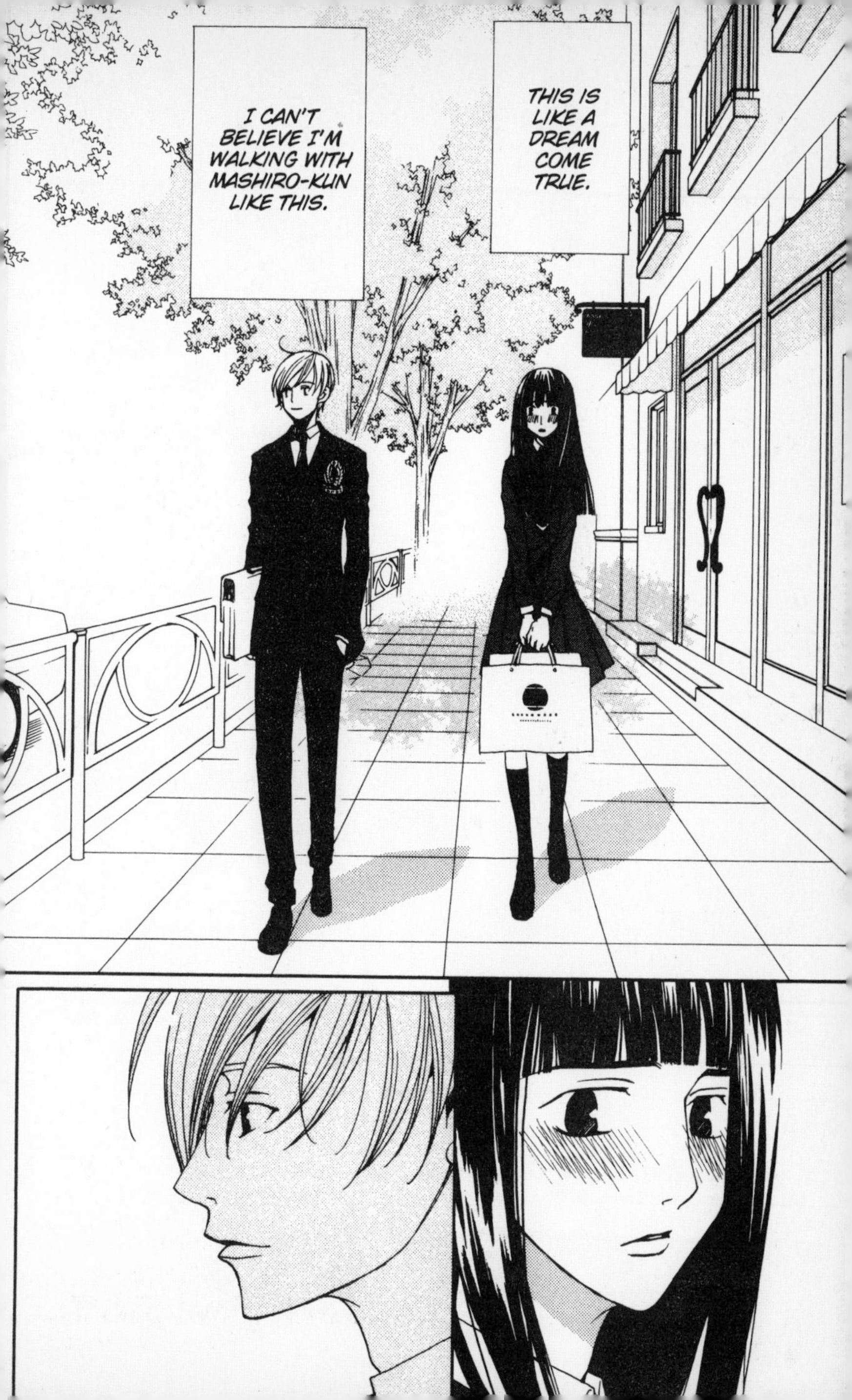
THIS IS LIKE A DREAM COME TRUE.
I CAN'T BELIEVE I'M WALKING WITH MASHIRO-KUN LIKE THIS.

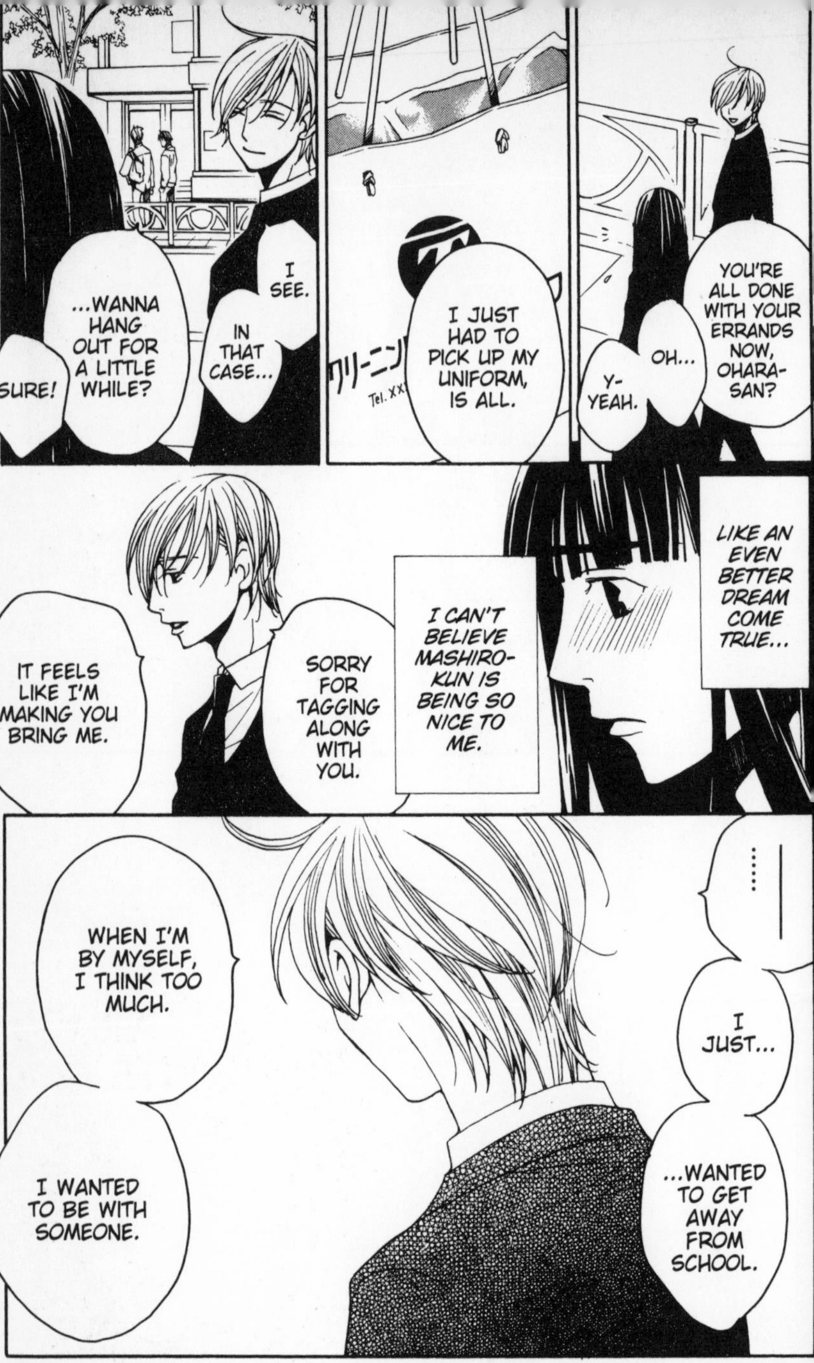
YOU'RE ALL DONE WITH YOUR ERRANDS NOW, OHARA-SAN?
OH...
Y-YEAH.
I JUST HAD TO PICK UP MY UNIFORM, IS ALL.
I SEE.
IN THAT CASE...
...WANNA HANG OUT FOR A LITTLE WHILE?
SURE!
LIKE AN EVEN BETTER DREAM COME TRUE...
I CAN'T BELIEVE MASHIRO-KUN IS BEING SO NICE TO ME.
SORRY FOR TAGGING ALONG WITH YOU.
IT FEELS LIKE I'M MAKING YOU BRING ME.
......
I JUST...
...WANTED TO GET AWAY FROM SCHOOL.
WHEN I'M BY MYSELF, I THINK TOO MUCH.
I WANTED TO BE WITH SOMEONE.

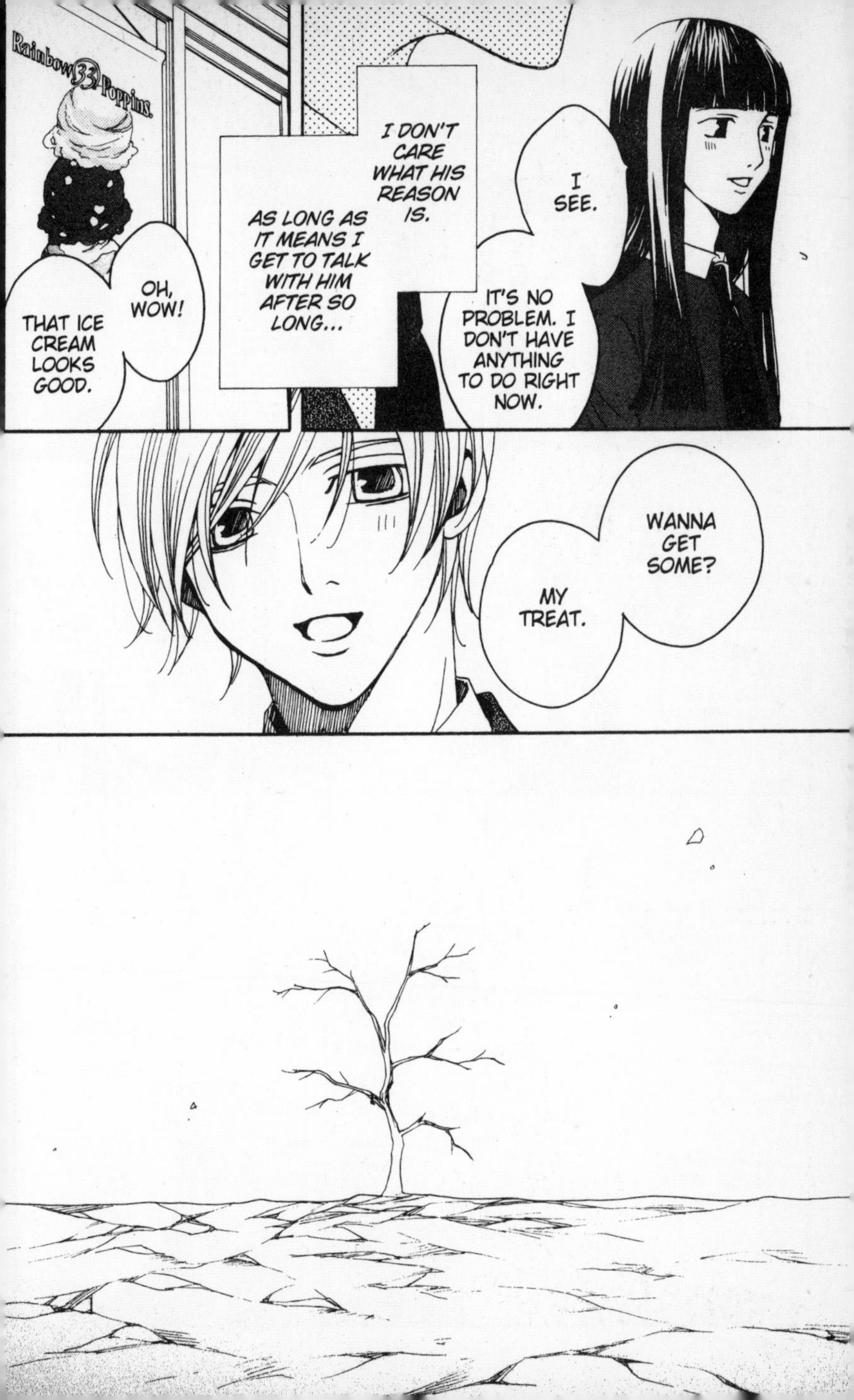
I SEE.
IT'S NO PROBLEM. I DON'T HAVE ANYTHING TO DO RIGHT NOW.
I DON'T CARE WHAT HIS REASON IS.
AS LONG AS IT MEANS I GET TO TALK WITH HIM AFTER SO LONG...
Rainbow 33 Poppins.
OH, WOW!
THAT ICE CREAM LOOKS GOOD.
WANNA GET SOME?
MY TREAT.

THERE'S HARDLY ANYONE HERE TODAY.

WHAT IS THIS?

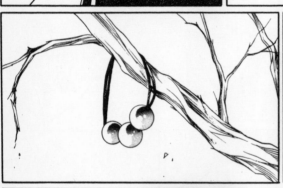

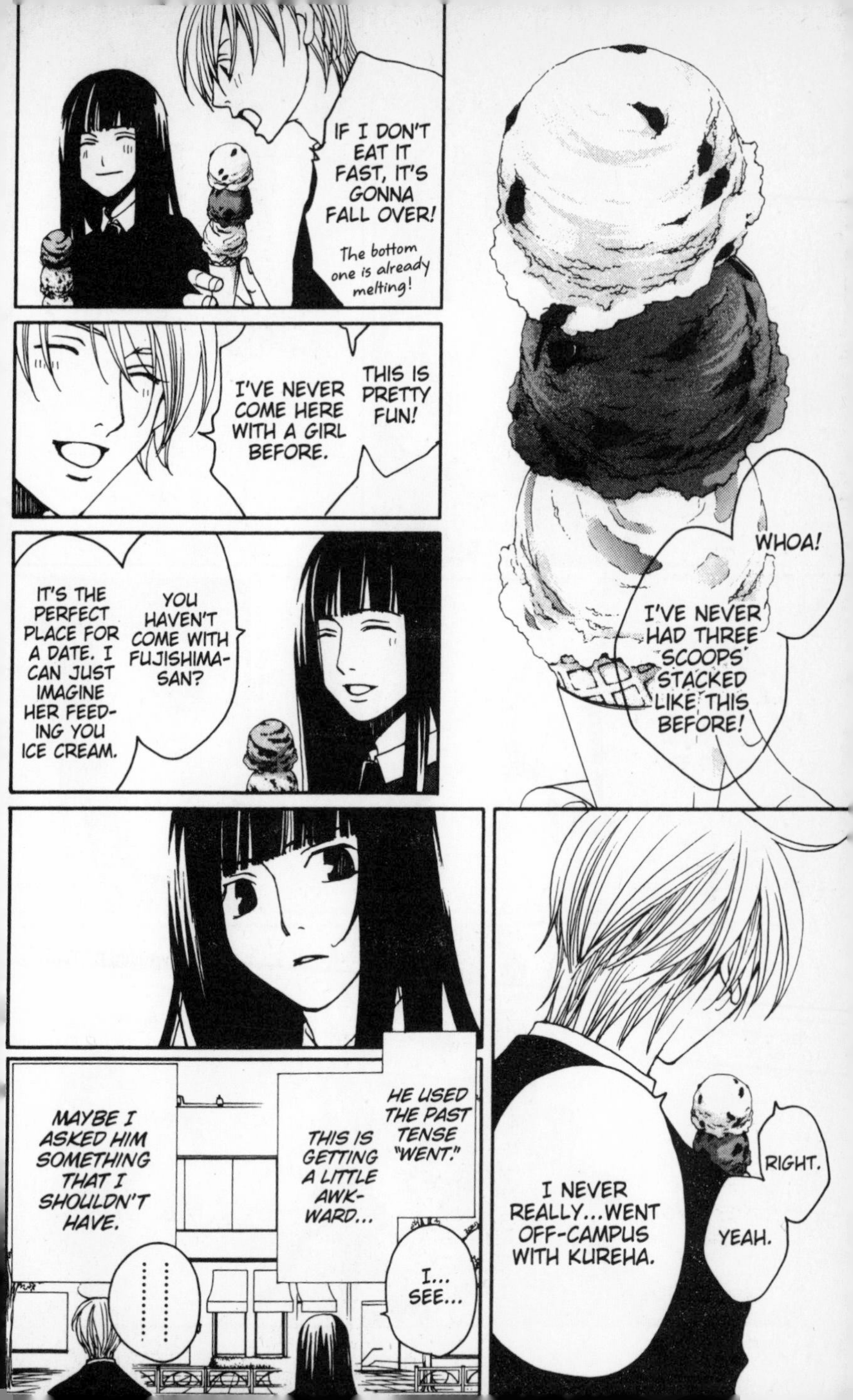
WHOA!
I'VE NEVER HAD THREE SCOOPS STACKED LIKE THIS BEFORE!
IF I DON'T EAT IT FAST, IT'S GONNA FALL OVER!
The bottom one is already melting!
THIS IS PRETTY FUN!
I'VE NEVER COME HERE WITH A GIRL BEFORE.
YOU HAVEN'T COME WITH FUJISHIMA-SAN?
IT'S THE PERFECT PLACE FOR A DATE. I CAN JUST IMAGINE HER FEEDING YOU ICE CREAM.
RIGHT.
YEAH.
I NEVER REALLY...WENT OFF-CAMPUS WITH KUREHA.
HE USED THE PAST TENSE "WENT."
THIS IS GETTING A LITTLE AWKWARD...
I... SEE...
......
MAYBE I ASKED HIM SOMETHING THAT I SHOULDN'T HAVE.

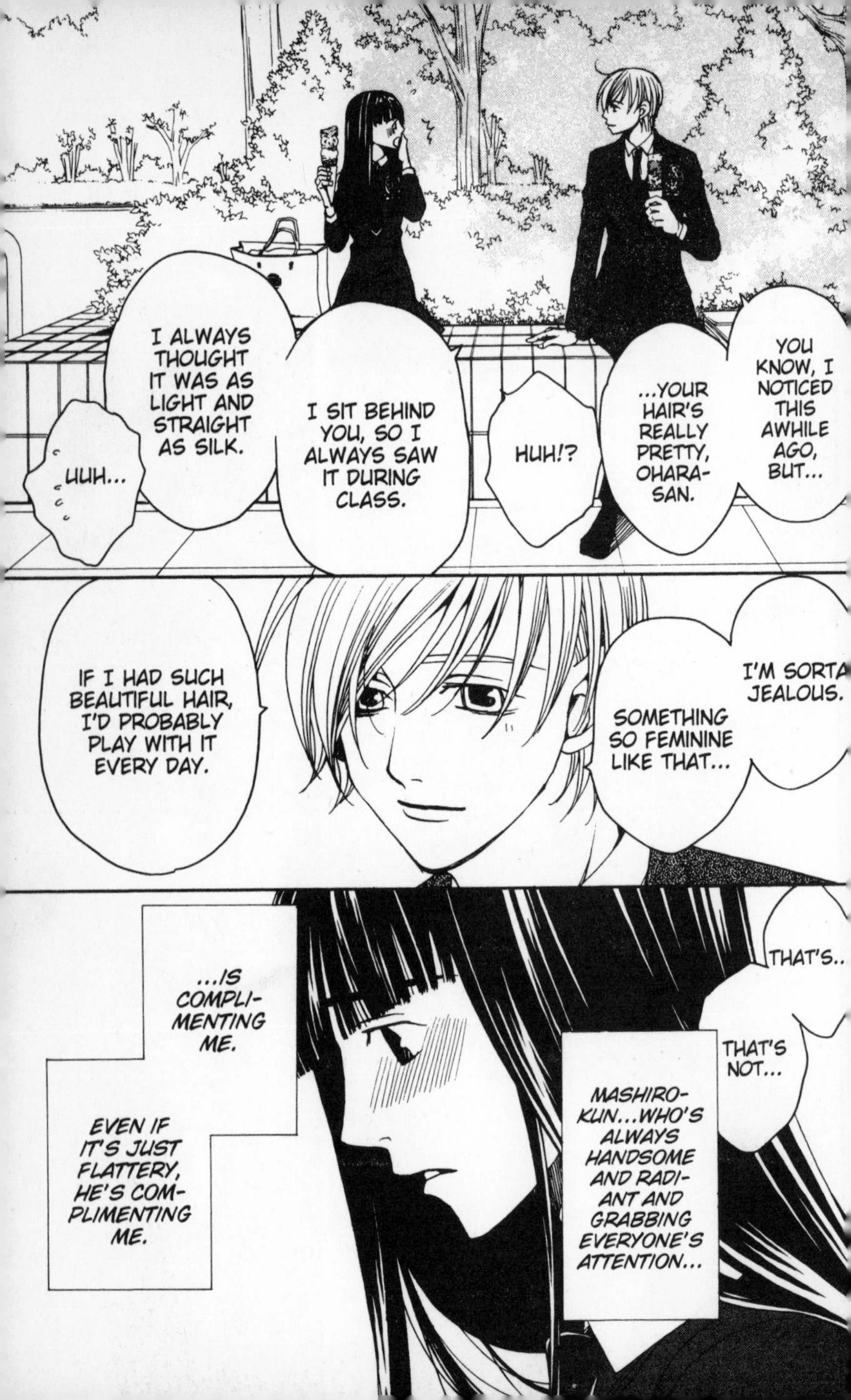
YOU KNOW, I NOTICED THIS AWHILE AGO, BUT...
...YOUR HAIR'S REALLY PRETTY, OHARA-SAN.
HUH!?
I SIT BEHIND YOU, SO I ALWAYS SAW IT DURING CLASS.
I ALWAYS THOUGHT IT WAS AS LIGHT AND STRAIGHT AS SILK.
UUH...
I'M SORTA JEALOUS.
SOMETHING SO FEMININE LIKE THAT...
IF I HAD SUCH BEAUTIFUL HAIR, I'D PROBABLY PLAY WITH IT EVERY DAY.
THAT'S..
THAT'S NOT...
MASHIRO-KUN...WHO'S ALWAYS HANDSOME AND RADIANT AND GRABBING EVERYONE'S ATTENTION...
...IS COMPLIMENTING ME.
EVEN IF IT'S JUST FLATTERY, HE'S COMPLIMENTING ME.

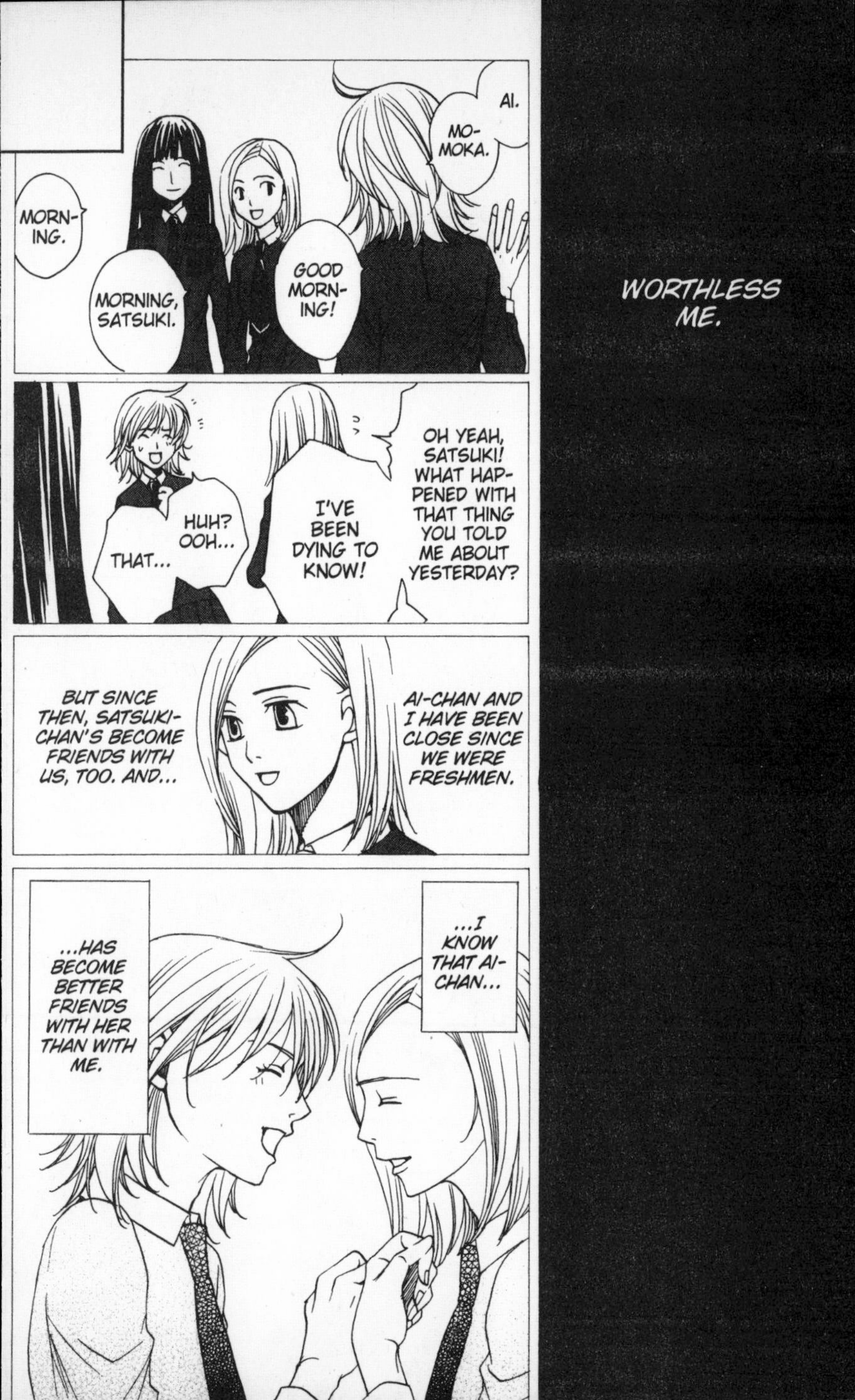
WORTHLESS ME.
AI.
MO-MOKA.
GOOD MORN-ING!
MORNING, SATSUKI.
MORN-ING.
OH YEAH, SATSUKI! WHAT HAP-PENED WITH THAT THING YOU TOLD ME ABOUT YESTERDAY?
I'VE BEEN DYING TO KNOW!
HUH? OOH...
THAT...
AI-CHAN AND I HAVE BEEN CLOSE SINCE WE WERE FRESHMEN.
BUT SINCE THEN, SATSUKI-CHAN'S BECOME FRIENDS WITH US, TOO. AND...
...I KNOW THAT AI-CHAN...
...HAS BECOME BETTER FRIENDS WITH HER THAN WITH ME.

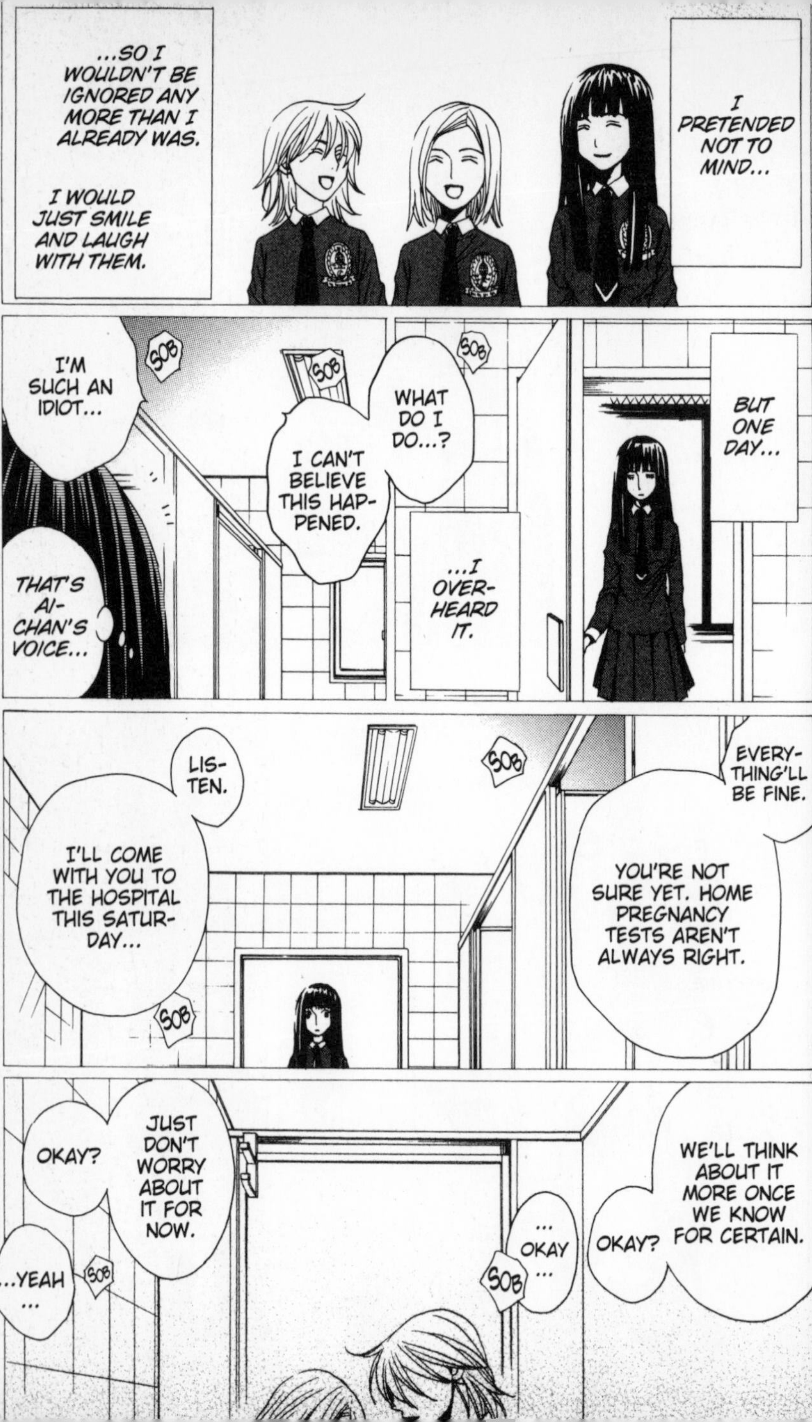
I PRETENDED NOT TO MIND...
...SO I WOULDN'T BE IGNORED ANY MORE THAN I ALREADY WAS.
I WOULD JUST SMILE AND LAUGH WITH THEM.
BUT ONE DAY...
SOB
WHAT DO I DO...?
...I OVERHEARD IT.
SOB
I CAN'T BELIEVE THIS HAPPENED.
SOB
I'M SUCH AN IDIOT...
THAT'S AI-CHAN'S VOICE...
EVERYTHING'LL BE FINE.
YOU'RE NOT SURE YET. HOME PREGNANCY TESTS AREN'T ALWAYS RIGHT.
SOB
LISTEN.
I'LL COME WITH YOU TO THE HOSPITAL THIS SATURDAY...
SOB
WE'LL THINK ABOUT IT MORE ONCE WE KNOW FOR CERTAIN.
OKAY?
...OKAY...
SOB
JUST DON'T WORRY ABOUT IT FOR NOW.
OKAY?
SOB
...YEAH...

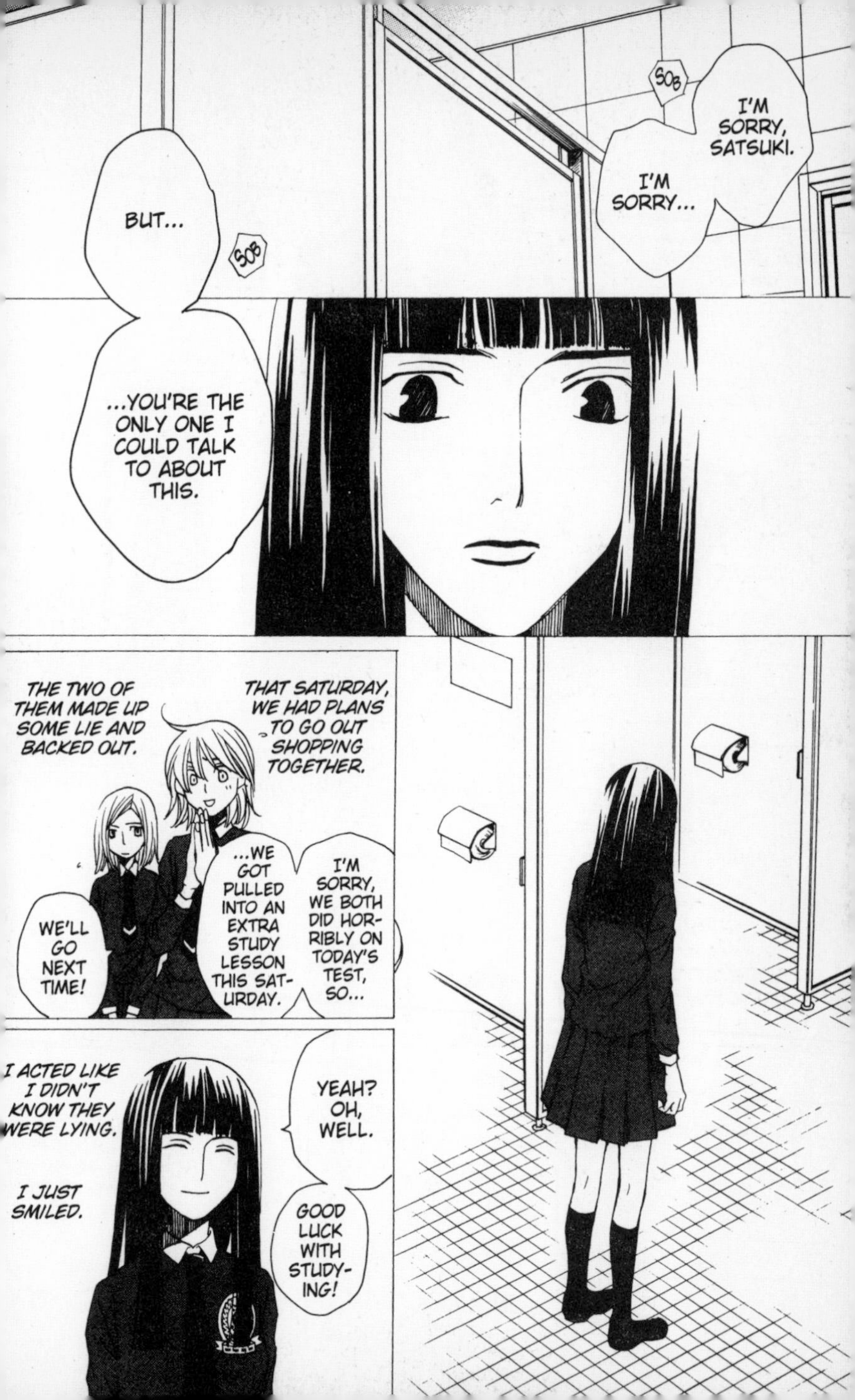
SOB
I'M SORRY, SATSUKI.
I'M SORRY...
BUT...
SOB
...YOU'RE THE ONLY ONE I COULD TALK TO ABOUT THIS.
THAT SATURDAY, WE HAD PLANS TO GO OUT SHOPPING TOGETHER.
THE TWO OF THEM MADE UP SOME LIE AND BACKED OUT.
I'M SORRY, WE BOTH DID HOR-RIBLY ON TODAY'S TEST, SO...
...WE GOT PULLED INTO AN EXTRA STUDY LESSON THIS SAT-URDAY.
WE'LL GO NEXT TIME!
YEAH? OH, WELL.
GOOD LUCK WITH STUDY-ING!
I ACTED LIKE I DIDN'T KNOW THEY WERE LYING.
I JUST SMILED.

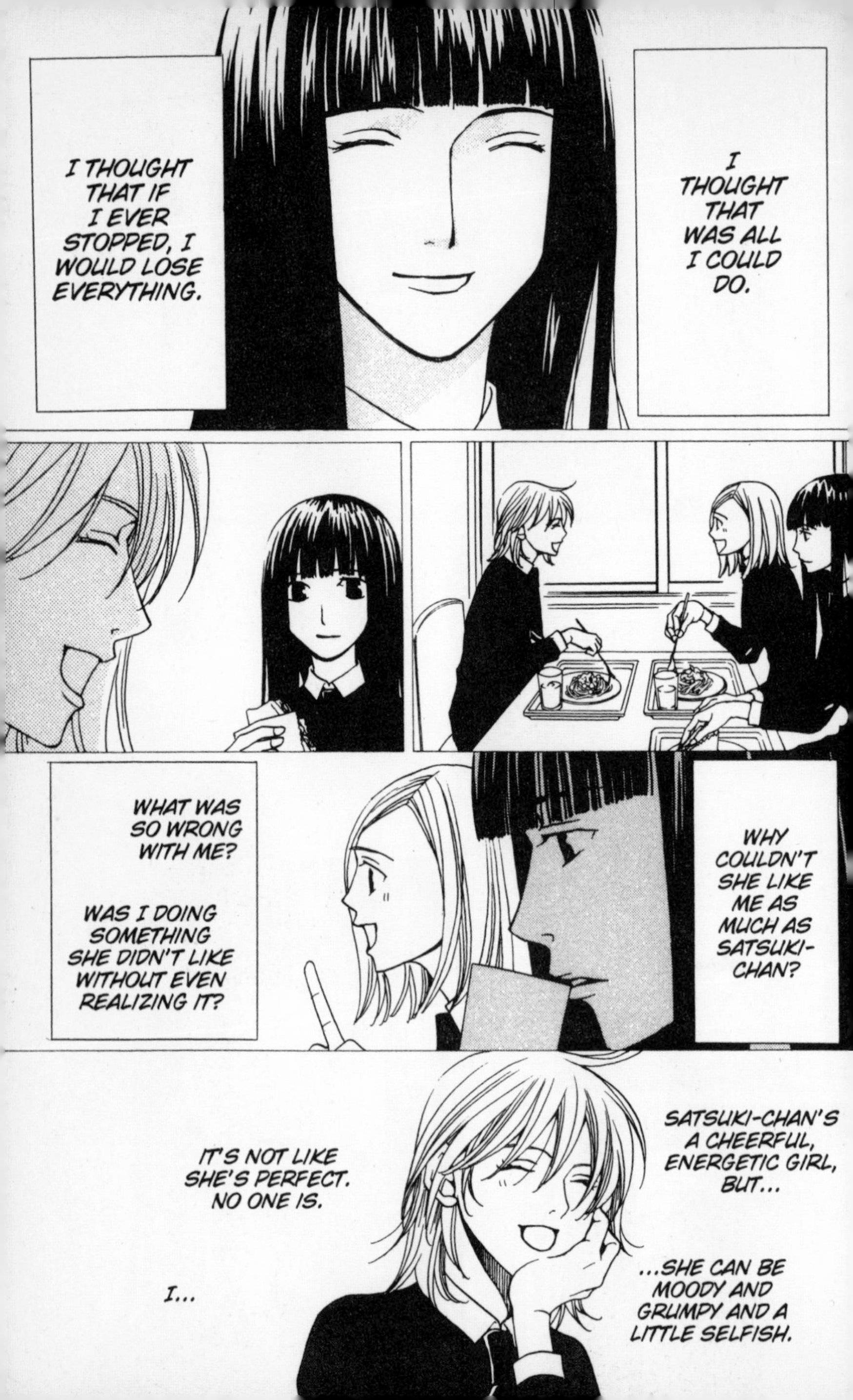
I THOUGHT THAT WAS ALL I COULD DO.
I THOUGHT THAT IF I EVER STOPPED, I WOULD LOSE EVERYTHING.
WHY COULDN'T SHE LIKE ME AS MUCH AS SATSUKI-CHAN?
WHAT WAS SO WRONG WITH ME?
WAS I DOING SOMETHING SHE DIDN'T LIKE WITHOUT EVEN REALIZING IT?
SATSUKI-CHAN'S A CHEERFUL, ENERGETIC GIRL, BUT...
...SHE CAN BE MOODY AND GRUMPY AND A LITTLE SELFISH.
IT'S NOT LIKE SHE'S PERFECT. NO ONE IS.
I...

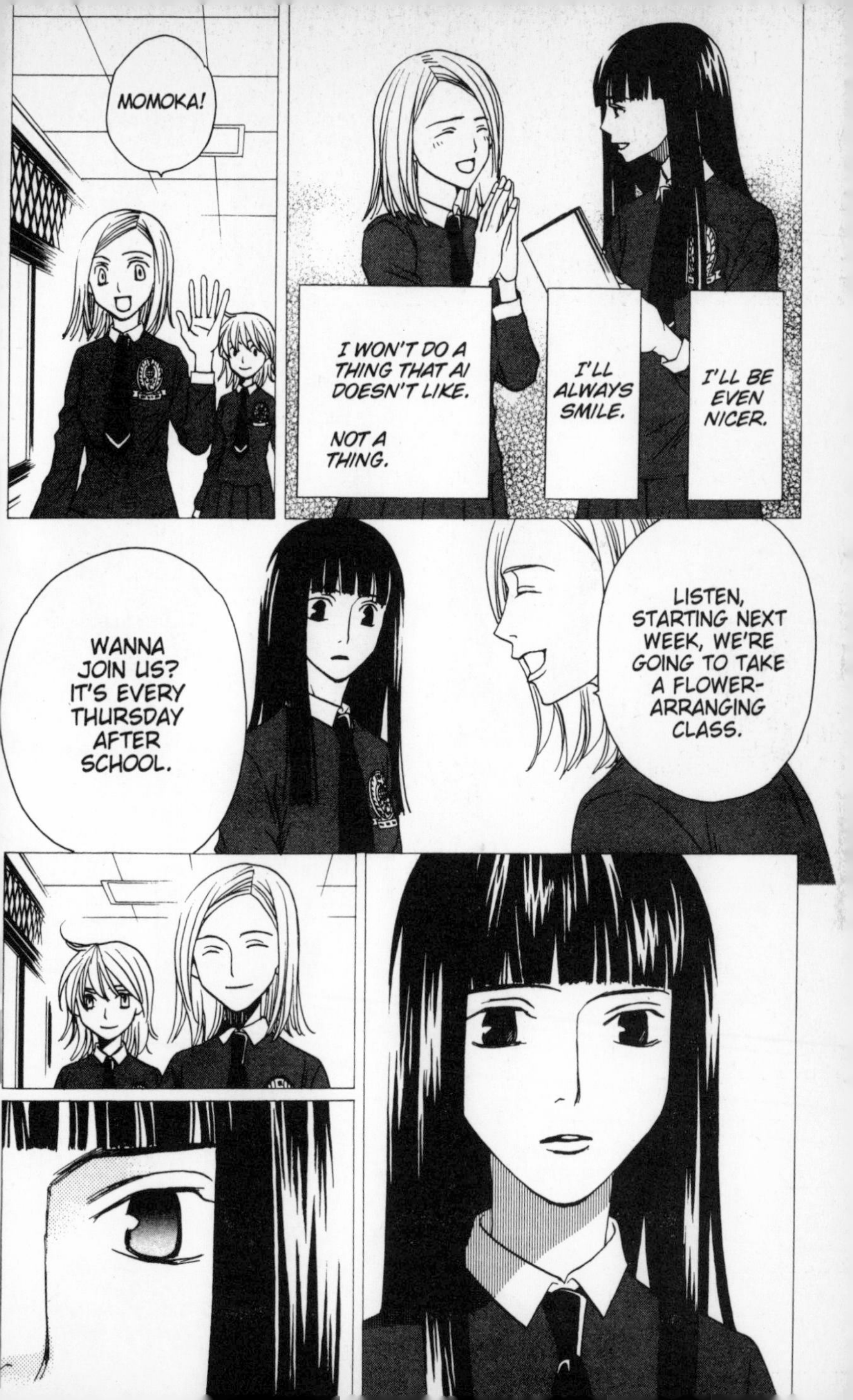
I'LL BE EVEN NICER.
I'LL ALWAYS SMILE.
I WON'T DO A THING THAT AI DOESN'T LIKE.
NOT A THING.
MOMOKA!
LISTEN, STARTING NEXT WEEK, WE'RE GOING TO TAKE A FLOWER-ARRANGING CLASS.
WANNA JOIN US? IT'S EVERY THURSDAY AFTER SCHOOL.

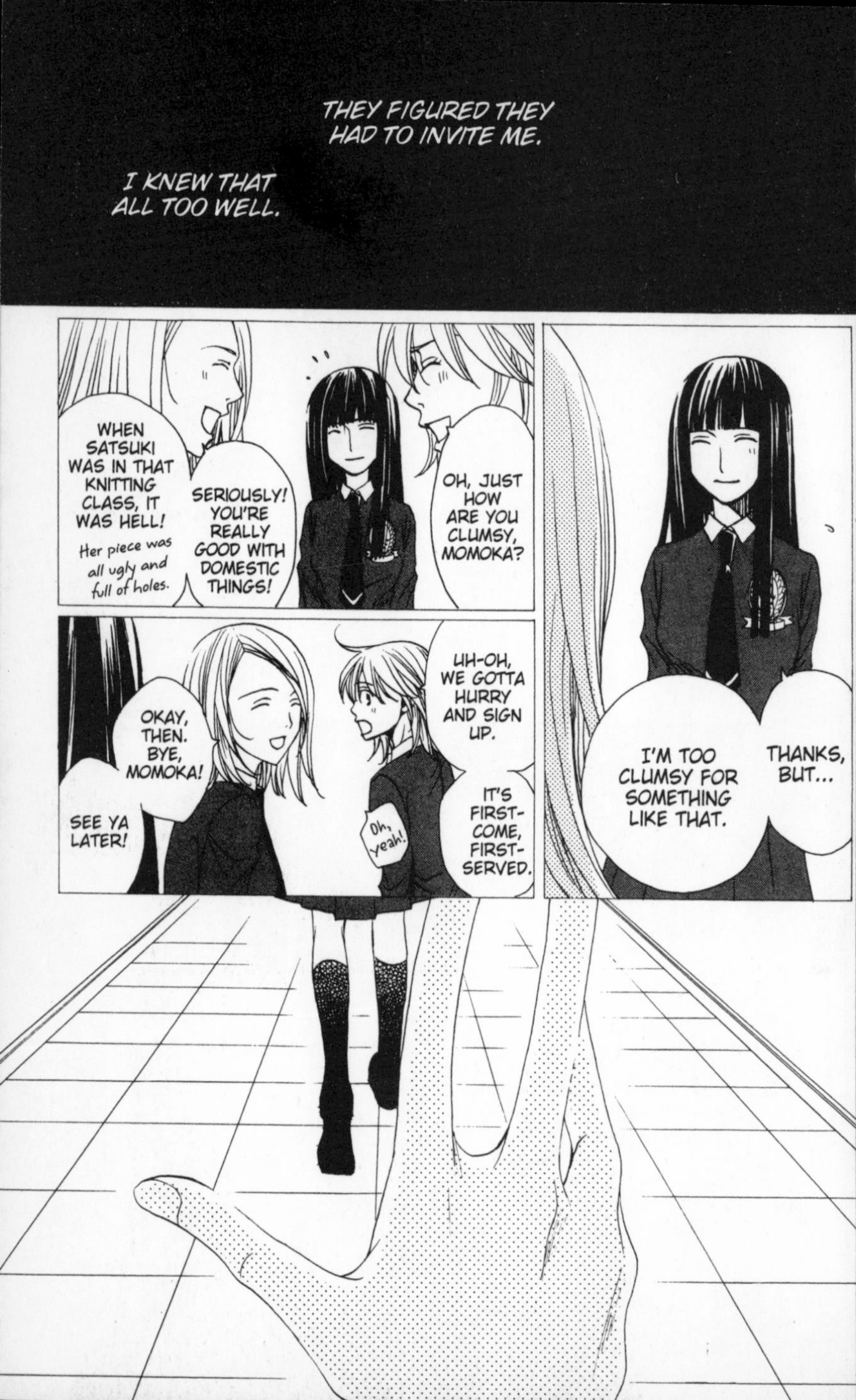
THEY FIGURED THEY HAD TO INVITE ME.
I KNEW THAT ALL TOO WELL.
THANKS, BUT...
I'M TOO CLUMSY FOR SOMETHING LIKE THAT.
OH, JUST HOW ARE YOU CLUMSY, MOMOKA?
SERIOUSLY! YOU'RE REALLY GOOD WITH DOMESTIC THINGS!
WHEN SATSUKI WAS IN THAT KNITTING CLASS, IT WAS HELL!
Her piece was all ugly and full of holes.
UH-OH, WE GOTTA HURRY AND SIGN UP.
IT'S FIRST-COME, FIRST-SERVED.
Oh, yeah!
OKAY, THEN. BYE, MOMOKA!
SEE YA LATER!

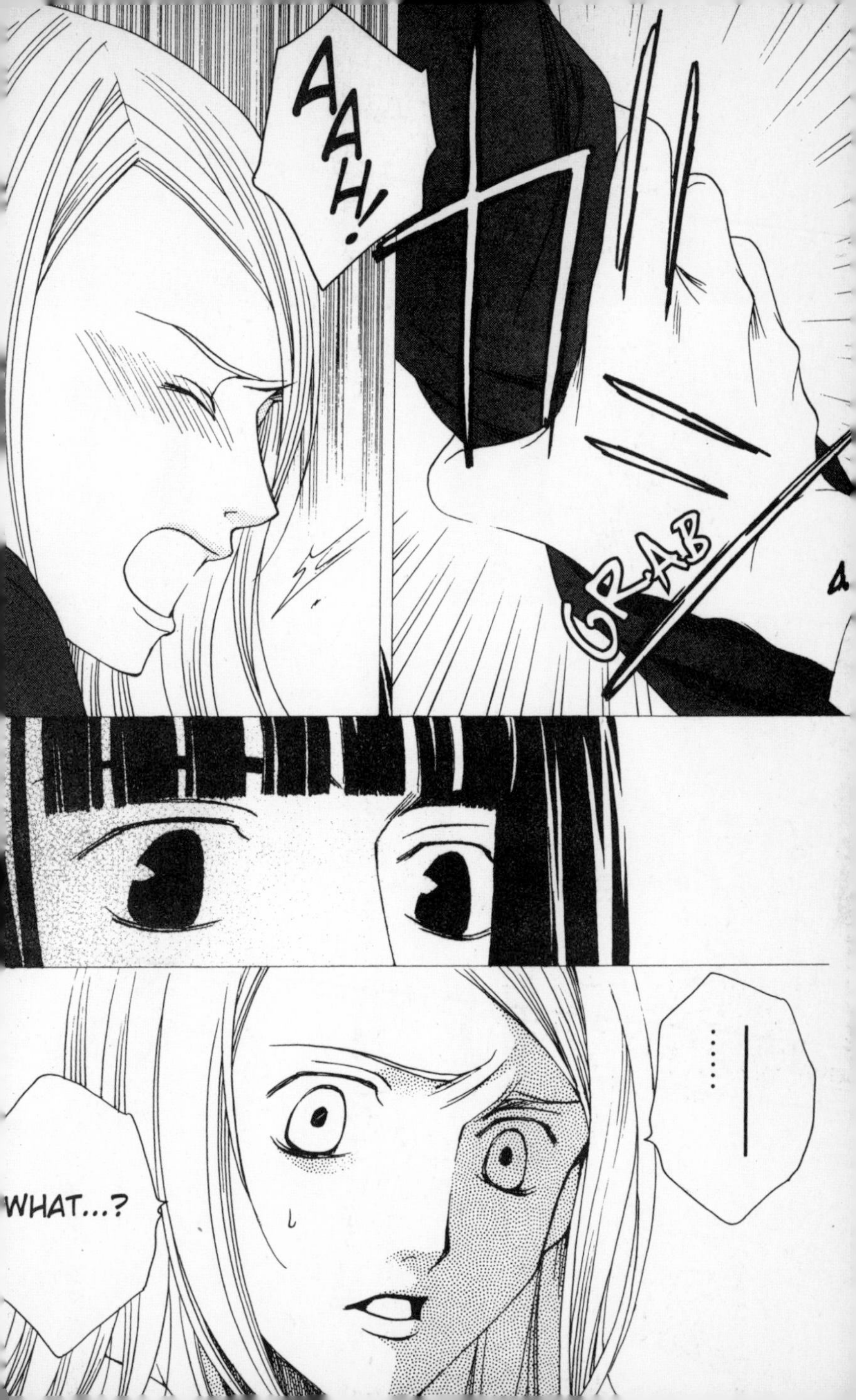
GRAB
AAH!
......
WHAT...?

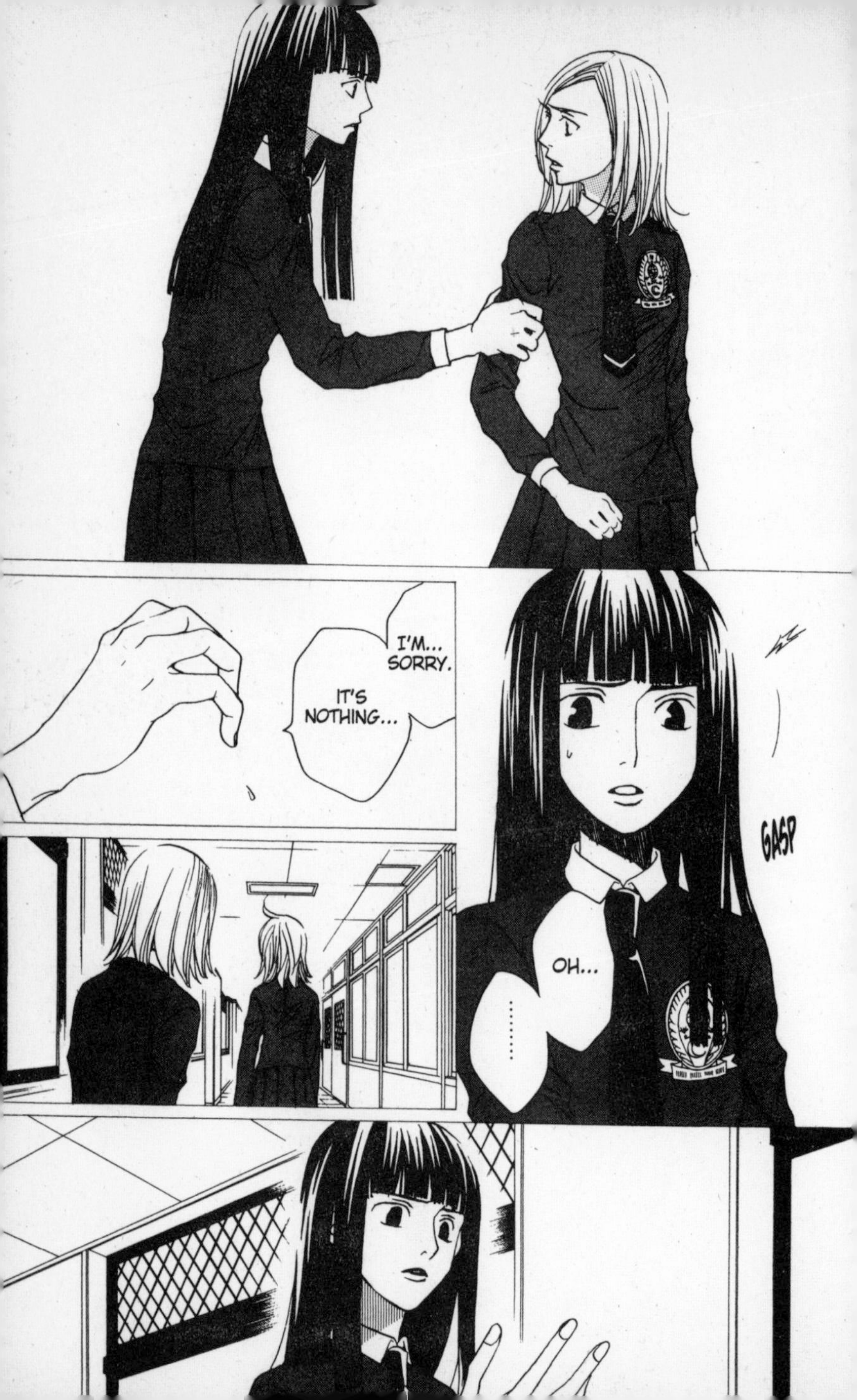
GASP
OH...
......
I'M... SORRY.
IT'S NOTHING...

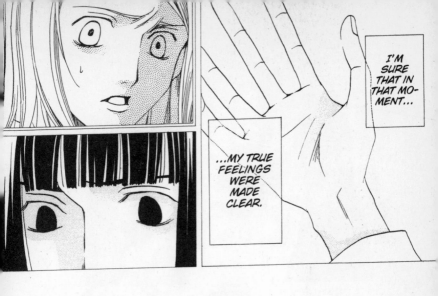

I'M SURE THAT IN THAT MOMENT...

...MY TRUE FEELINGS WERE MADE CLEAR.

THE REAL ME...

...IS SO SELFISH.

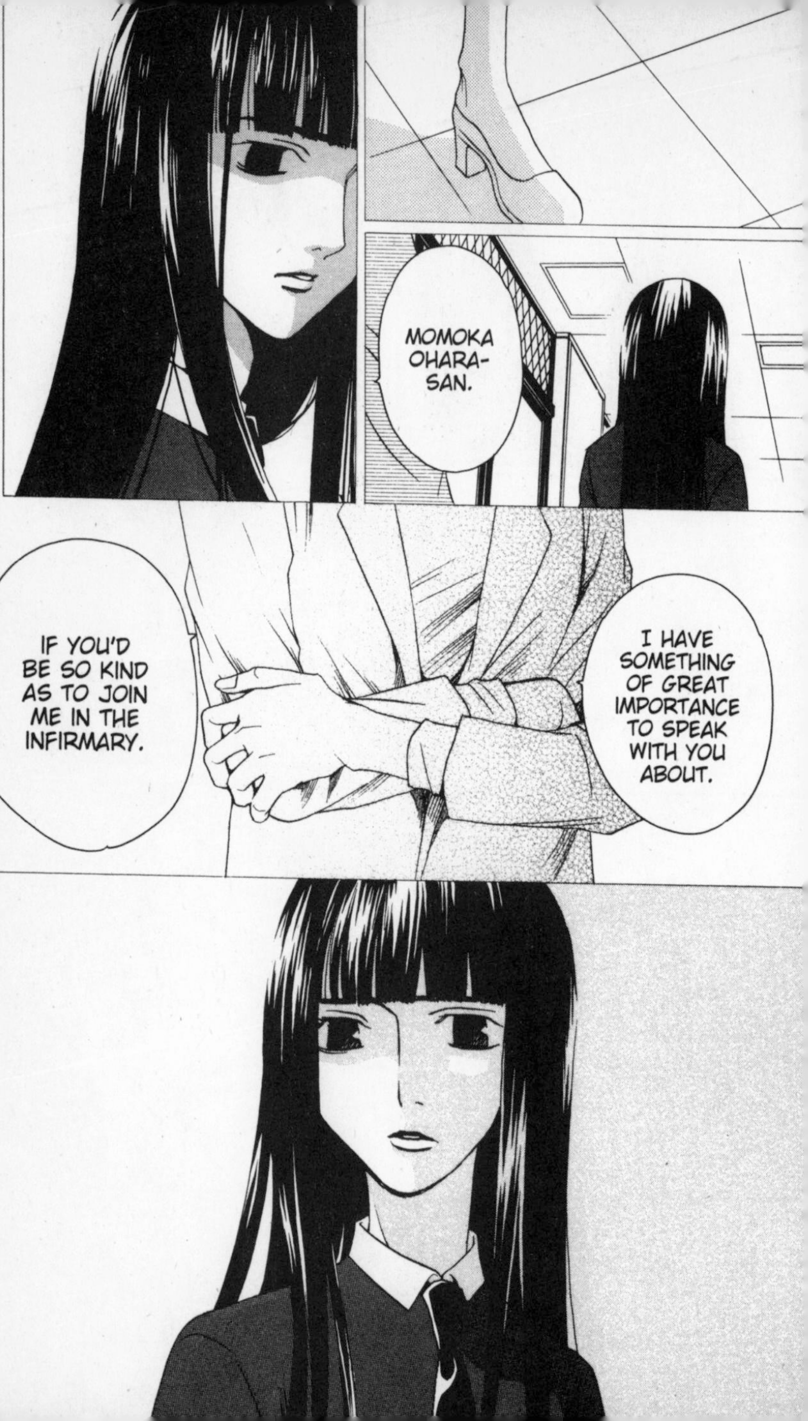
MOMOKA OHARA-SAN.
I HAVE SOMETHING OF GREAT IMPORTANCE TO SPEAK WITH YOU ABOUT.
IF YOU'D BE SO KIND AS TO JOIN ME IN THE INFIRMARY.

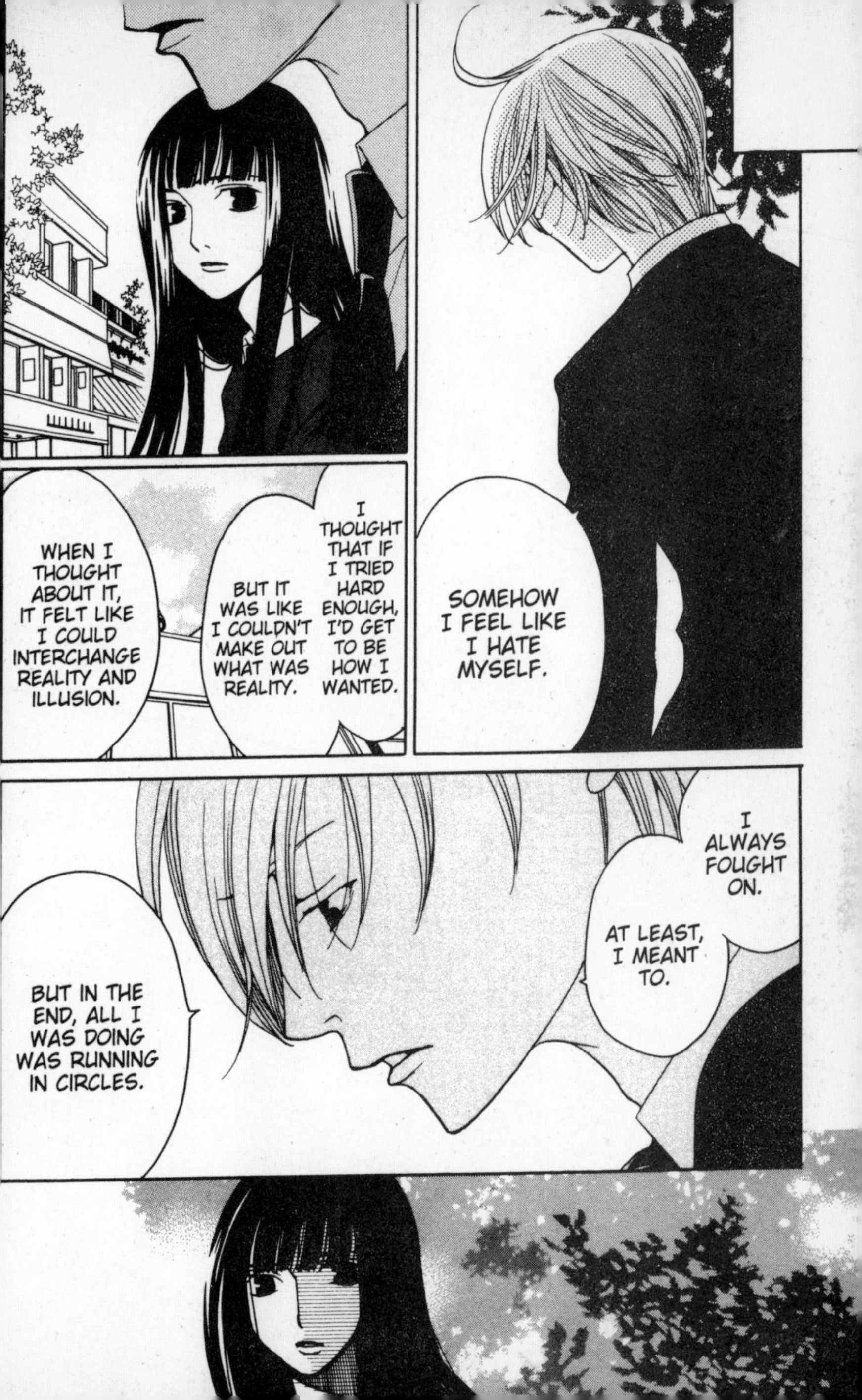
SOMEHOW I FEEL LIKE I HATE MYSELF.
I THOUGHT THAT IF I TRIED HARD ENOUGH, I'D GET TO BE HOW I WANTED.
BUT IT WAS LIKE I COULDN'T MAKE OUT WHAT WAS REALITY.
WHEN I THOUGHT ABOUT IT, IT FELT LIKE I COULD INTERCHANGE REALITY AND ILLUSION.
I ALWAYS FOUGHT ON.
AT LEAST, I MEANT TO.
BUT IN THE END, ALL I WAS DOING WAS RUNNING IN CIRCLES.

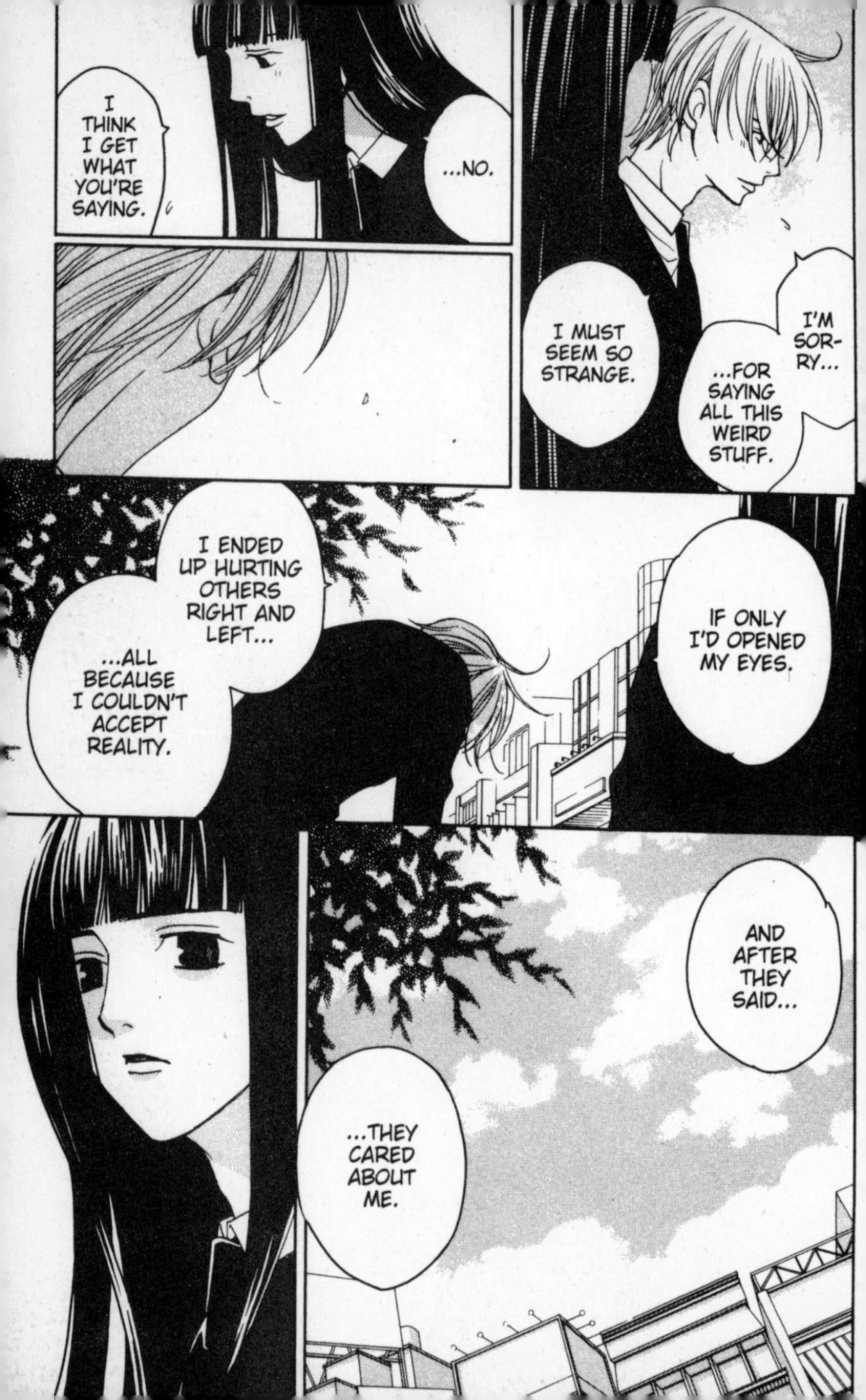
I'M SORRY...
...FOR SAYING ALL THIS WEIRD STUFF.
I MUST SEEM SO STRANGE.
...NO.
I THINK I GET WHAT YOU'RE SAYING.
IF ONLY I'D OPENED MY EYES.
I ENDED UP HURTING OTHERS RIGHT AND LEFT...
...ALL BECAUSE I COULDN'T ACCEPT REALITY.
AND AFTER THEY SAID...
...THEY CARED ABOUT ME.

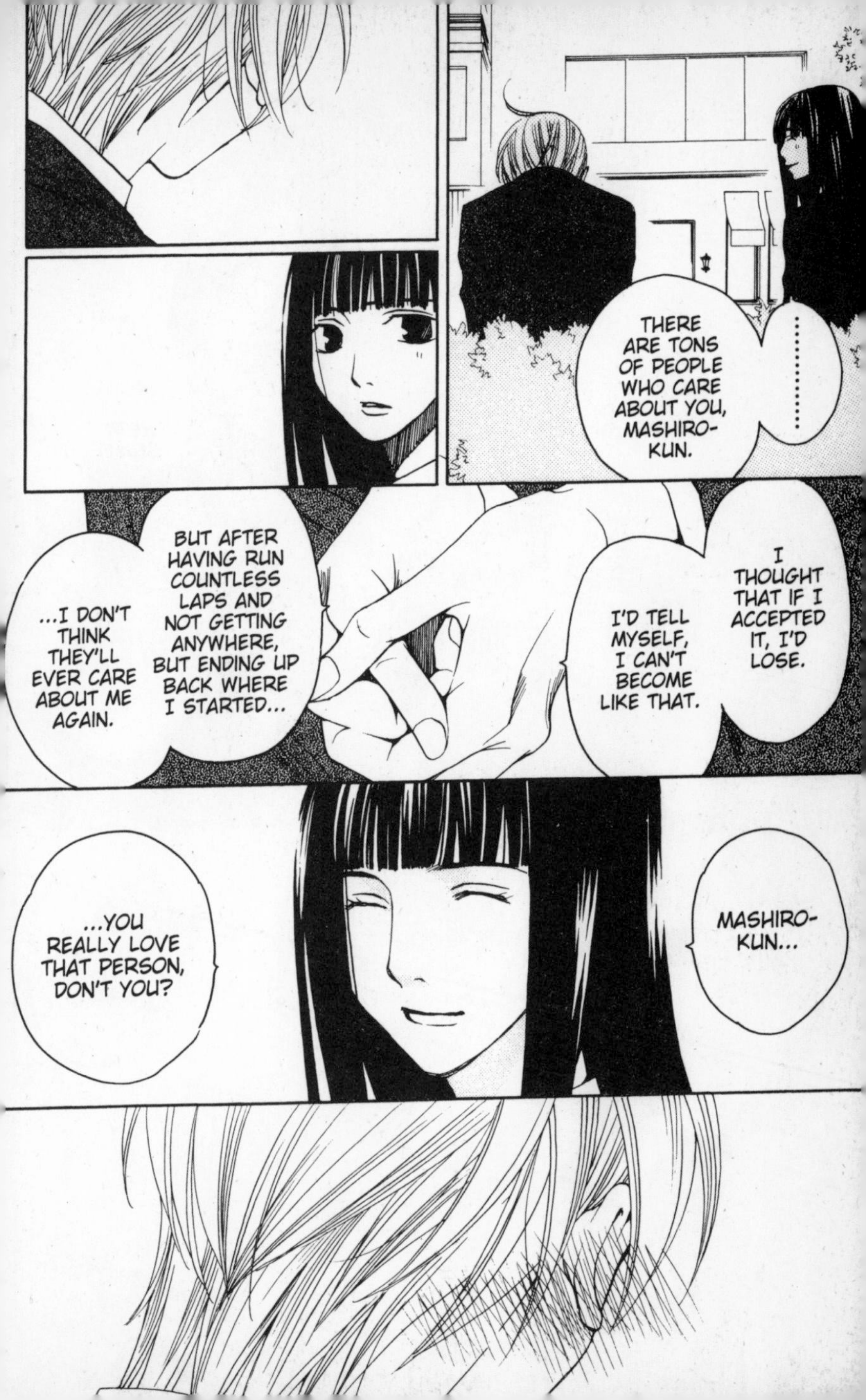
......
THERE ARE TONS OF PEOPLE WHO CARE ABOUT YOU, MASHIRO-KUN.
I THOUGHT THAT IF I ACCEPTED IT, I'D LOSE.
I'D TELL MYSELF, I CAN'T BECOME LIKE THAT.
BUT AFTER HAVING RUN COUNTLESS LAPS AND NOT GETTING ANYWHERE, BUT ENDING UP BACK WHERE I STARTED...
...I DON'T THINK THEY'LL EVER CARE ABOUT ME AGAIN.
MASHIRO-KUN...
...YOU REALLY LOVE THAT PERSON, DON'T YOU?

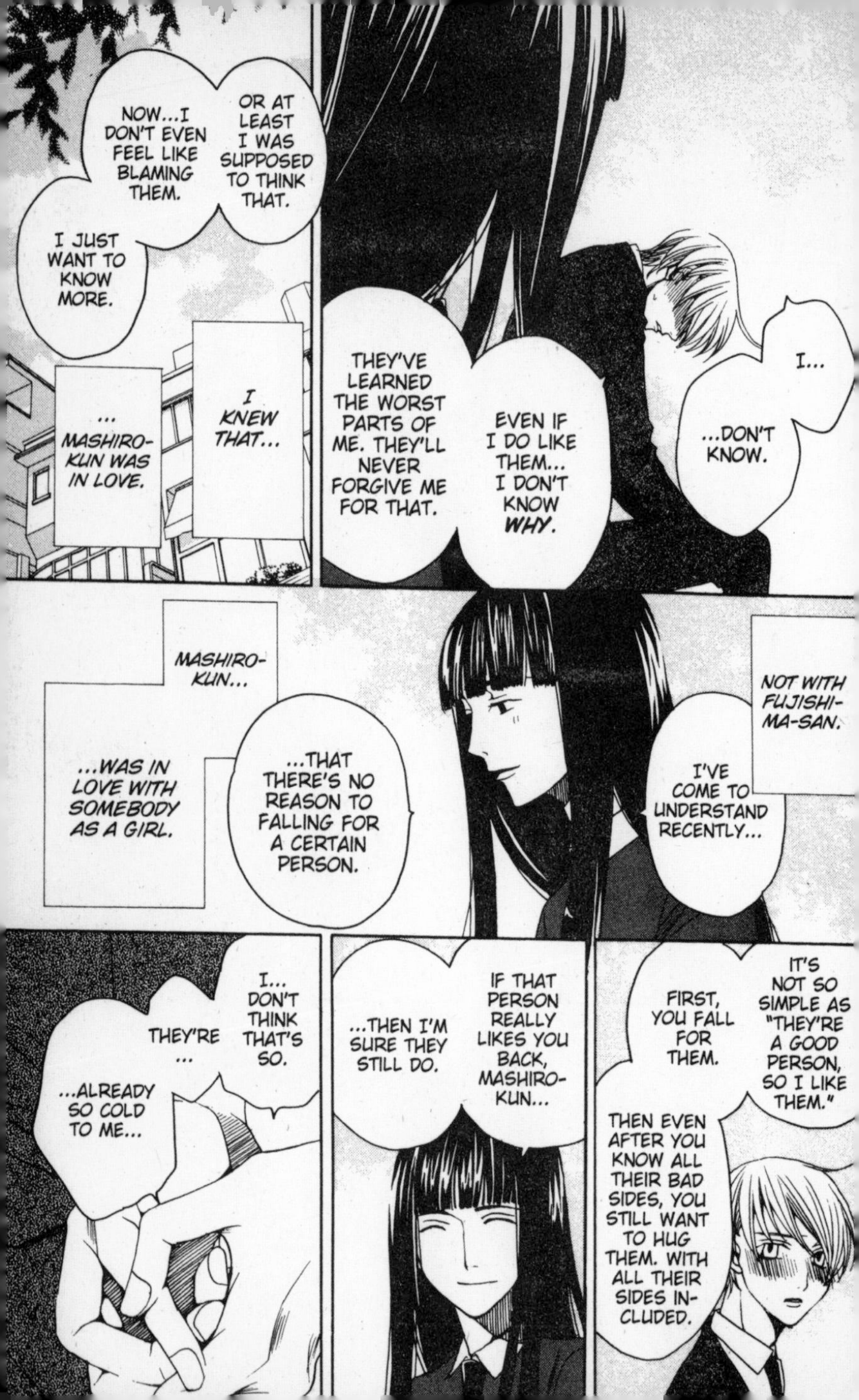
I...
...DON'T KNOW.
EVEN IF I DO LIKE THEM... I DON'T KNOW *WHY*.
THEY'VE LEARNED THE WORST PARTS OF ME. THEY'LL NEVER FORGIVE ME FOR THAT.
OR AT LEAST I WAS SUPPOSED TO THINK THAT.
NOW...I DON'T EVEN FEEL LIKE BLAMING THEM.
I JUST WANT TO KNOW MORE.
I KNEW THAT...
...MASHIRO-KUN WAS IN LOVE.
NOT WITH FUJISHIMA-SAN.
I'VE COME TO UNDERSTAND RECENTLY...
...THAT THERE'S NO REASON TO FALLING FOR A CERTAIN PERSON.
MASHIRO-KUN...
...WAS IN LOVE WITH SOMEBODY AS A GIRL.
IT'S NOT SO SIMPLE AS "THEY'RE A GOOD PERSON, SO I LIKE THEM."
FIRST, YOU FALL FOR THEM.
THEN EVEN AFTER YOU KNOW ALL THEIR BAD SIDES, YOU STILL WANT TO HUG THEM. WITH ALL THEIR SIDES INCLUDED.
IF THAT PERSON REALLY LIKES YOU BACK, MASHIRO-KUN...
...THEN I'M SURE THEY STILL DO.
I... DON'T THINK THAT'S SO.
THEY'RE ...
...ALREADY SO COLD TO ME...

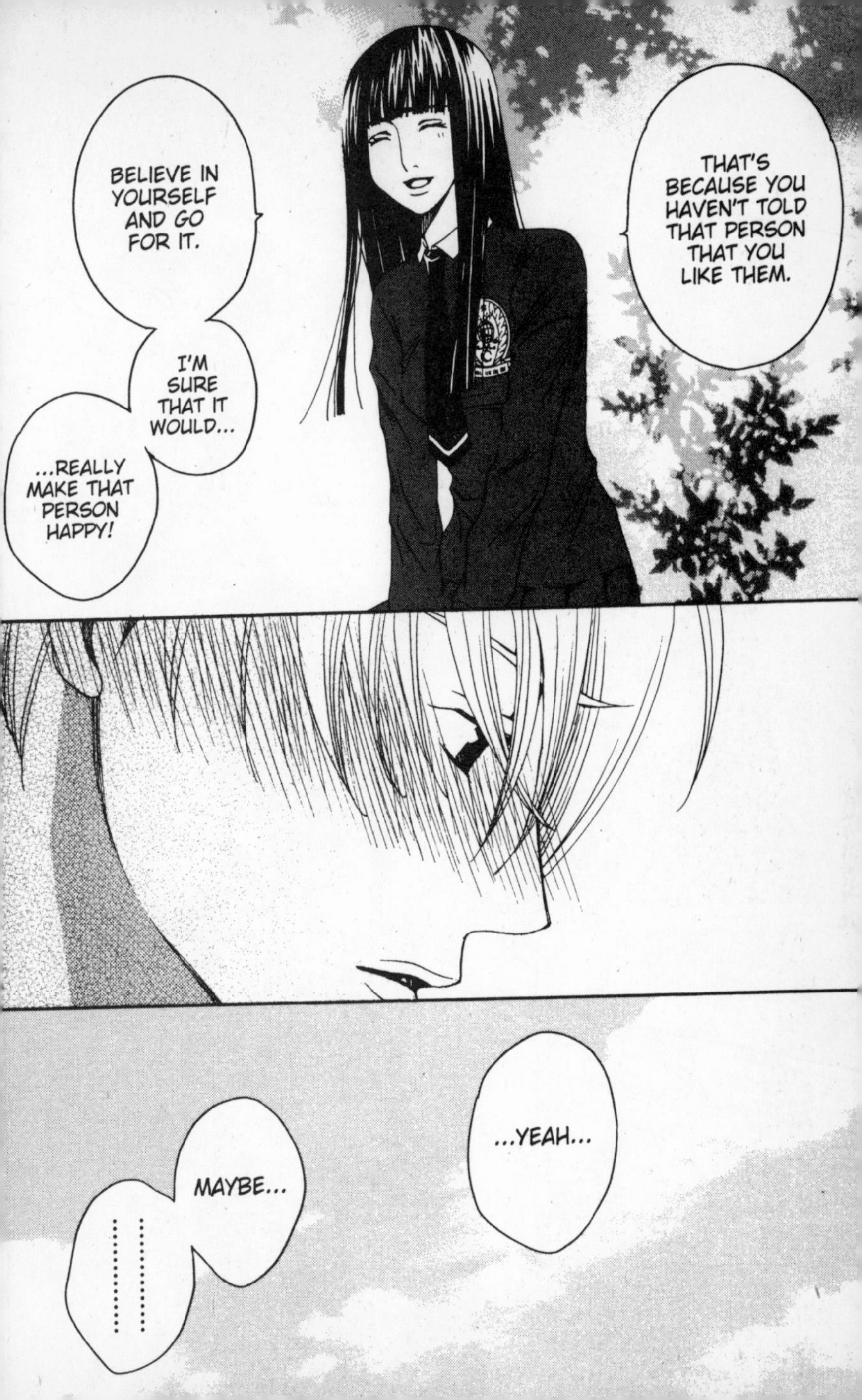
THAT'S BECAUSE YOU HAVEN'T TOLD THAT PERSON THAT YOU LIKE THEM.
BELIEVE IN YOURSELF AND GO FOR IT.
I'M SURE THAT IT WOULD...
...REALLY MAKE THAT PERSON HAPPY!
...YEAH...
MAYBE...
......

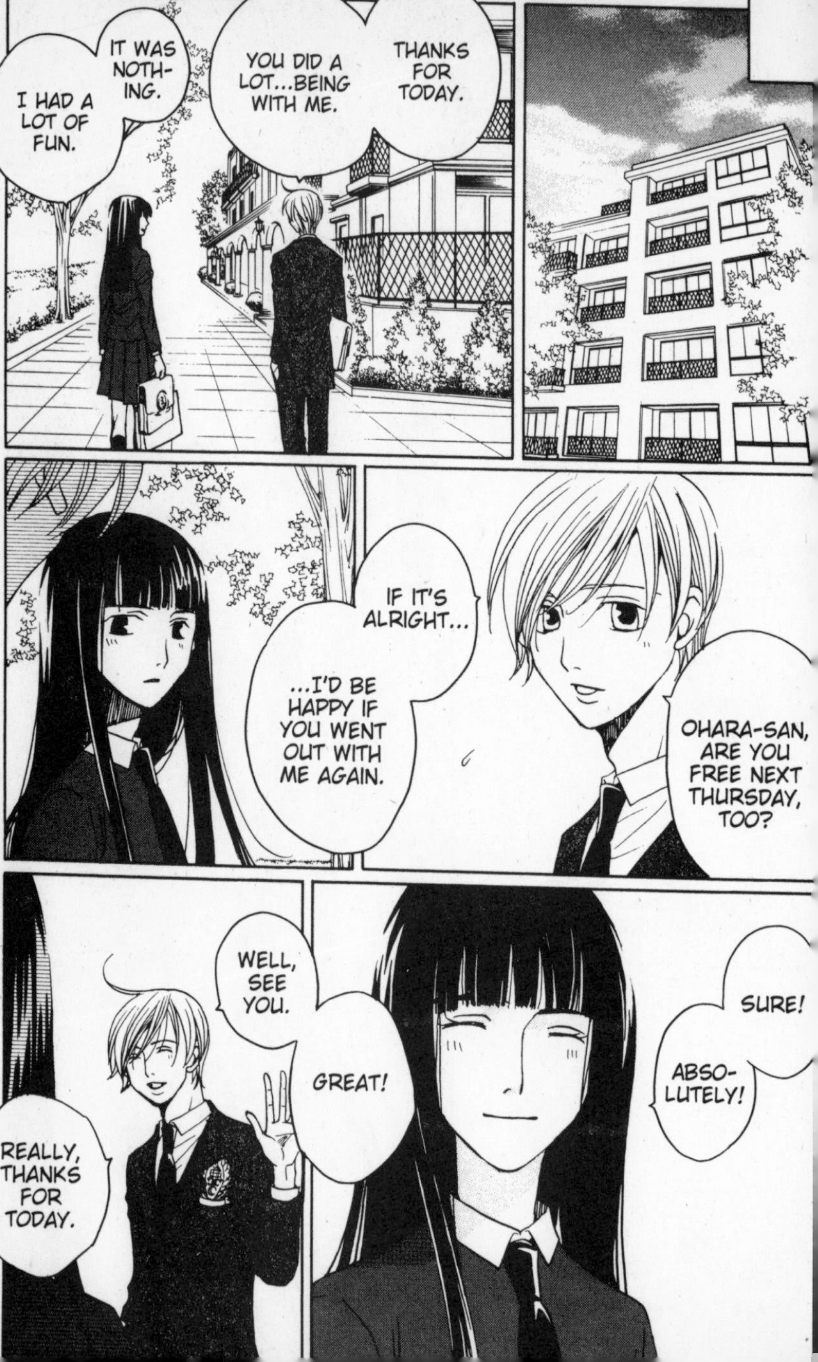
THANKS FOR TODAY.
YOU DID A LOT...BEING WITH ME.
IT WAS NOTHING.
I HAD A LOT OF FUN.
OHARA-SAN, ARE YOU FREE NEXT THURSDAY, TOO?
IF IT'S ALRIGHT...
...I'D BE HAPPY IF YOU WENT OUT WITH ME AGAIN.
SURE!
ABSOLUTELY!
GREAT!
WELL, SEE YOU.
REALLY, THANKS FOR TODAY.

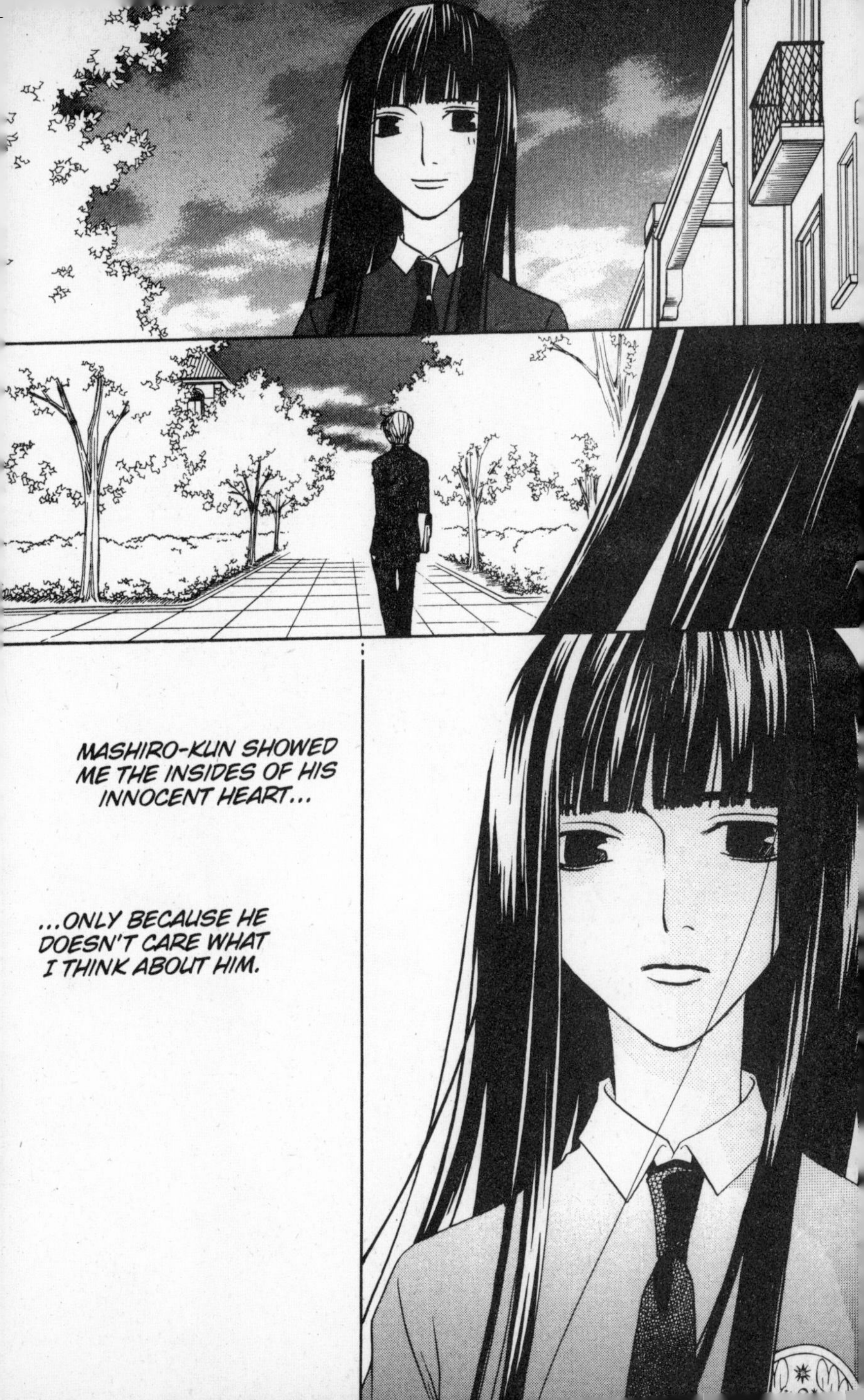
MASHIRO-KUN SHOWED ME THE INSIDES OF HIS INNOCENT HEART...
...ONLY BECAUSE HE DOESN'T CARE WHAT I THINK ABOUT HIM.

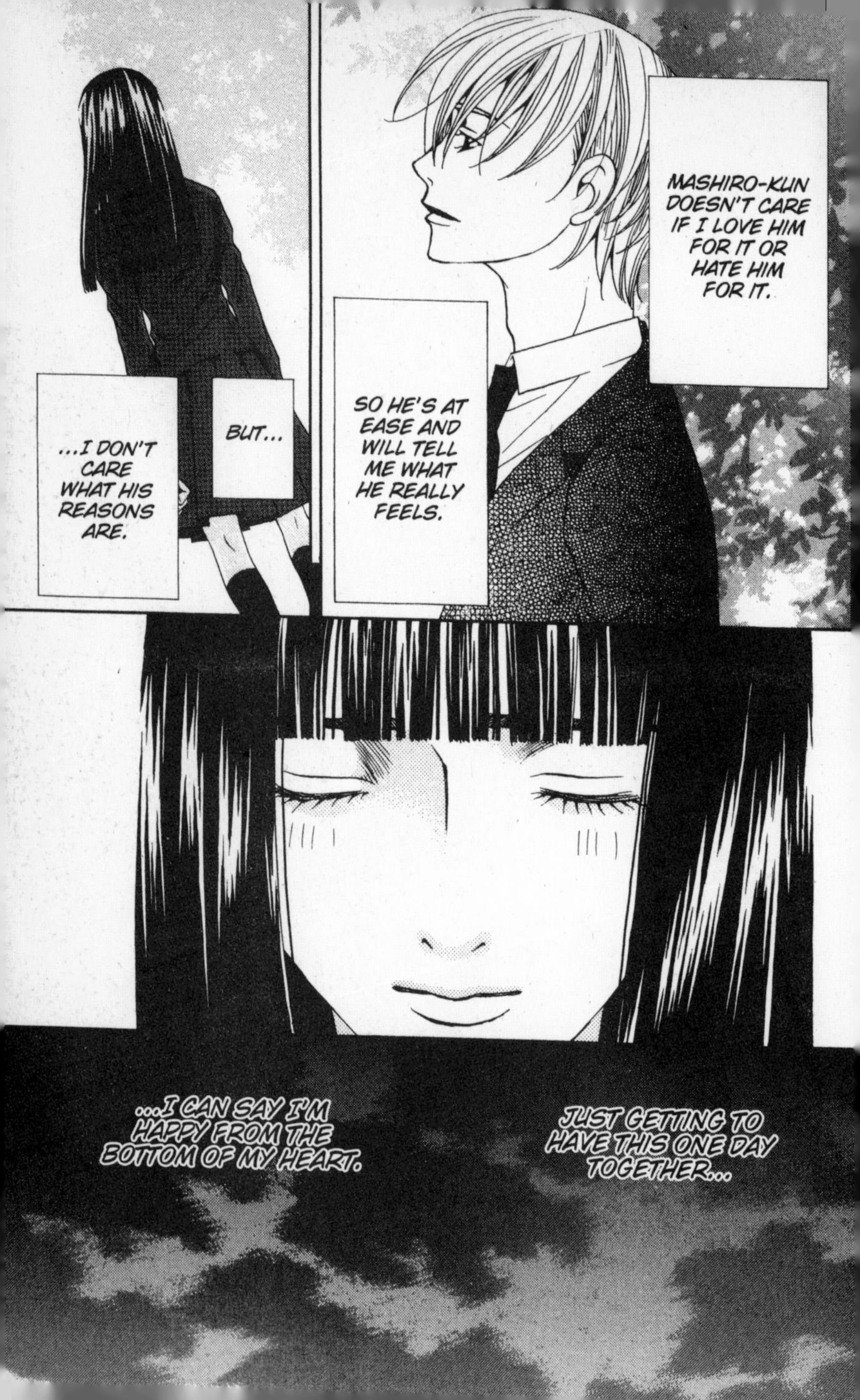
MASHIRO-KUN DOESN'T CARE IF I LOVE HIM FOR IT OR HATE HIM FOR IT.
SO HE'S AT EASE AND WILL TELL ME WHAT HE REALLY FEELS.
BUT...
...I DON'T CARE WHAT HIS REASONS ARE.
JUST GETTING TO HAVE THIS ONE DAY TOGETHER...
...I CAN SAY I'M HAPPY FROM THE BOTTOM OF MY HEART.

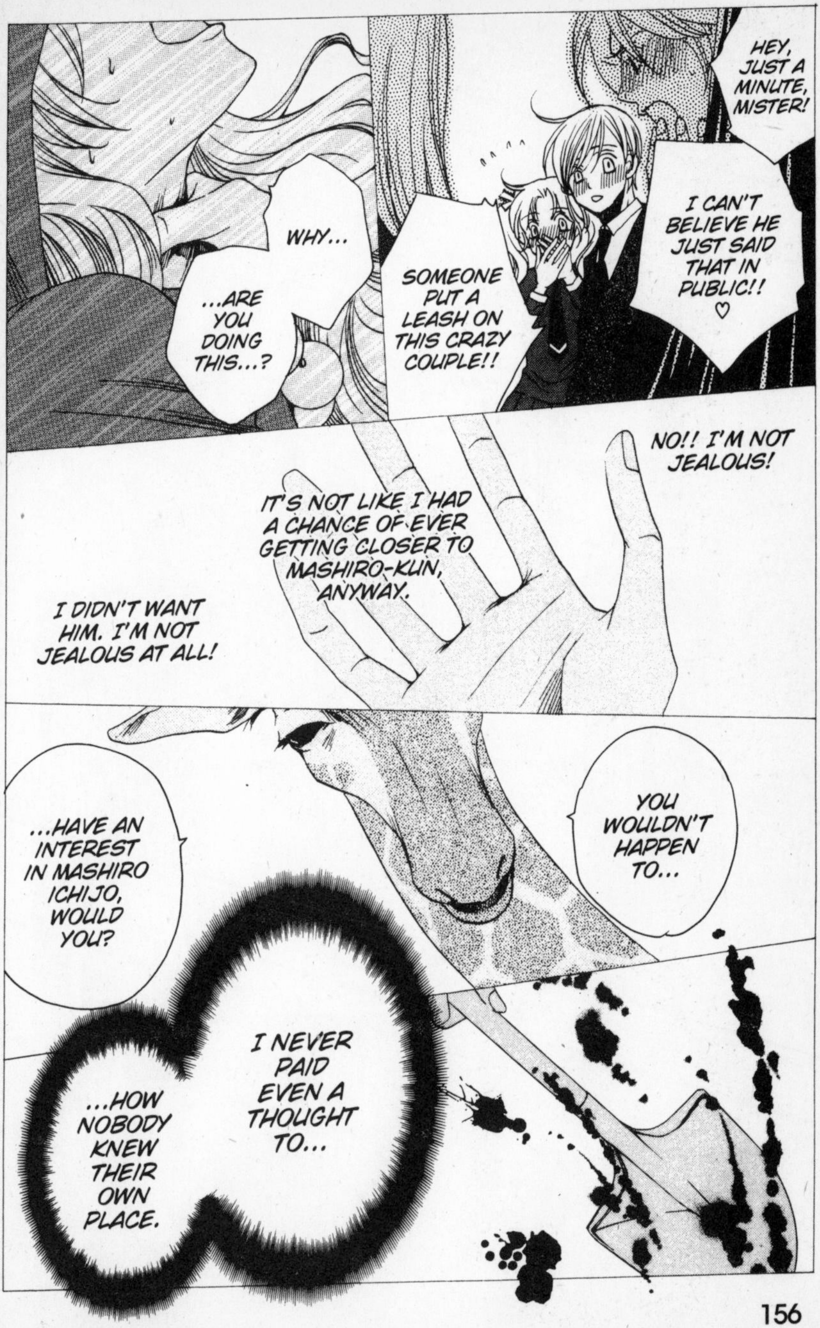
HEY, JUST A MINUTE, MISTER!
I CAN'T BELIEVE HE JUST SAID THAT IN PUBLIC!! ♡
SOMEONE PUT A LEASH ON THIS CRAZY COUPLE!!
WHY...
...ARE YOU DOING THIS...?
NO!! I'M NOT JEALOUS!
IT'S NOT LIKE I HAD A CHANCE OF EVER GETTING CLOSER TO MASHIRO-KUN, ANYWAY.
I DIDN'T WANT HIM. I'M NOT JEALOUS AT ALL!
YOU WOULDN'T HAPPEN TO...
...HAVE AN INTEREST IN MASHIRO ICHIJO, WOULD YOU?
I NEVER PAID EVEN A THOUGHT TO...
...HOW NOBODY KNEW THEIR OWN PLACE.

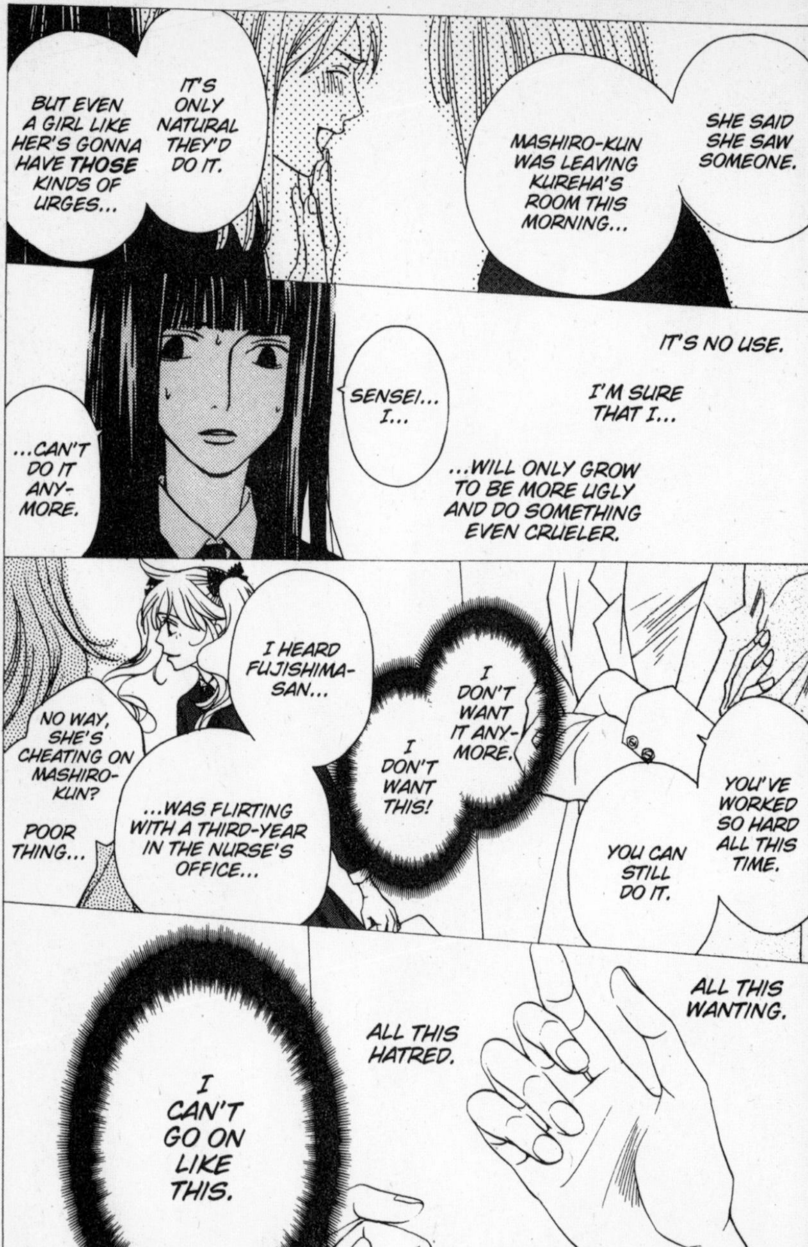
SHE SAID SHE SAW SOMEONE.
MASHIRO-KUN WAS LEAVING KUREHA'S ROOM THIS MORNING...
IT'S ONLY NATURAL THEY'D DO IT.
BUT EVEN A GIRL LIKE HER'S GONNA HAVE THOSE KINDS OF URGES...
IT'S NO USE.
I'M SURE THAT I...
...WILL ONLY GROW TO BE MORE UGLY AND DO SOMETHING EVEN CRUELER.
SENSEI... I...
...CAN'T DO IT ANYMORE.
YOU'VE WORKED SO HARD ALL THIS TIME.
YOU CAN STILL DO IT.
I DON'T WANT IT ANYMORE.
I DON'T WANT THIS!
I HEARD FUJISHIMA-SAN...
...WAS FLIRTING WITH A THIRD-YEAR IN THE NURSE'S OFFICE...
NO WAY, SHE'S CHEATING ON MASHIRO-KUN?
POOR THING...
ALL THIS WANTING.
ALL THIS HATRED.
I CAN'T GO ON LIKE THIS.

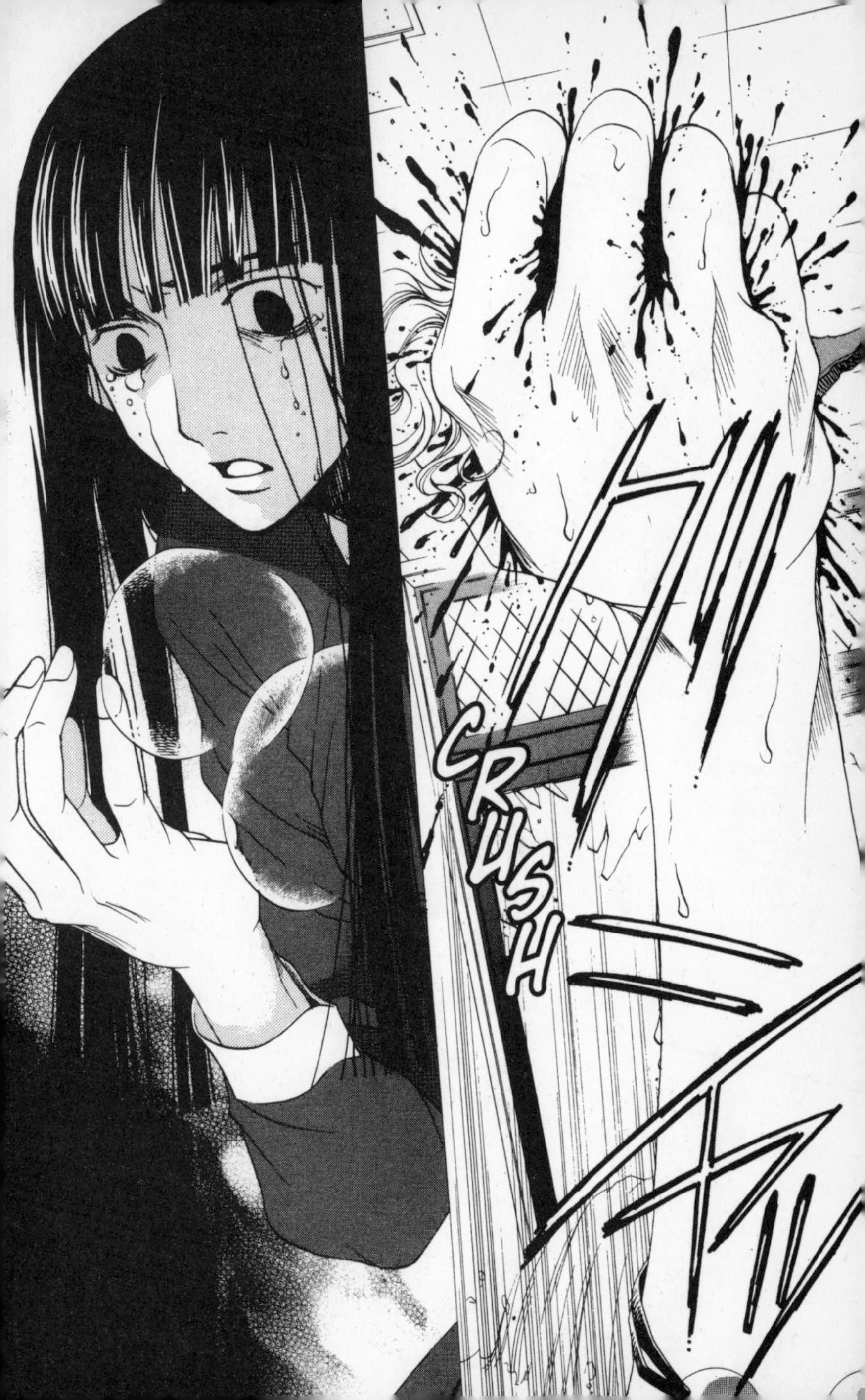
CRUSH

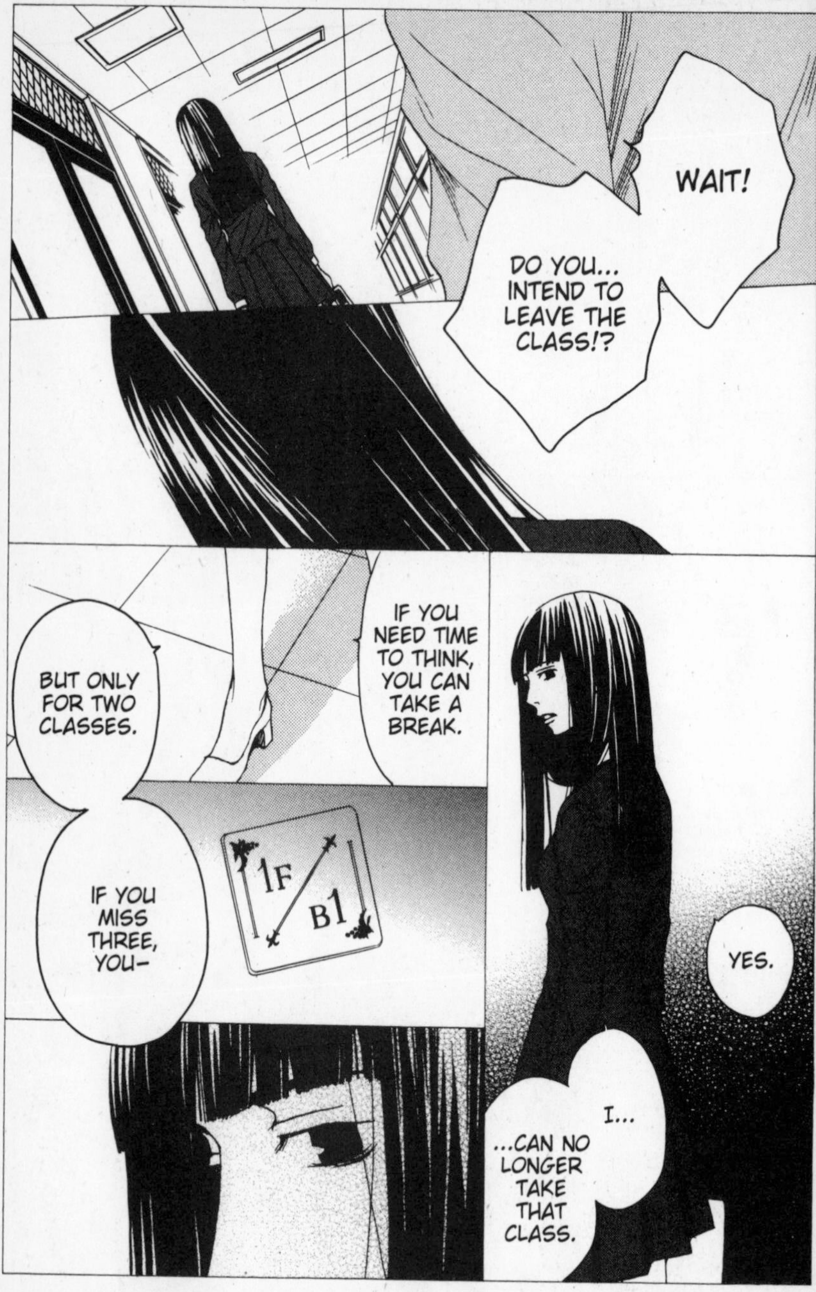
WAIT!
DO YOU... INTEND TO LEAVE THE CLASS!?
IF YOU NEED TIME TO THINK, YOU CAN TAKE A BREAK.
BUT ONLY FOR TWO CLASSES.
1F B1
IF YOU MISS THREE, YOU-
YES.
I...
...CAN NO LONGER TAKE THAT CLASS.

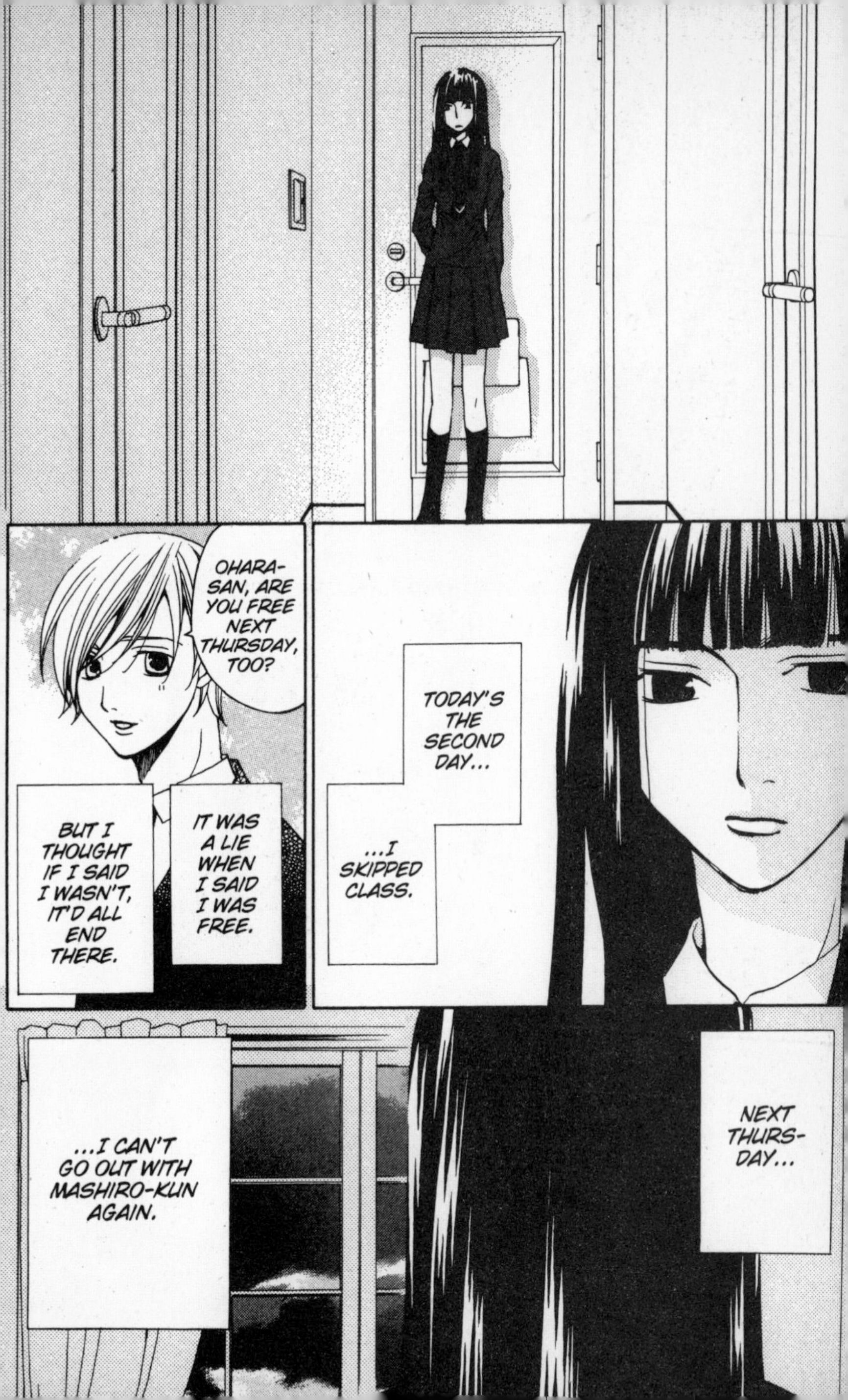
TODAY'S THE SECOND DAY...
...I SKIPPED CLASS.
OHARA-SAN, ARE YOU FREE NEXT THURSDAY, TOO?
IT WAS A LIE WHEN I SAID I WAS FREE.
BUT I THOUGHT IF I SAID I WASN'T, IT'D ALL END THERE.
NEXT THURS-DAY...
...I CAN'T GO OUT WITH MASHIRO-KUN AGAIN.

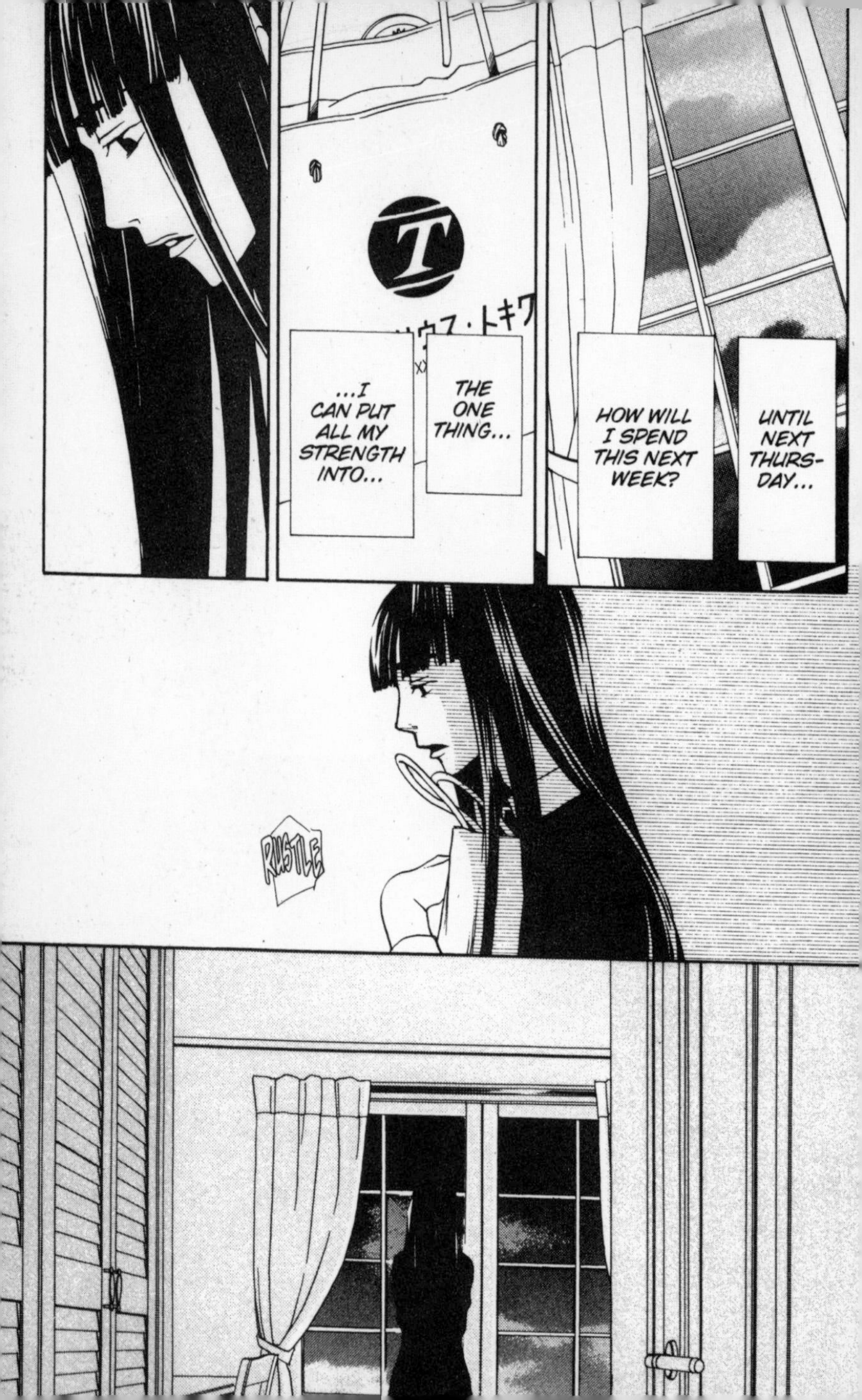
UNTIL NEXT THURS-DAY...
HOW WILL I SPEND THIS NEXT WEEK?
THE ONE THING...
...I CAN PUT ALL MY STRENGTH INTO...
RUSTLE

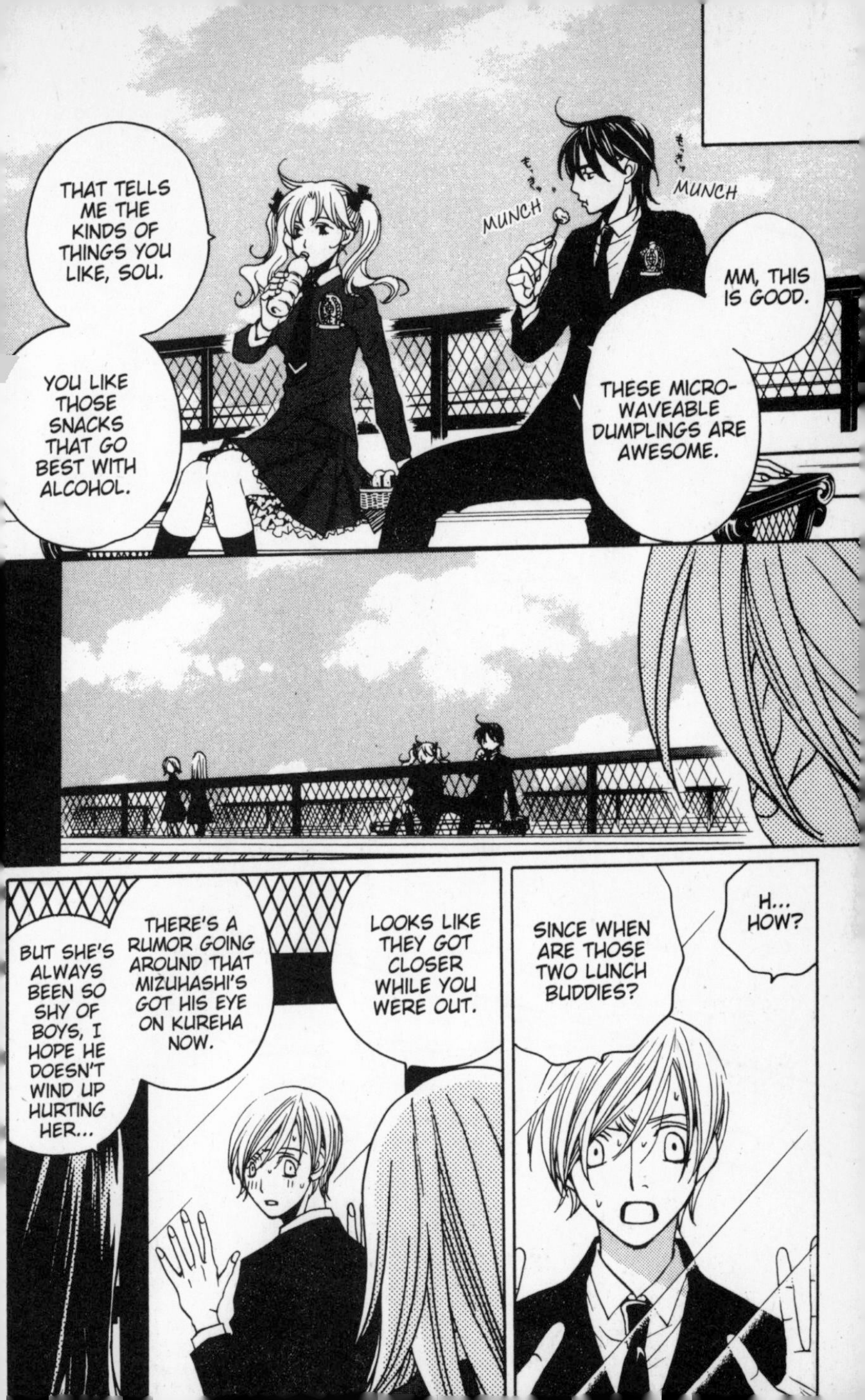
MUNCH
MUNCH
MM, THIS IS GOOD.
THESE MICRO-WAVEABLE DUMPLINGS ARE AWESOME.
THAT TELLS ME THE KINDS OF THINGS YOU LIKE, SOU.
YOU LIKE THOSE SNACKS THAT GO BEST WITH ALCOHOL.
H... HOW?
SINCE WHEN ARE THOSE TWO LUNCH BUDDIES?
LOOKS LIKE THEY GOT CLOSER WHILE YOU WERE OUT.
THERE'S A RUMOR GOING AROUND THAT MIZUHASHI'S GOT HIS EYE ON KUREHA NOW.
BUT SHE'S ALWAYS BEEN SO SHY OF BOYS, I HOPE HE DOESN'T WIND UP HURTING HER...

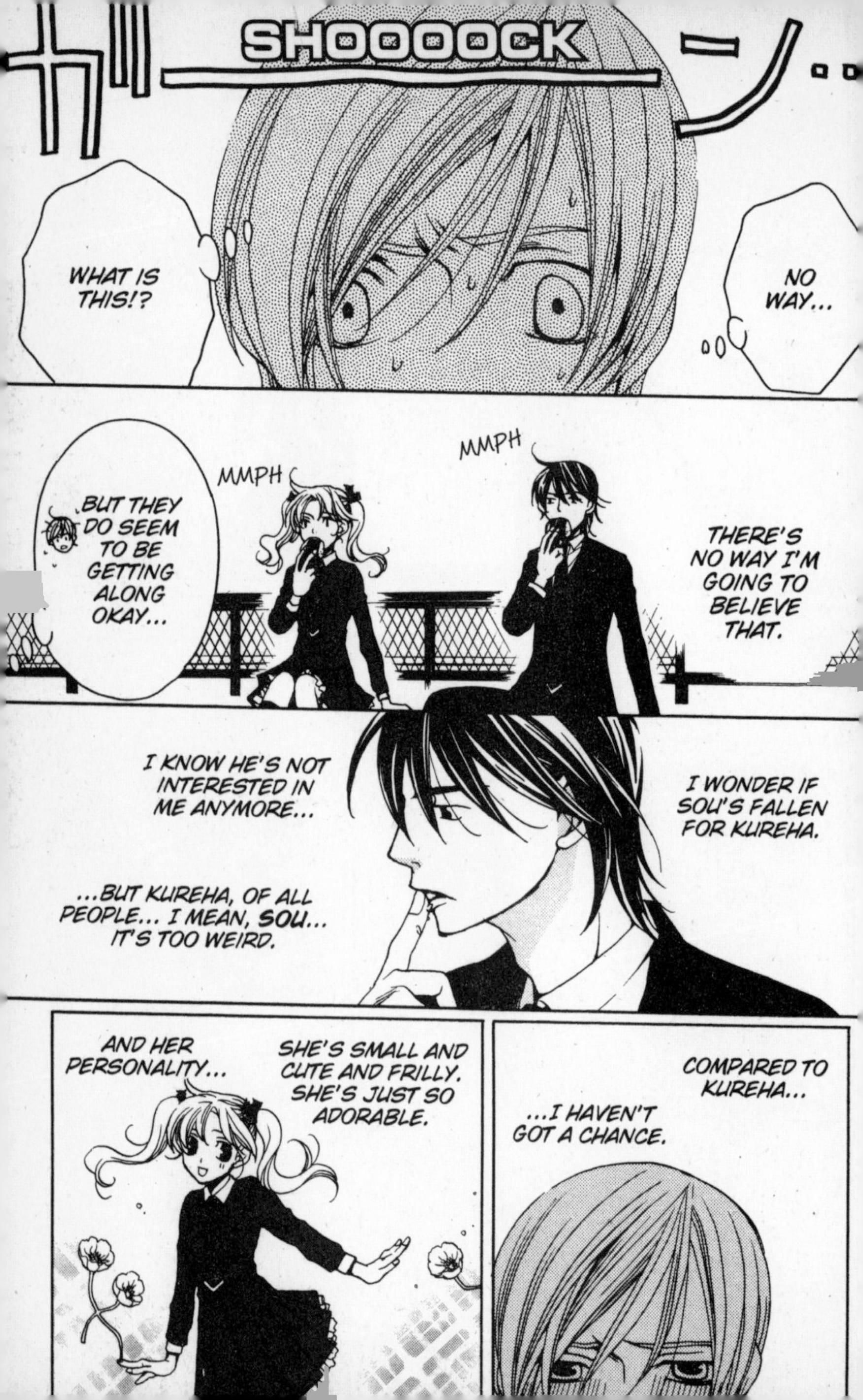
SHOOOOCK
NO WAY...
WHAT IS THIS!?
THERE'S NO WAY I'M GOING TO BELIEVE THAT.
MMPH
MMPH
BUT THEY DO SEEM TO BE GETTING ALONG OKAY...
I WONDER IF SOU'S FALLEN FOR KUREHA.
I KNOW HE'S NOT INTERESTED IN ME ANYMORE...
...BUT KUREHA, OF ALL PEOPLE... I MEAN, SOU... IT'S TOO WEIRD.
COMPARED TO KUREHA...
...I HAVEN'T GOT A CHANCE.
SHE'S SMALL AND CUTE AND FRILLY. SHE'S JUST SO ADORABLE.
AND HER PERSONALITY...

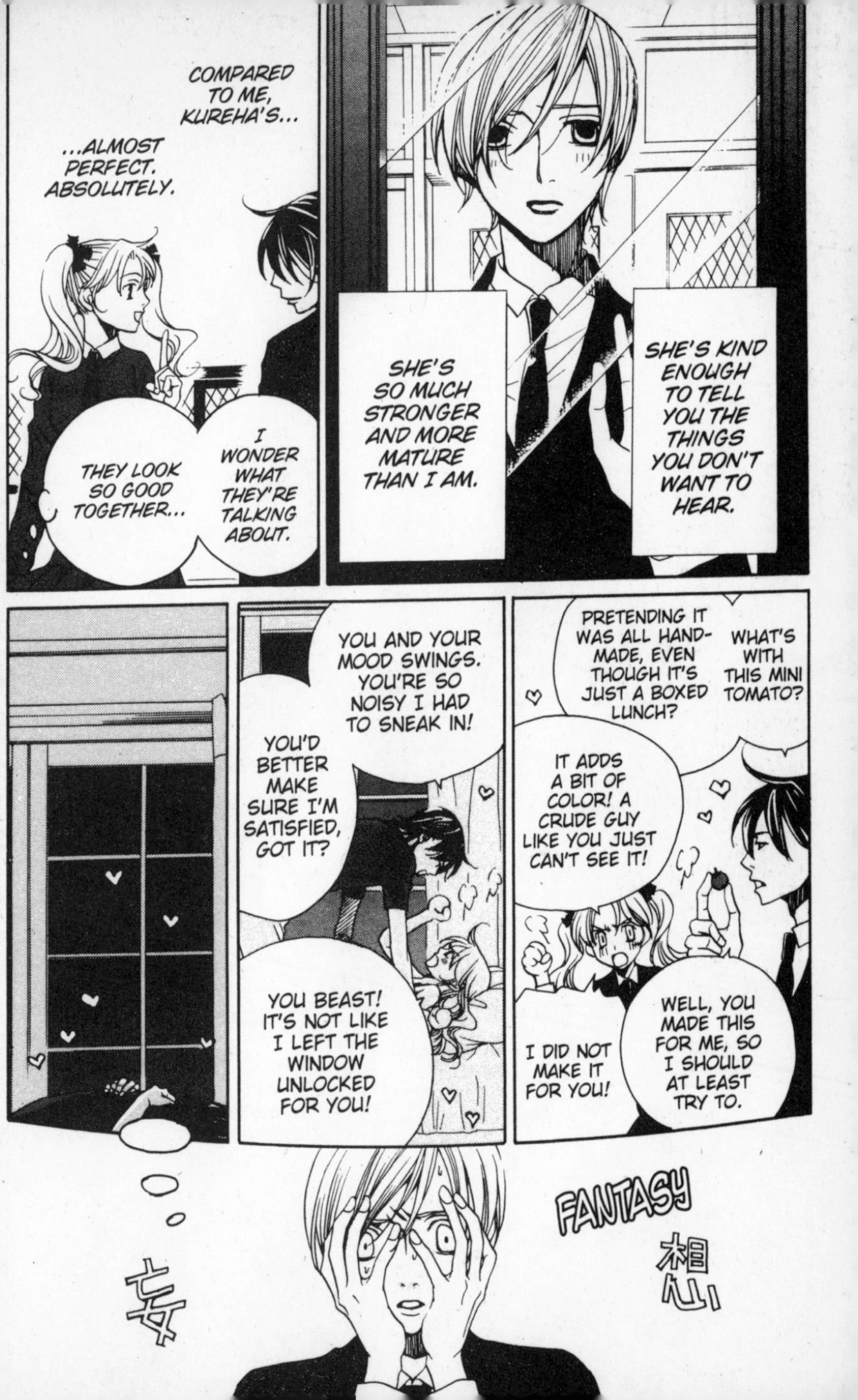
SHE'S KIND ENOUGH TO TELL YOU THE THINGS YOU DON'T WANT TO HEAR.
SHE'S SO MUCH STRONGER AND MORE MATURE THAN I AM.
COMPARED TO ME, KUREHA'S...
...ALMOST PERFECT. ABSOLUTELY.
I WONDER WHAT THEY'RE TALKING ABOUT.
THEY LOOK SO GOOD TOGETHER...
WHAT'S WITH THIS MINI TOMATO?
PRETENDING IT WAS ALL HAND-MADE, EVEN THOUGH IT'S JUST A BOXED LUNCH?
IT ADDS A BIT OF COLOR! A CRUDE GUY LIKE YOU JUST CAN'T SEE IT!
WELL, YOU MADE THIS FOR ME, SO I SHOULD AT LEAST TRY TO.
I DID NOT MAKE IT FOR YOU!
YOU AND YOUR MOOD SWINGS. YOU'RE SO NOISY I HAD TO SNEAK IN!
YOU'D BETTER MAKE SURE I'M SATISFIED, GOT IT?
YOU BEAST! IT'S NOT LIKE I LEFT THE WINDOW UNLOCKED FOR YOU!
FANTASY
想い

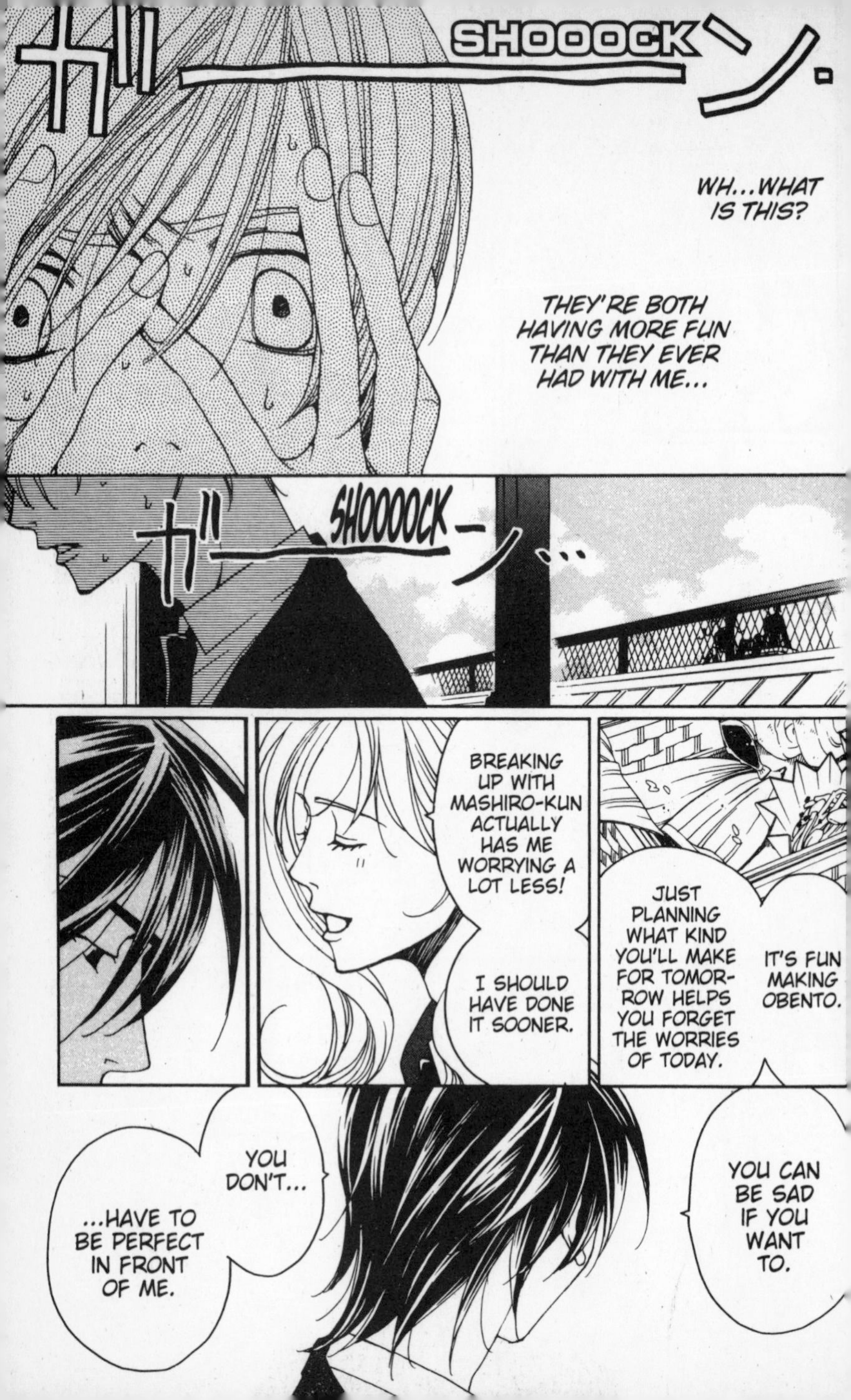

SHOOOCK
WH...WHAT IS THIS?
THEY'RE BOTH HAVING MORE FUN THAN THEY EVER HAD WITH ME...
SHOOOOCK
IT'S FUN MAKING OBENTO.
JUST PLANNING WHAT KIND YOU'LL MAKE FOR TOMORROW HELPS YOU FORGET THE WORRIES OF TODAY.
BREAKING UP WITH MASHIRO-KUN ACTUALLY HAS ME WORRYING A LOT LESS!
I SHOULD HAVE DONE IT SOONER.
YOU CAN BE SAD IF YOU WANT TO.
YOU DON'T...
...HAVE TO BE PERFECT IN FRONT OF ME.

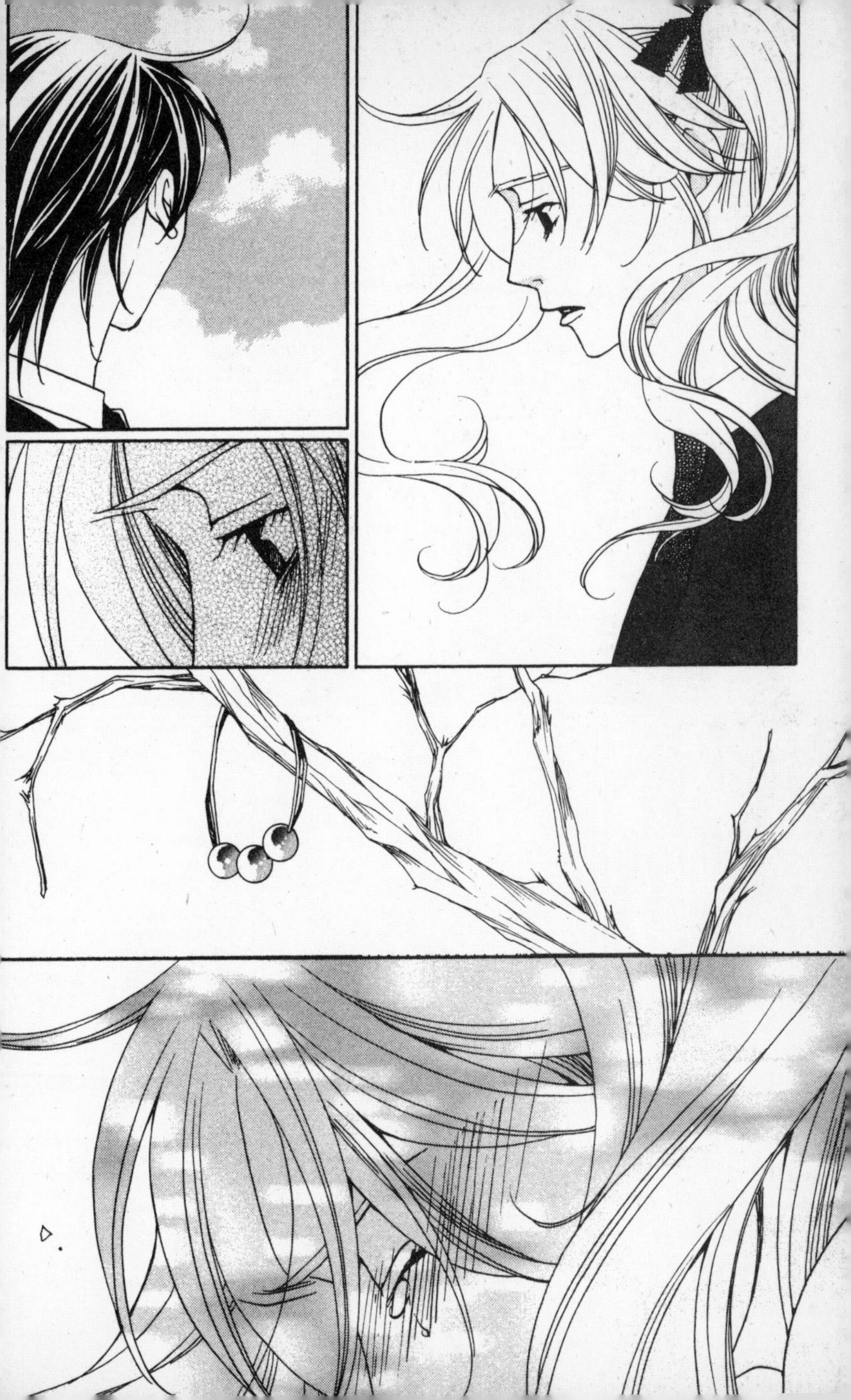

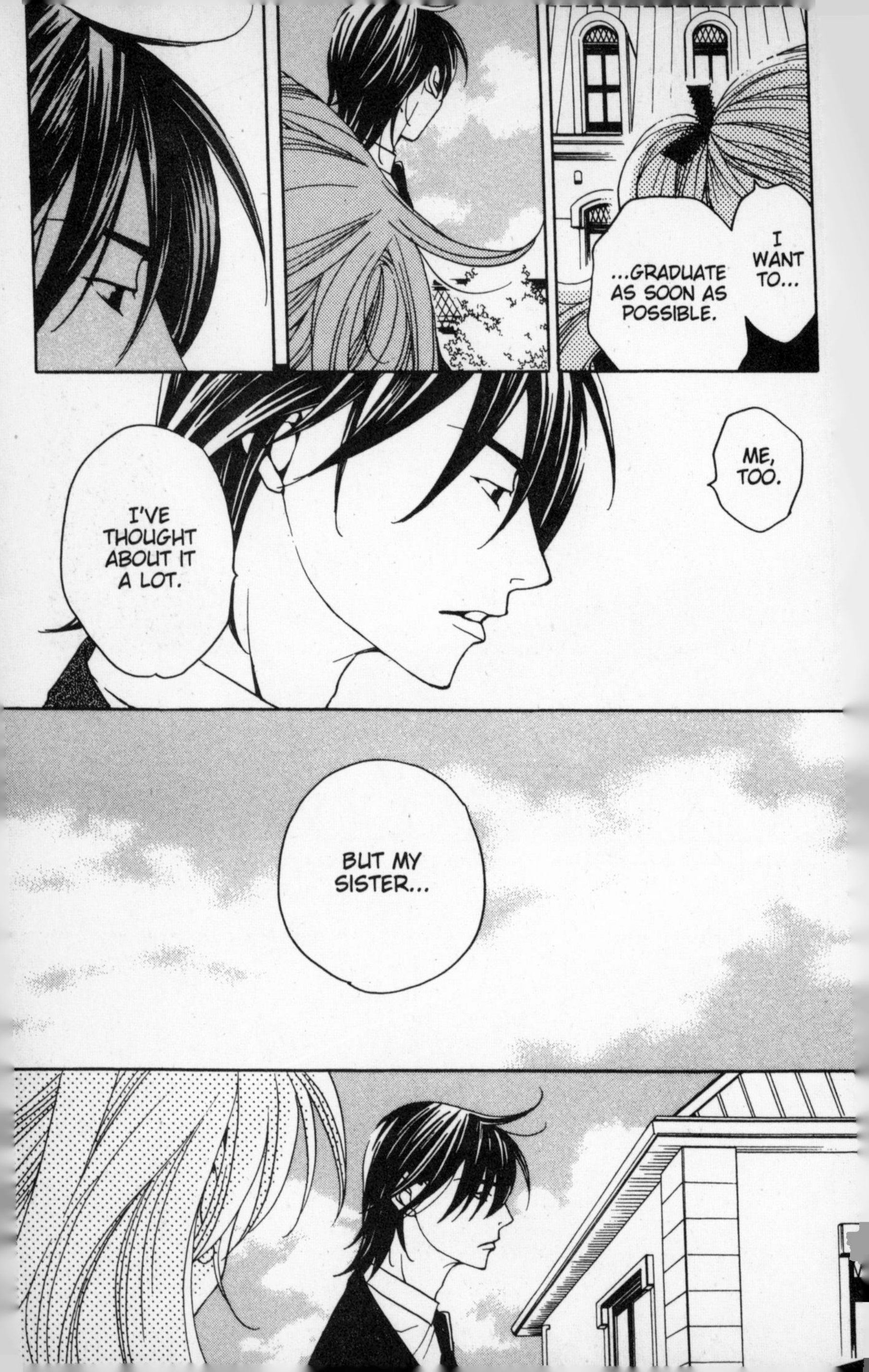

I WANT TO...
...GRADUATE AS SOON AS POSSIBLE.
ME, TOO.
I'VE THOUGHT ABOUT IT A LOT.
BUT MY SISTER...

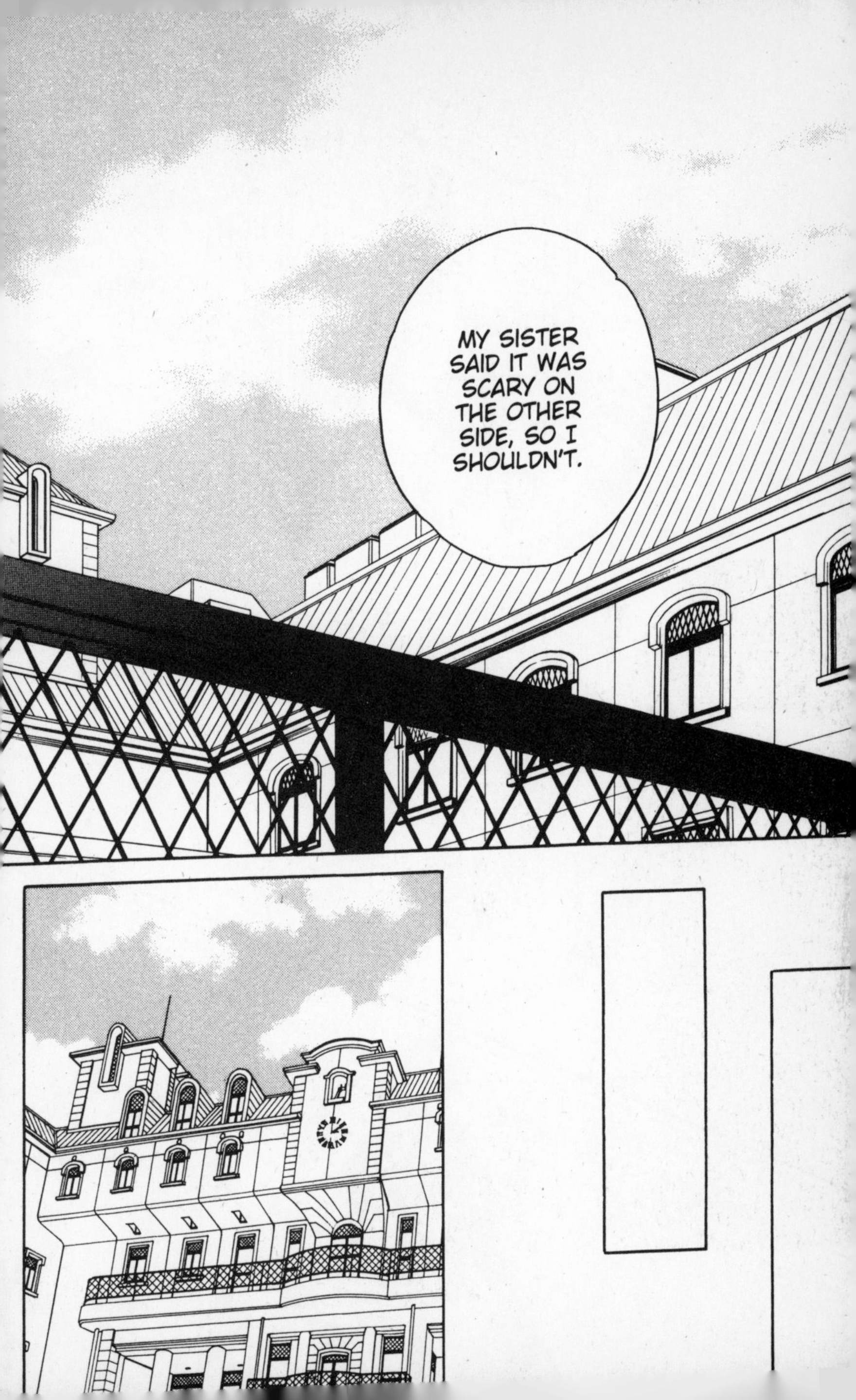
MY SISTER SAID IT WAS SCARY ON THE OTHER SIDE, SO I SHOULDN'T.

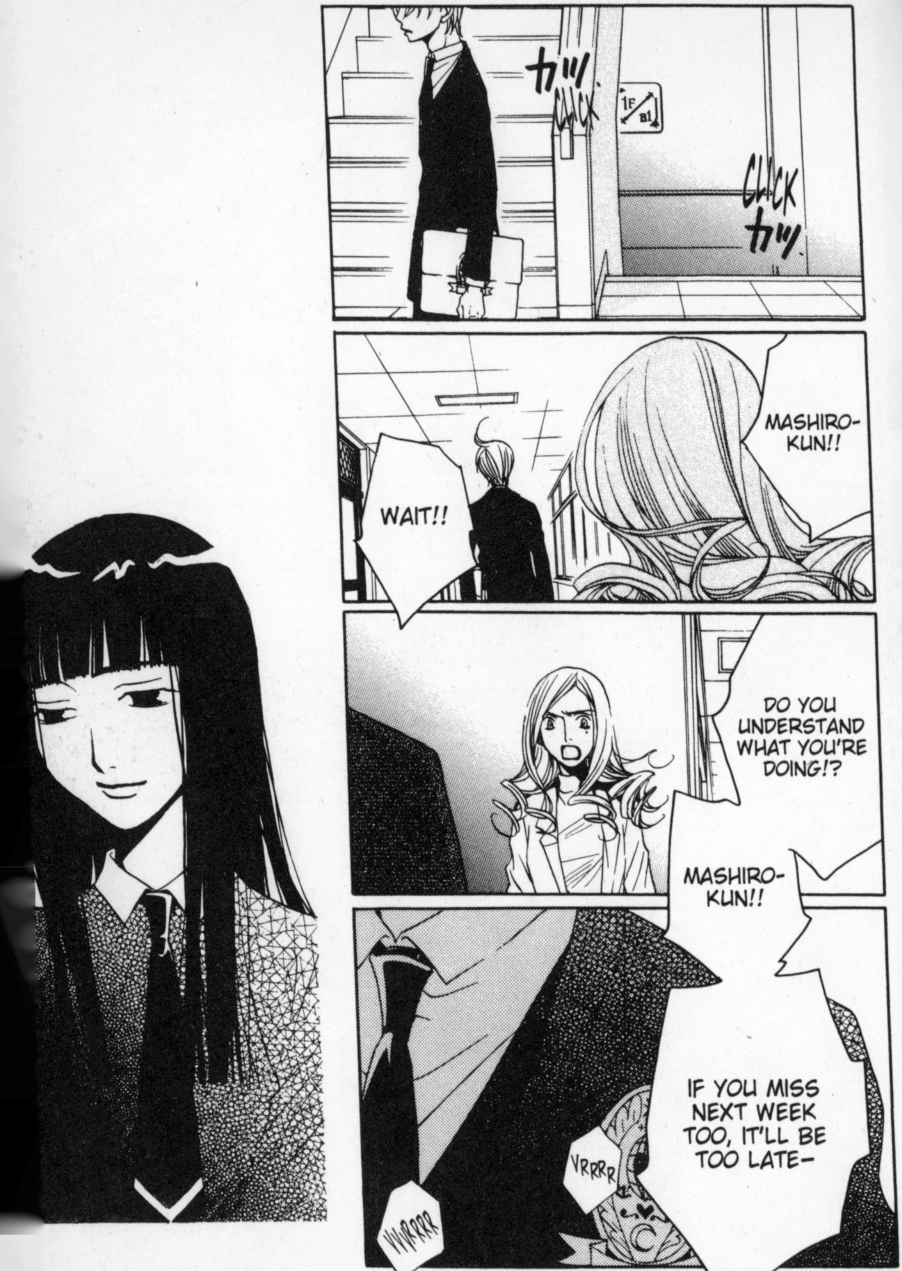
カッ
CLICK
1F
B1
CLICK
カッ
MASHIRO-KUN!!
WAIT!!
DO YOU UNDERSTAND WHAT YOU'RE DOING!?
MASHIRO-KUN!!
IF YOU MISS NEXT WEEK TOO, IT'LL BE TOO LATE-
VRRRR
VVVRRRR

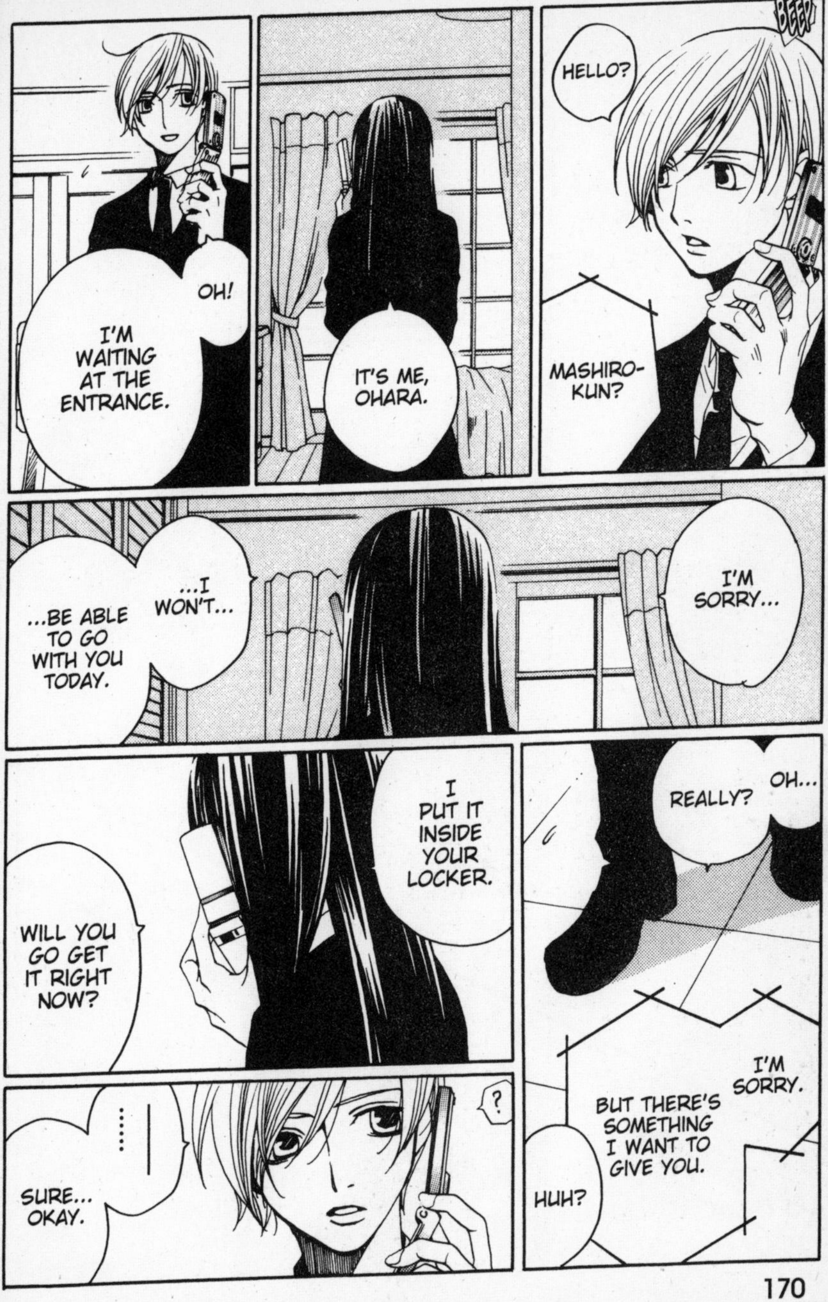
BEEP
HELLO?
MASHIRO-KUN?
IT'S ME, OHARA.
OH!
I'M WAITING AT THE ENTRANCE.
I'M SORRY...
...I WON'T...
...BE ABLE TO GO WITH YOU TODAY.
OH...
REALLY?
I'M SORRY.
BUT THERE'S SOMETHING I WANT TO GIVE YOU.
HUH?
I PUT IT INSIDE YOUR LOCKER.
WILL YOU GO GET IT RIGHT NOW?
?
......
SURE... OKAY.

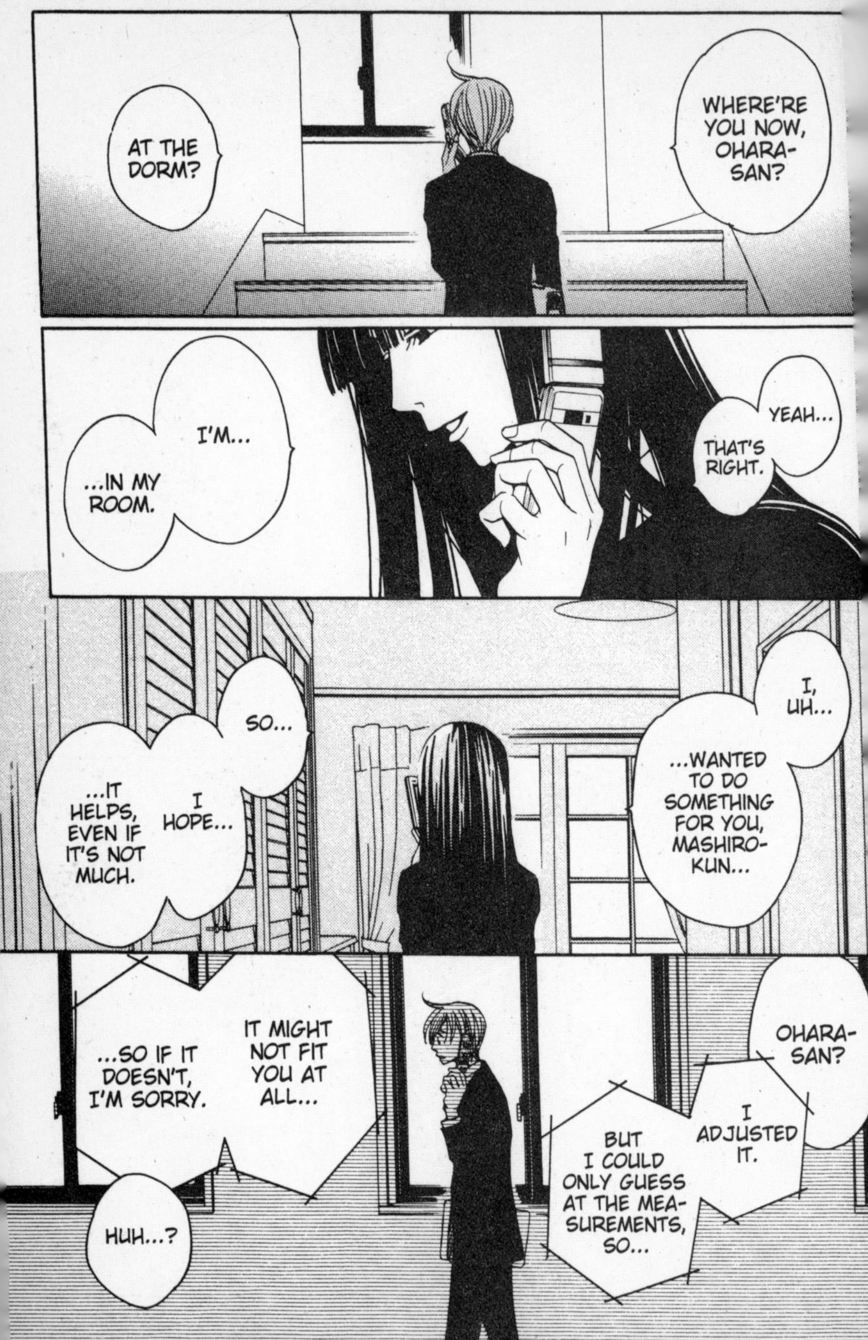
WHERE'RE YOU NOW, OHARA-SAN?
AT THE DORM?
YEAH... THAT'S RIGHT.
I'M...
...IN MY ROOM.
I, UH...
...WANTED TO DO SOMETHING FOR YOU, MASHIRO-KUN...
SO...
I HOPE...
...IT HELPS, EVEN IF IT'S NOT MUCH.
OHARA-SAN?
I ADJUSTED IT.
BUT I COULD ONLY GUESS AT THE MEA-SUREMENTS, SO...
IT MIGHT NOT FIT YOU AT ALL...
...SO IF IT DOESN'T, I'M SORRY.
HUH...?

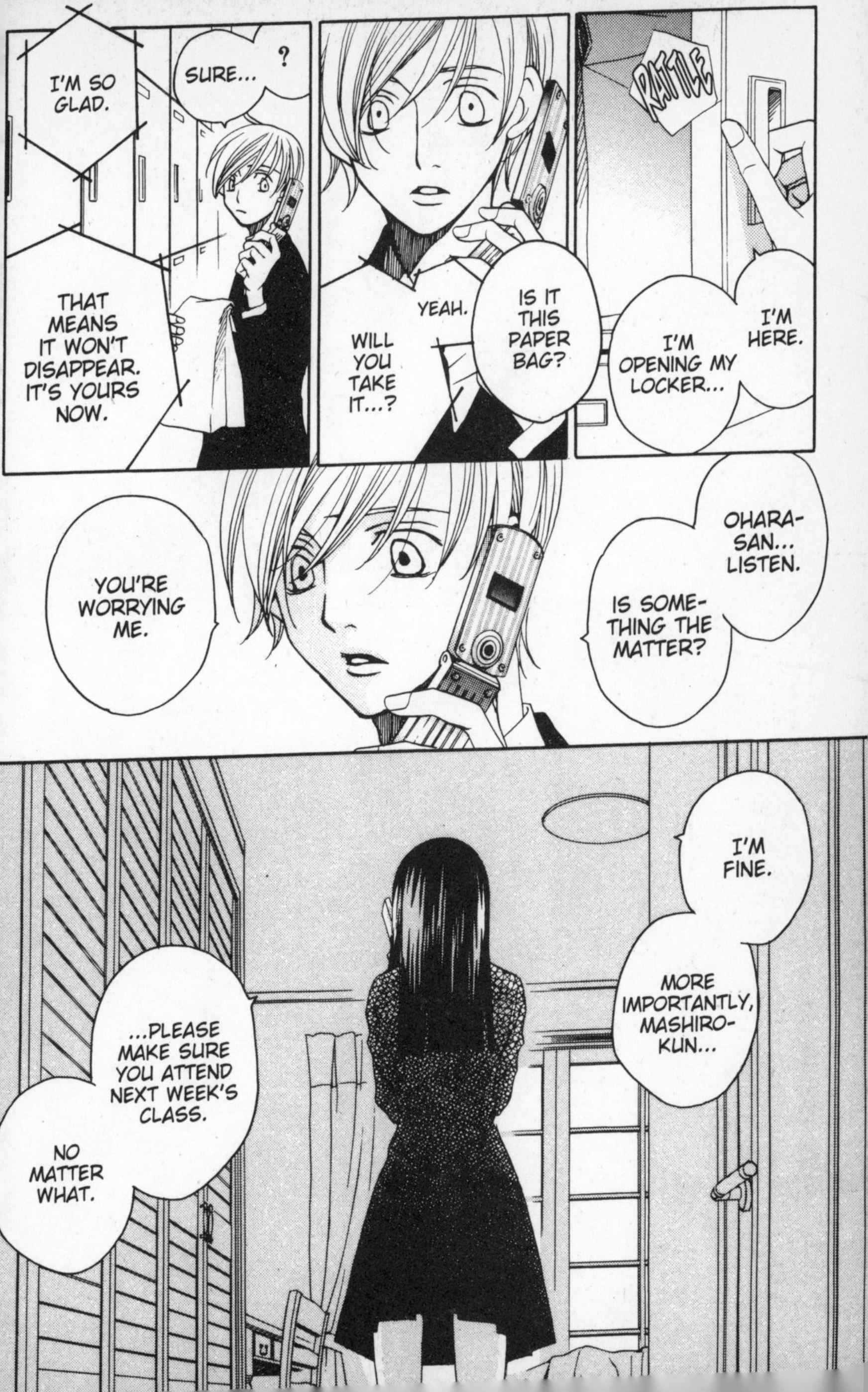
RATTLE
I'M HERE.
I'M OPENING MY LOCKER...
IS IT THIS PAPER BAG?
YEAH.
WILL YOU TAKE IT...?
?
SURE...
I'M SO GLAD.
THAT MEANS IT WON'T DISAPPEAR. IT'S YOURS NOW.
OHARA-SAN... LISTEN.
IS SOME-THING THE MATTER?
YOU'RE WORRYING ME.
I'M FINE.
MORE IMPORTANTLY, MASHIRO-KUN...
...PLEASE MAKE SURE YOU ATTEND NEXT WEEK'S CLASS.
NO MATTER WHAT.

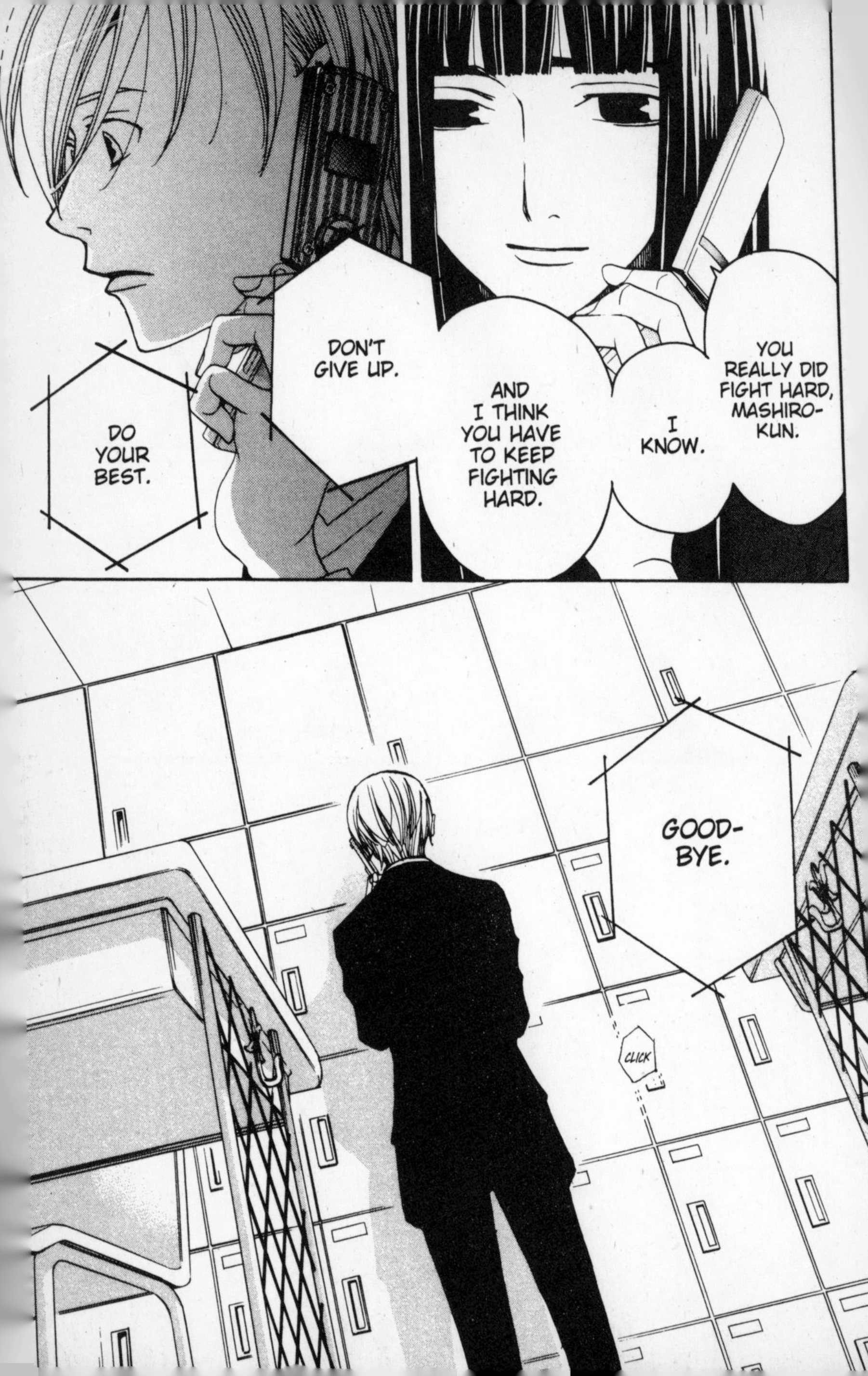

YOU REALLY DID FIGHT HARD, MASHIRO-KUN.
I KNOW.
AND I THINK YOU HAVE TO KEEP FIGHTING HARD.
DON'T GIVE UP.
DO YOUR BEST.
GOOD-BYE.
CLICK

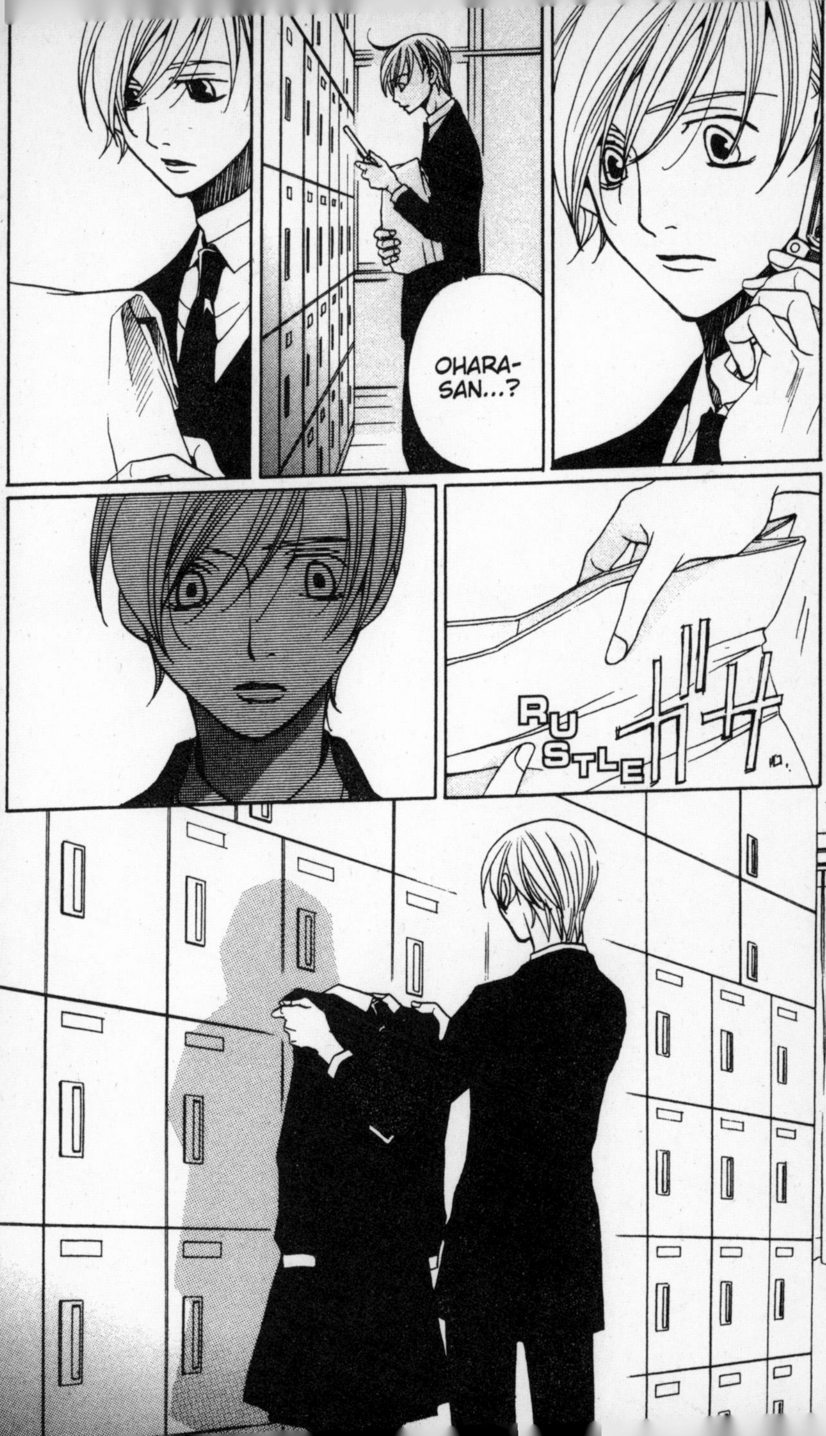
OHARA-
SAN...?
RUSTLE

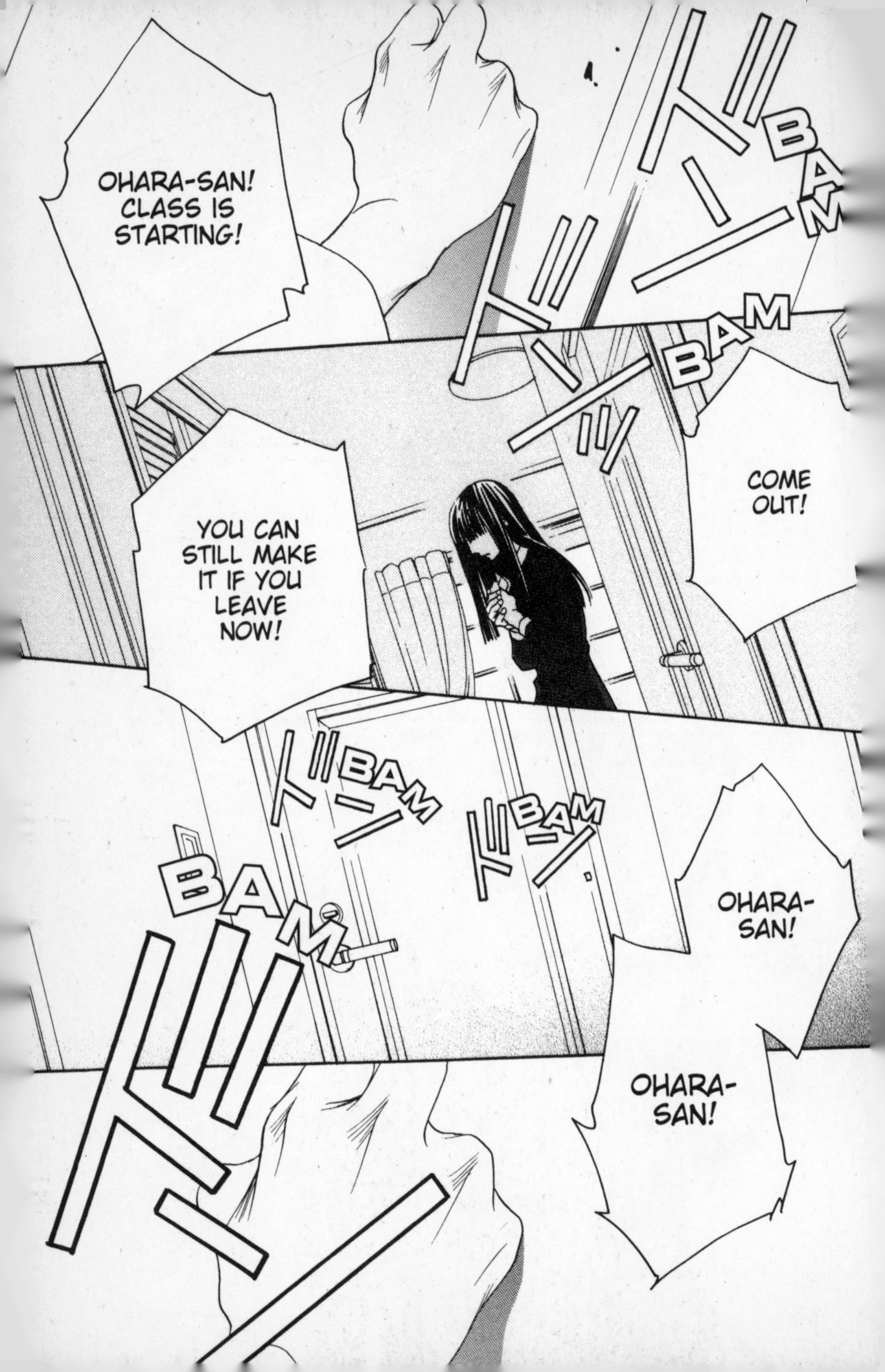
BAM
OHARA-SAN! CLASS IS STARTING!
BAM
COME OUT!
YOU CAN STILL MAKE IT IF YOU LEAVE NOW!
OHARA-SAN!
BAM
BAM
OHARA-SAN!
BAM

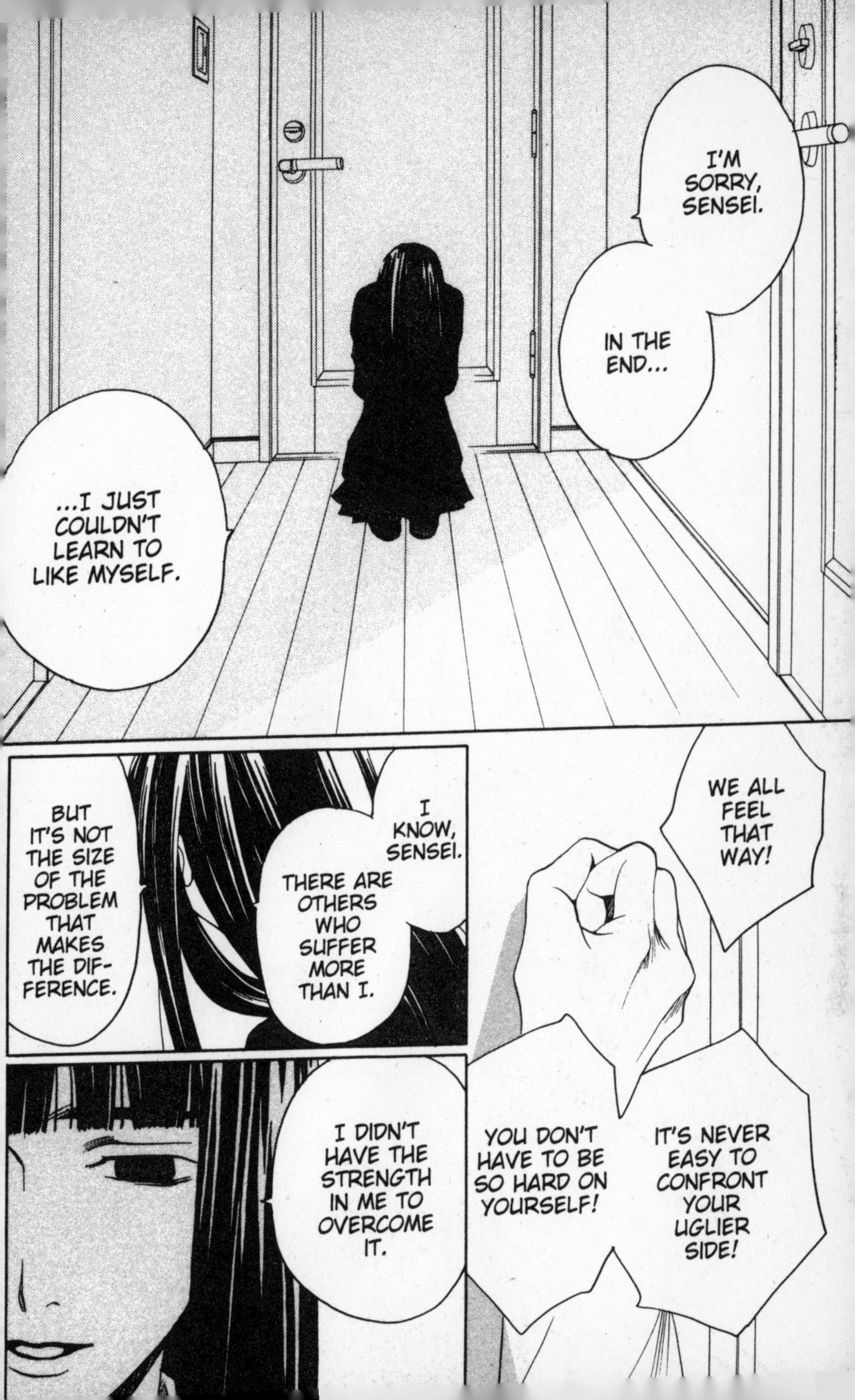
I'M SORRY, SENSEI.
IN THE END...
...I JUST COULDN'T LEARN TO LIKE MYSELF.
WE ALL FEEL THAT WAY!
IT'S NEVER EASY TO CONFRONT YOUR UGLIER SIDE!
YOU DON'T HAVE TO BE SO HARD ON YOURSELF!
I KNOW, SENSEI. THERE ARE OTHERS WHO SUFFER MORE THAN I.
BUT IT'S NOT THE SIZE OF THE PROBLEM THAT MAKES THE DIFFERENCE.
I DIDN'T HAVE THE STRENGTH IN ME TO OVERCOME IT.

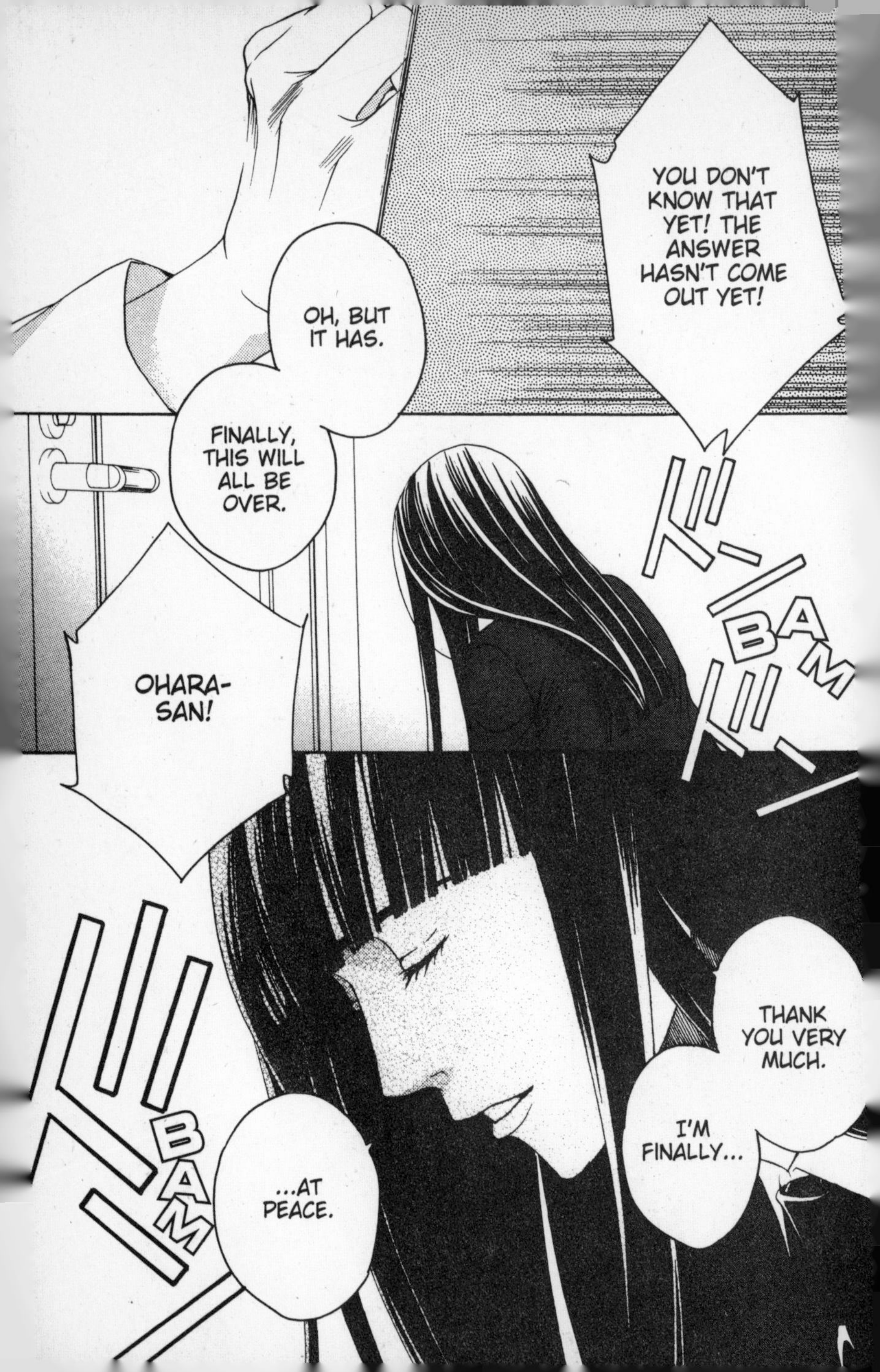
YOU DON'T KNOW THAT YET! THE ANSWER HASN'T COME OUT YET!
OH, BUT IT HAS.
FINALLY, THIS WILL ALL BE OVER.
BAM
OHARA-SAN!
THANK YOU VERY MUCH.
I'M FINALLY...
...AT PEACE.
BAM

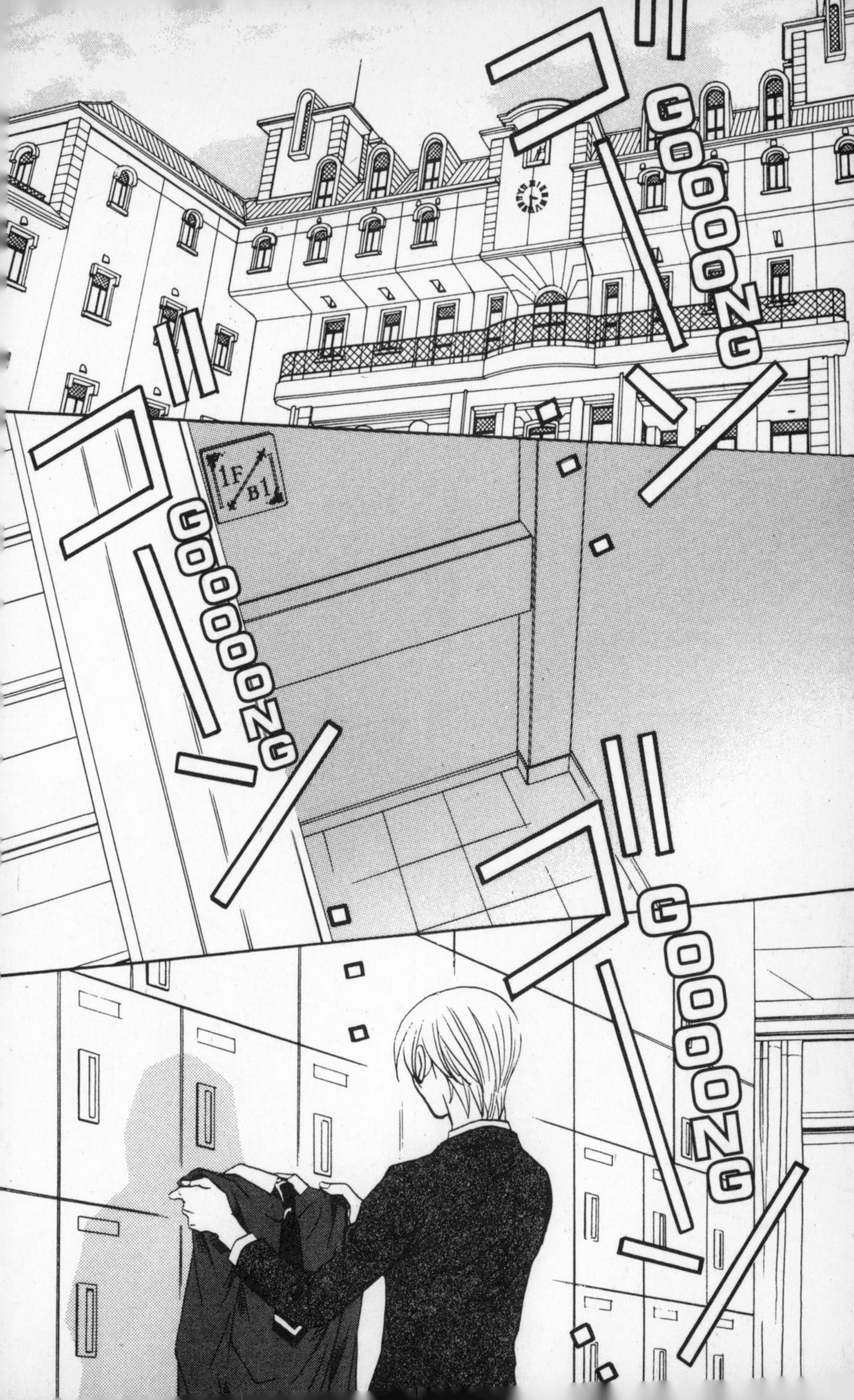
GOOOONG
1F
B1
GOOOOONG
GOOOONG

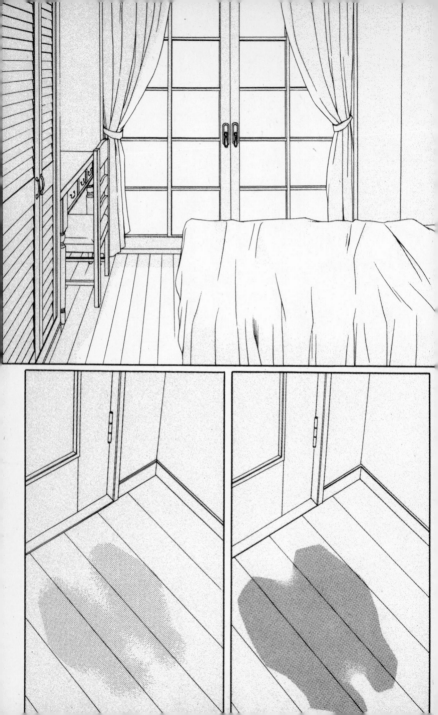

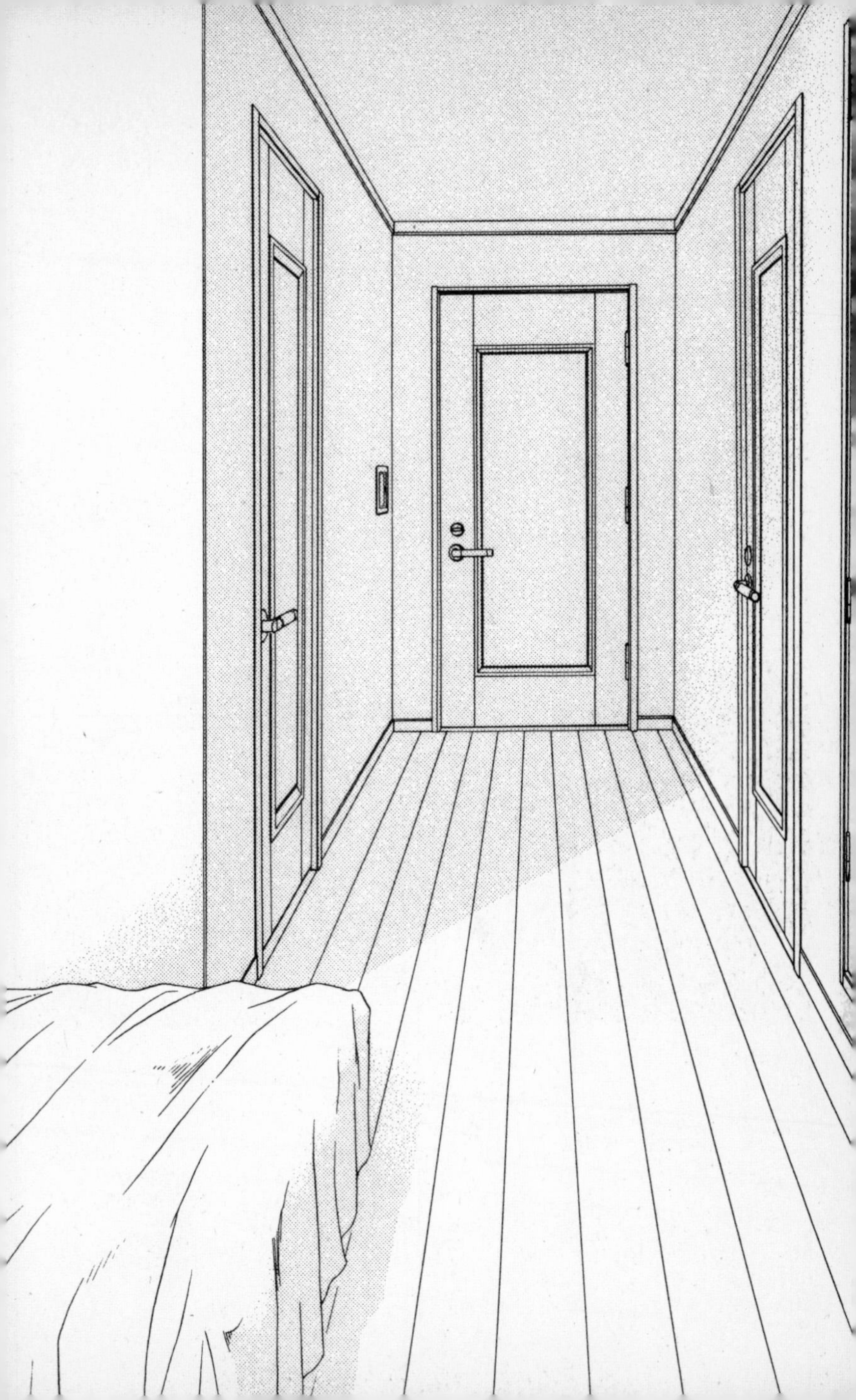

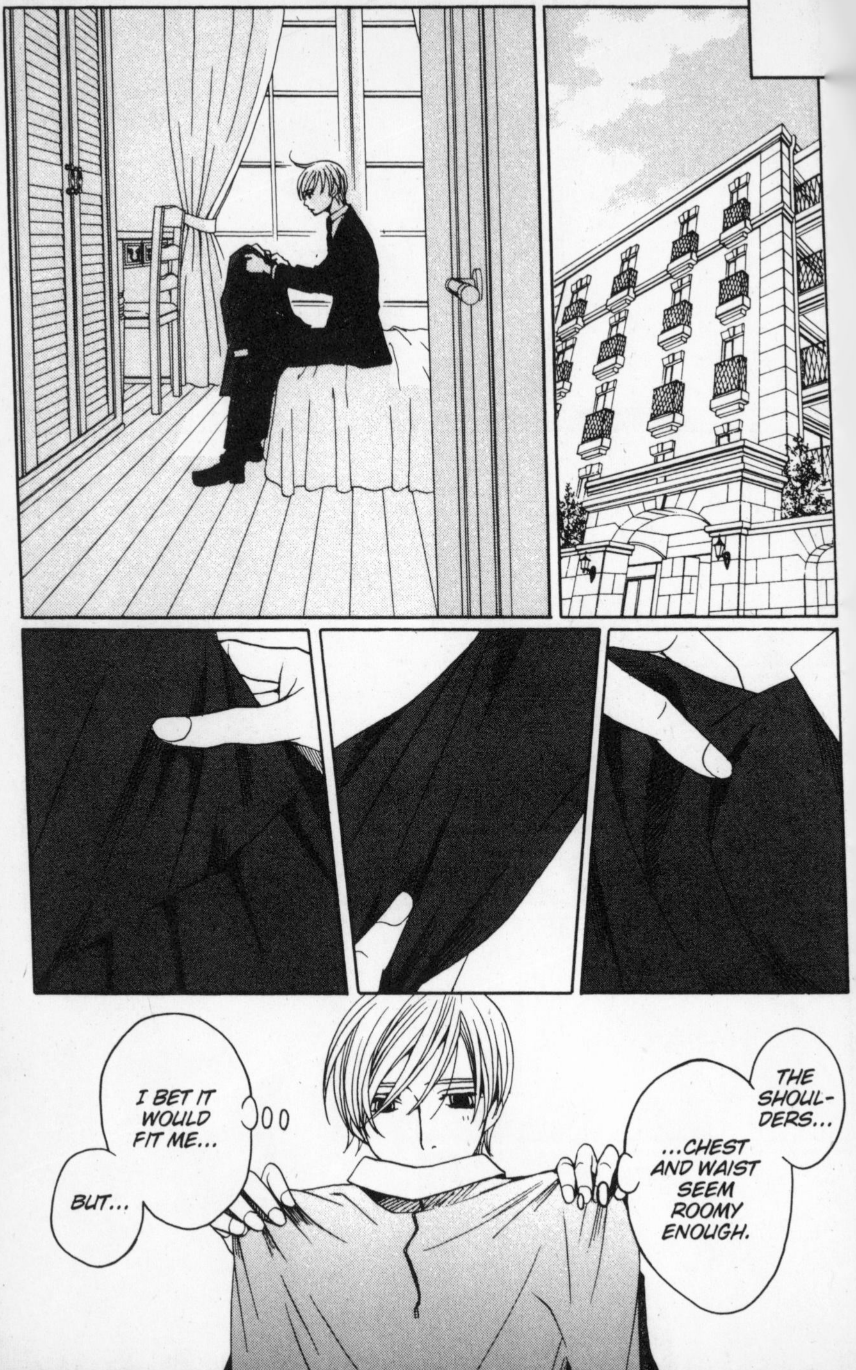
THE SHOUL-DERS...
...CHEST AND WAIST SEEM ROOMY ENOUGH.
I BET IT WOULD FIT ME...
BUT...

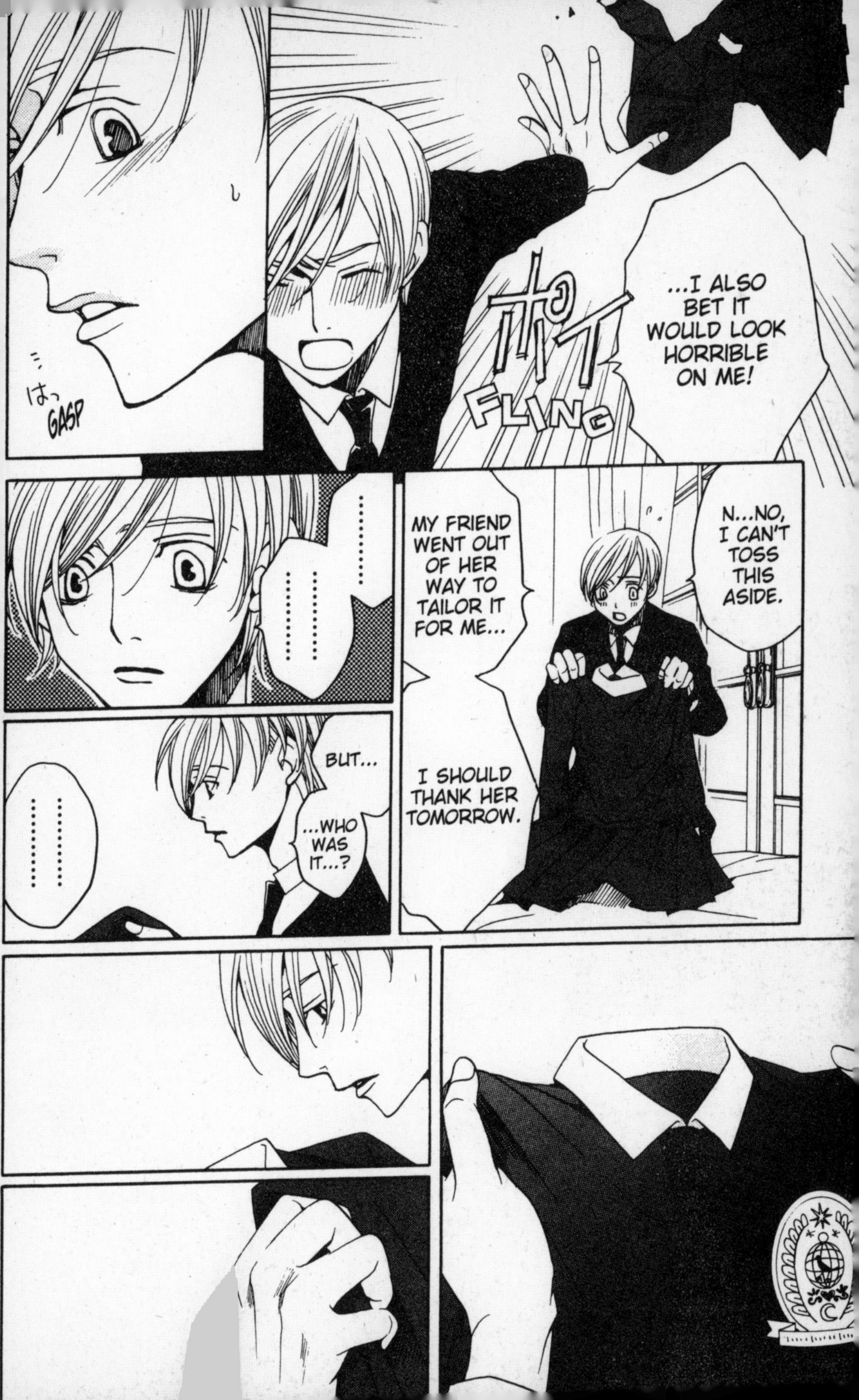
...I ALSO BET IT WOULD LOOK HORRIBLE ON ME!
ホイ
FLING
はっ
GASP
N...NO, I CAN'T TOSS THIS ASIDE.
MY FRIEND WENT OUT OF HER WAY TO TAILOR IT FOR ME...
I SHOULD THANK HER TOMORROW.
......
BUT...
...WHO WAS IT...?
......

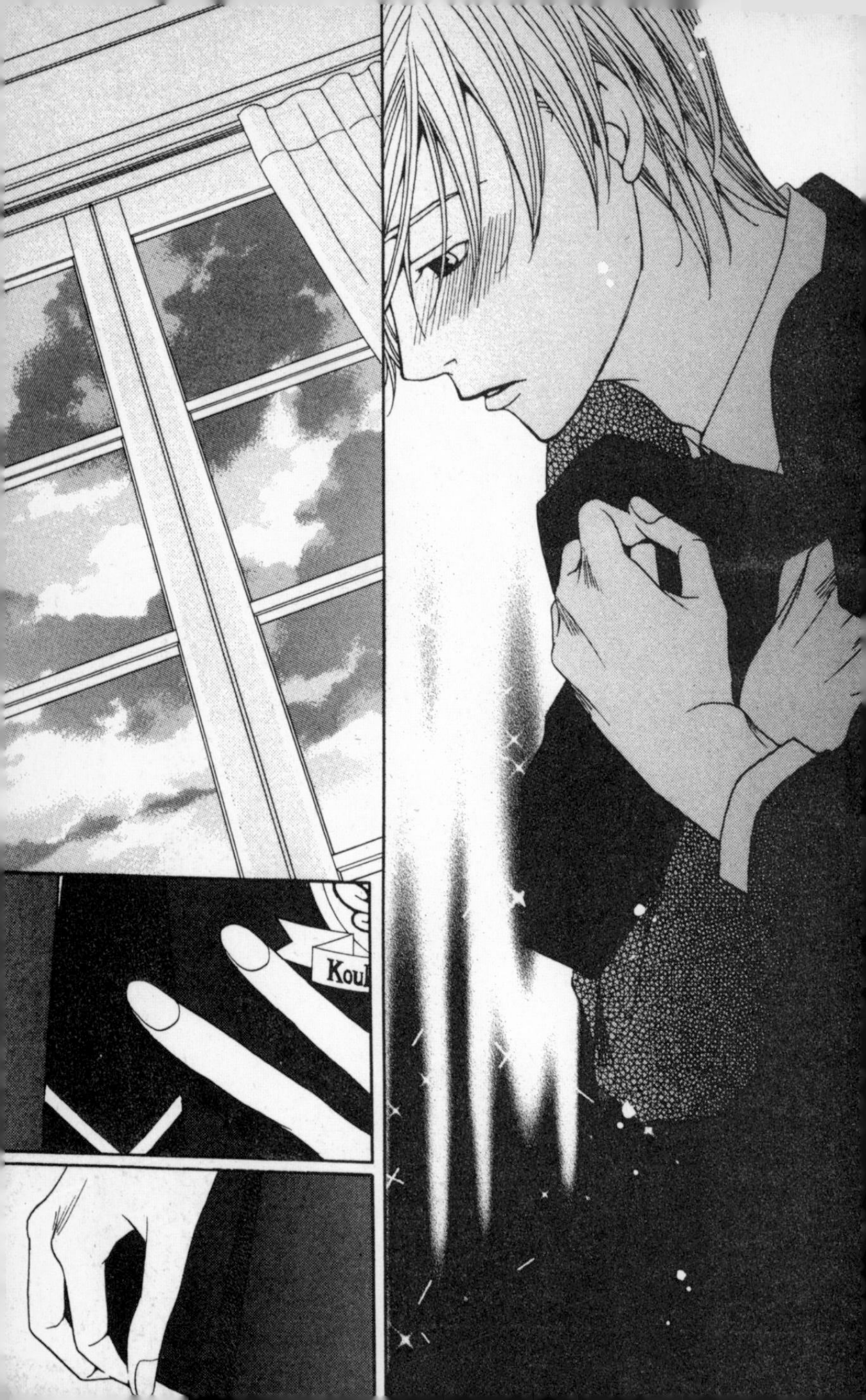
Kou

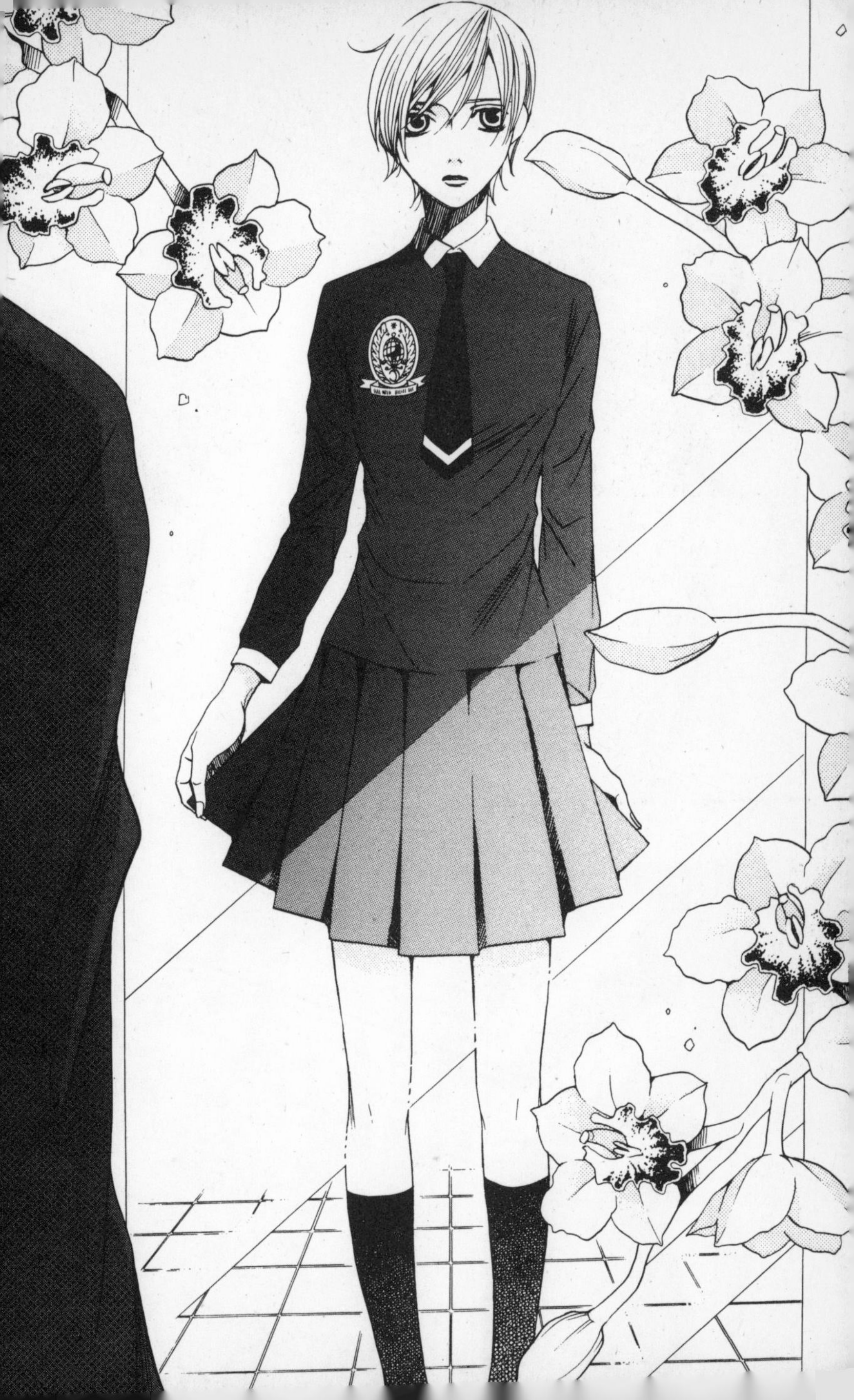

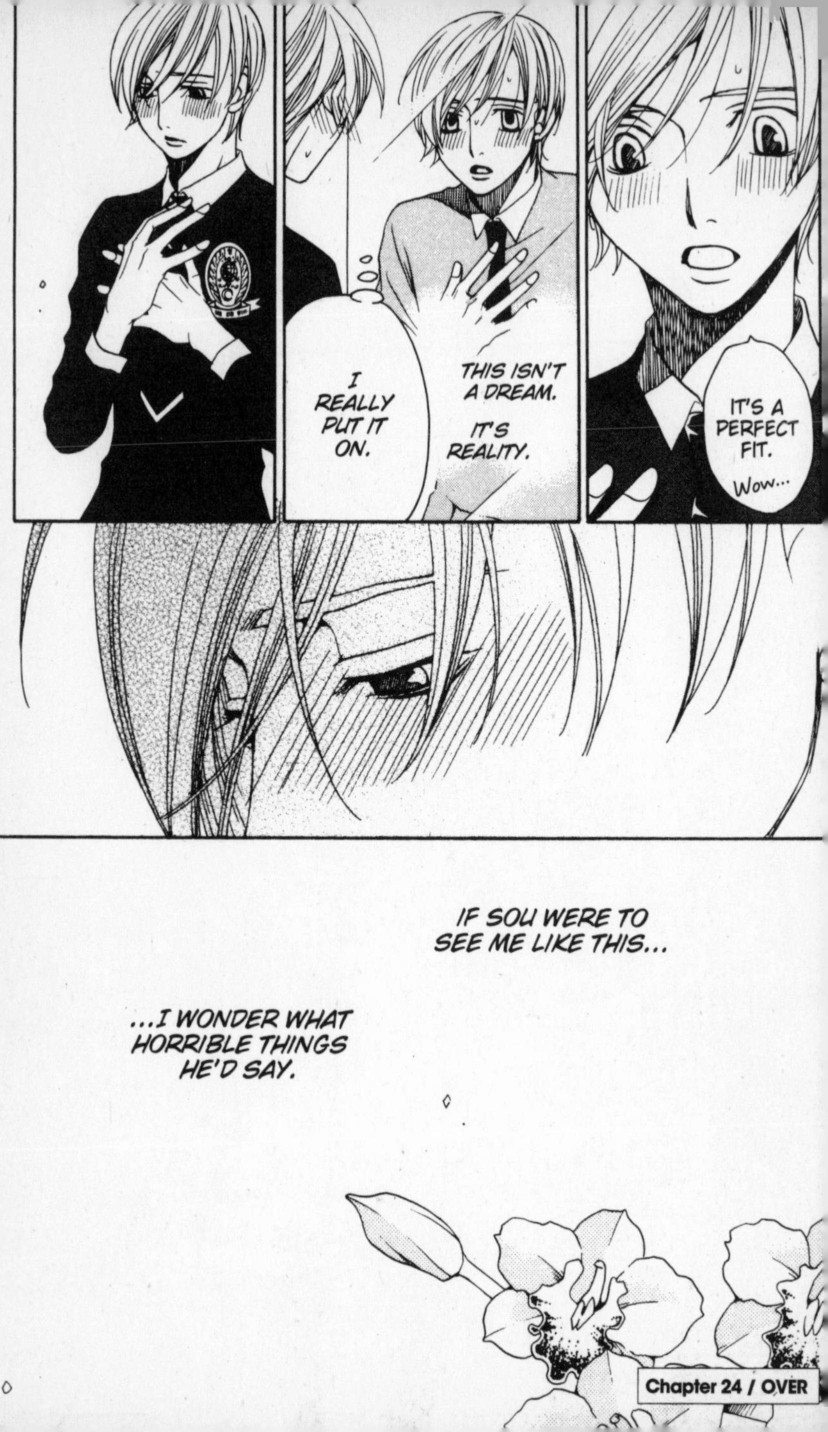
IT'S A PERFECT FIT.
Wow...
THIS ISN'T A DREAM.
IT'S REALITY.
I REALLY PUT IT ON.
IF SOU WERE TO SEE ME LIKE THIS...
...I WONDER WHAT HORRIBLE THINGS HE'D SAY.
Chapter 24 / OVER

After School Nightmare 6 / OVER

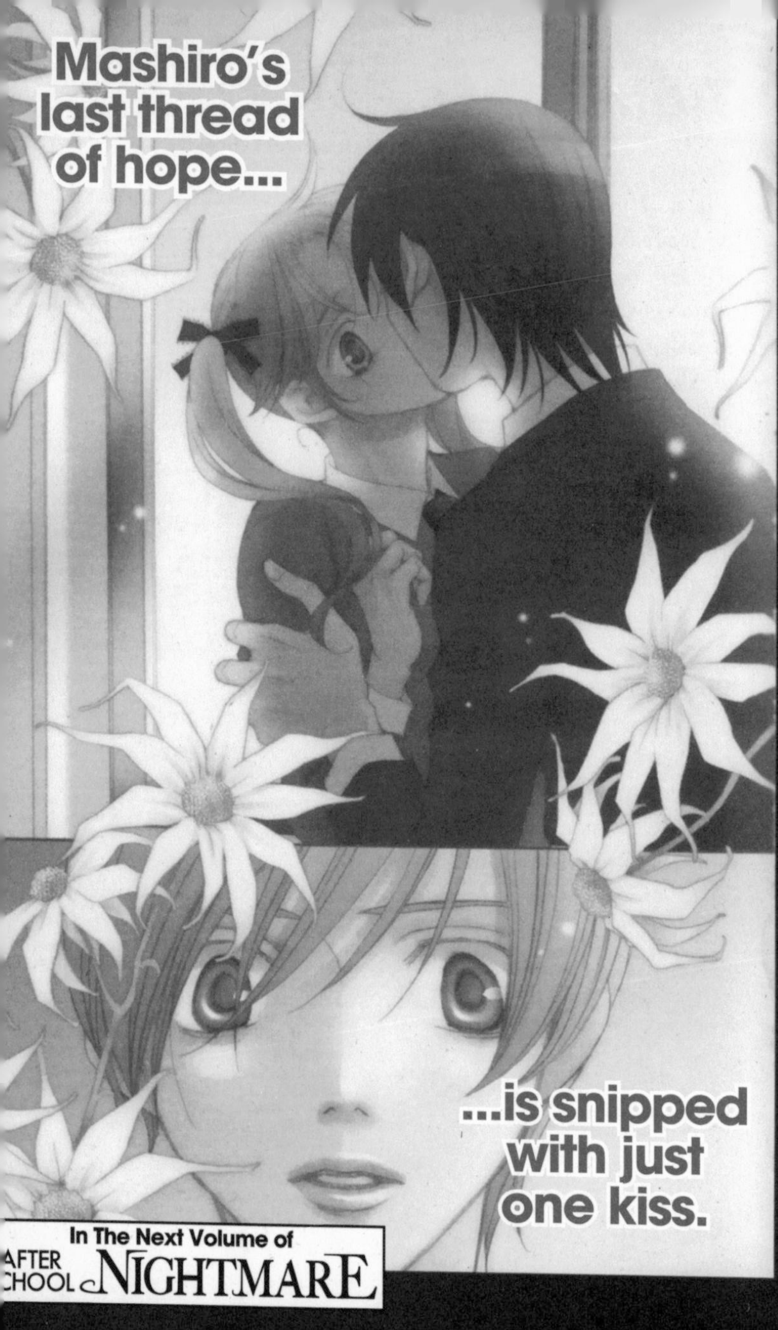
Mashiro's last thread of hope...
...is snipped with just one kiss.
In The Next Volume of
AFTER SCHOOL NIGHTMARE

Translator's Notes:

Pg. 8 – "Mother Courage"
Mother Courage is a character from a novel called "The Runagate Courage" from the late 1600's and was made famous in "Mother Courage and Her Children". She's a strong-minded woman who is a walking contradiction as she tries to protect her children from the war and yet seeks to profit from it.

Pg. 12 – obento
A boxed lunch very popular with all ages. They usually include rice, fish or meat and pickled vegetables. Fabulous for an easy picnic!

Pg. 97 - Asuka Suo
蘇芳 Keeping up the tradition of color-oriented names in this series, Asuka Suo's last name is a layered color of brown on the top and red beneath.

Pg. 127 - Momoka Ohara
大原桃花 Both the first and last name of this girl are colors. "Momo" means peach and thereby denotes the same pinkish beige color. Her last name "Ohara" means "big field" thereby denoting grassy greens of nature.

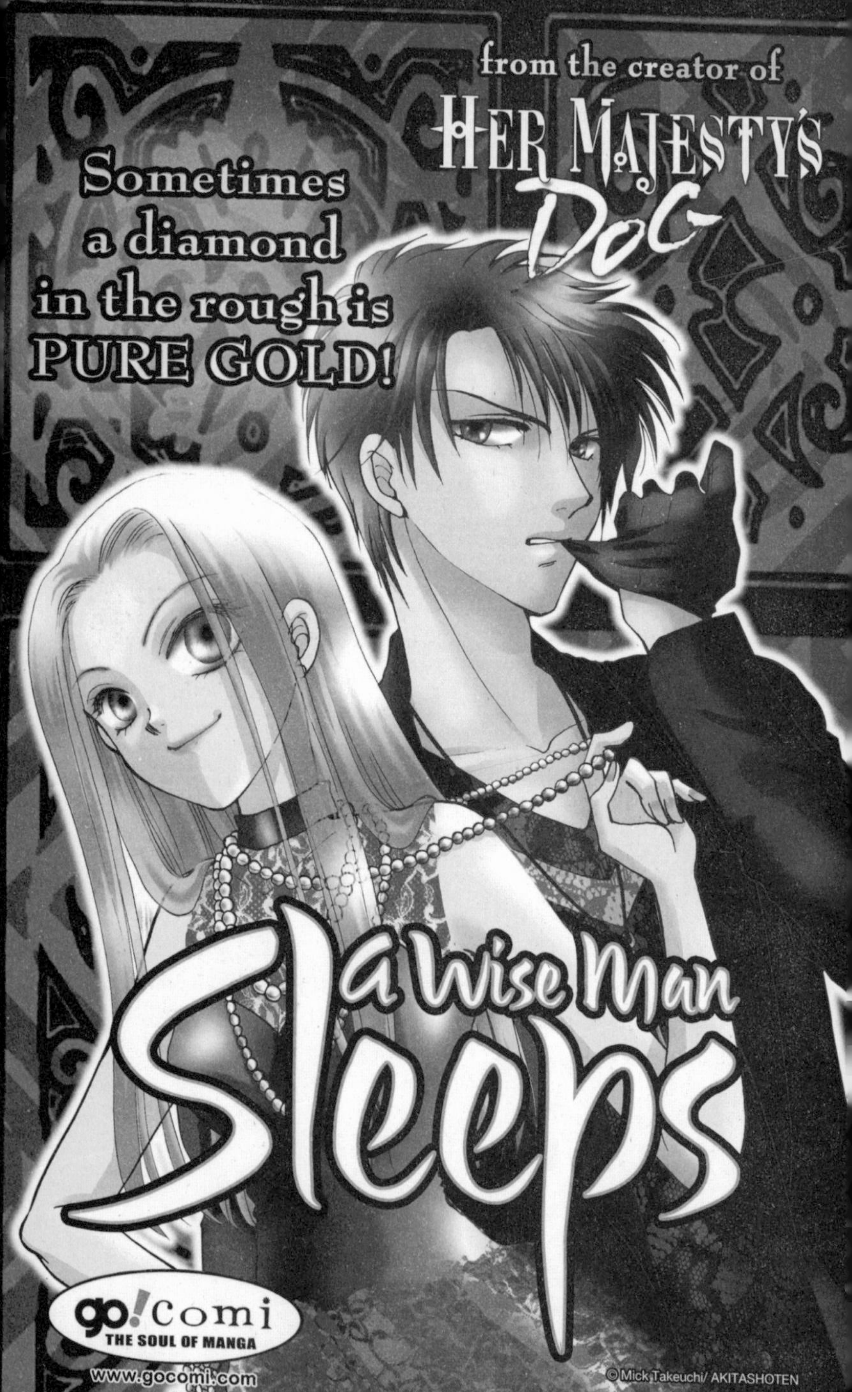
from the creator of
HER MAJESTY'S DOG
Sometimes a diamond in the rough is PURE GOLD!
A Wise Man Sleeps
go!comi
THE SOUL OF MANGA
www.gocomi.com
© Mick Takeuchi/ AKITASHOTEN

BLACK SUN ● SILVER MOON

SAVING THE WORLD...
ONE ZOMBIE AT A TIME.

go!comi
THE SOUL OF MANGA

Black Sun Silver Moon ©TOMO MAEDA/SHINSHOKAN
First published in Japan in 2005 by SHINSHOKAN Co., Ltd. Tokyo

SETONA MIZUSHIRO

Since this story was inspired by what I remembered from watching *F1*, at first I imagined the characters fighting in a cramped cockpit.

In the beginning, I looked at it from a more sci-fi viewpoint, and the cockpit that the characters were thrown into changed into a class capsule-type thing. After a lot of time passed, I thought to myself, "If I don't make this more like a shojo manga, I won't get it entered into a shojo manga magazine," so I re-thought it , and arranged it to be more like a shojo manga...and the cockpit was transfigured into a canopied bed. (ha)

It's a race everyone's competing in as they loop the same course time and time again. In a motor car race, once the checkered flag at the finish line is waved, a champagne shower awaits the winner. But just what lies beyond the graduation goal in After School Nightmare?

ABOUT THE MANGA-KA

Setona Mizushiro's first real dabble in the world of creating manga was in 1985 when she participated in the publication of a dojinshi (amateur manga). She remained active in the dojinshi world until she debuted in April of 1993 with her short single *Fuyu ga Owarou Toshiteita* (Winter Was Ending) that ran in Shogakukan's *Puchi Comic* magazine. Mizushiro-sensei is well-known for her series *X-Day* in which she exhibits an outstanding ability to delve into psychological issues of every nature. Besides manga, Mizushiro-sensei has an affinity for chocolate, her two cats (Jam and Nene), and round sparkly objects.